MW01659786

SHOW

PHOTOGRAPHS BY ANTOINE BOOTZ

First published in the United States
of America in 2009 by

Glitterati Incorporated

Glitterati Incorporated
225 Central Park West, Suite 305
New York, New York 10024
www.GlitteratiIncorporated.com
Telephone: 212 362 9119
glitterati@verizon.net for inquiries

Copyright © 2009 by Ralph Pucci

All photographs copyright Antoine Bootz
except Josef Astor, pages 8, 108, and 109

All rights reserved. No part of this publication may
be reproduced in any form or by any electronic or
mechanical means, including information storage
and retrieval systems, without permission in writing
from Glitterati Incorporated, except by a reviewer
who may quote brief passages in a review.

First edition, 2009

Creative Director: Ken Smart
Design: Sarah Morgan Karp/smk-design.com

Library of Congress Cataloging-in-Publication data
is available from the publisher.

Hardcover edition ISBN 13:
978-0-9801557-8-5

Printed and bound in China by Hong Kong
Graphics & Printing Ltd.
10 9 8 7 6 5 4 3 2 1

RALPH**PUCCI**

SHOW

Glitterati
INCORPORATED
New York, New York

A C K N O W L E D G M E N T S

Special Thanks to My Family:

Ann, Nicole, Michael, Will and Maria Pucci

Andrew Markopoulos
Salvatore Marra
Jim Elliott
Bill Withers
Frank Kellar
Wilmer Weiss
Robert Currie
Joe Powers
Lowell Nesbitt
Stephen Sprouse
Angel Estrada
Fernando Bengoechea
Adel Rootstein
Rob Unger
Joseph Cicio
Karen Smith-Harvey
Steve Kornajcik
John Roscio
Jamie Becker
James Damian
Timothy Opsomer
Joe Feszko
James Bellante
Brian Preussker
Mark Minichiello
Ignaz Gorischek
William Herbst
Guy Scarengelo
Mary Alice Hughes
James Mansour

Susan Homan
Janis Bell
Jim Apruzzese
Gratia Morgan
Ron Gosses
Simon Doonan
Margaret Russell
Cindy Allen
Michael Wollaeger
Pilar Viladas
David Moin
Tom Beebe
Sarah Medford
Wendy Goodman
Barbara Thornburg
Adele Cygelman
Mayer Rus
Donna Warner
Allyn Magrino
Paul Wilmont
John Ceriale
Greg Mills
Linda Fargo
David Lachapelle
Marcus Leatherdale
Larissa
Antoine Bootz
Tibor Kalman
Chris Fortuna
Philip Cozzi

Ruven Afanador
Peter Morello
Jack Lenor Larsen
Richard David Story
Dietmar Busse
John Wigmore
Christine Belich
Fran Taubman
Olivier Gagnere
Roberto Dutesco
Mark Gagnon
Tobie Giddio
Giselle
James Maharg
Mallory Andrews
Richard Gluckman
Stephen Johanknect
Jack Hruska
Judy Niedermaier
Eddie Mock
Stephen Allen
Donn Copa
Wade Williams
Ed Schilling
Will Nguyen
Nancy Holcomb
Joseph Batchelor
Ken Smart
Michael Evert
Michael J. McLeod

Dedicated to my parents, Nick & Lee Pucci

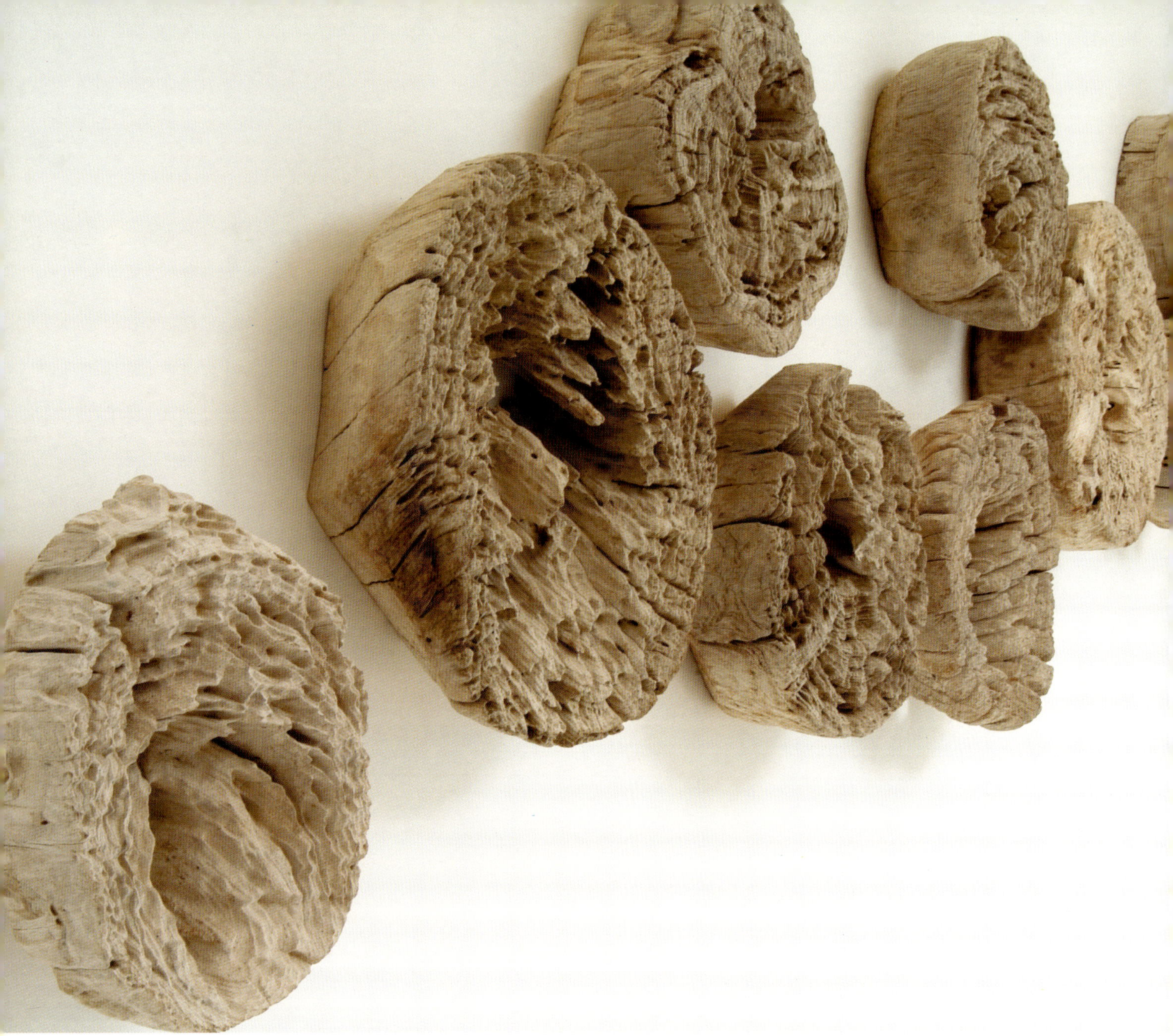

CONTENTS

INTRODUCTION 8 Andrée Putman 12 Ruben Toledo 16 Hiroshi Tanabe 24 Paul Mathieu 26 Abigail Simpson 30 Ralph Pucci 34, 48, 80, 182, 184, 186 Jerome Abel Seguin 38 Christy Turlington 44 Christopher Farr 50 Laura Ljunkvist 56 John Tanji Koga 60 Patrick Naggar 64 Herve Van Der Straeten 72 Jens Risom 90 India Mahdavi 96 Christopher Makos 100 Antoine Bootz 104 Paul Solberg 106 Josef Astor 108 Nicholas Howey 110 Gail Leboff 112 Diego Uchitel 114 James Brown 116 Jim Zivic 118

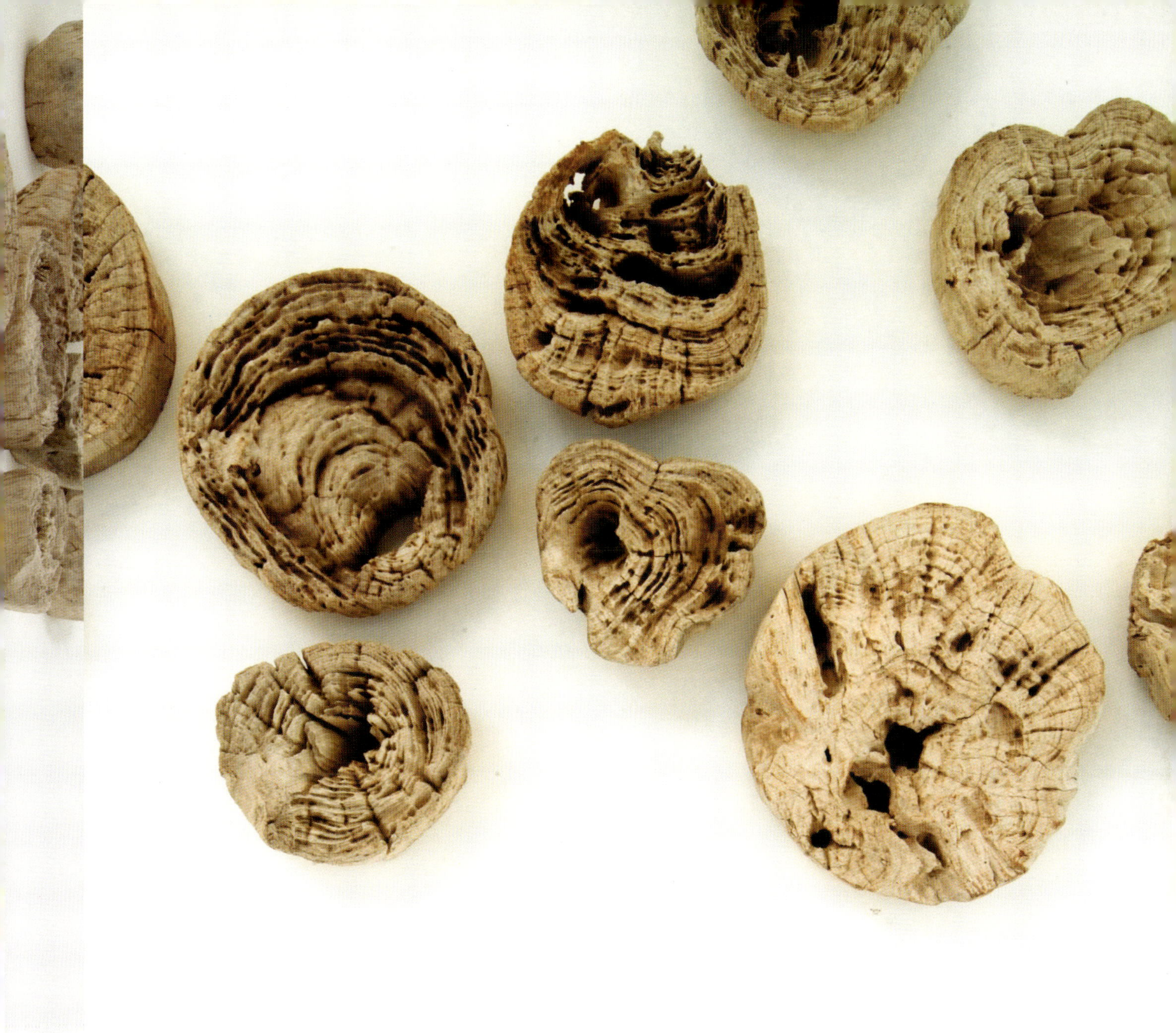

Jerome Abel Seguin, wall sculpture, 2002

Jonathan Kline 122 Chris Lehrecke 124 Vladimir Kagan 130 Maira Kalman 136 Michael Bartalos 139 Kenny Scharf 140 Jeffrey Fulvimari 146 Madeline Weinrib 149 Chesley Mclaren 150 Anna Sui 152 Robert Clyde Anderson 153 Stephen Campbell 154 Anja Kroencke 155 Vicente Wolf 156 Ecart International 158 Trace Simple 160 Christophe Delcourt 162 Vorucchka 164 Kevin Walz 166 Robert Bristow 170 Eric Schmitt 174 David Weeks 176 Philippe Hiquily 180 Laurent Elie Badessi 188 ABOUT THE AUTHOR 192

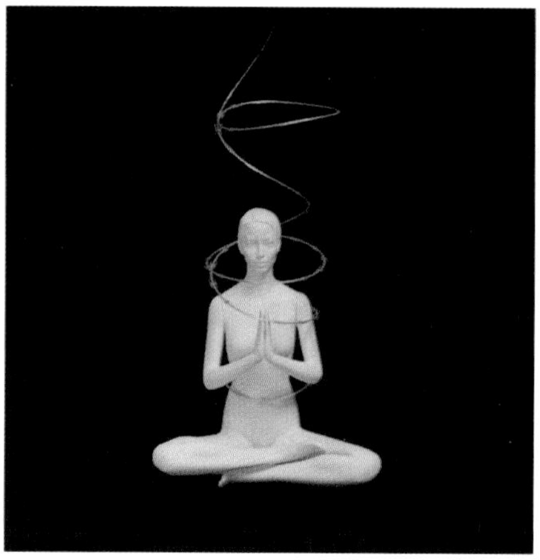

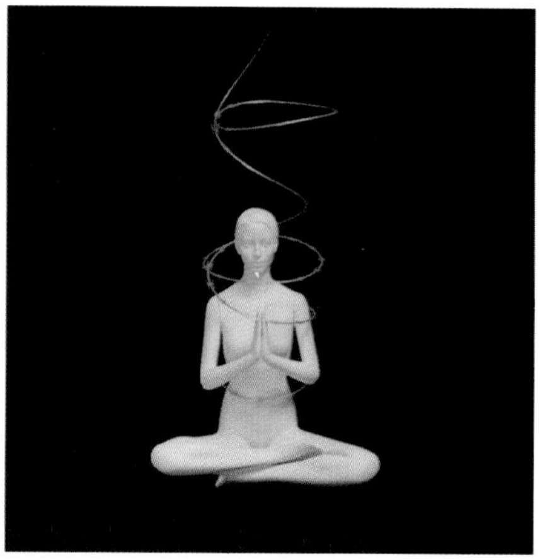

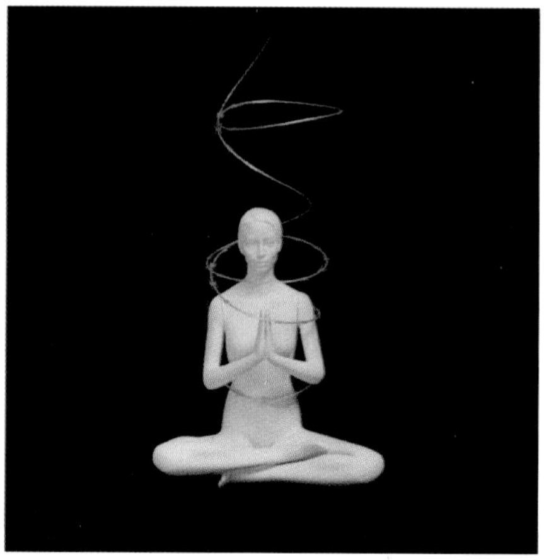

Christy Turlington, *Yoga*, 2002, photograph by Josef Astor

INTRODUCTION

ABOUT THE SHOW

ACT 1 The "show" begins in 1954 when my parents, Nick and Lee, open a mannequin repair shop in the basement of their Mt. Vernon, New York, home.

Over the next 22 years, the repair business grows into a successful company repairing mannequins in the New York metropolitan area. The repair shop is now located on 20th Street in New York City.

I join the family business in 1976. We hire a sculptor and start to make our own original mannequins.

End of Act 1

ACT 2 After learning the ropes, enjoying the "creative types" who purchase the mannequins, I begin to see great opportunities in the mannequin business. A collection in 1980 of male and female mannequins in athletic poses called "WORKOUT" is our first hit. Macy's buys hundreds, painted high-gloss black, and uses them as "sculpture" to create an Olympic environment. Gimbels in New York, Marshall Field's in Chicago, J. Wanamaker's in Philadelphia and The Broadway in Los Angeles all use "WORKOUT" with great success. I hit on something unique and different—all the other mannequin companies (there are about ten good companies worldwide) are making very proper, lady-like mannequins with makeup, wigs and nail polish. "WORKOUT" is totally different. It is sculpture.

I realize that I can take the inspiration, creativity and spirit of the pop culture of the early 1980s and create mannequins that are consistent to the times we live in. We move our factory and showroom to a 15,000 square-foot loft in Soho.

End of Act 2

ACT 3 Mannequin collections that follow are reclining mannequins as Greek and Roman statues designed for lingerie departments in finishes evoking ancient marble. Mannequins in catlike/dance poses sprayed bright red, yellow and blue with wild white wigs ("NY Dolls' Johnny Thunders"), which are created by the amazingly talented Angel Estrada, who works with me before becoming one of the most promising fashion designers and before AIDS takes him at a very young age. Another collection I am very proud of is "Avalon," a series inspired by the Roxy Music album—mannequins in severe, static poses with new wave pompadour, sculpted hair, (made "totally original" by leaving the mannequins raw, unpainted and-just sanded, so they look like stone). The collection has a chic punk feel, so I commission Stephen Sprouse to dress the collection for the show (this is before Stephen Sprouse has his first historic fashion show at the Ritz in New York City).

1985. This is a very important year. I meet the legendary Andrée Putman, who is in New York to design the first boutique hotel, Morgans. We create the "Olympian Goddess," a 6-foot, very severe, art-deco-esque mannequin for Barney's downtown store. A very young Isabel Toledo dresses the mannequin for the *Show*—hundreds attend the opening party at our Soho showroom to meet the "grand dame of design"—then Andy Warhol and Keith Haring arrive. The party goes into a frenzy as they sign autographs on T-shirts, breasts, anything their jumbo markers can sign. Pucci makes "Page Six" of the *New York Post* the next day.

Intermission

ACT 4 Andrée Putman asks me to represent her furniture collection, Ecart International, for the entire country—the year is 1990. I am now in the furniture business!

1992. We move to a very spacious 30,000 square-foot factory/showroom at 44 West 18th Street. We take the penthouse floor of this amazing warehouse in a landmark building with extraordinary NYC views and two, 20-foot skylights. We expose the aged brick and make a very raw, chic space. Our mannequin factory takes 15,000 square feet on the 11th floor of the building.

Retail goes into its biggest turmoil since the great depression with the filing of Chapter 11 by Bloomingdales, Macy's, and many others.

End of Act 4

ACT 5 My showroom is truly one of the great spaces in New York City—maybe in the world. I see so many opportunities. I start to invite artists from all the different artistic worlds to design my mannequins: to create something new, fresh, different and unique.

Ruben Toledo (not yet the greatest living fashion illustrator) collaborates on numerous collections. Architect Patrick Naggar creates a mannequin inspired by Egyptian vases. I ask Maira Kalman—the children's book author—whose *Max Makes a Million* I read a million times to my children before the lightbulb goes off in my head—to turn Max and Ada into mannequins. I'm most proud of the "Tango" collection because it takes lots of courage to transform the zany characters into high-fashion mannequins, and the idea is a hit—a big hit. "Tango" goes on to sell in the thousands all over the world.

Kenny Scharf, the pop artist, creates a one-eyed, green Flintstone-esque mannequin, which lands on the front page of the *Wall Street Journal*.

End of Act 5

ACT 6 Each *Show* gets more and more interesting, fun and successful. The crowd that each *Show* attracts becomes a New York happening, with a mix of artists, businessman, models, musicians, actors, visual directors and architects in attendance.

End of Act 6

ACT 7 Furniture becomes more and more important to me, professionally and artistically. My love of sculptural mannequins easily evolves into the sculptural wooden furniture pieces of Chris Lehrecke. Other furniture designers sign up to show exclusively at RALPH PUCCI—Patrick Naggar, Paul Mathieu, and the legends Jens Risom and Vladimir Kagan.

Each *Show* is a mix of the arts: a mural painted by an up-and-coming artist, to complement the furniture. Art and photography enhance the total vision; music by Miles Davis, Philip Glass; operas by Vivaldi—they all complete the scene.

We take an additional 15,000 square-foot floor in the building, call it "Nine" gallery, paint it white. We now have 30,000 square feet in which to put on a *Show*. We take the same gallery "Nine" concepts (all white) out west and open a Los Angeles showroom.

End of Act 7

ACT 8 I continue looking for the hand of the artist to be seen—nothing mass produced. I'm constantly looking for something new and different; timeless not trendy.

I've always felt that mannequins should be elegant, modern, edgy and hip. Furniture should be eternal, exquisitely made, something cherished forever. Art should make you think. A successful *Show* should be a "wow." The passion, love, excitement and creativity of each *Show* must be felt and enjoyed. There is no final act to this book because there is much more of the *Show* to experience.

Enjoy this *SHOW*!

Ralph Pucci
New York City

Note: Titles appearing in quotation marks denote the title of the exhibition at Pucci International; when cited in italics, the artist's own title is indicated. If no title is given, the work is untitled.

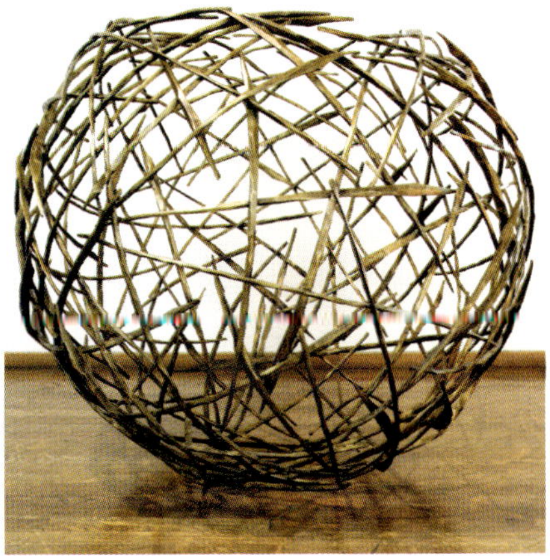

Herve Van Der Straeten, 2008

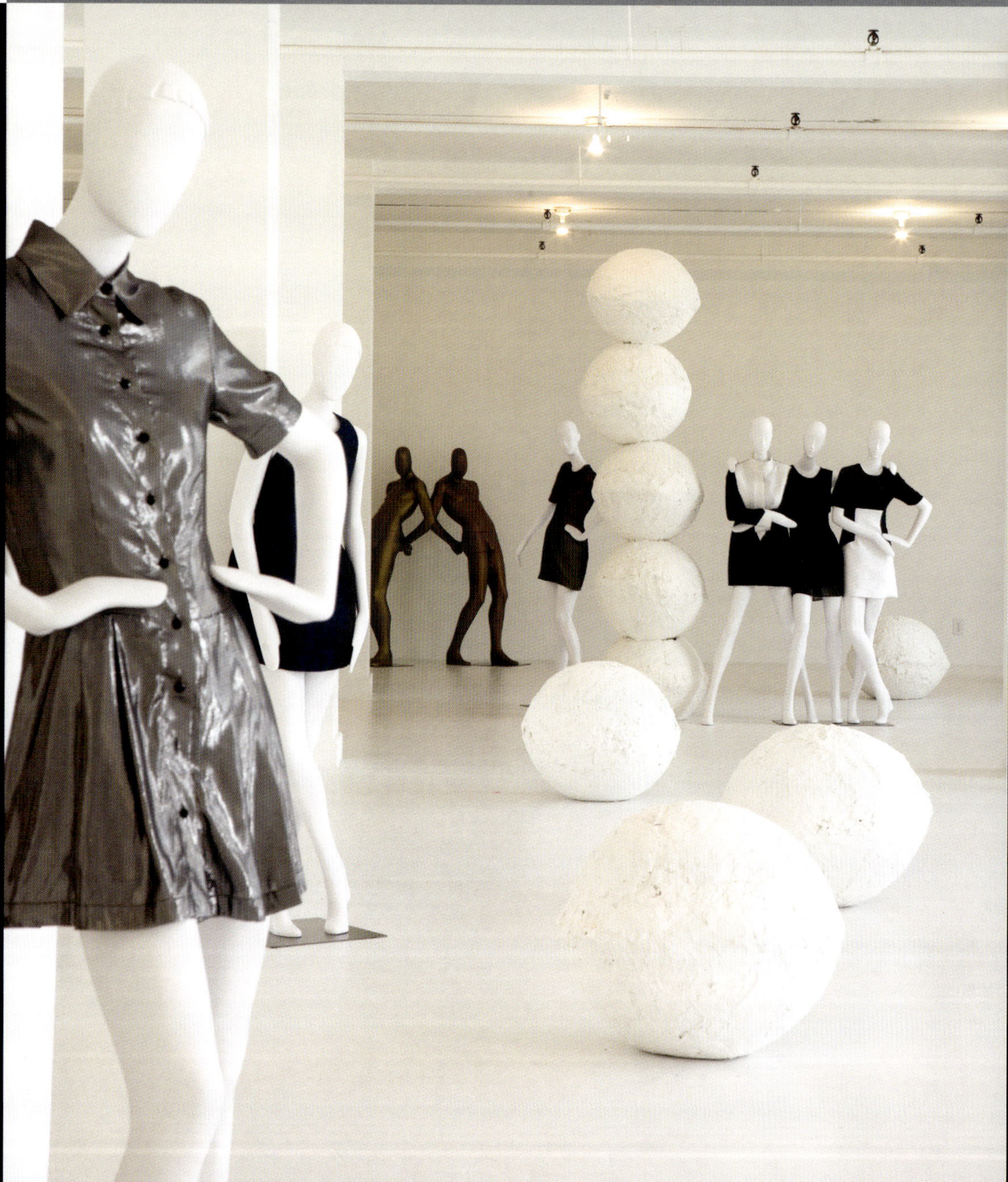

SHOW

(shō), v.,

To cause or allow to be seen, exhibit, display. To present or perform as public entertainment or spectacle. To indicate, point out, to show the way. To guide, escort, or usher. To explain, or make clear, make known.

Ralph Pucci, *Girl Mannequin*, 2008, fashion by Frank Tell

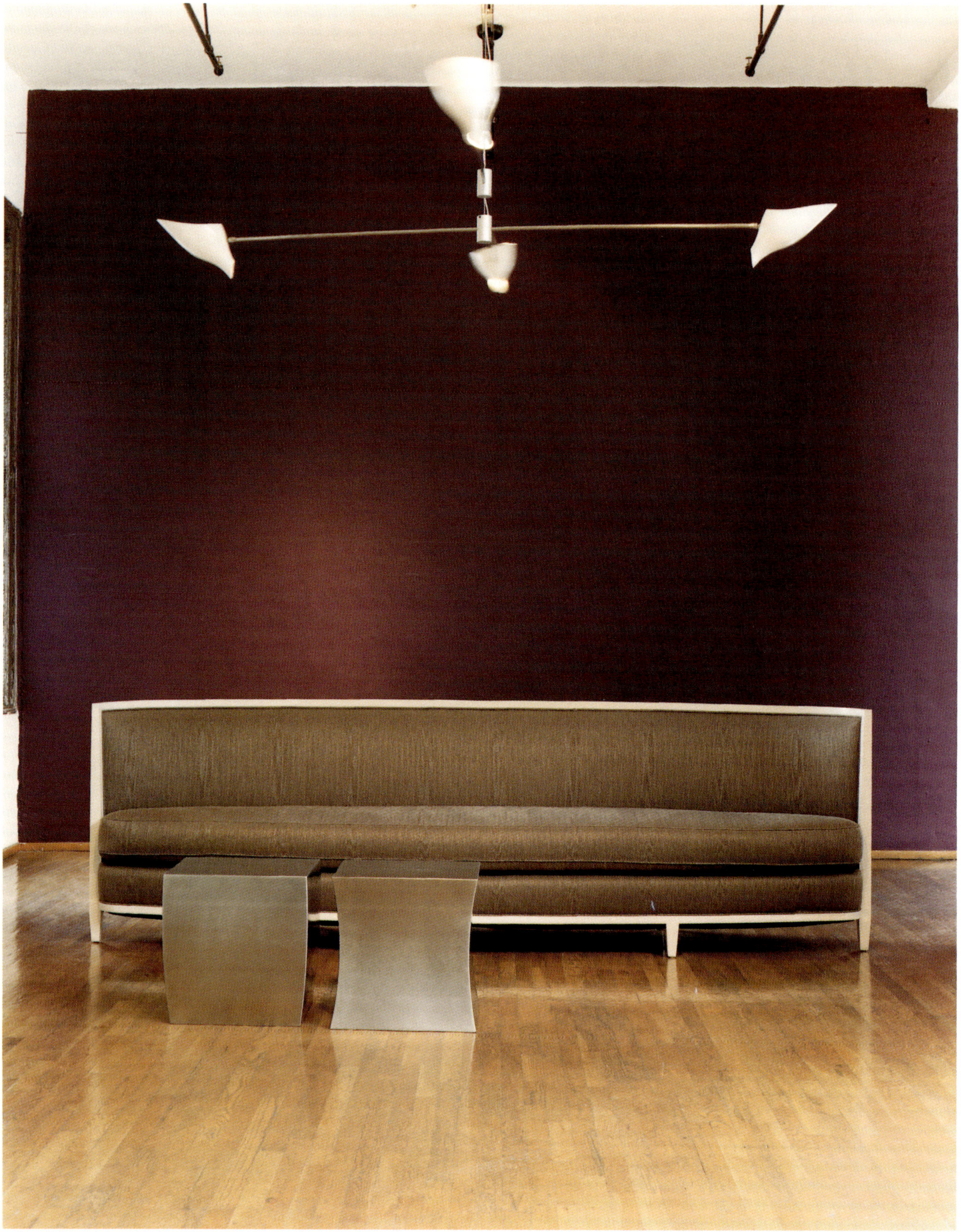

 andrée putman *Crescent Moon* sofa, 2000, tables by Chris Lehrecke, lamp by David Weeks (above); *Playing with Drawers* cabinet, 2000 (right)

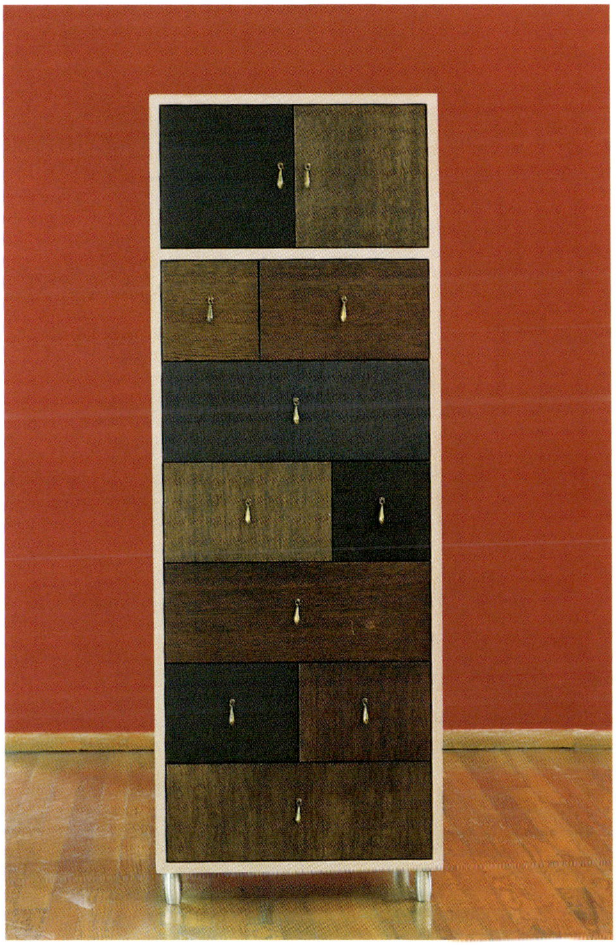

"I enjoy working primarily on space and light, and with special care taken for the sobriety, naturalness and elegance of details."

—Andrée Putman

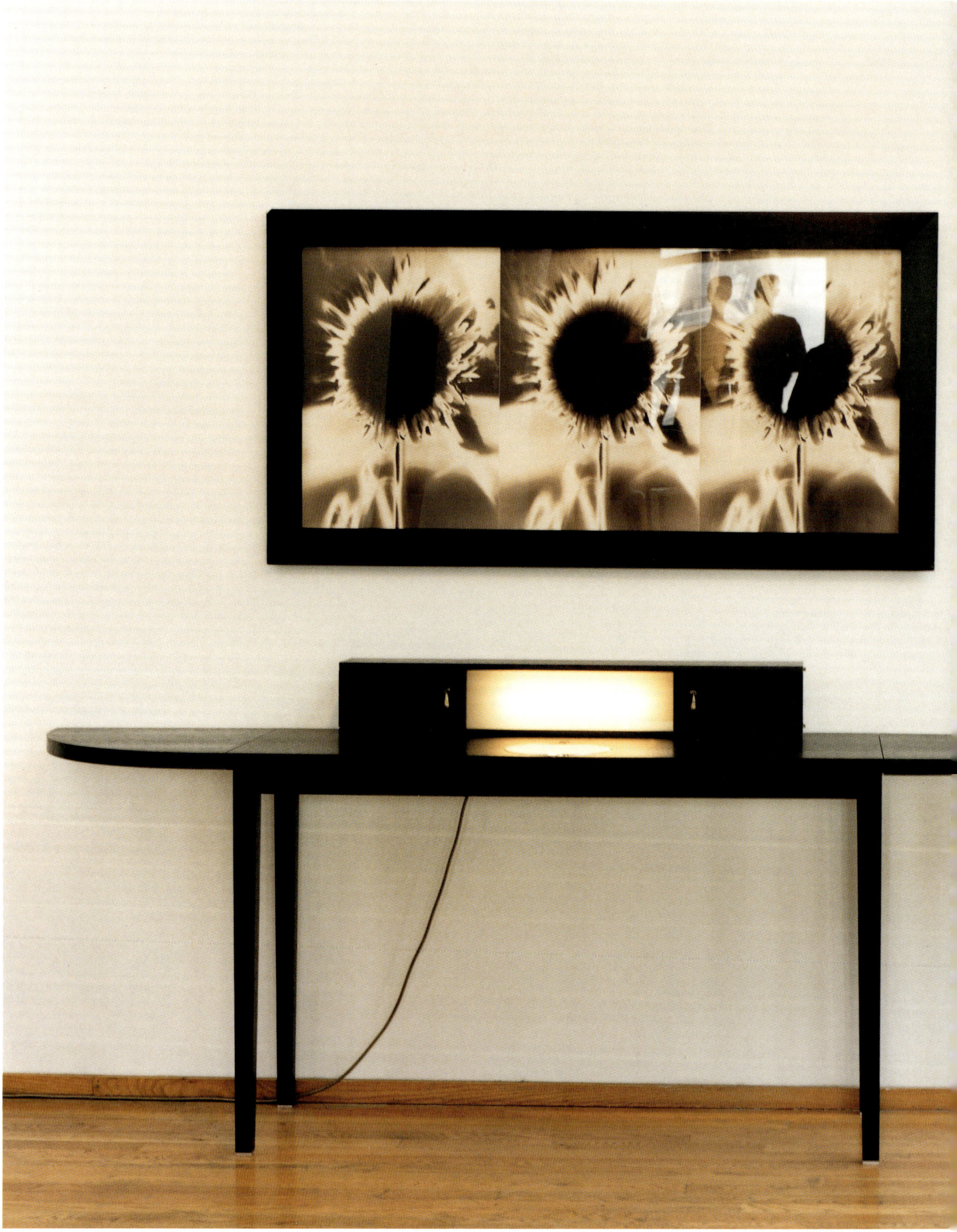

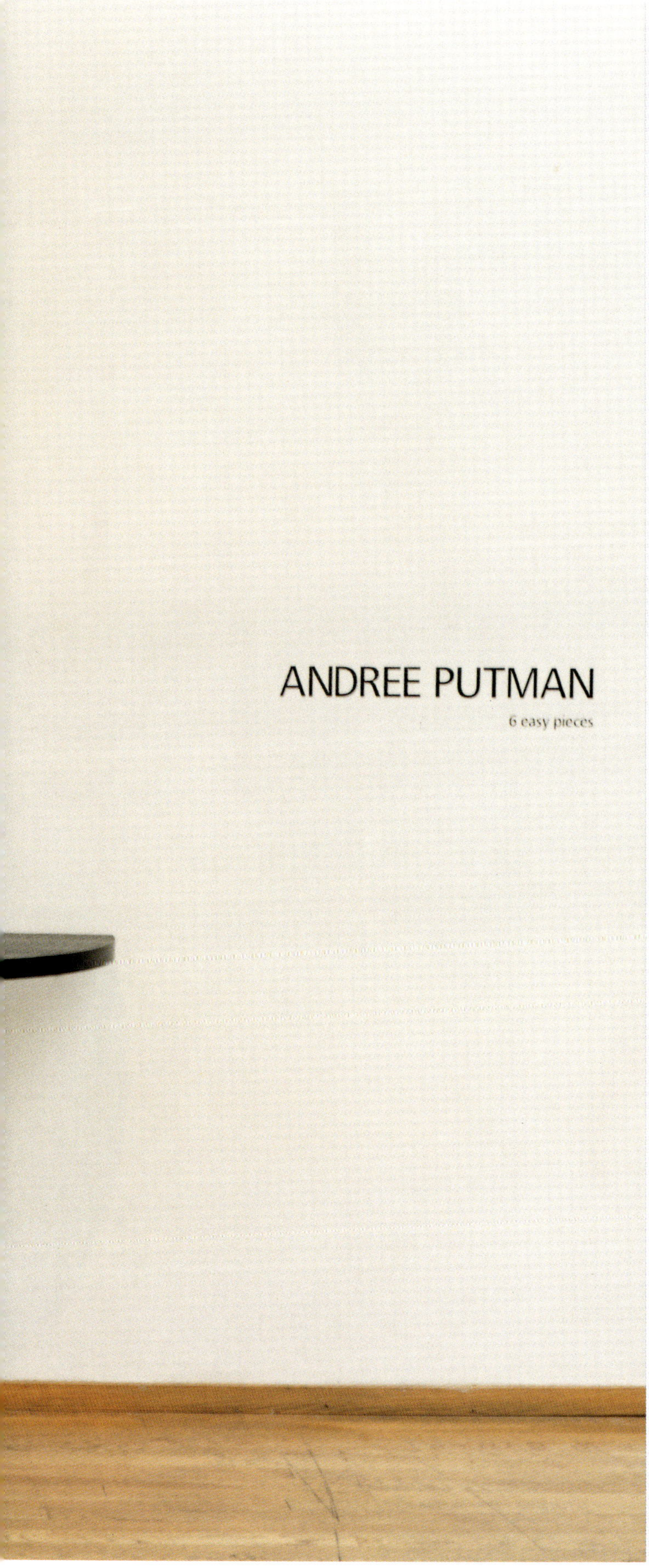

ANDREE PUTMAN

6 easy pieces

Double Play vanity, 2000, photograph by Gail LeBoff

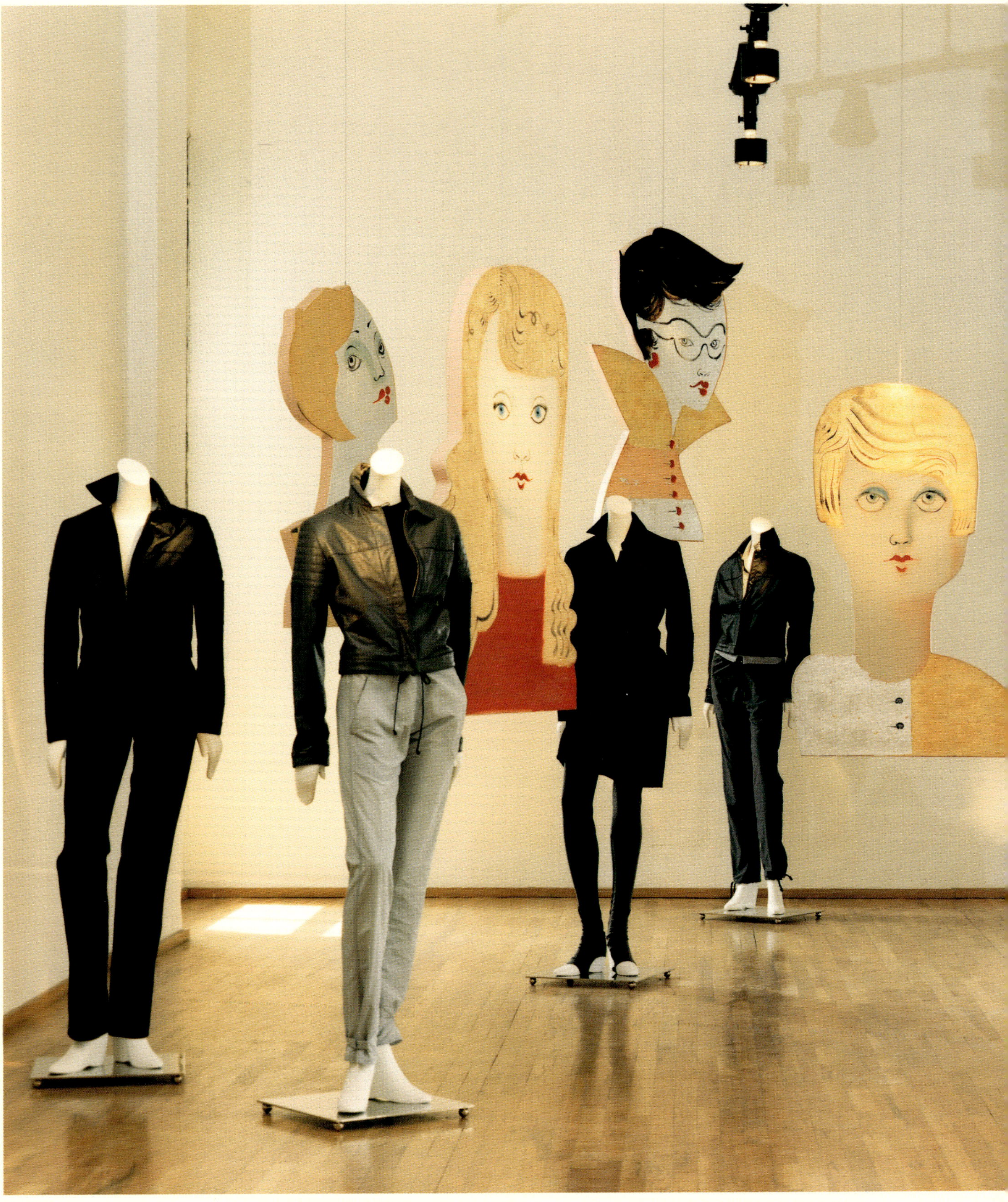

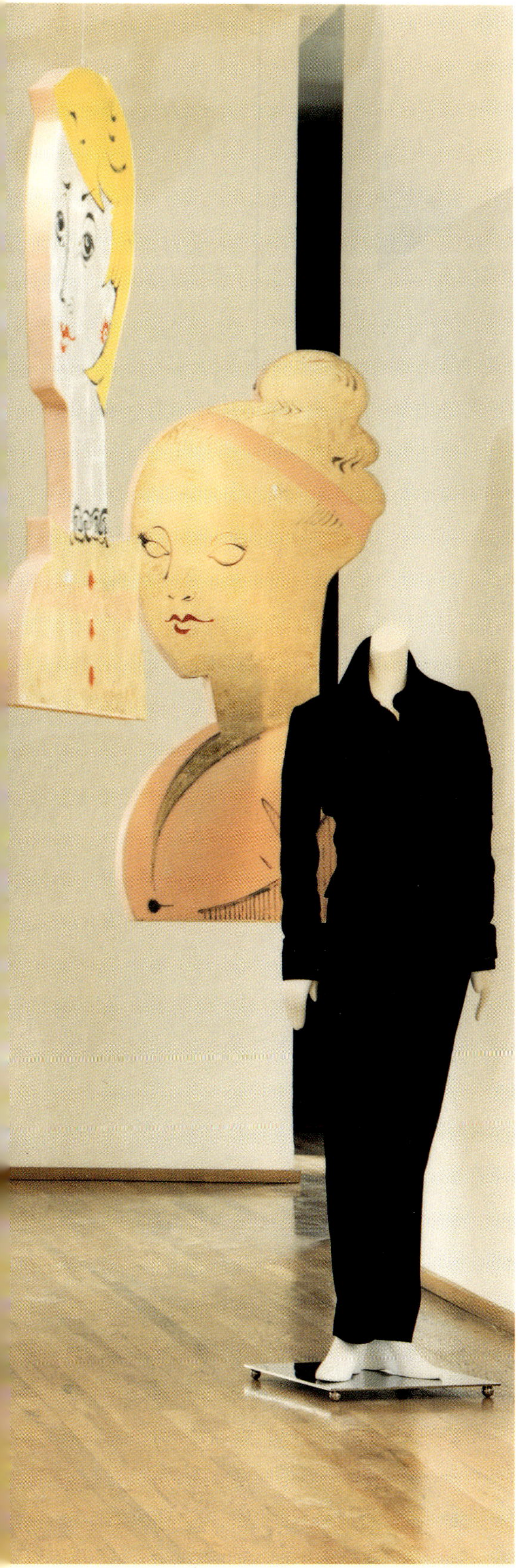

"For artists to give the world their very best work, we have to work among friends; we have to feel comfortable to create, and Ralph Pucci has created an atmosphere of freedom of design."

—Ruben Toledo

ruben toledo mannequins and mobiles, 1997, fashions by Darryl K

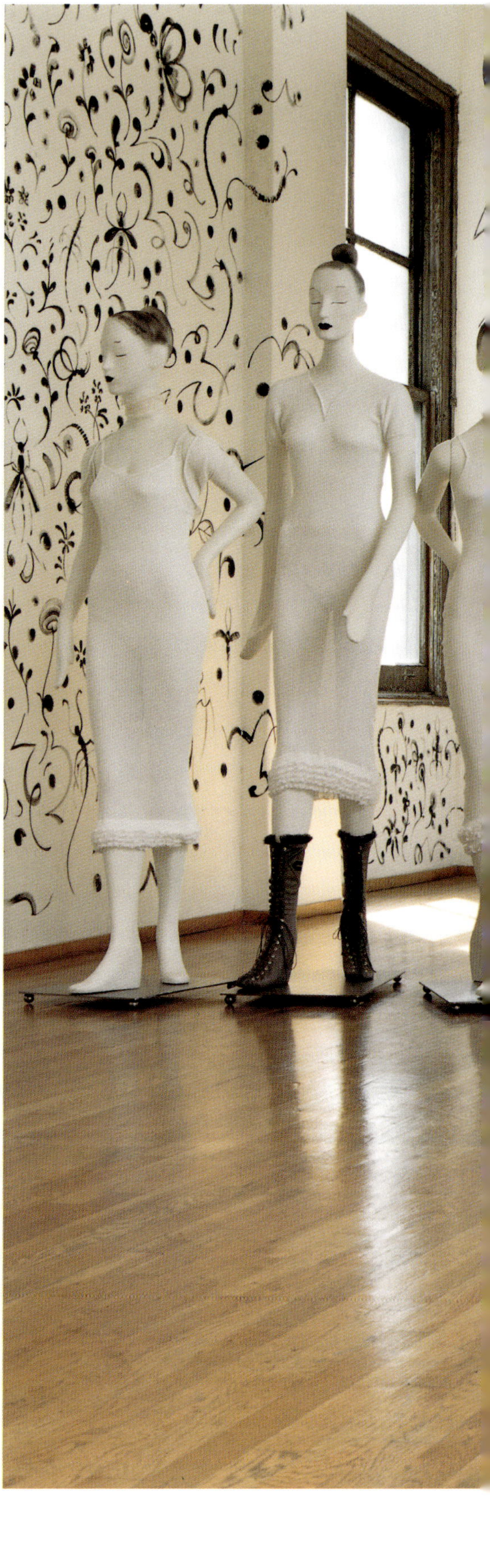

Birdie mannequins and mural, 2000, fashions by Isabel Toledo

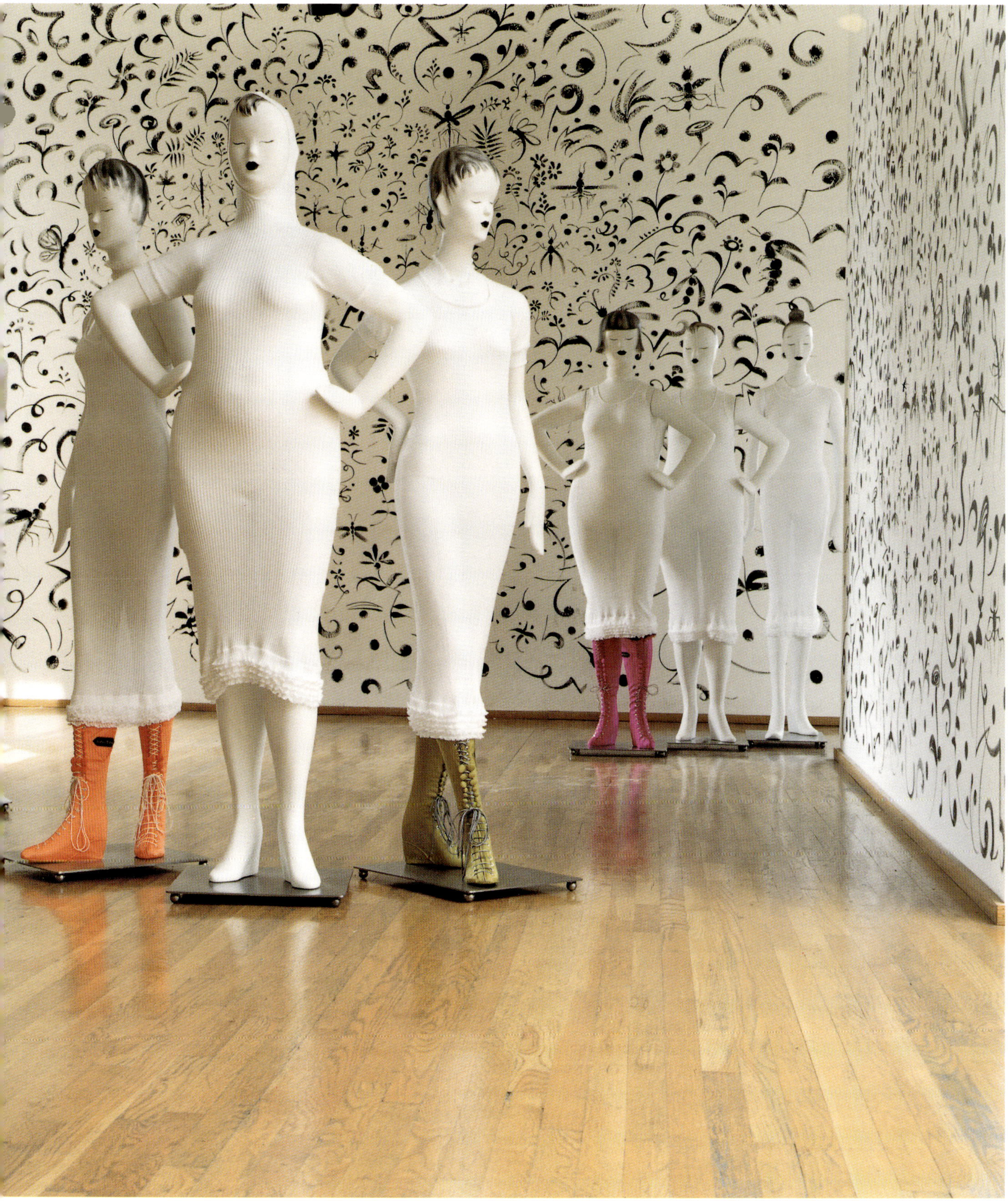

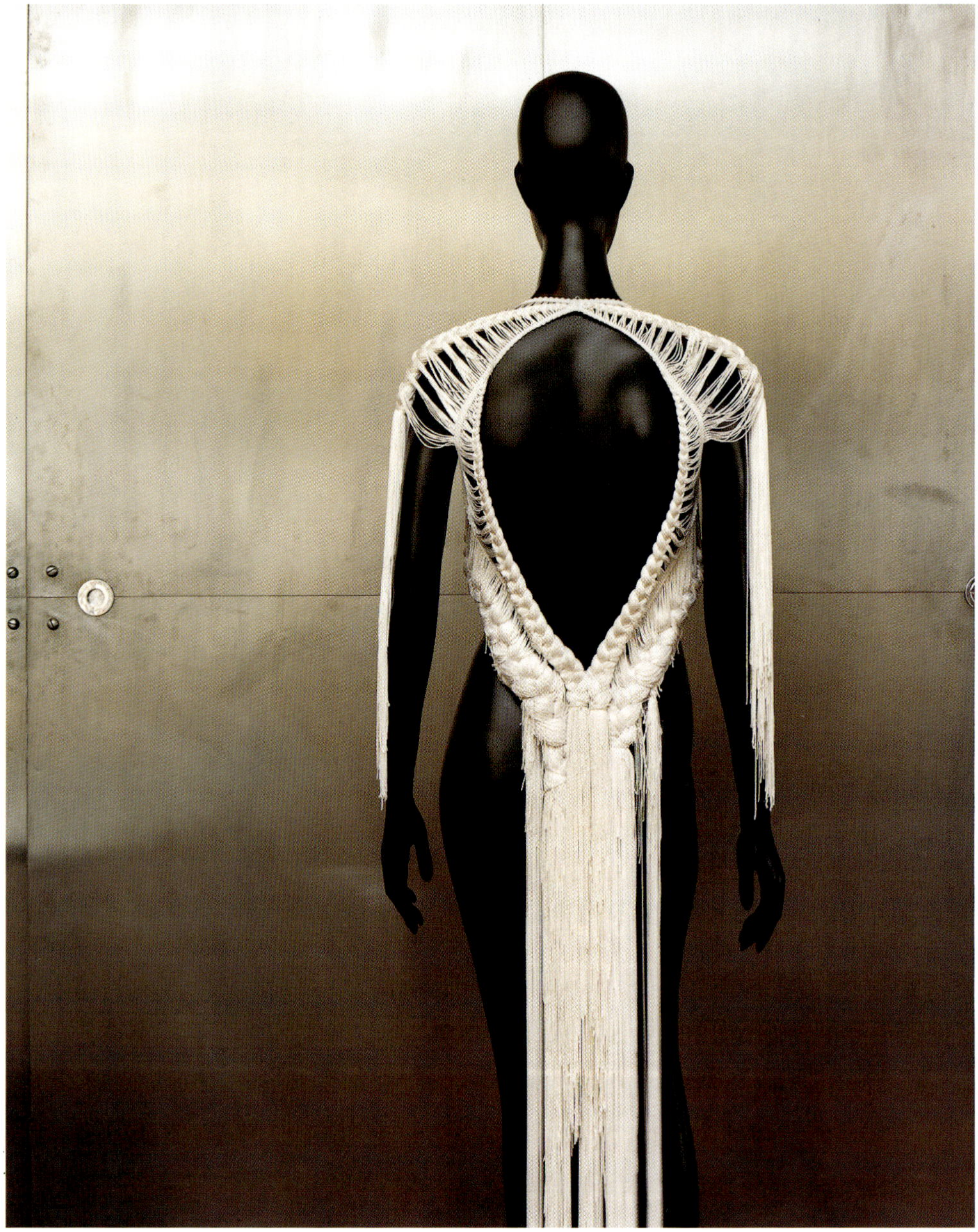

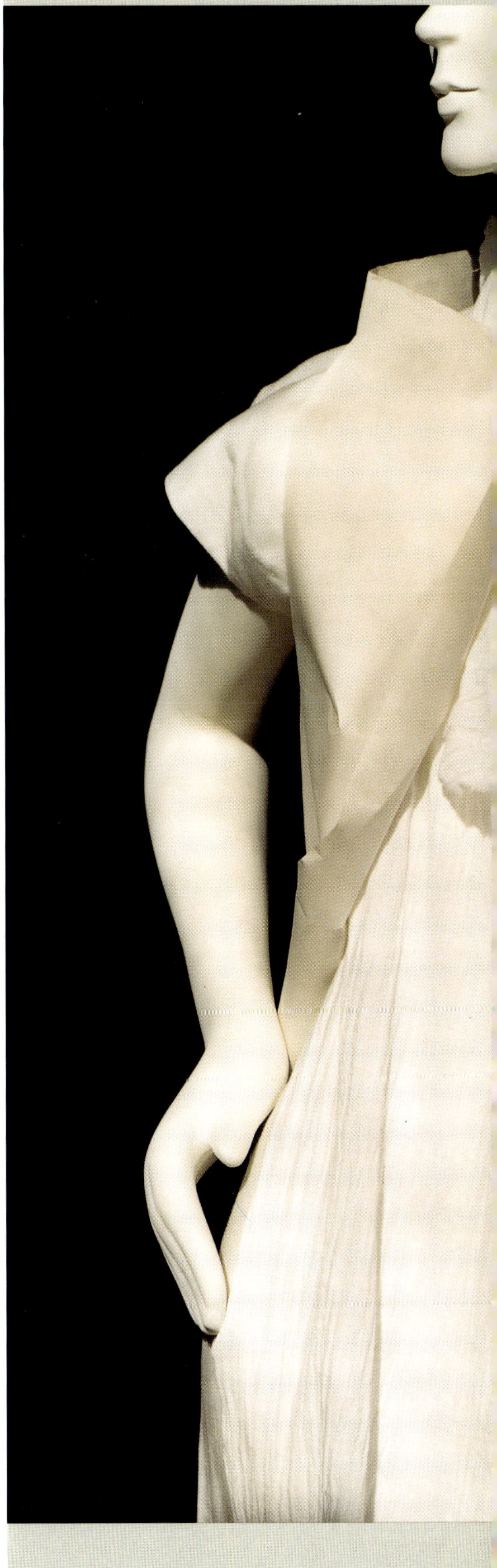

Fashions by Benjamin Cho (left); fashions by Susan Cianciolo (right)

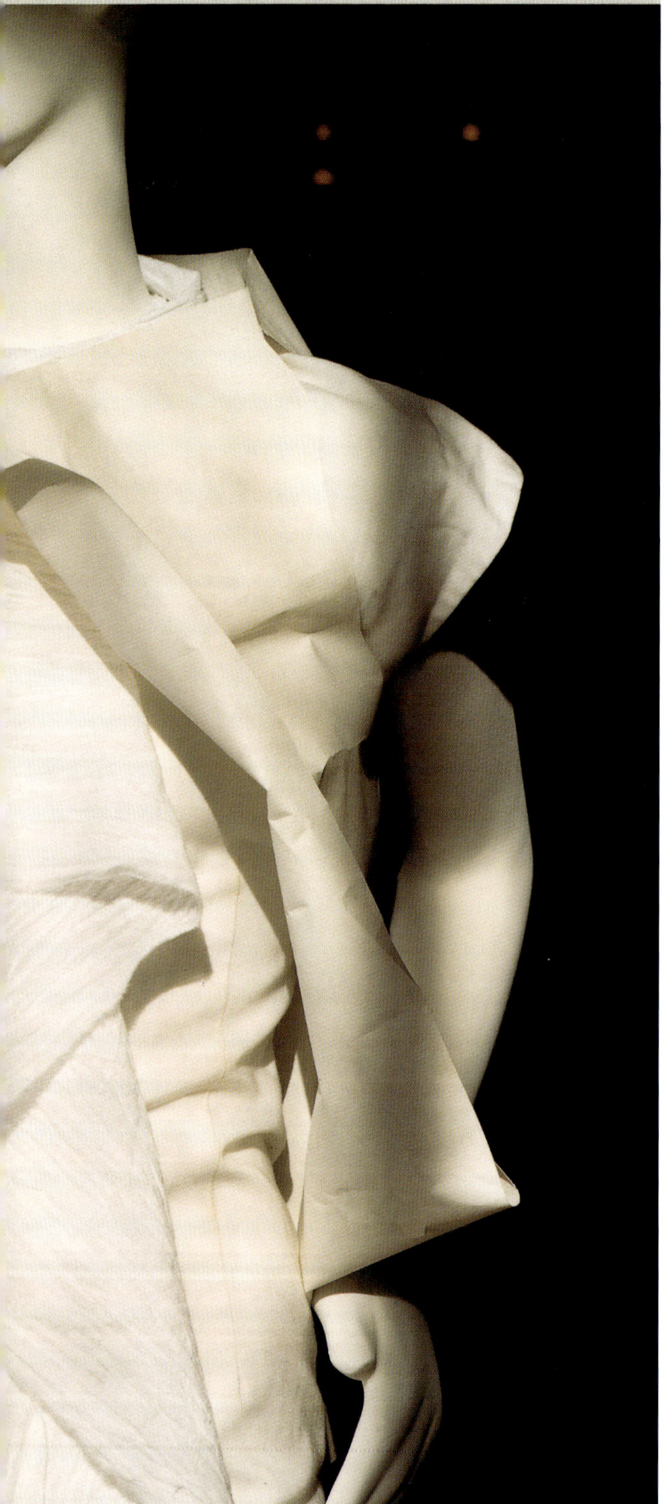

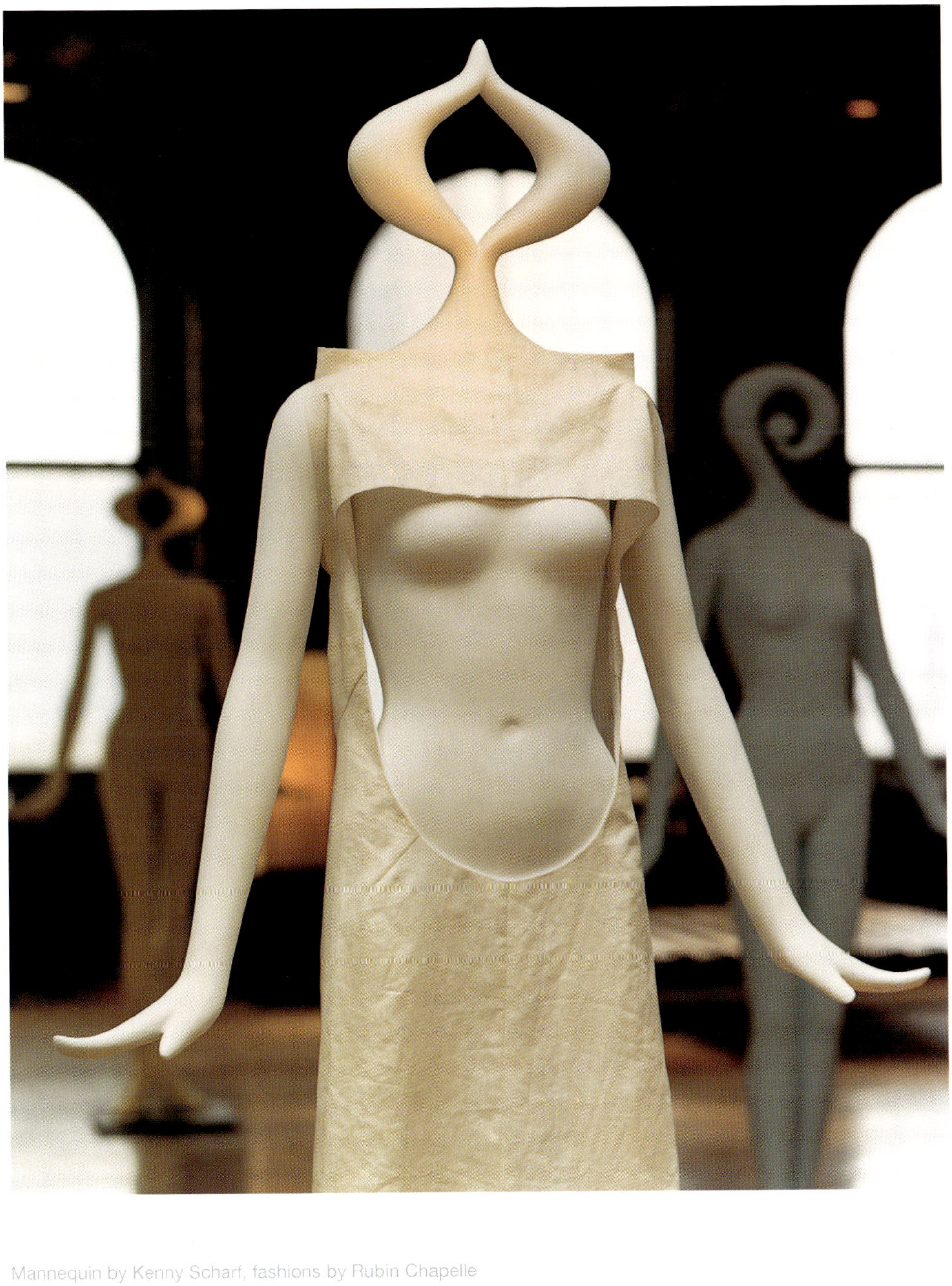

Mannequin by Kenny Scharf, fashions by Rubin Chapelle

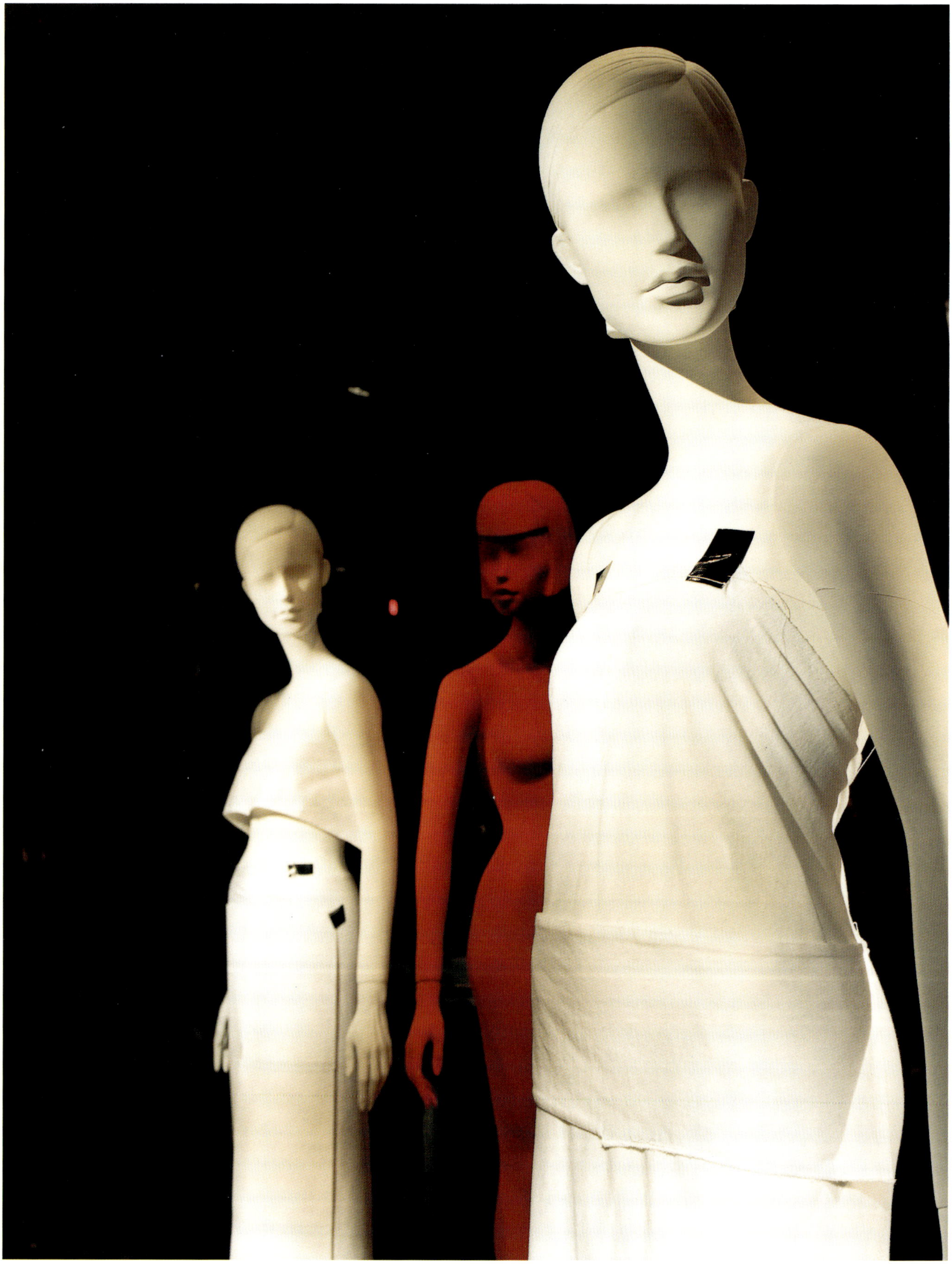

 hiroshi tanabe mannequins, 1997, fashions by Susan Cianciolo

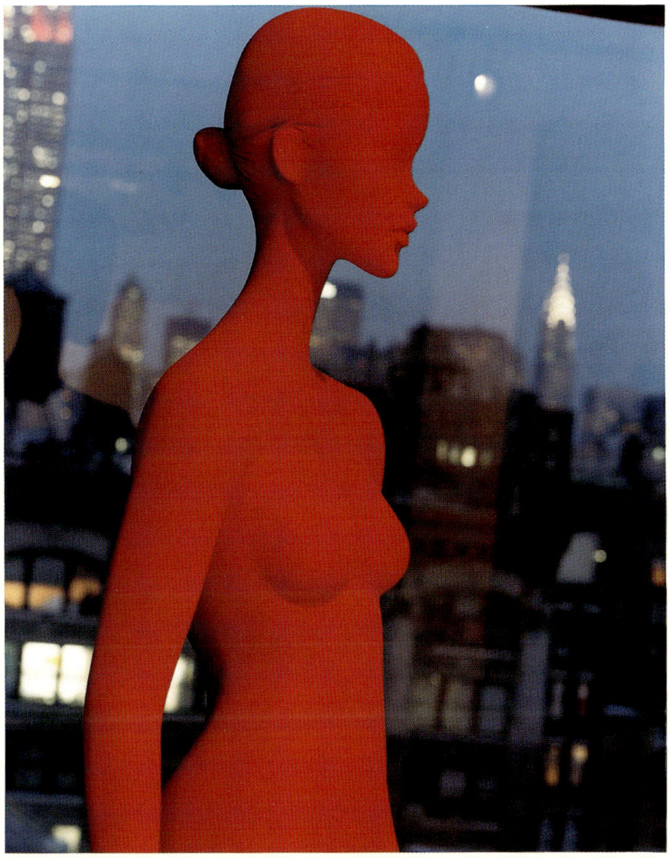

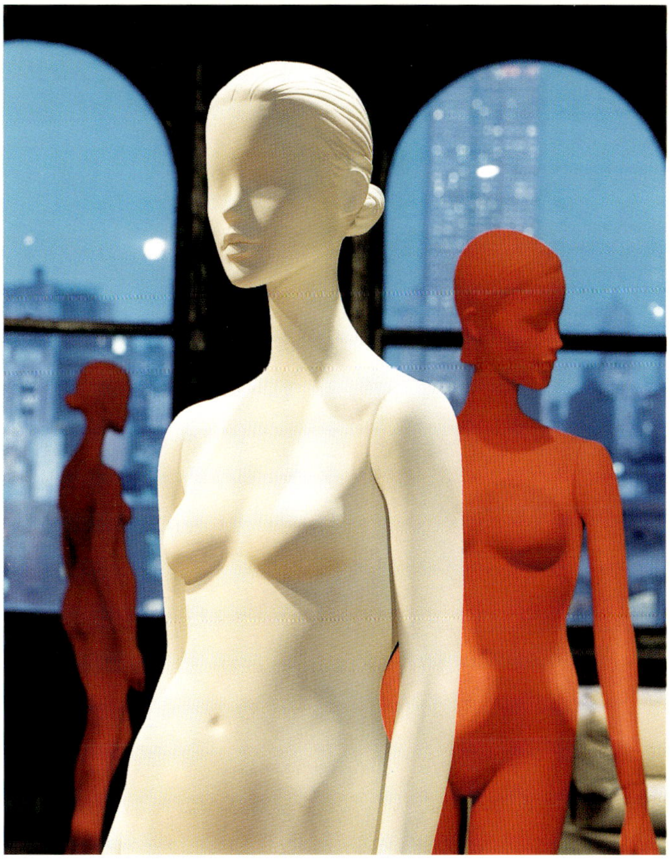

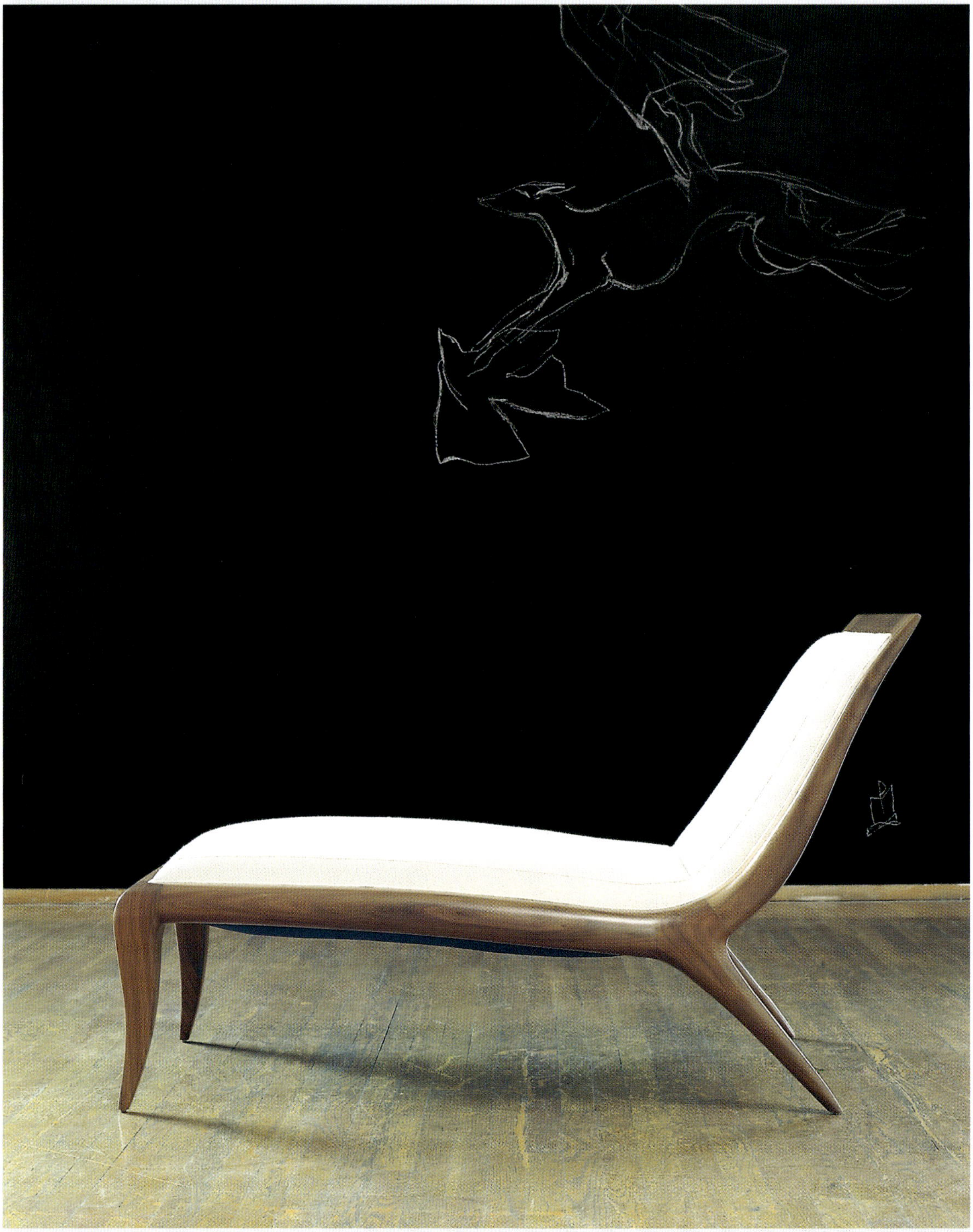

paul mathieu *Havana* chaise and drawing, 2006

"The first impression should never be the last; the first emotion should be a constant source of inspiration."

—Paul Mathieu

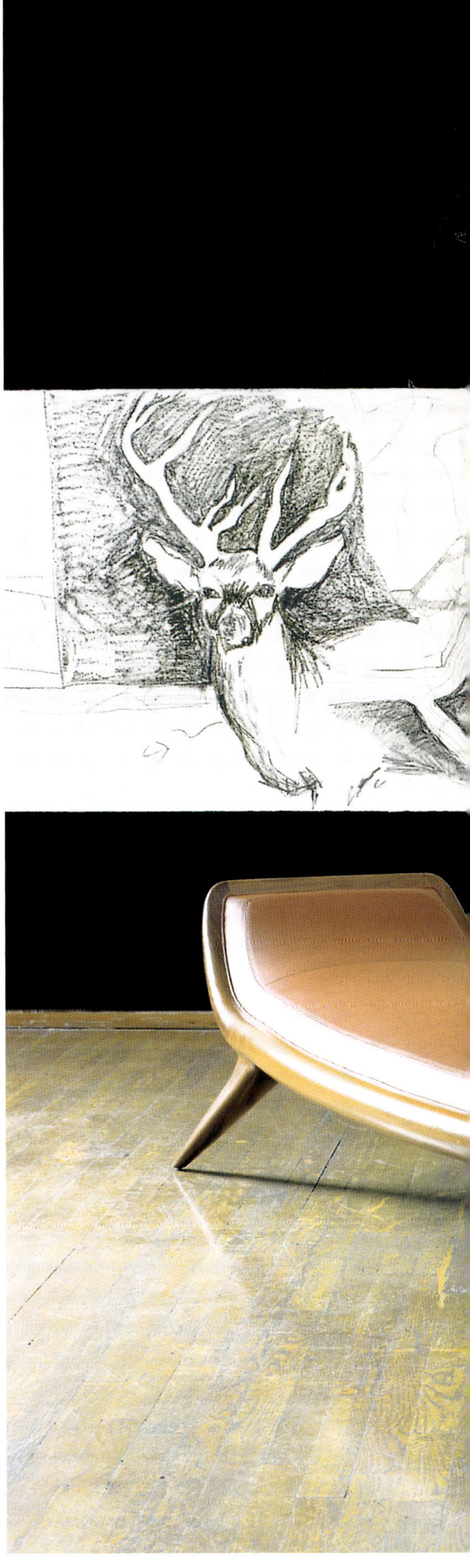

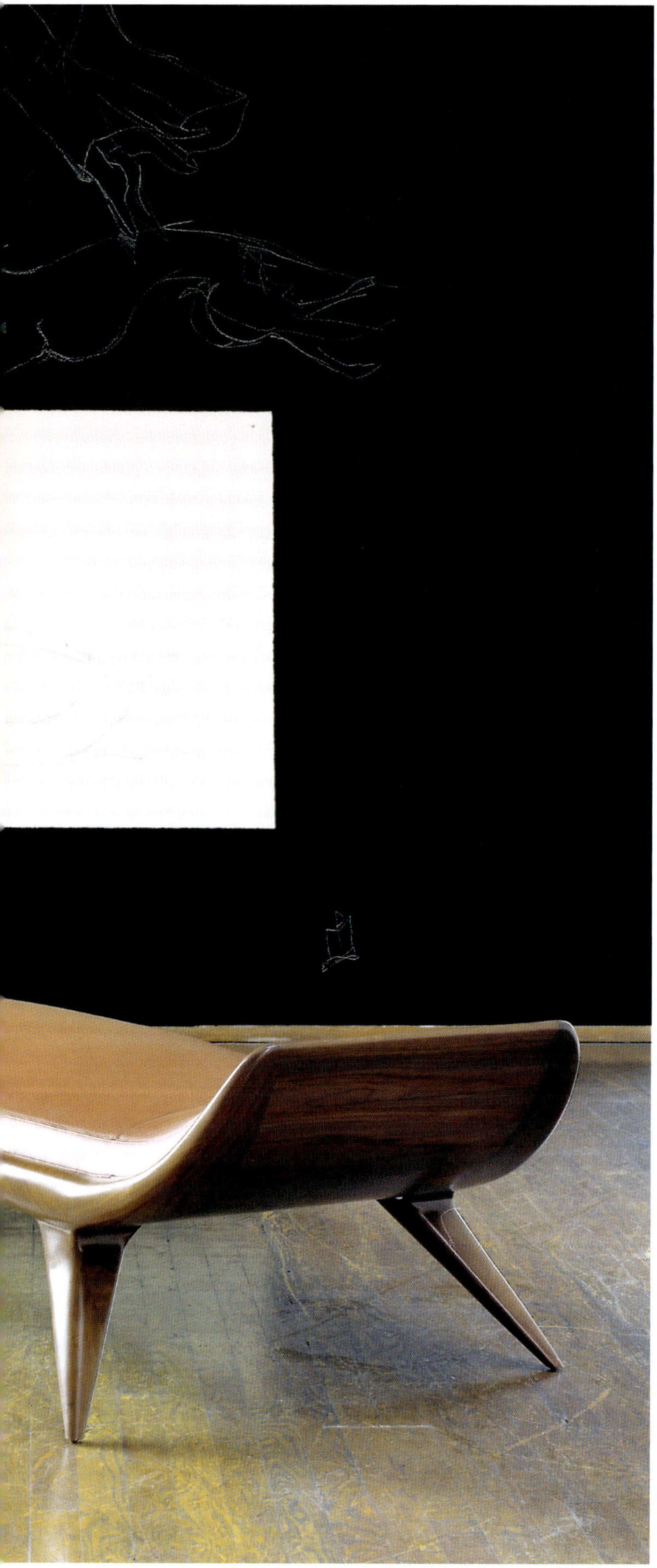

Havana day bed, 2006 (left); *Havana* console, 2006 (right)

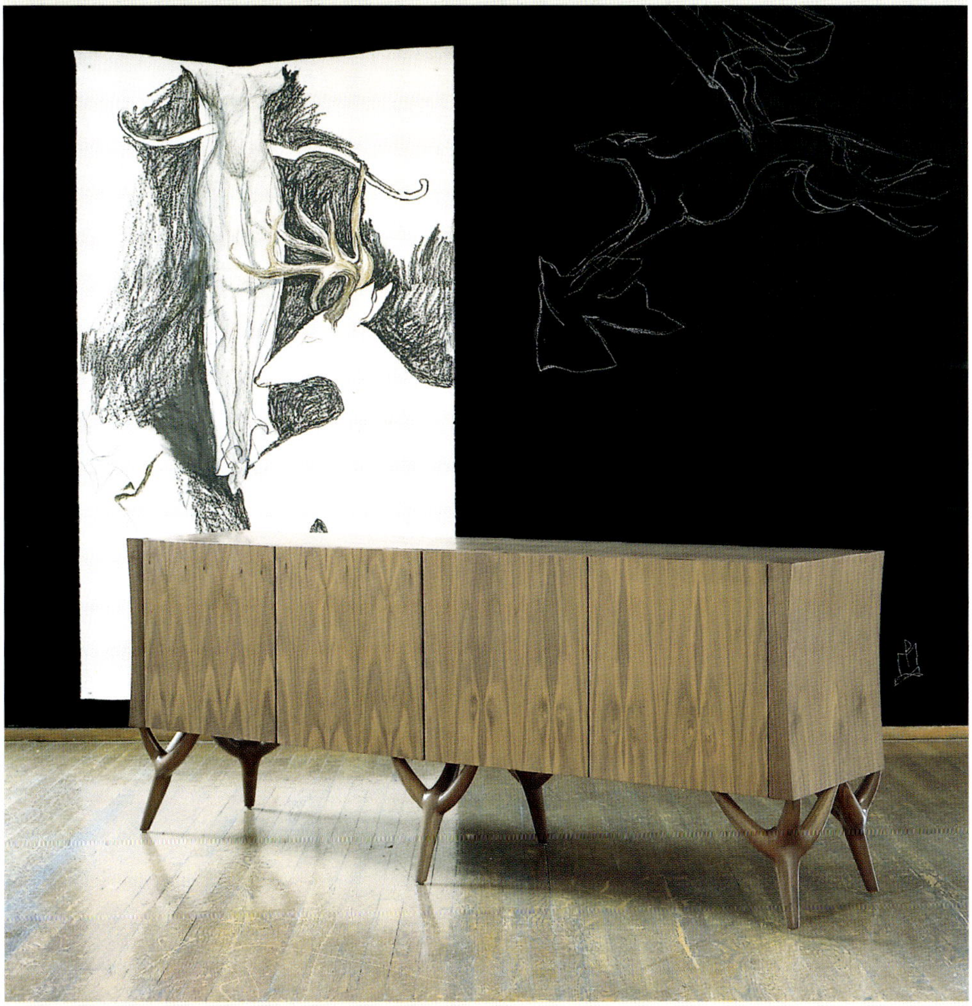

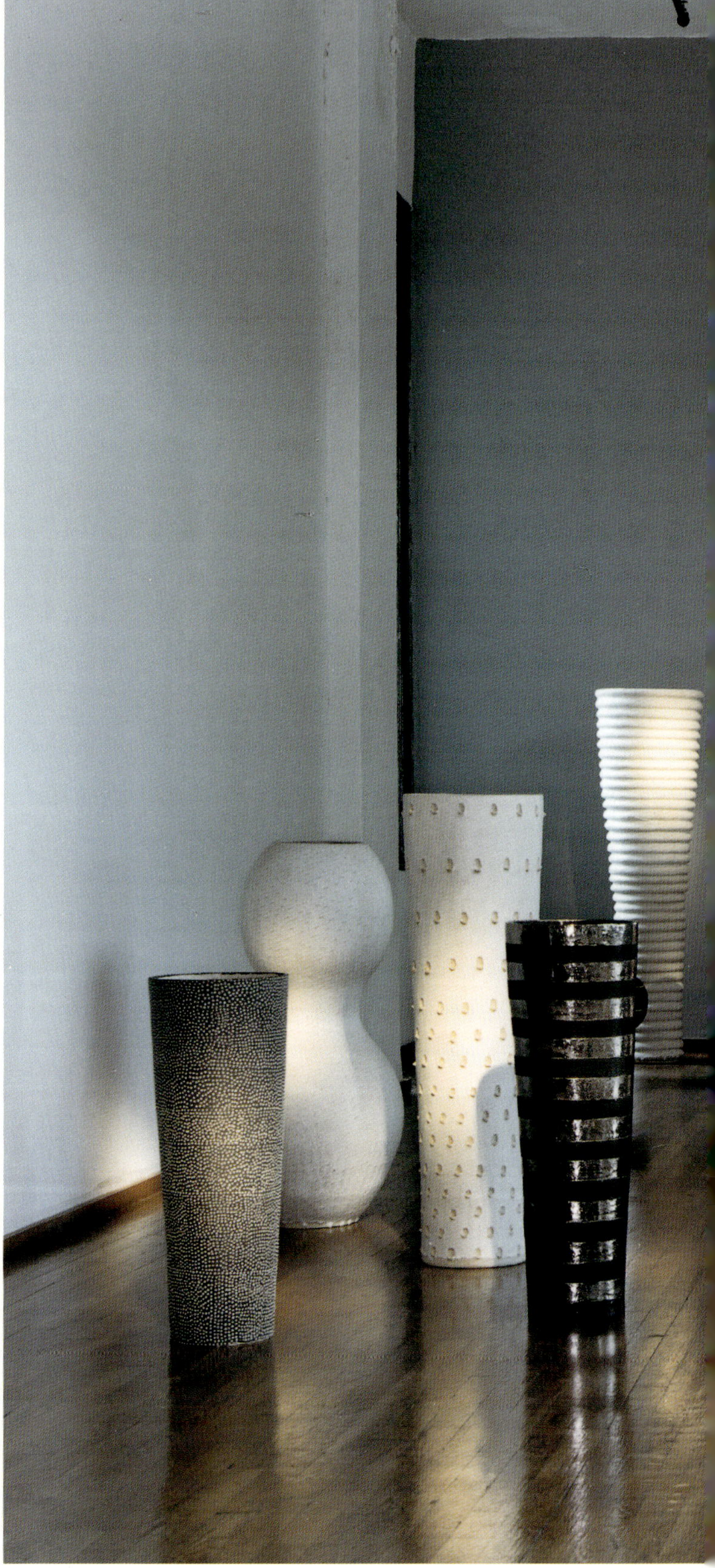

abigail simpson "Ceramic Vessels," 2001

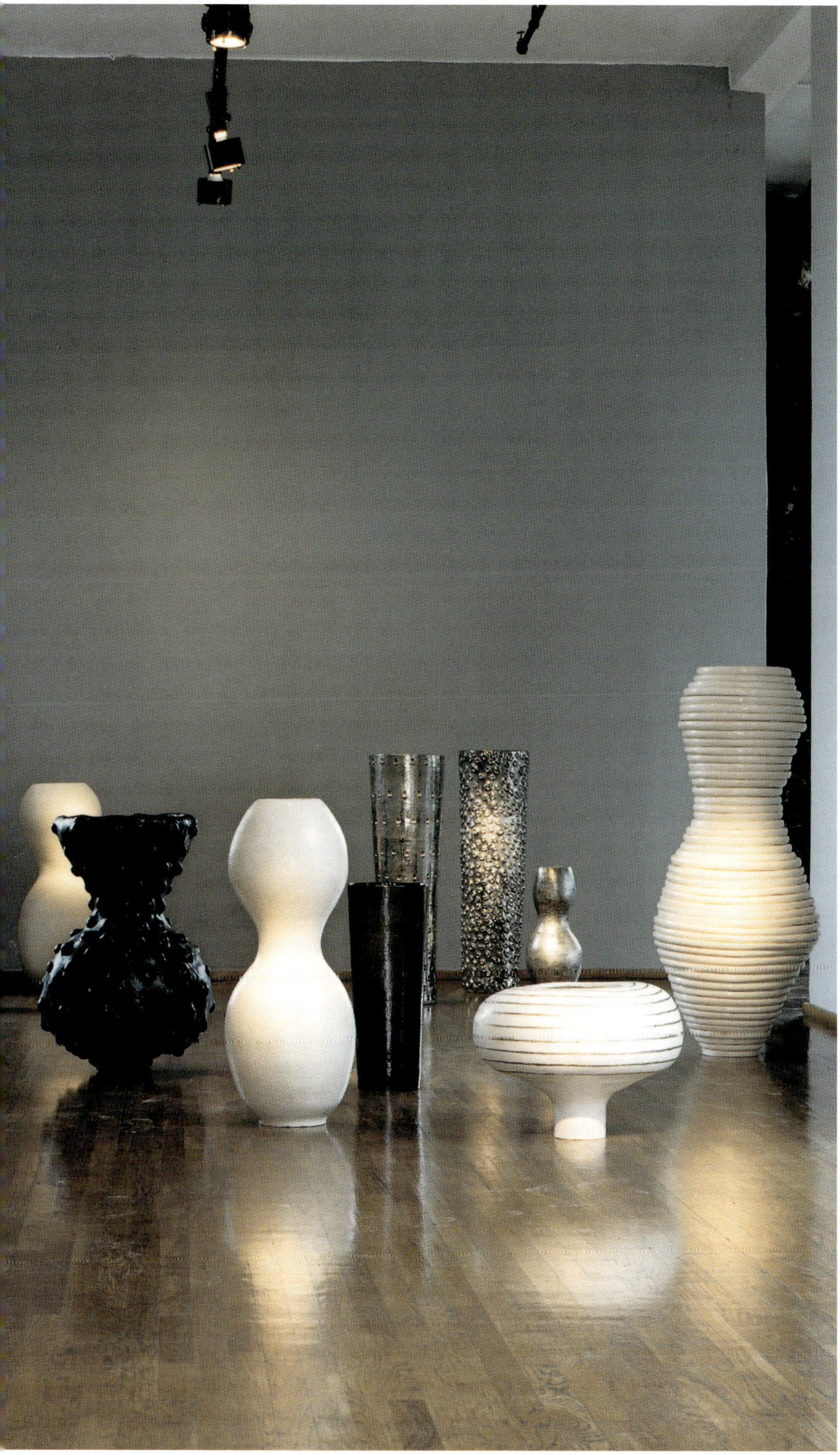

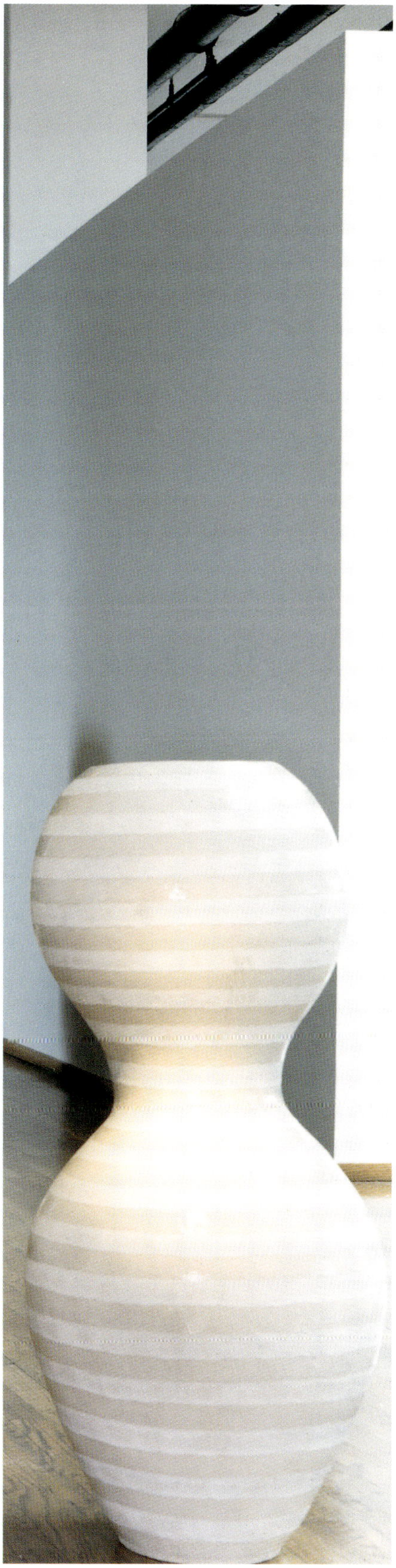

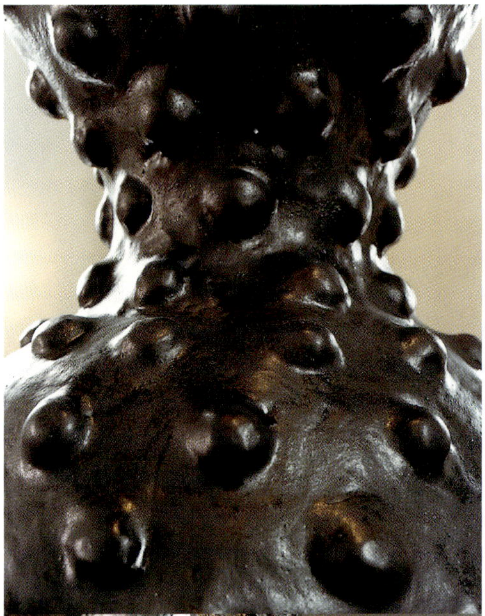
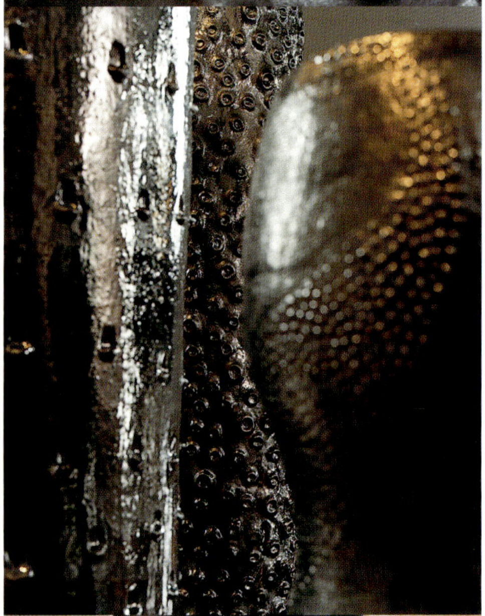
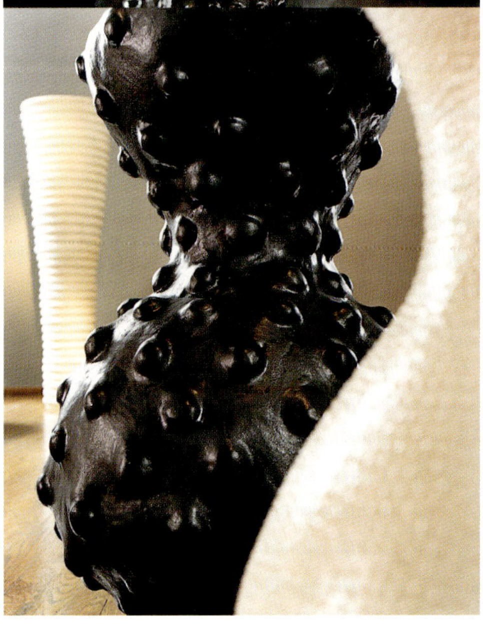
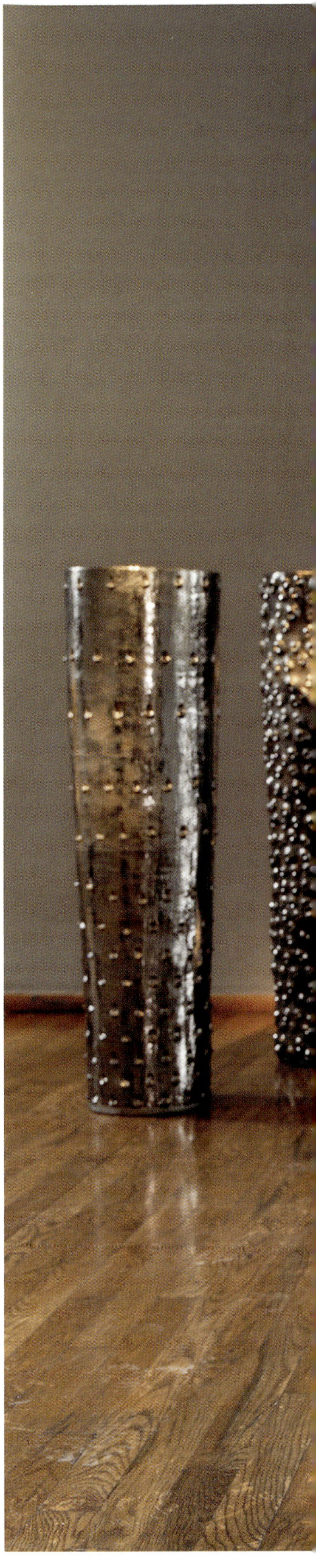

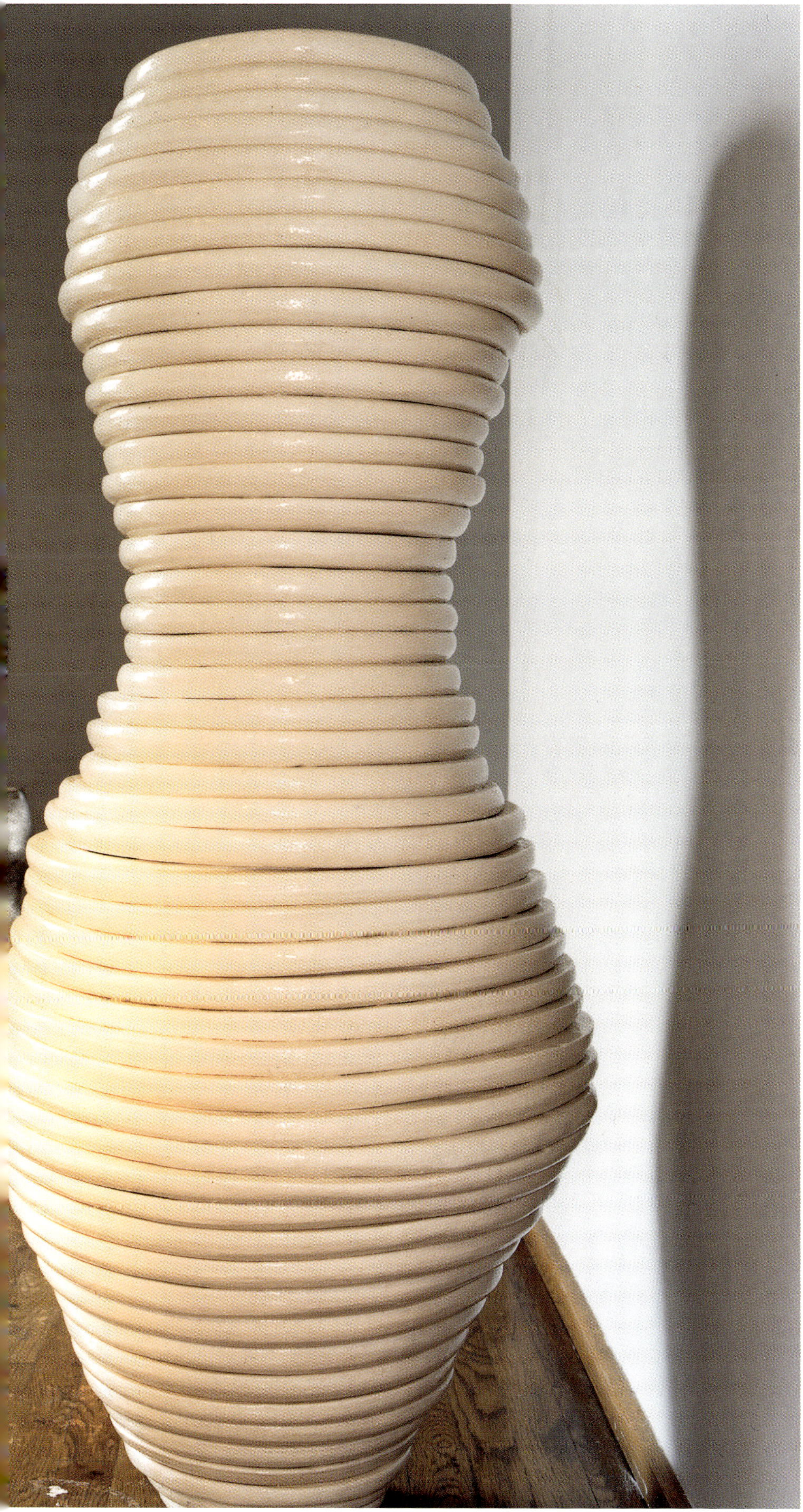

"Ceramic Vessels," 2001

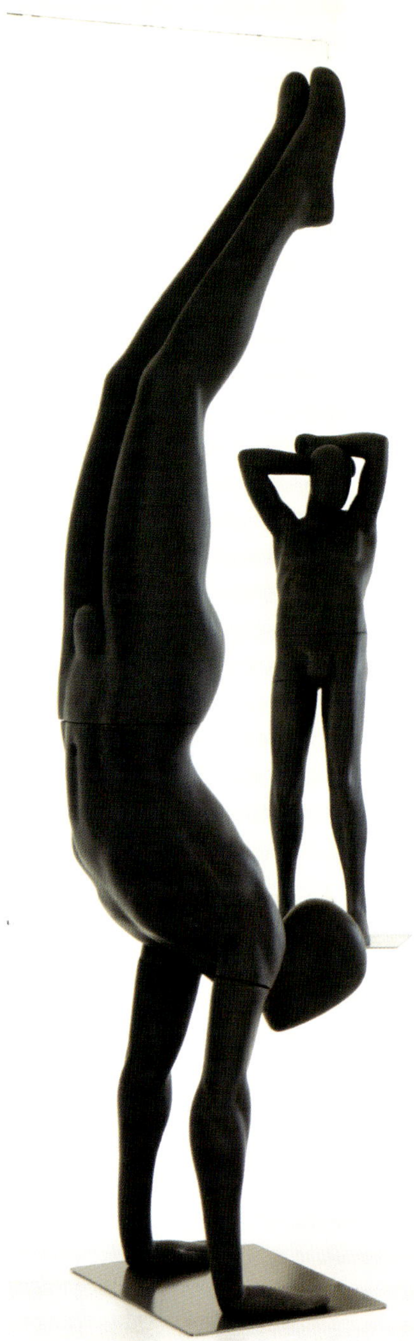

ralph pucci *SPORT* mannequins, 2007

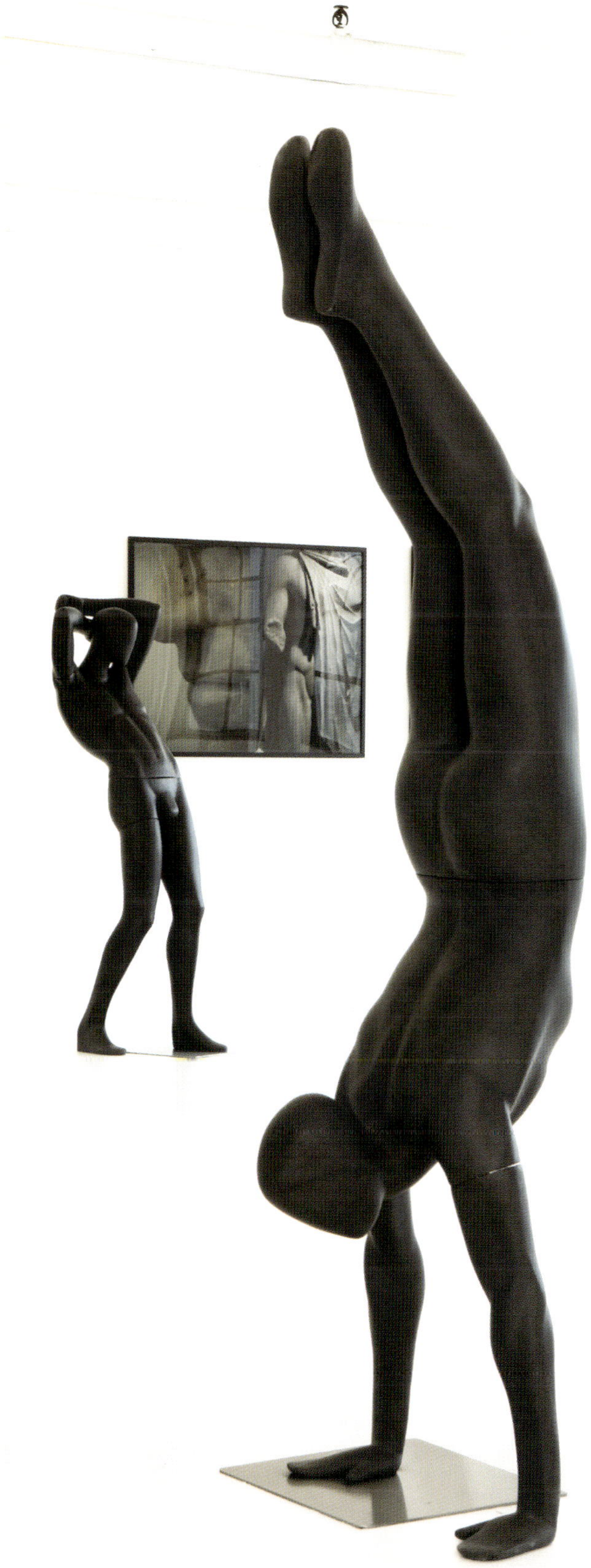

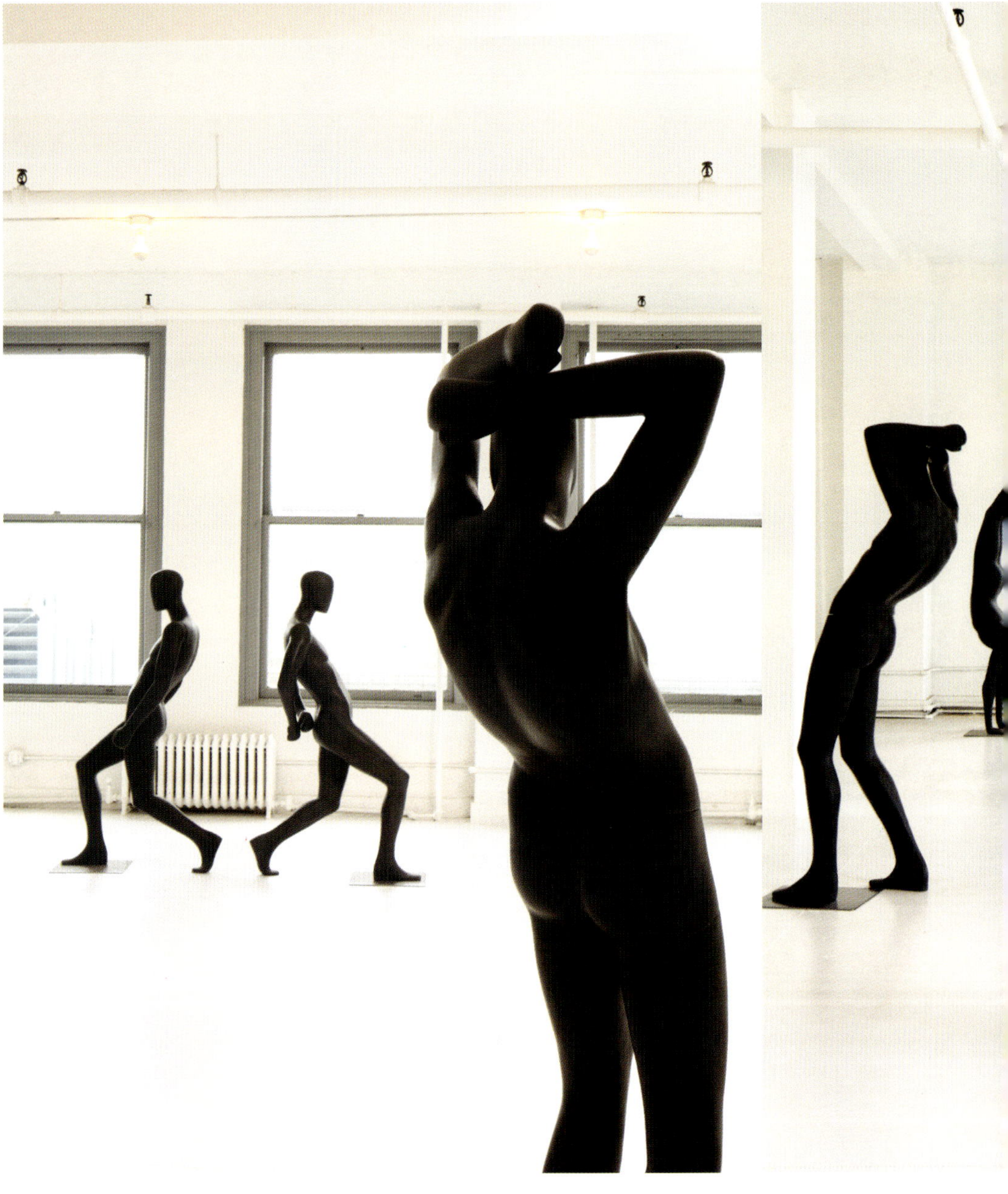

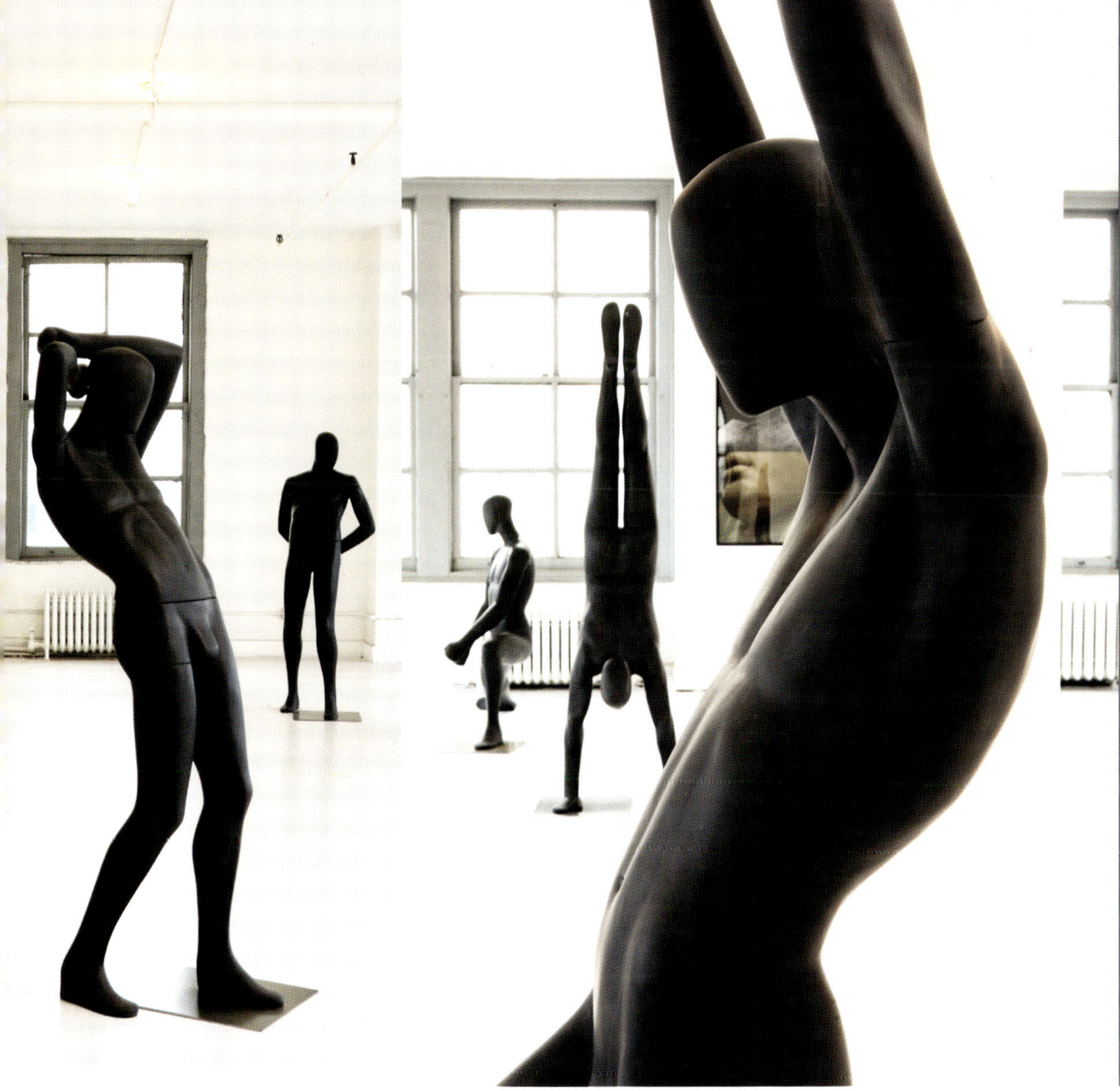

SPORT mannequins, 2007

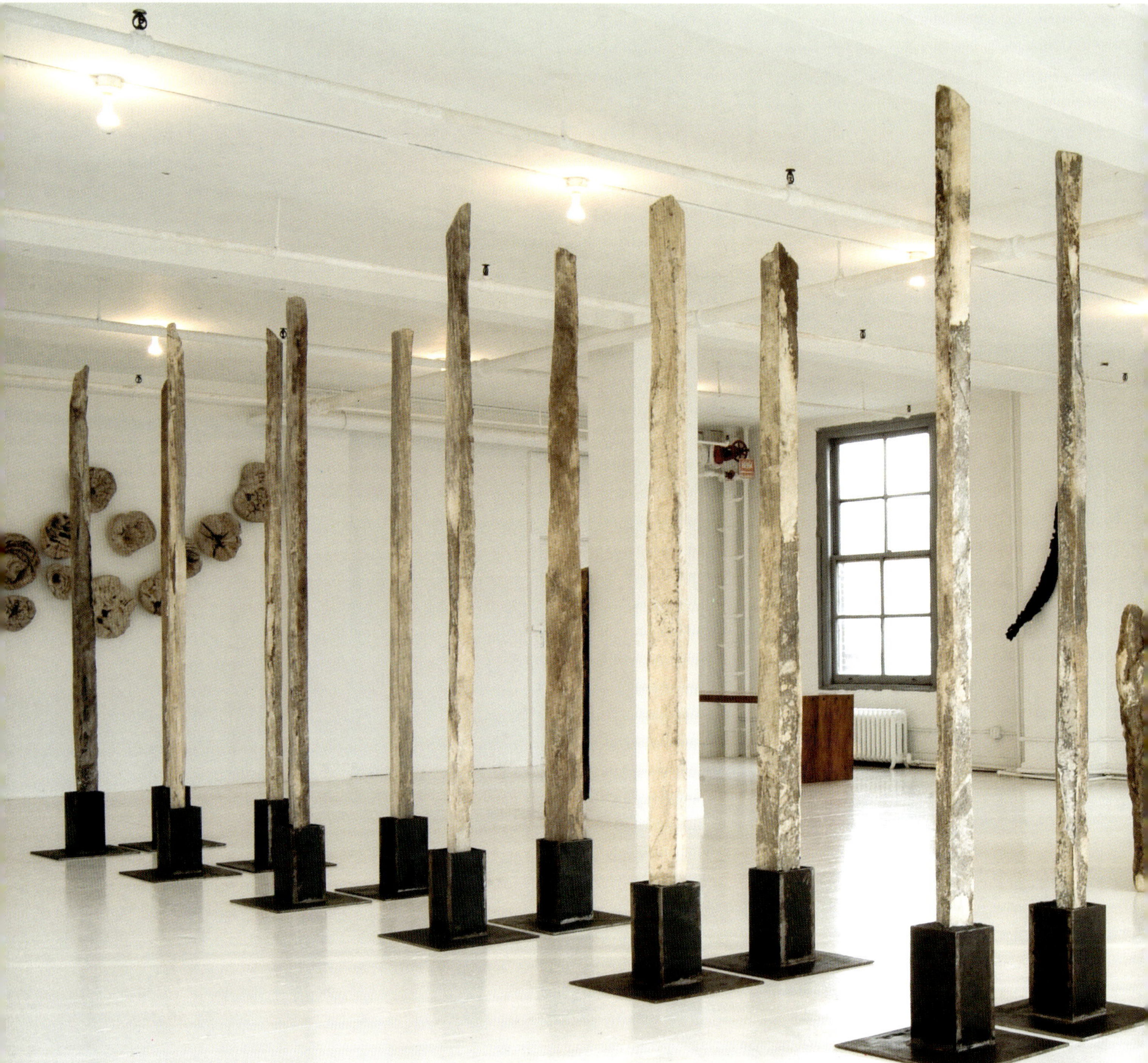

 jerome abel seguin stone, 2002

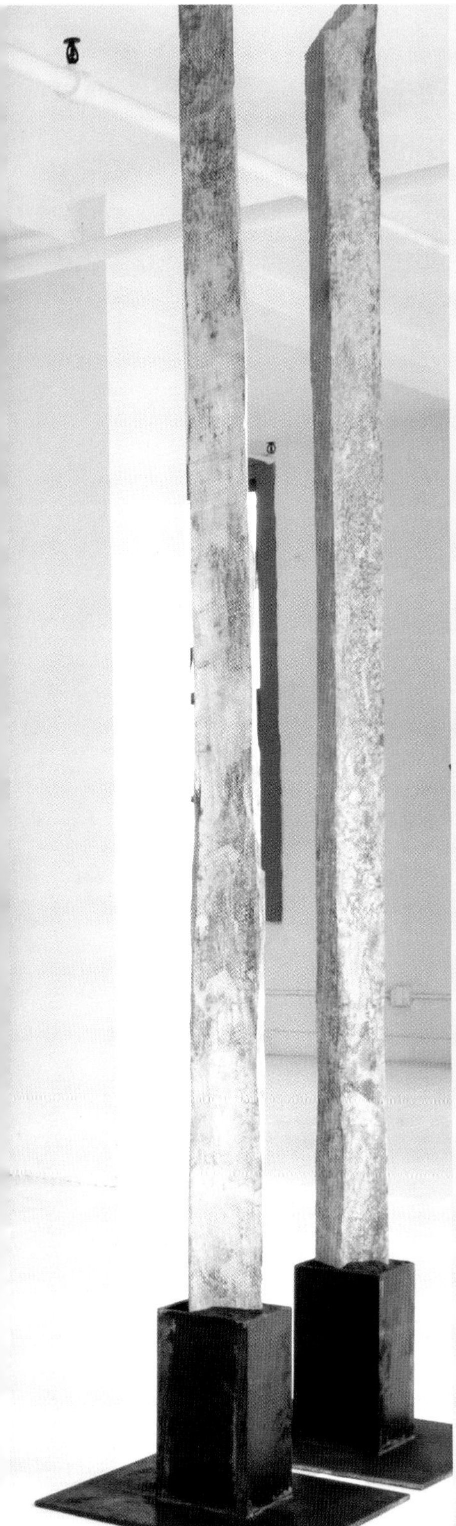

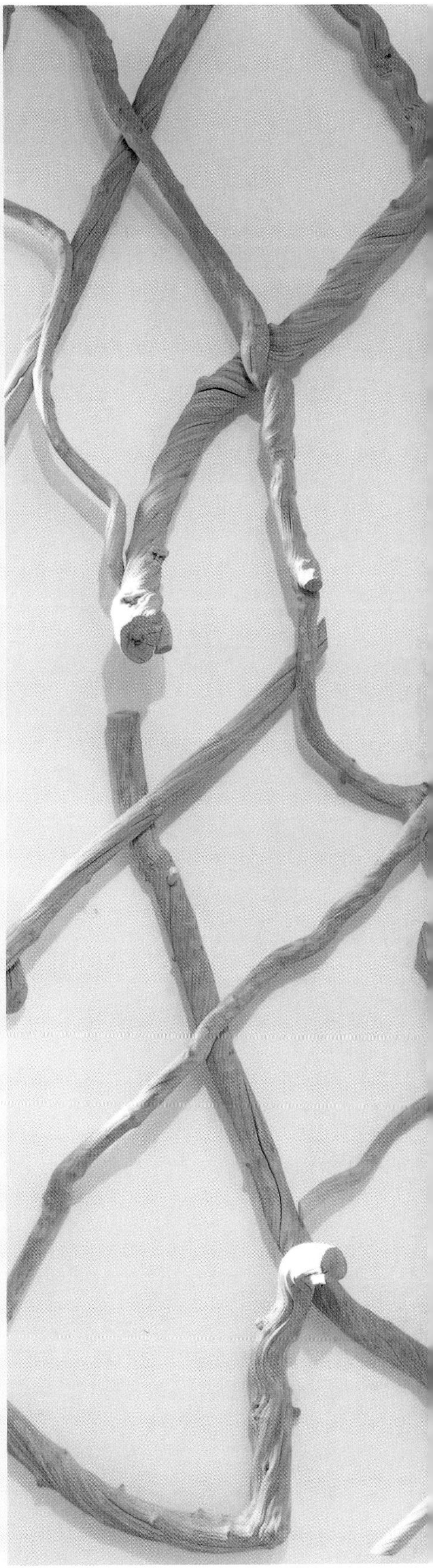

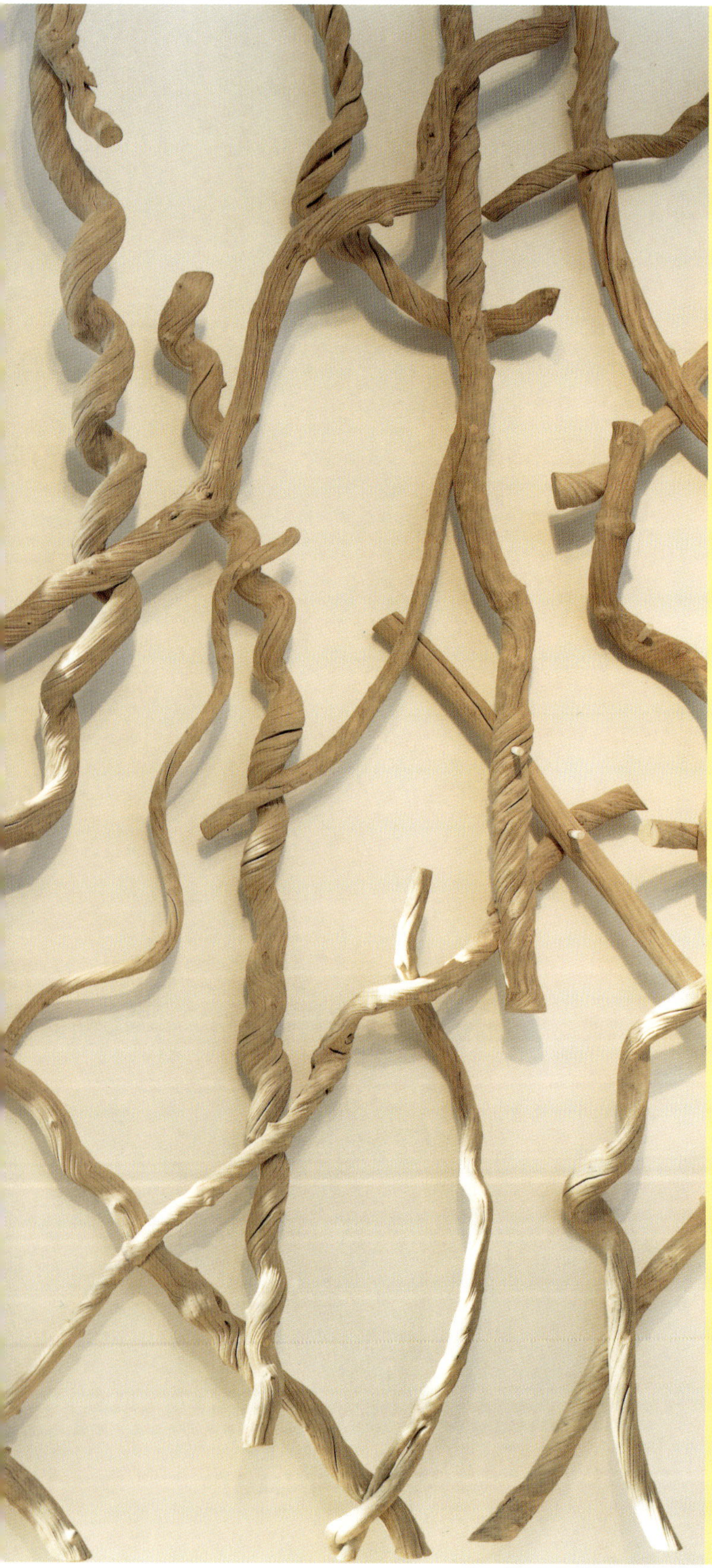

bench, 2000

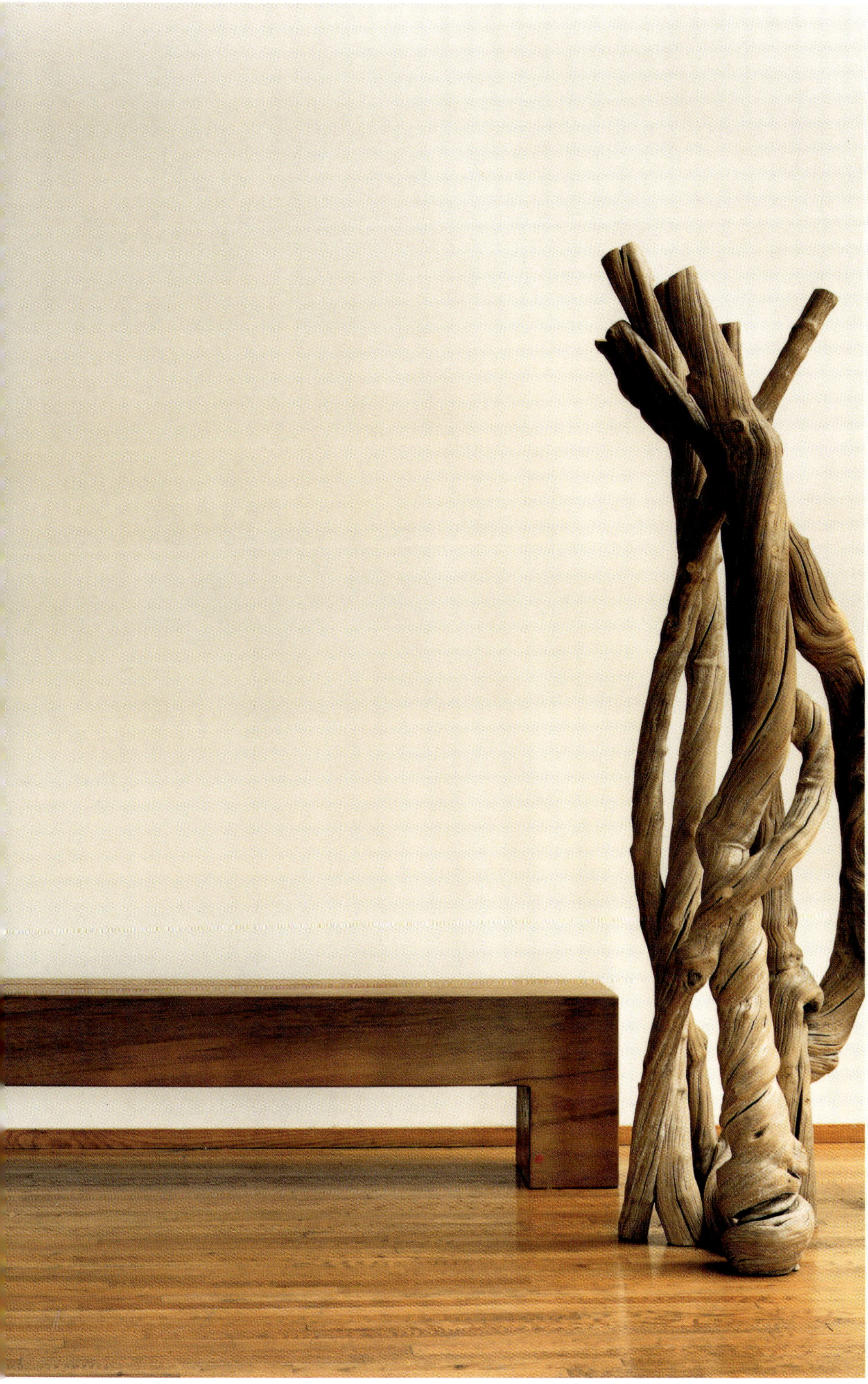

“What does it matter if the work is beautiful in configuration, generous in space, free from clutter, sophisticated in details, pure in materials, unless it reveals the soul?”

—Jerome Abel Seguin

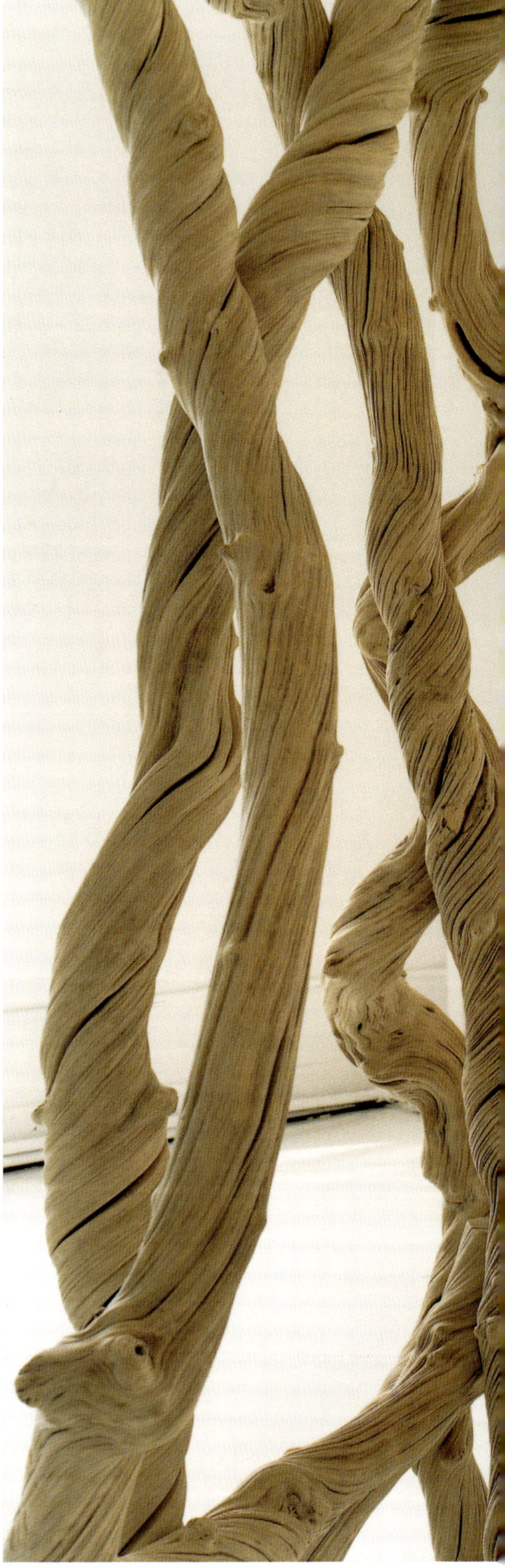

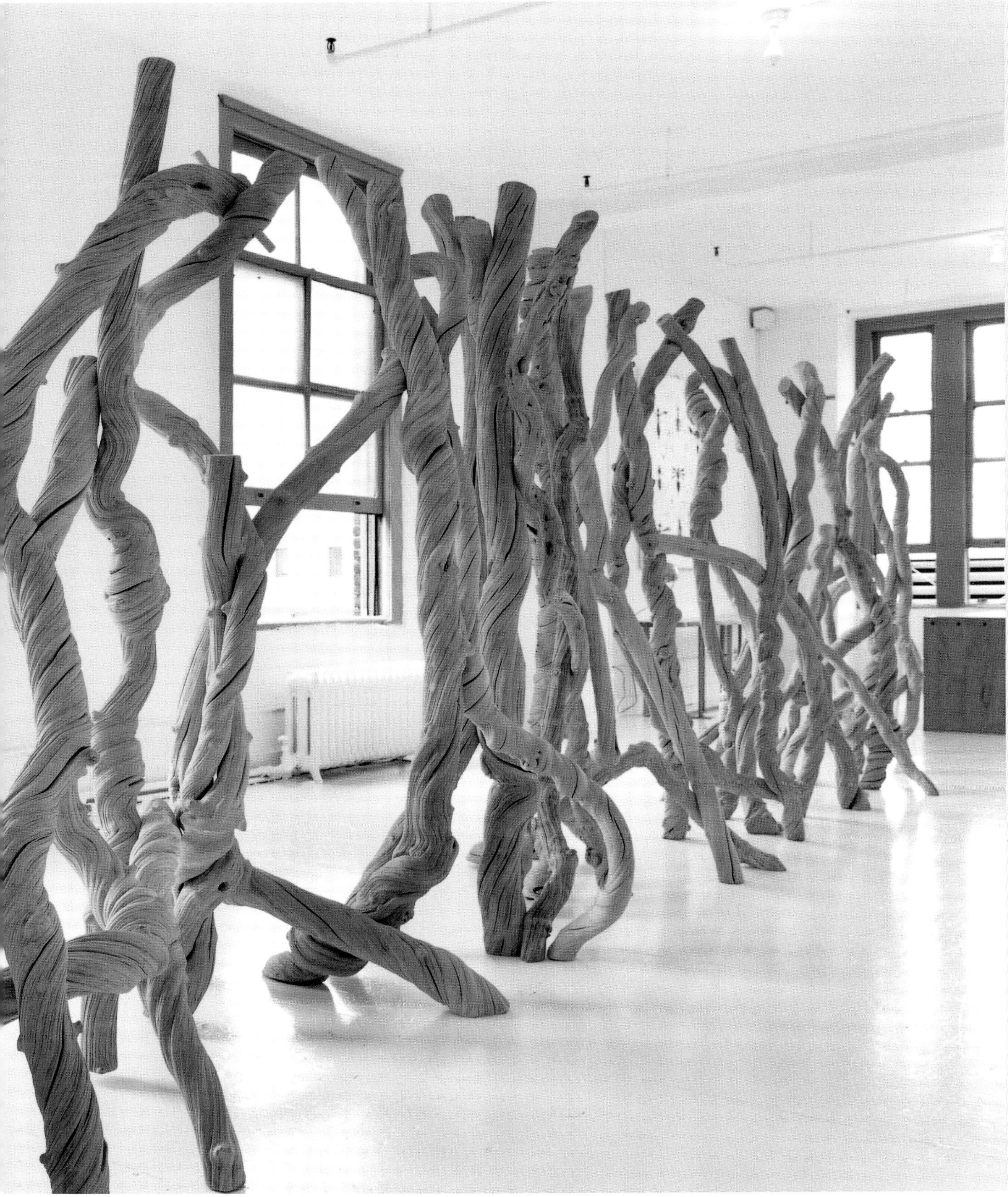

Dance of Lliana, 2002

christy turlington *Yoga, 2002, fashions by Nuala*

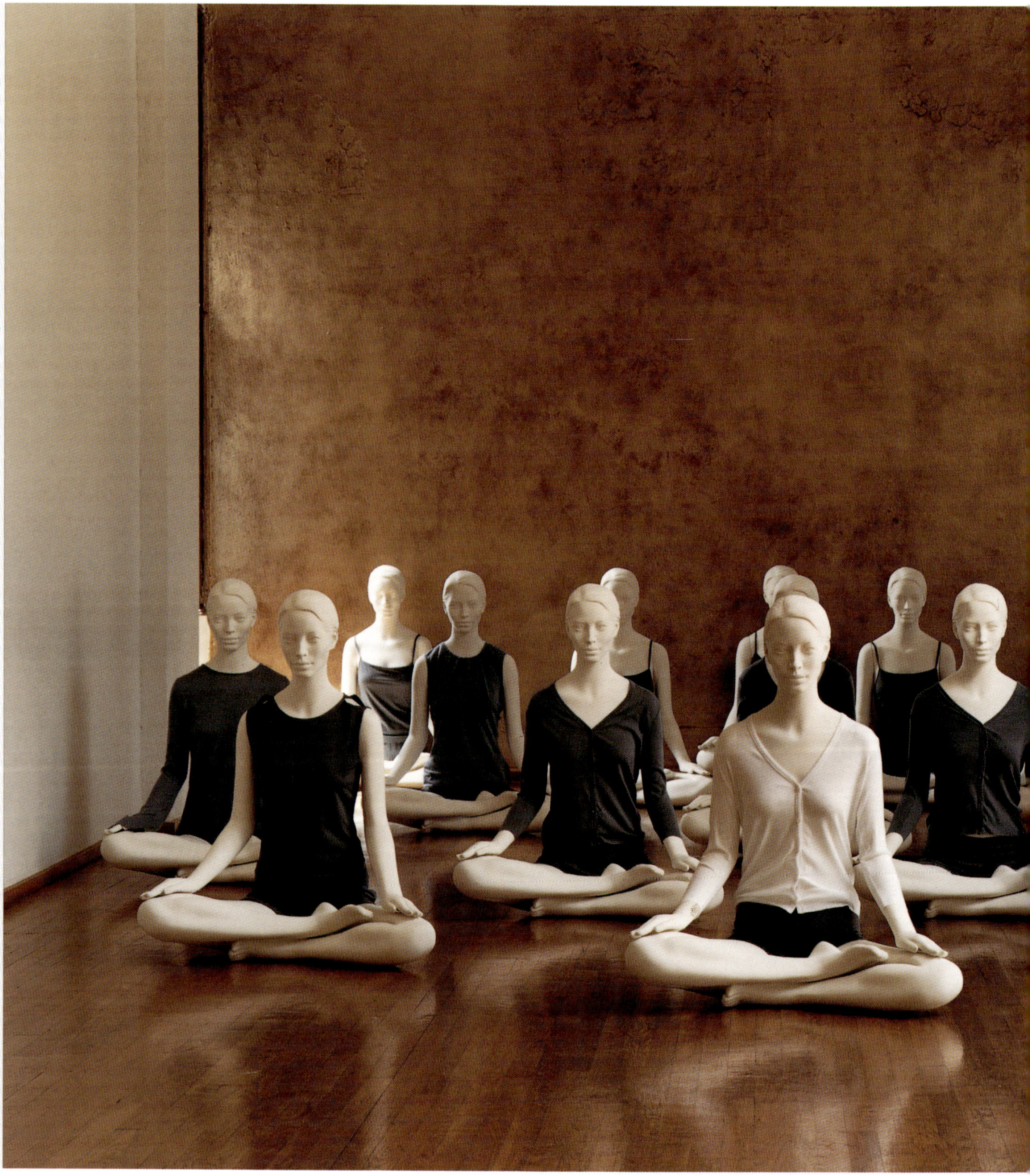

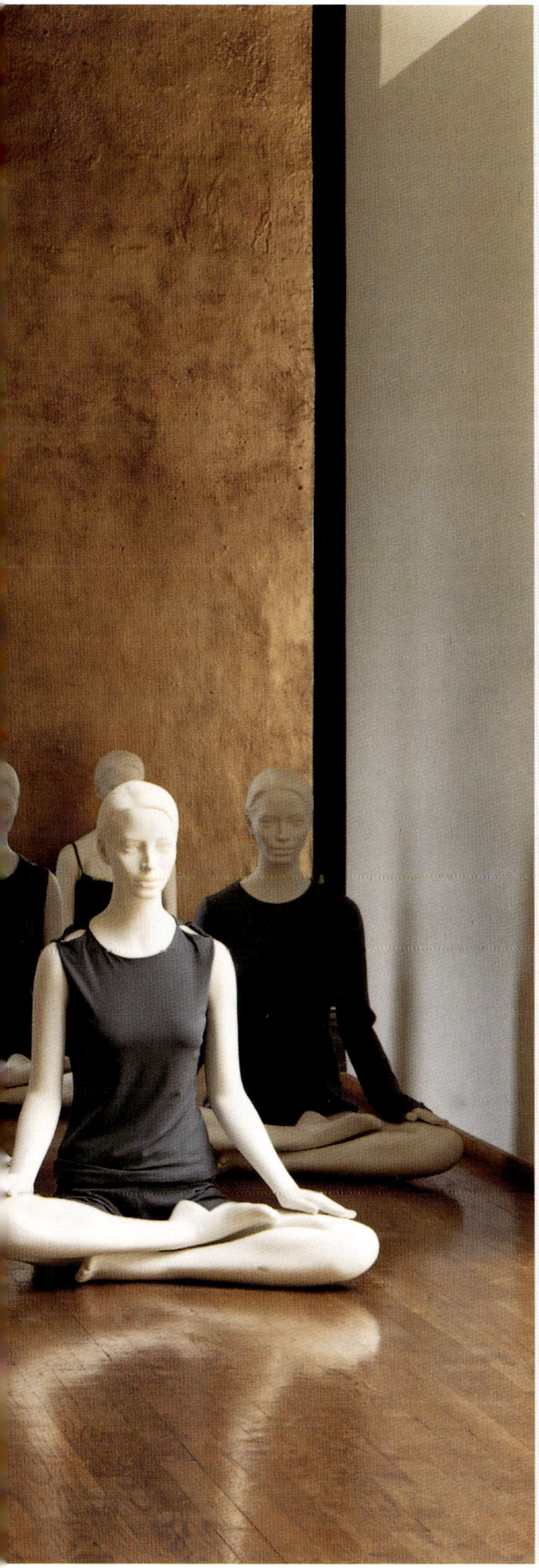

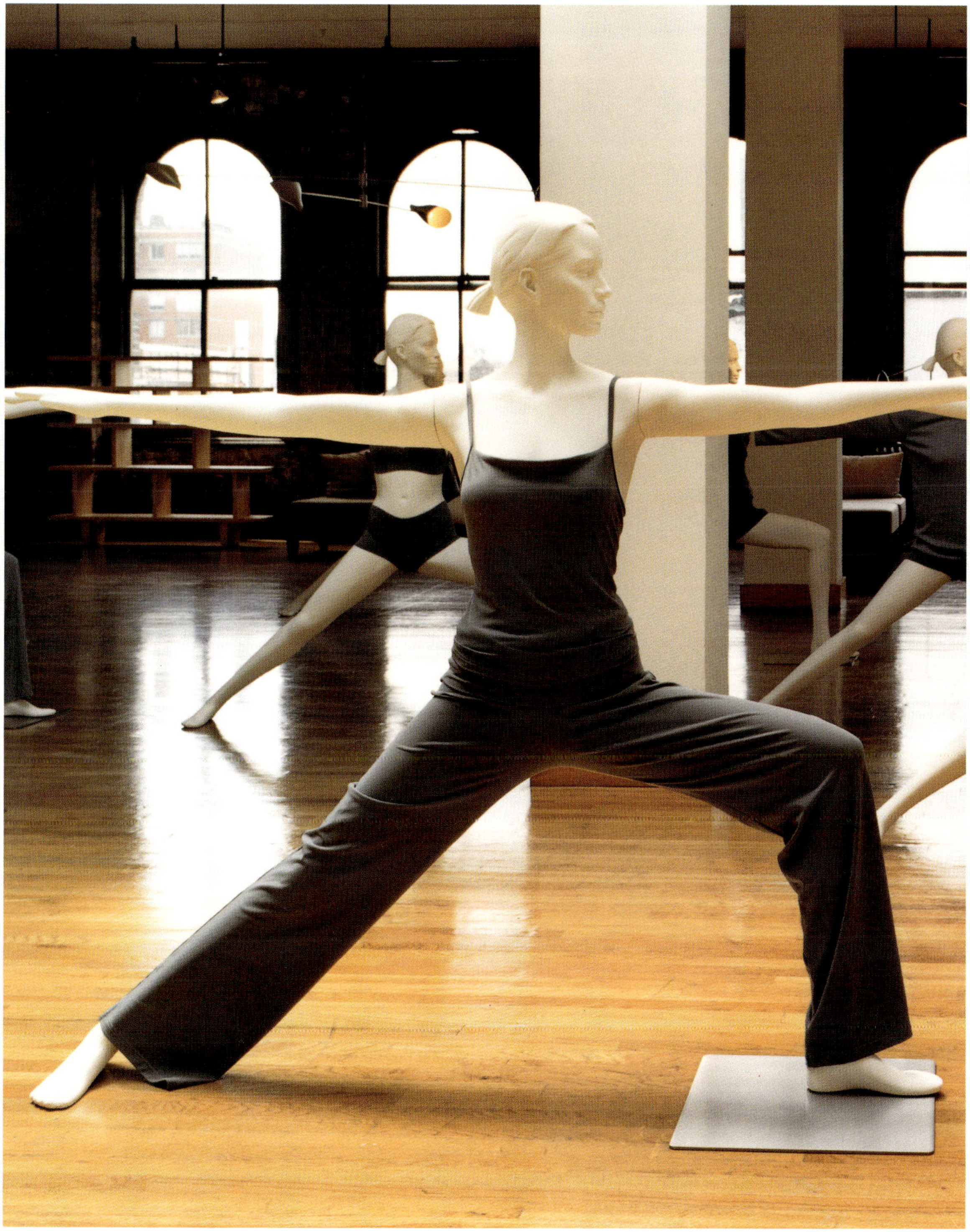

Yoga, 2002

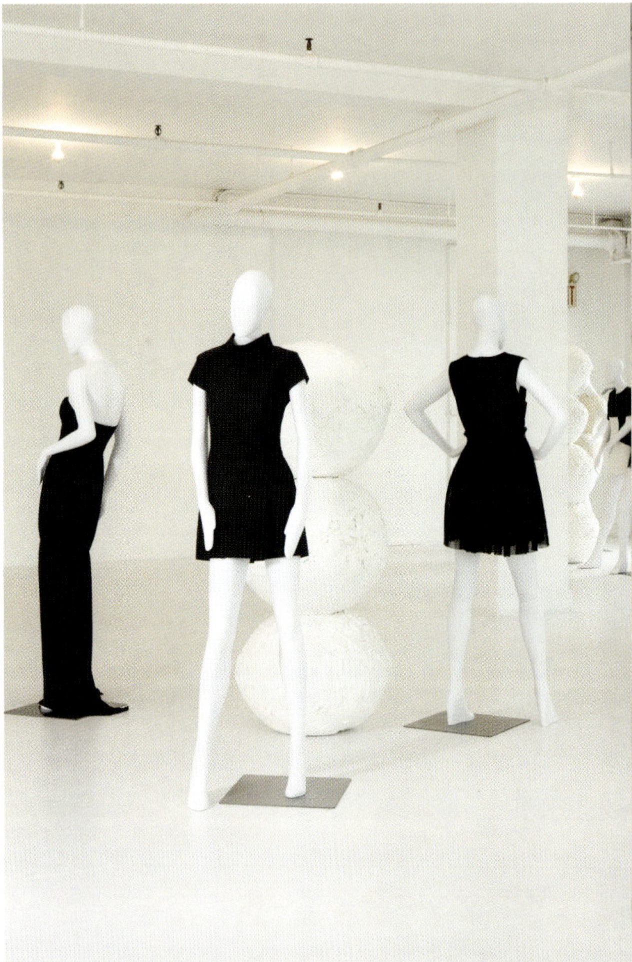
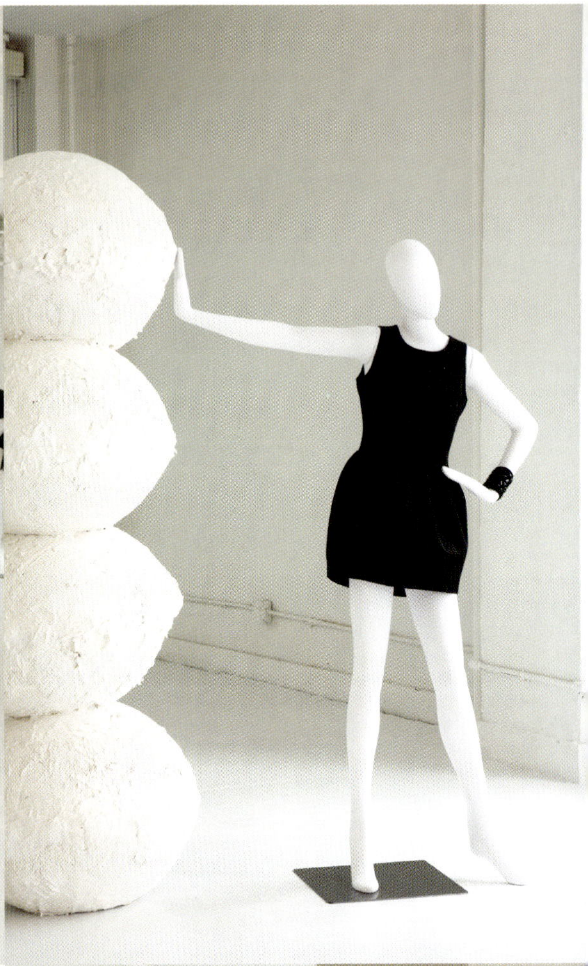
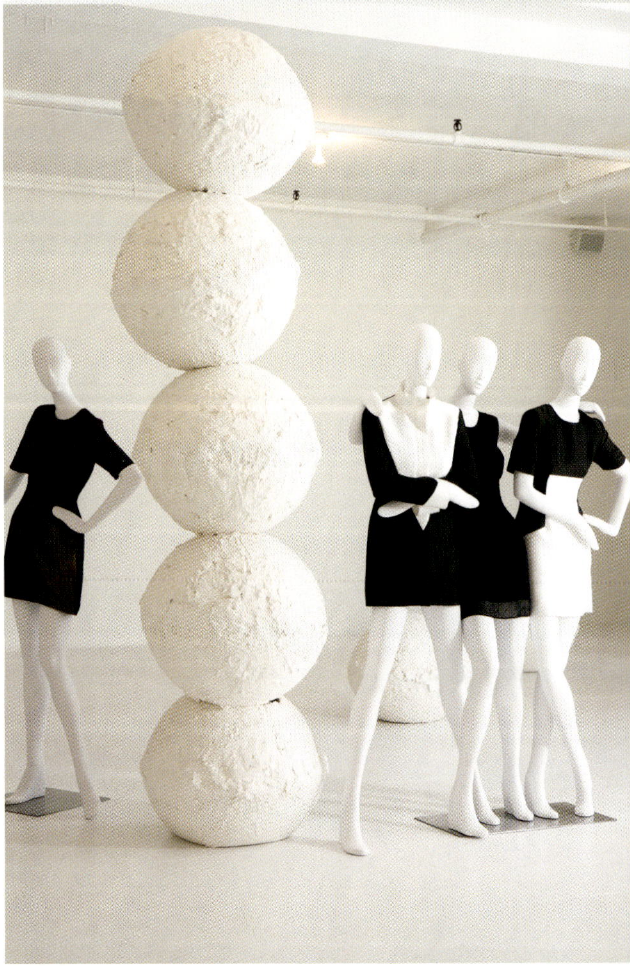
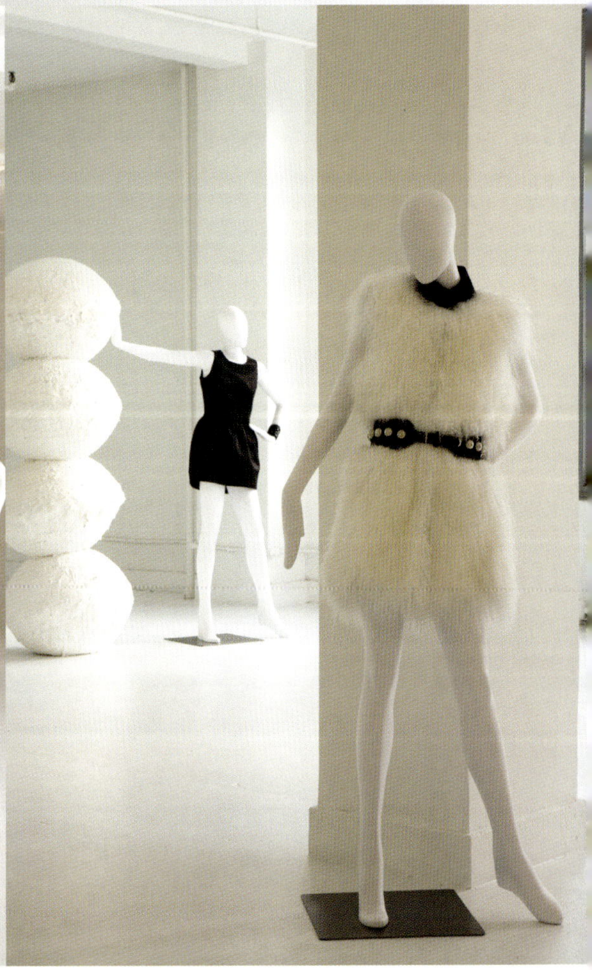

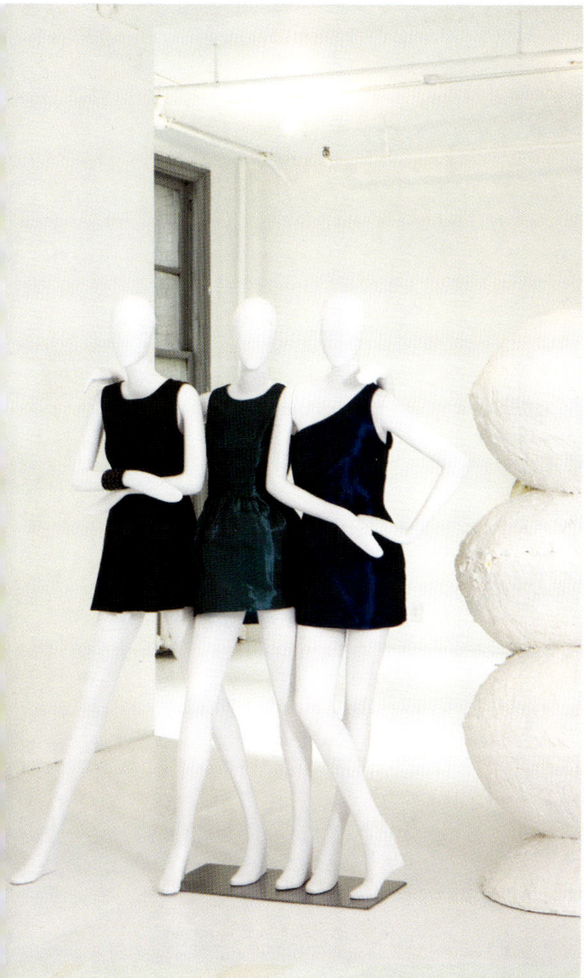

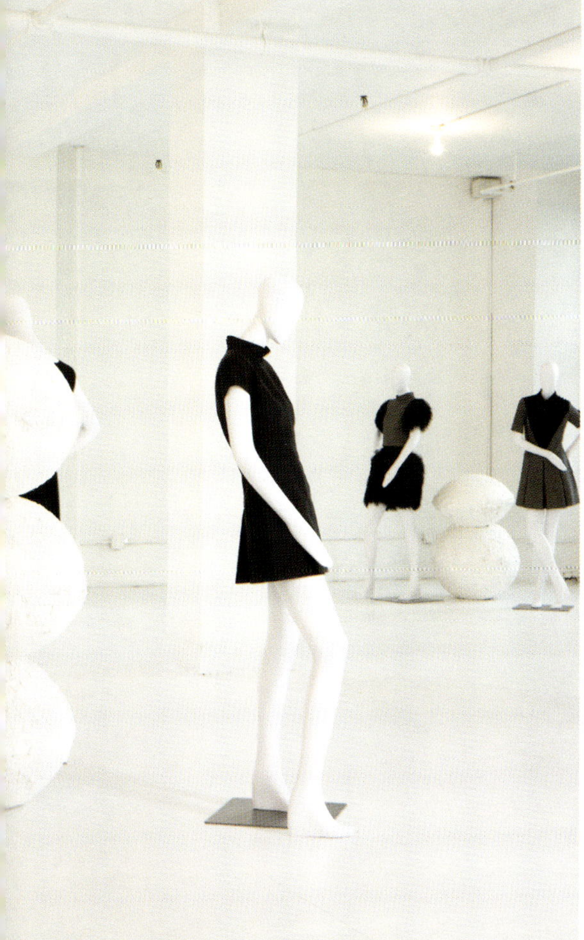

Ralph Pucci, *Girl Mannequin*, 2008, fashion by Frank Tell

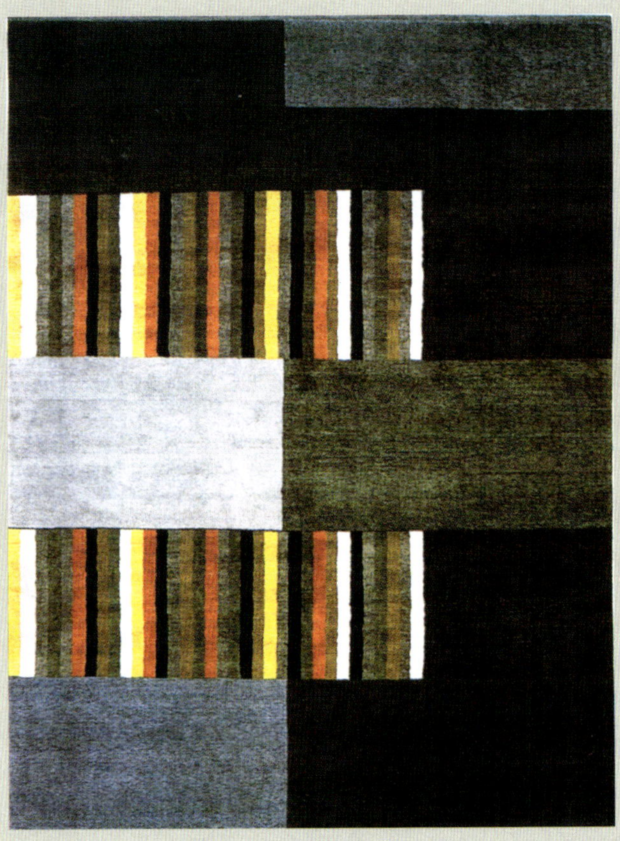

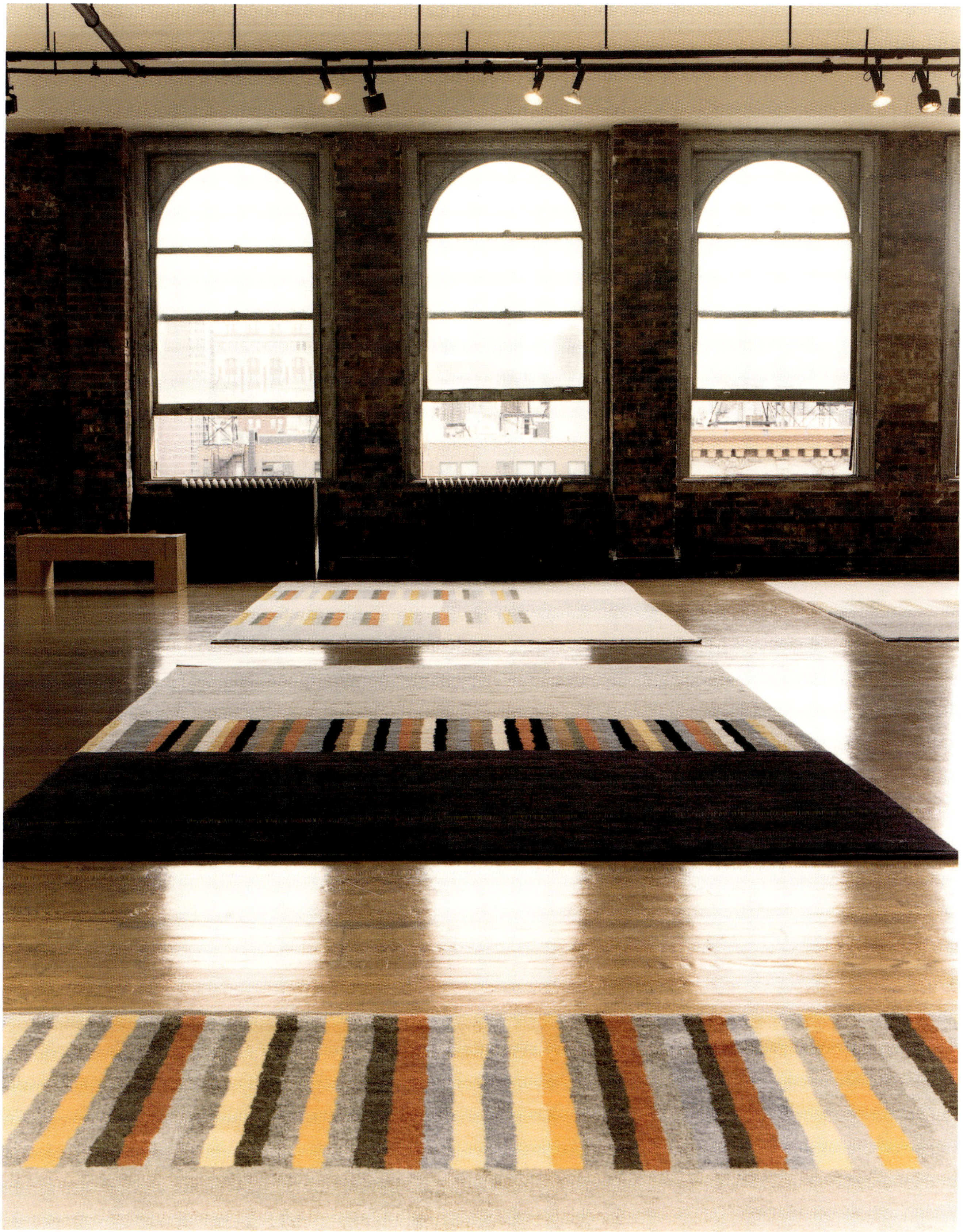

christopher farr *Code*, 2002

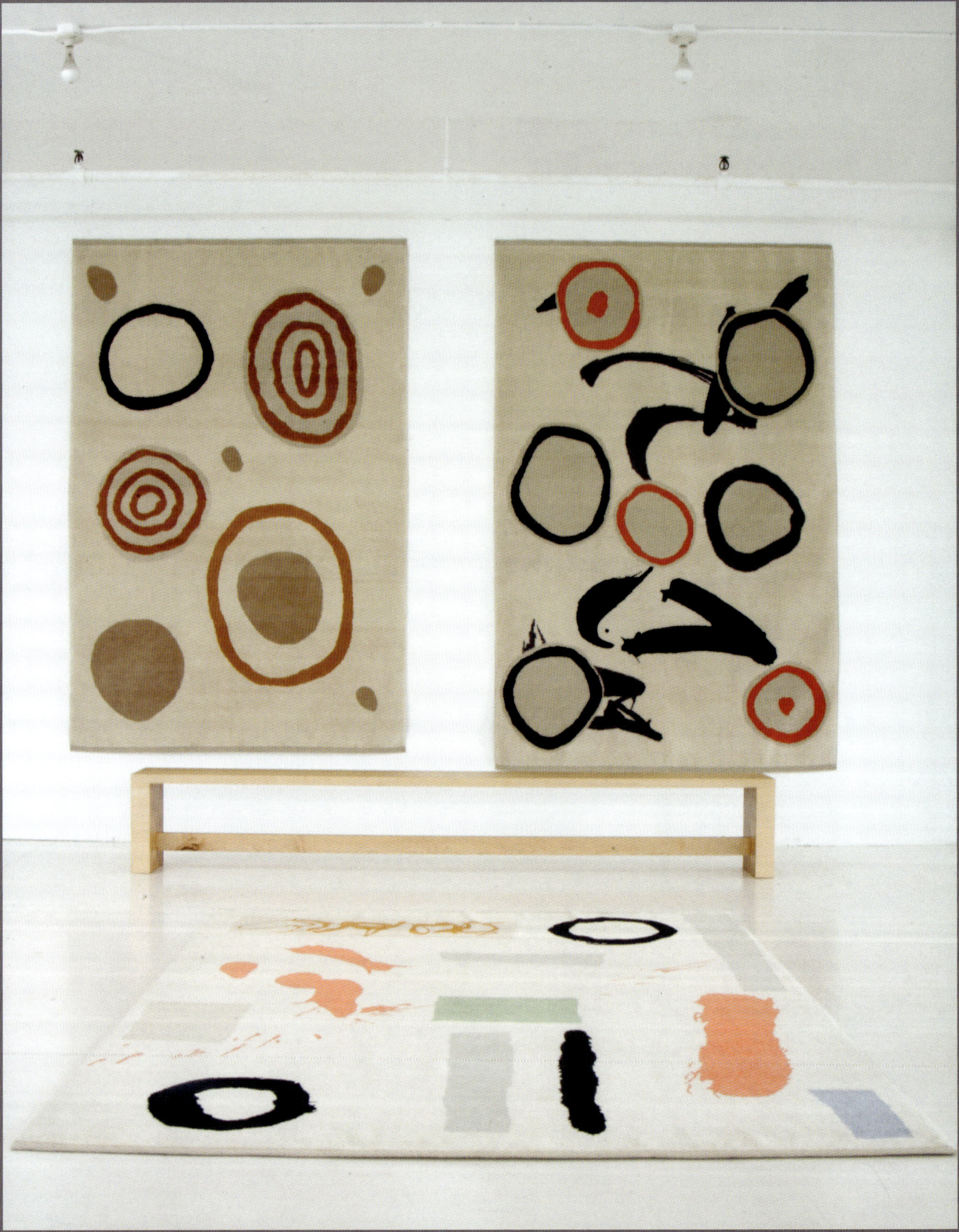

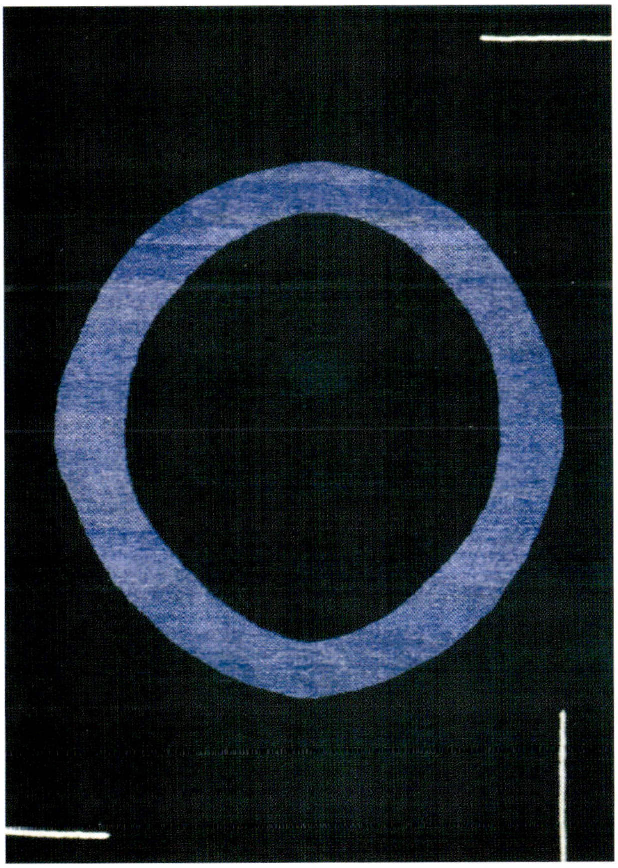

Gregory Evans, design for Christopher Farr, 2004, bench by Robert Bristow (left), Kate Blee, design for Christopher Farr, 2001 (above)

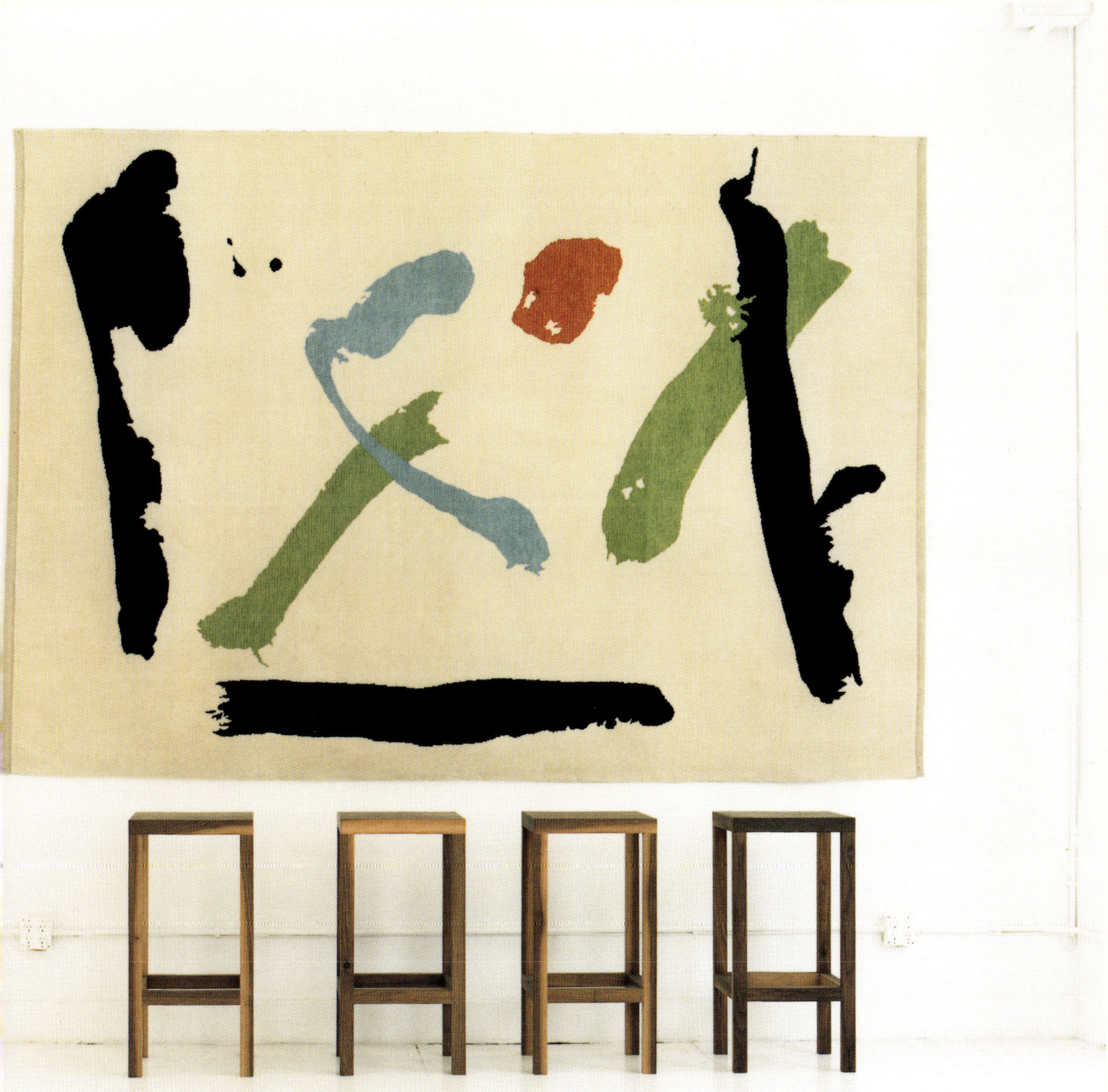

Gregory Evans, design for Christopher Farr, 2004, barstool by Robert Bristow, sculpture by Jerome Abel Seguin

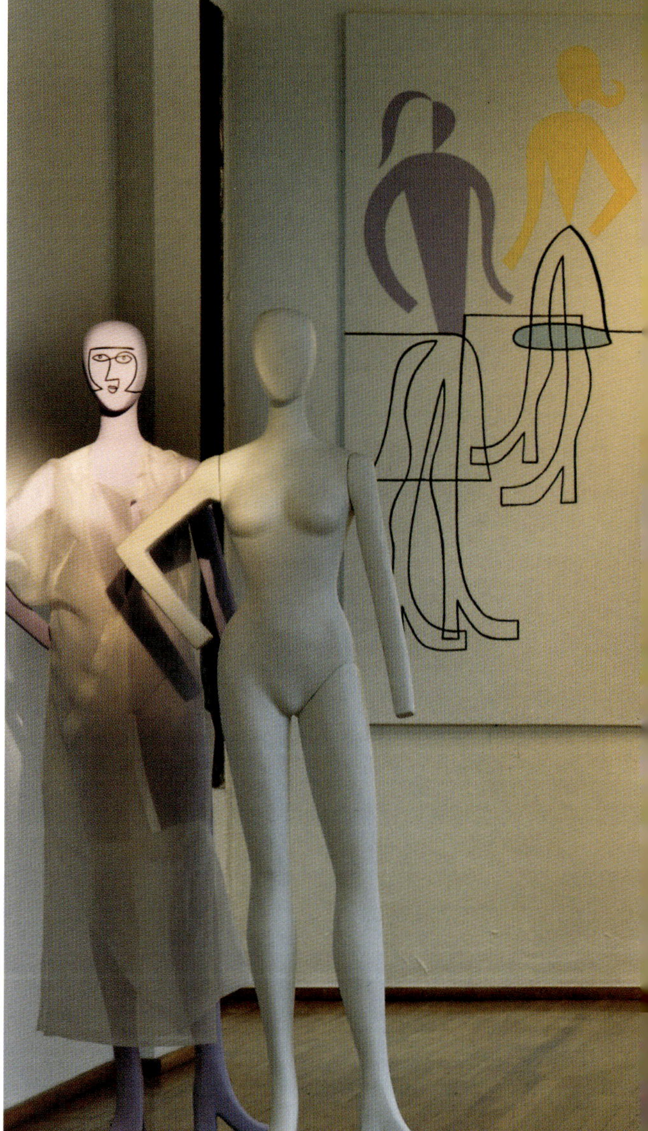

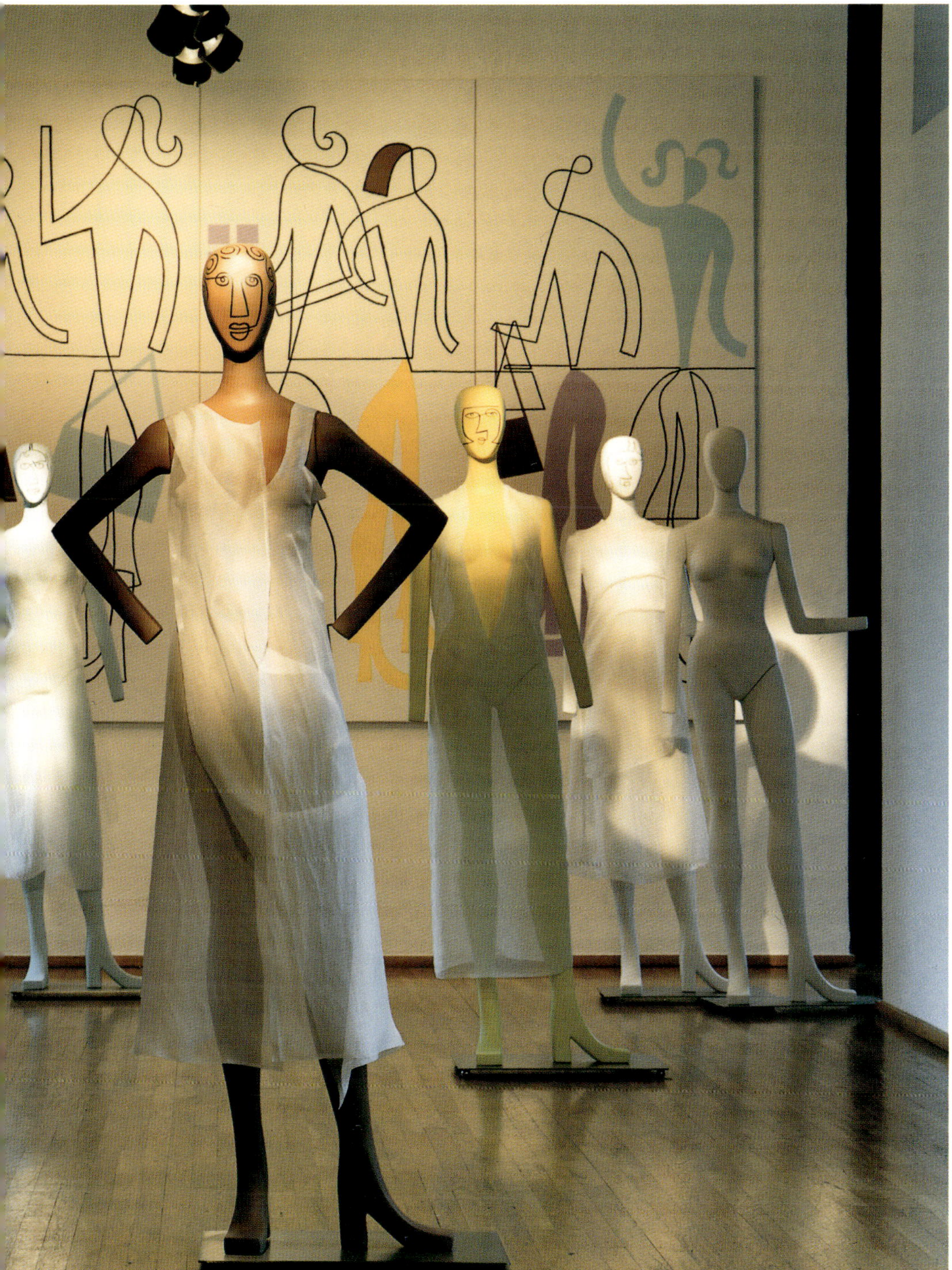

laura ljunkvist mannequin and mural, 2000, fashions by Ruben Chapelle

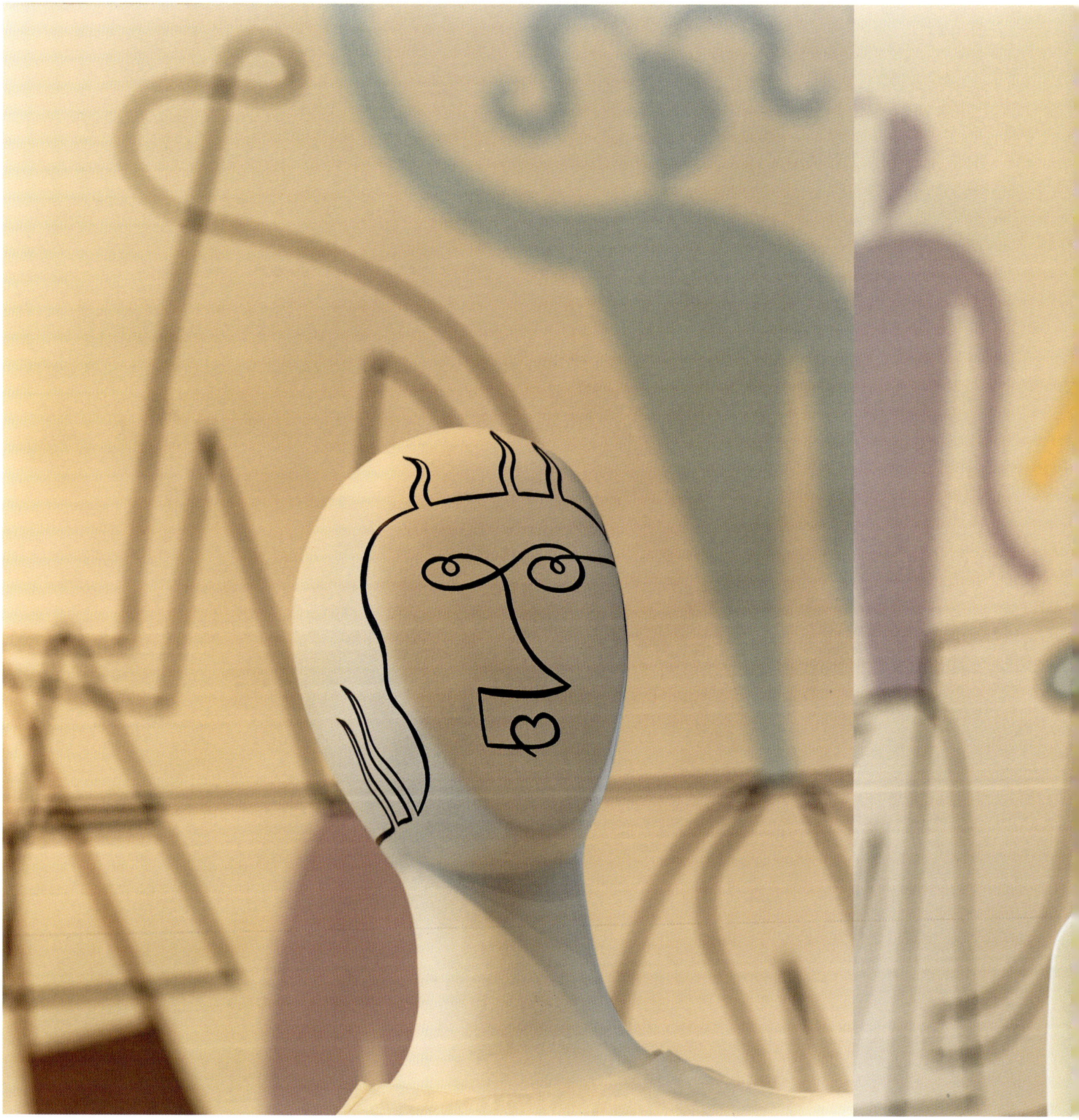

 Mannequin, 2000

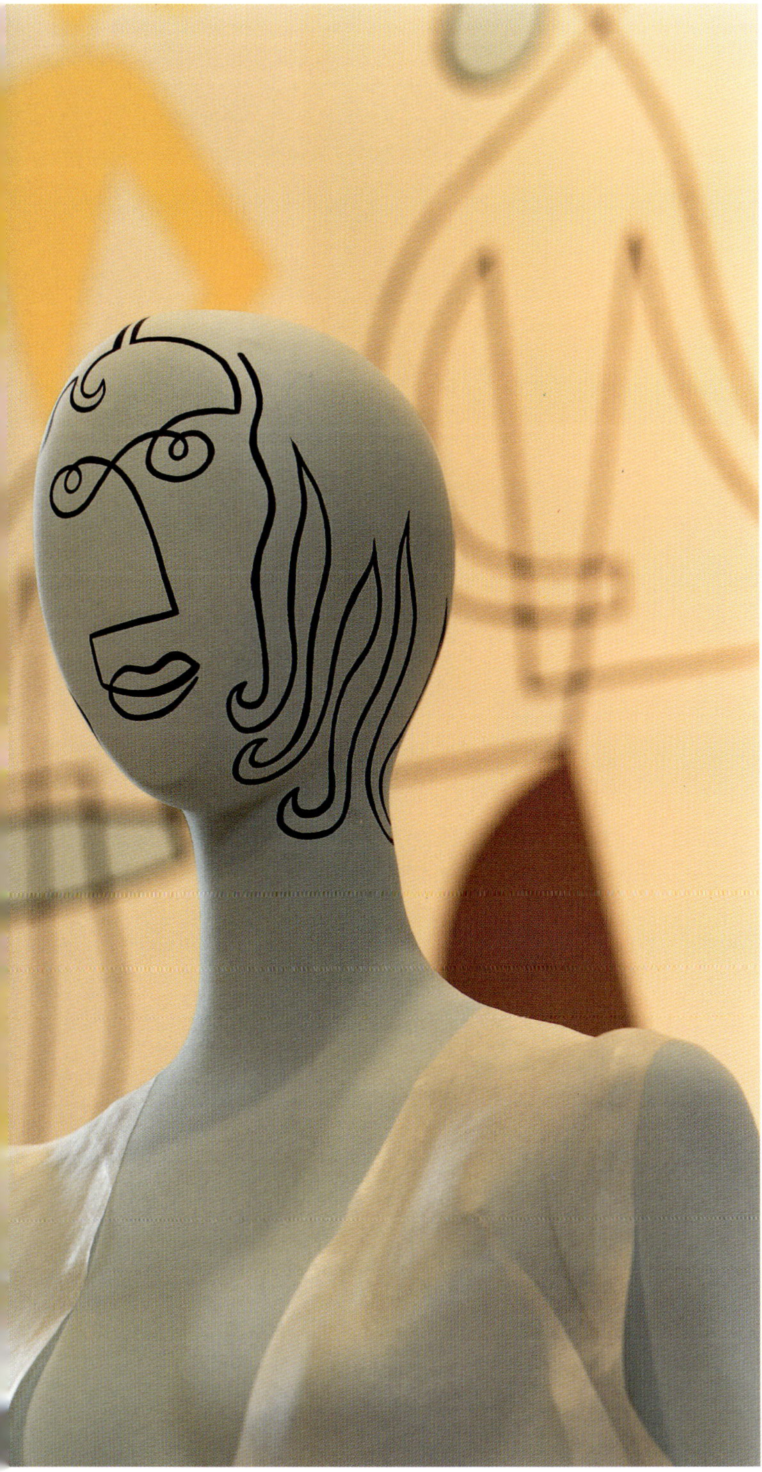

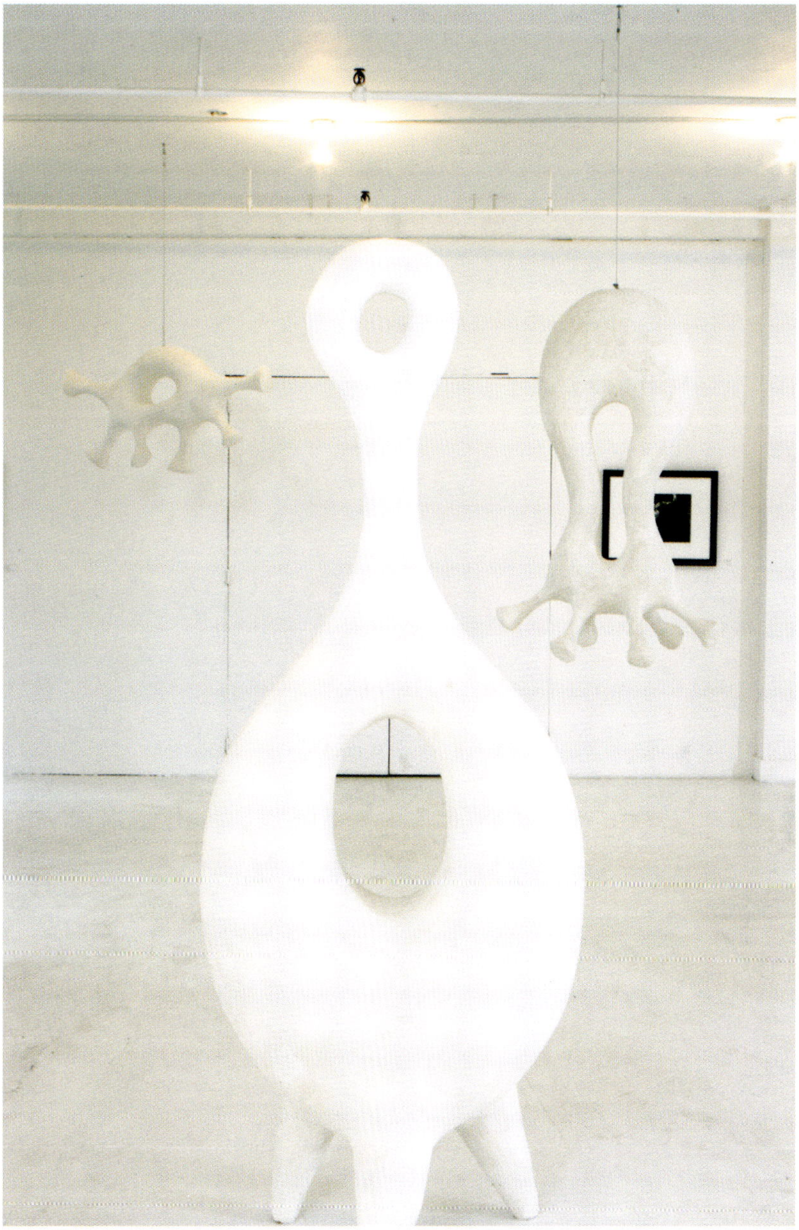

John Tanji Koga "Garden of Spirits," 2007

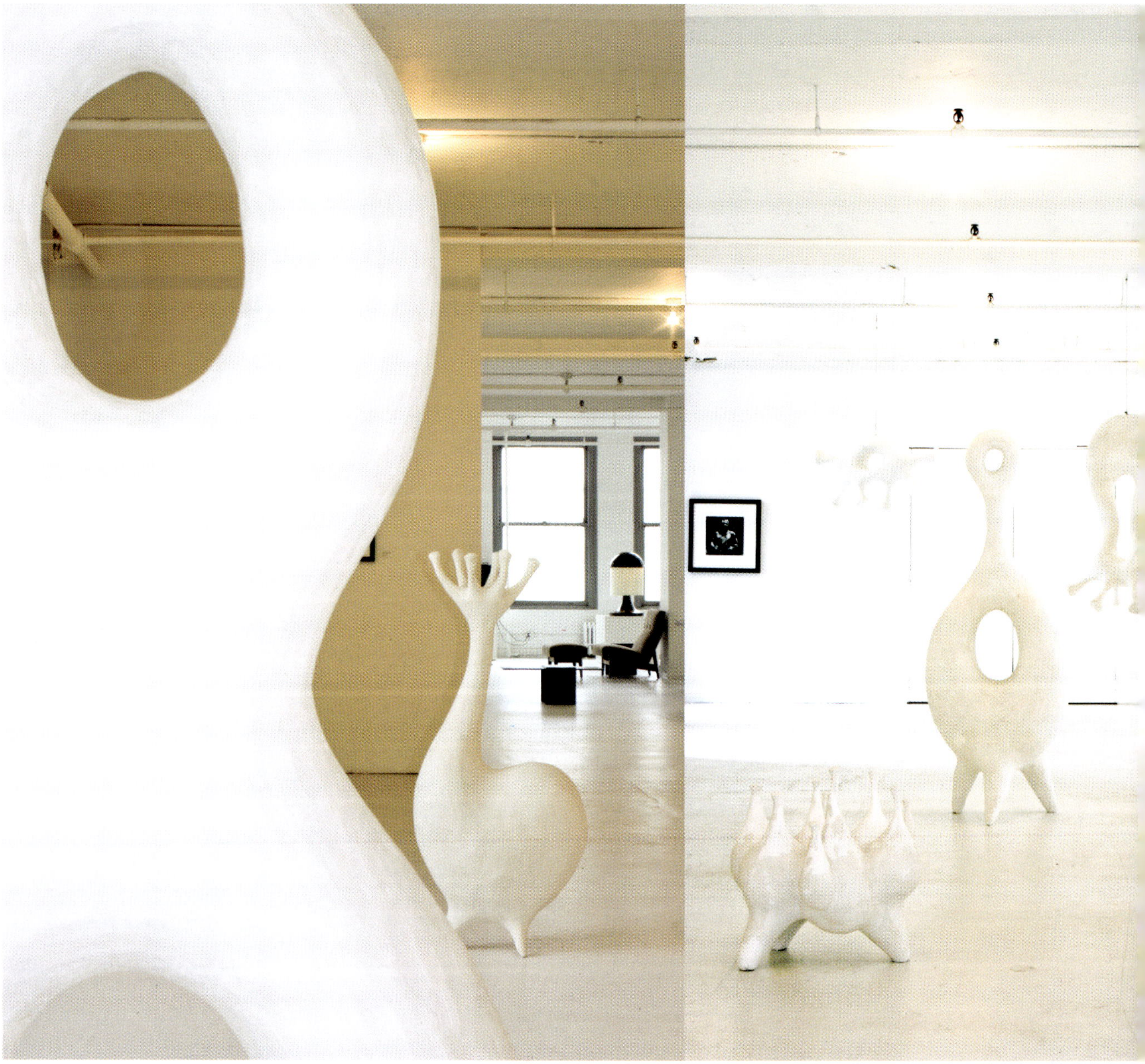

"Garden of Spirits," 2007

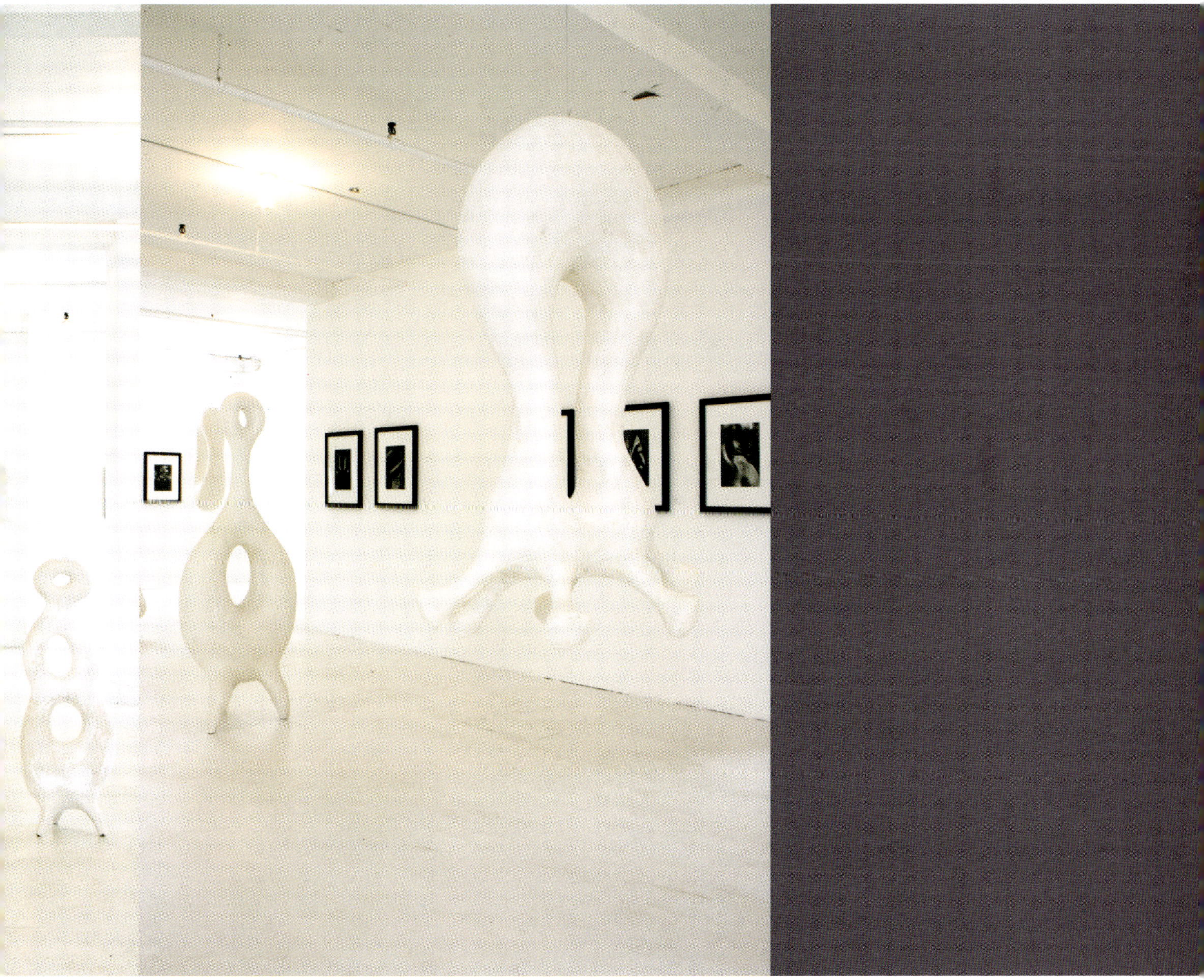

"We are, at the same moment, very ancient and very modern."

—Patrick Naggar

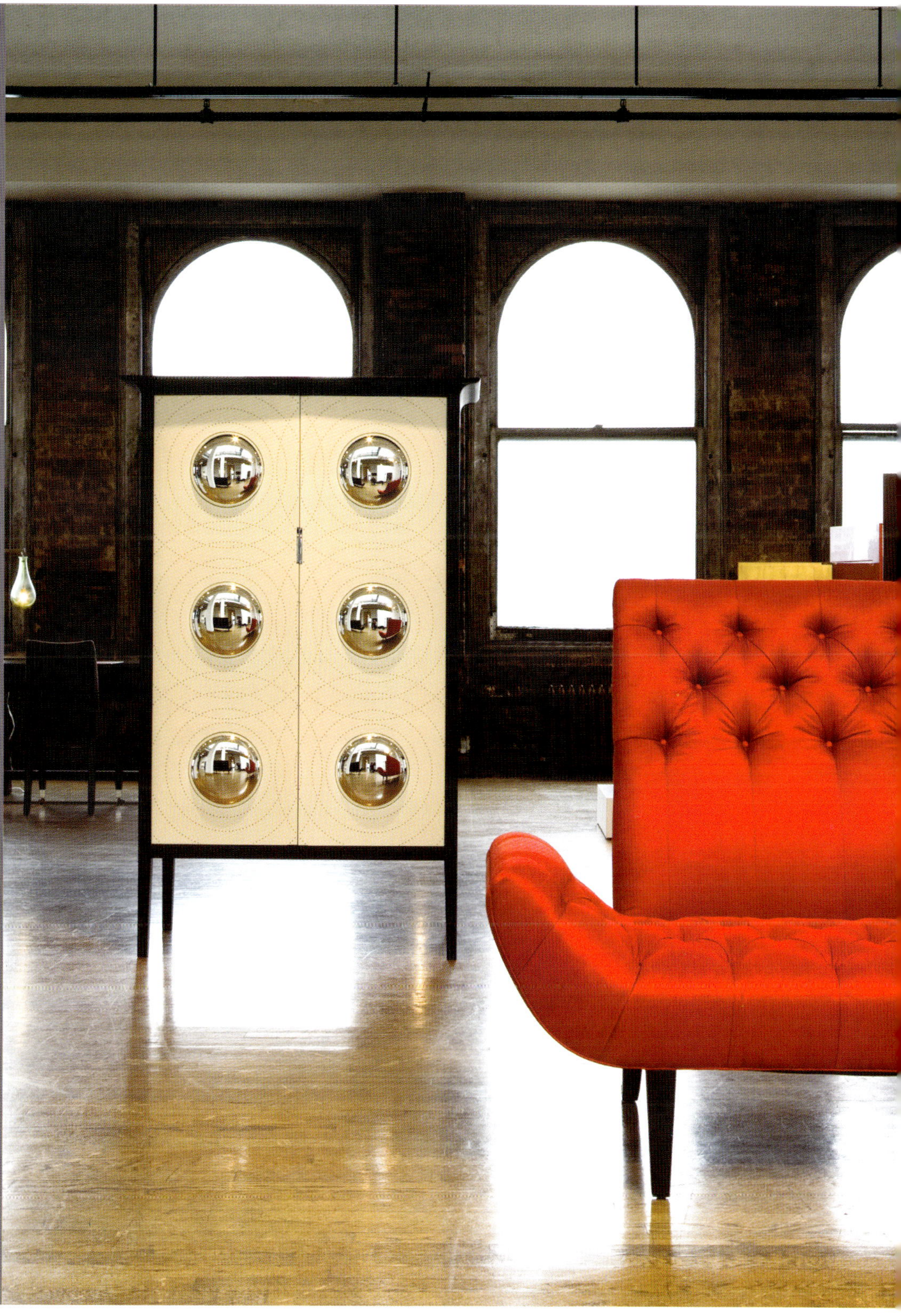

patrick naggar *Transitions* collection, *Pharos* cabinet and *Neo-Chester Sofa*, 2008

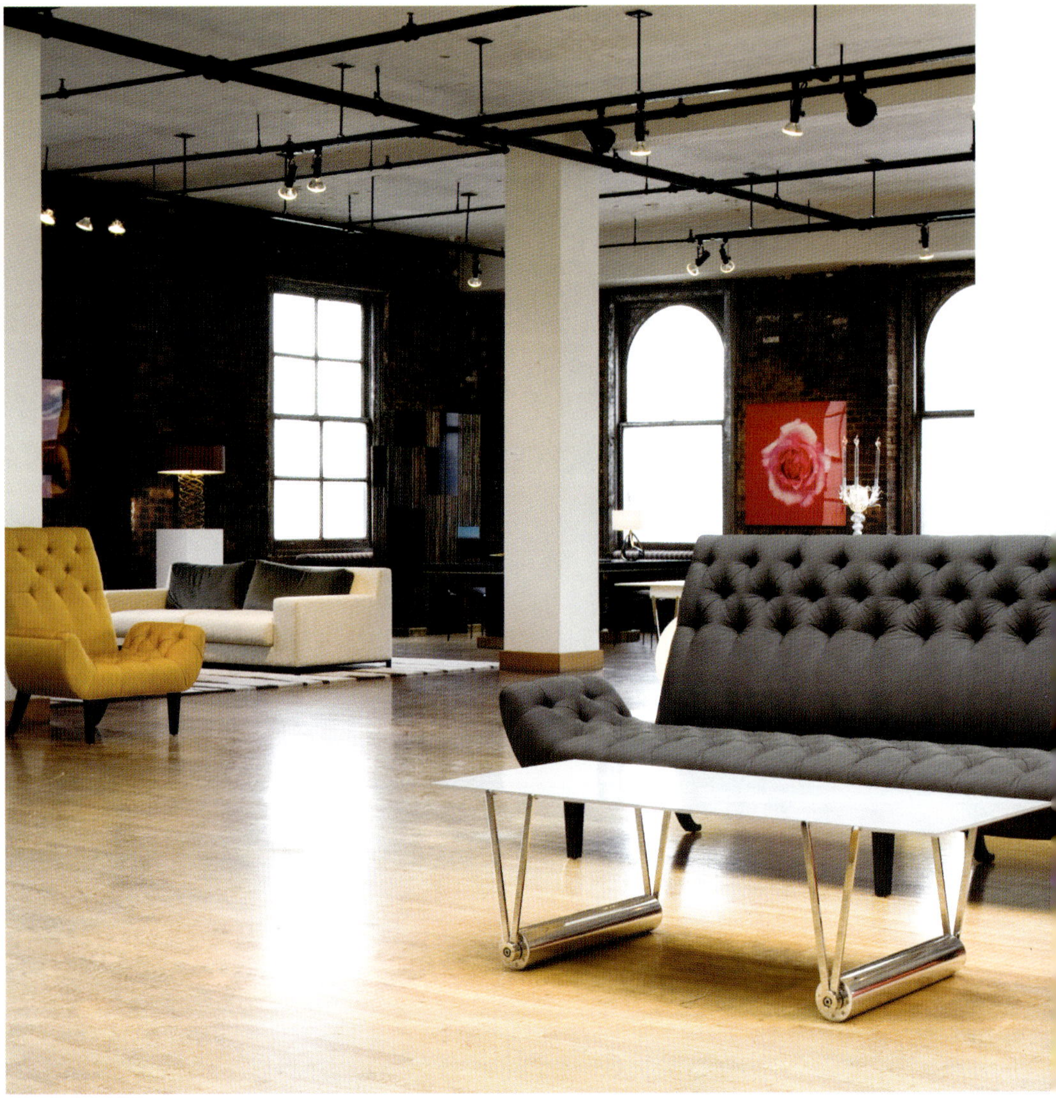

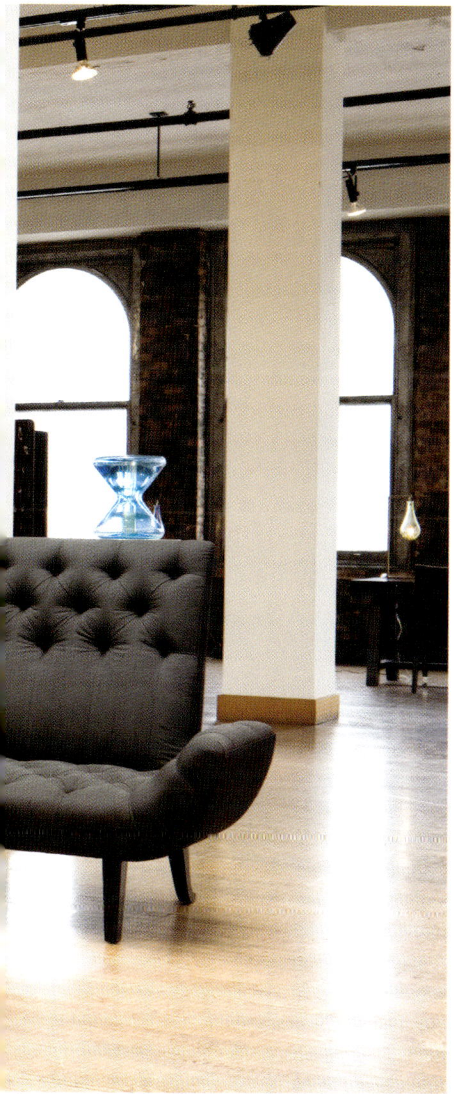

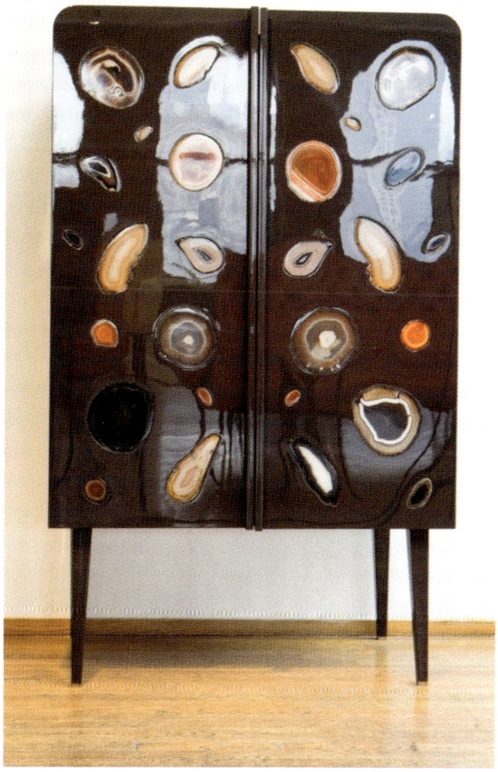

Transitions collection *Neo-Chester Sofa* with *Cylinder* table (left), *Gem* cabinet (above))

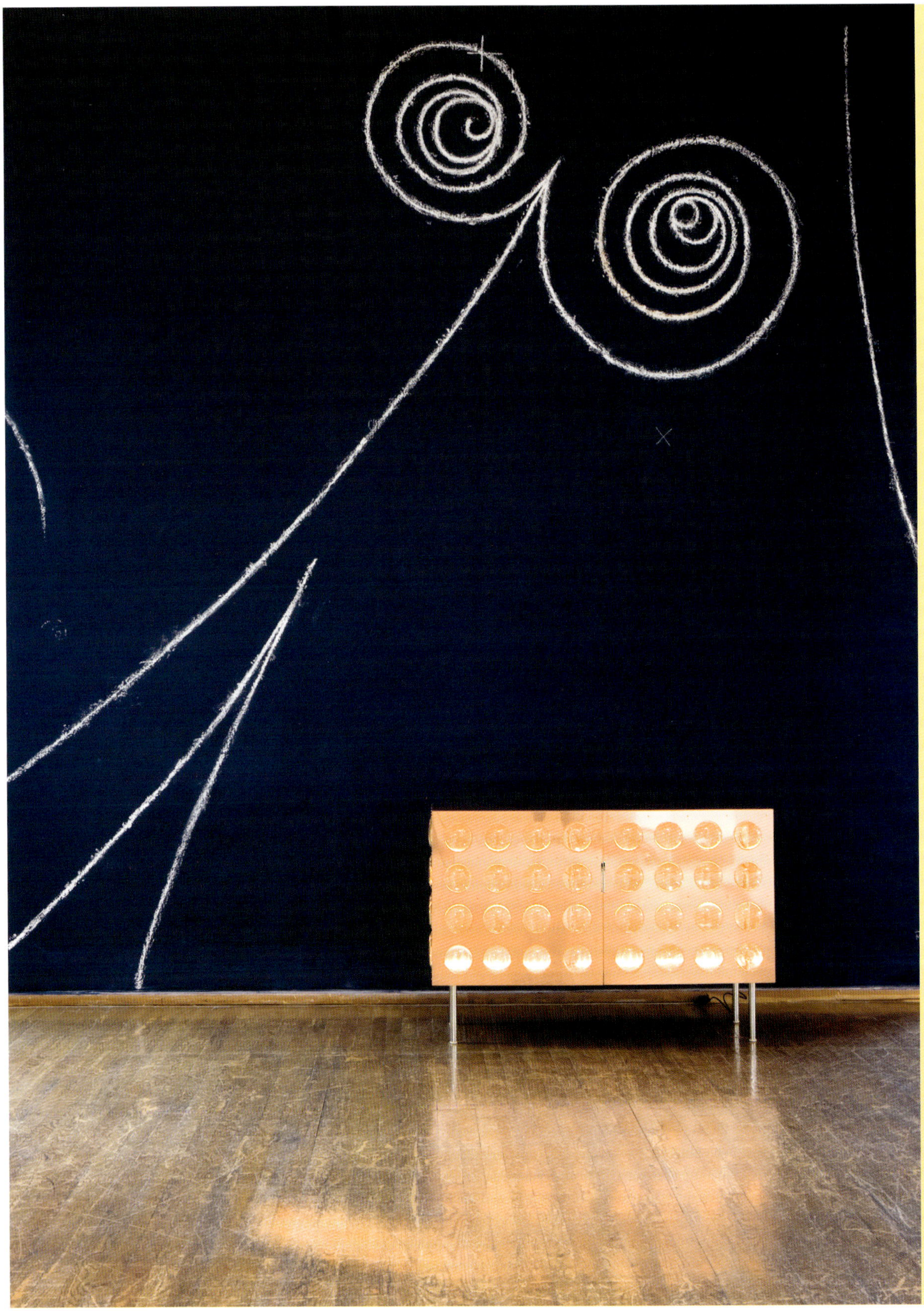

 Transitions collection, *Spinoza* console, 2008, mural by Partick Naggar

"It is not about using the past as a quotation, but using it instead as a source of renewal."

—Patrick Naggar

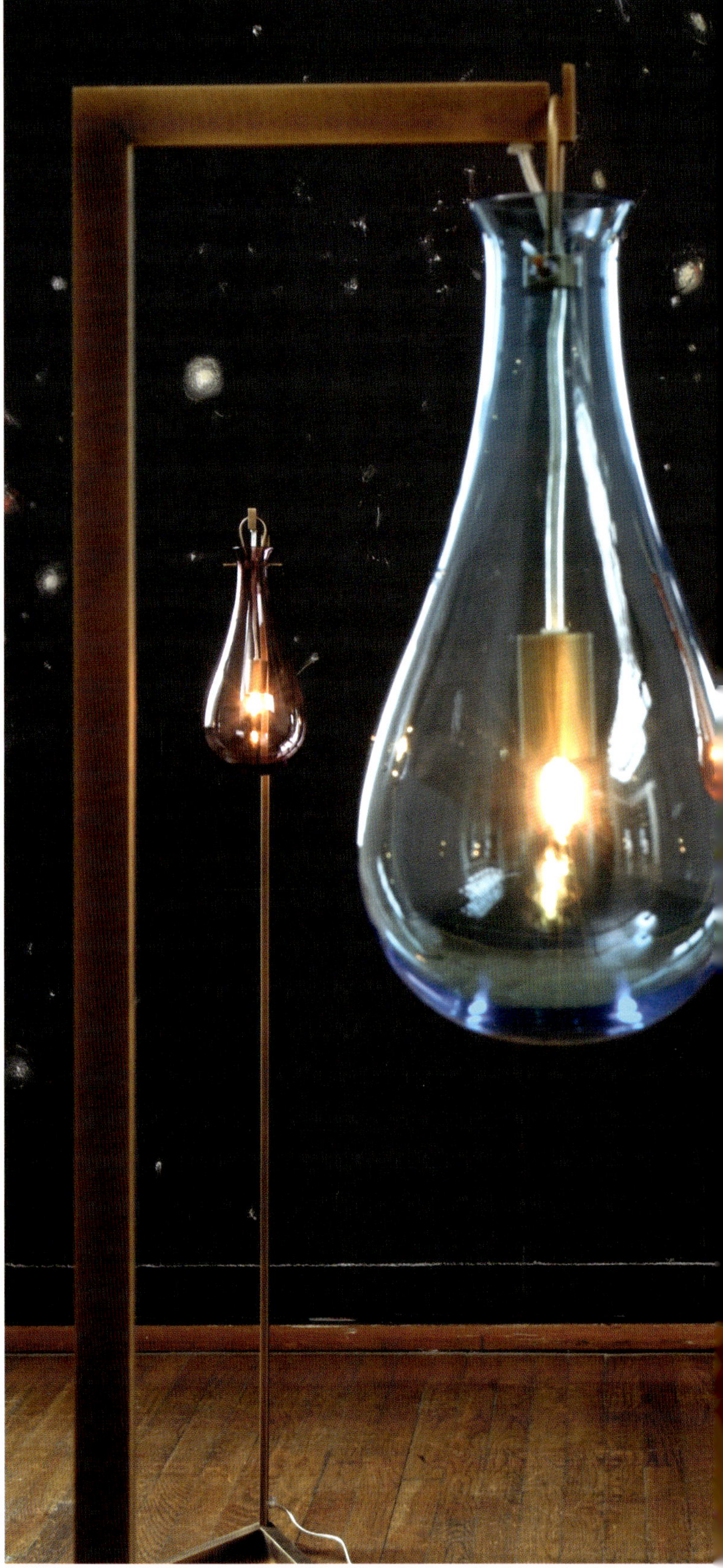

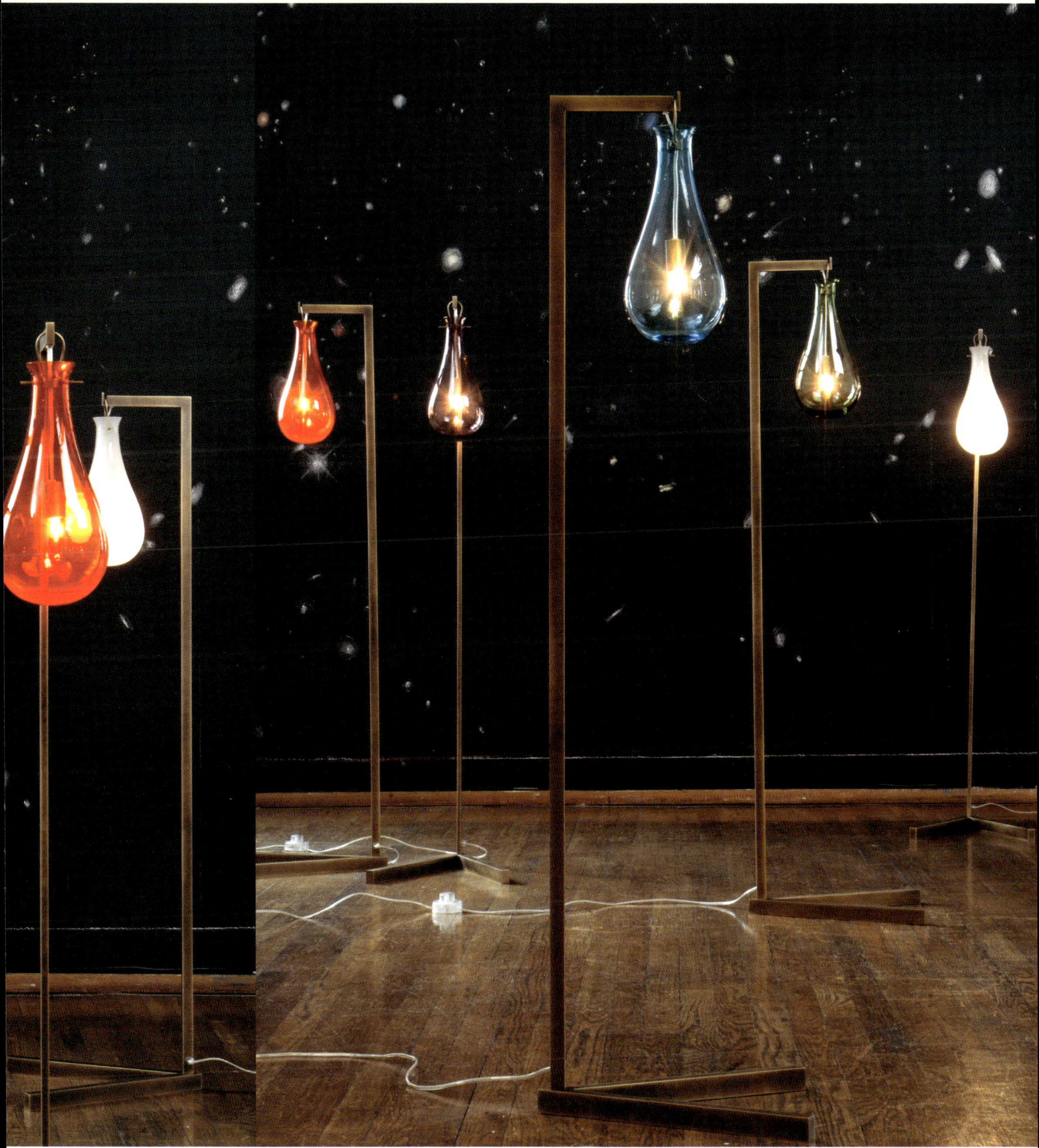

Bubble lamp and mural, 2004

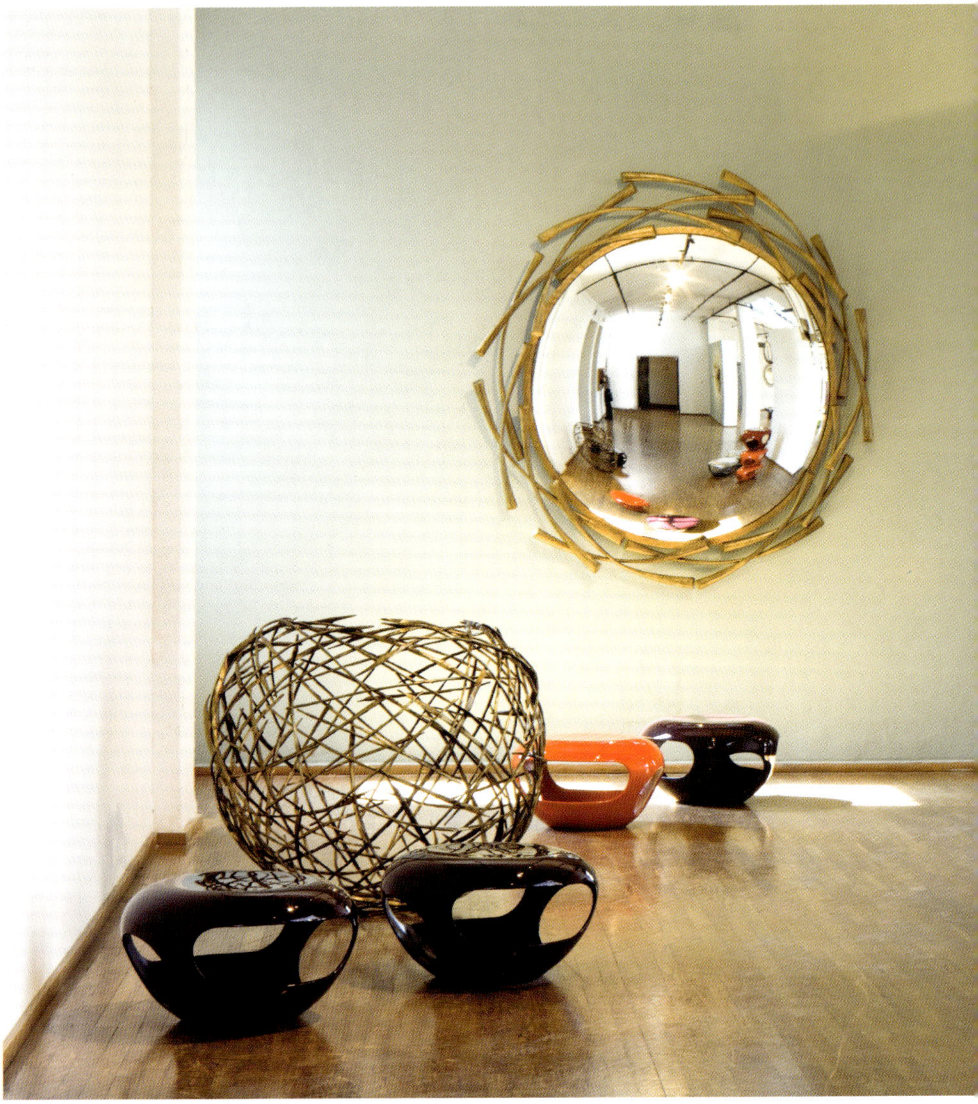

herve van der straeten "Turbulence," 2007

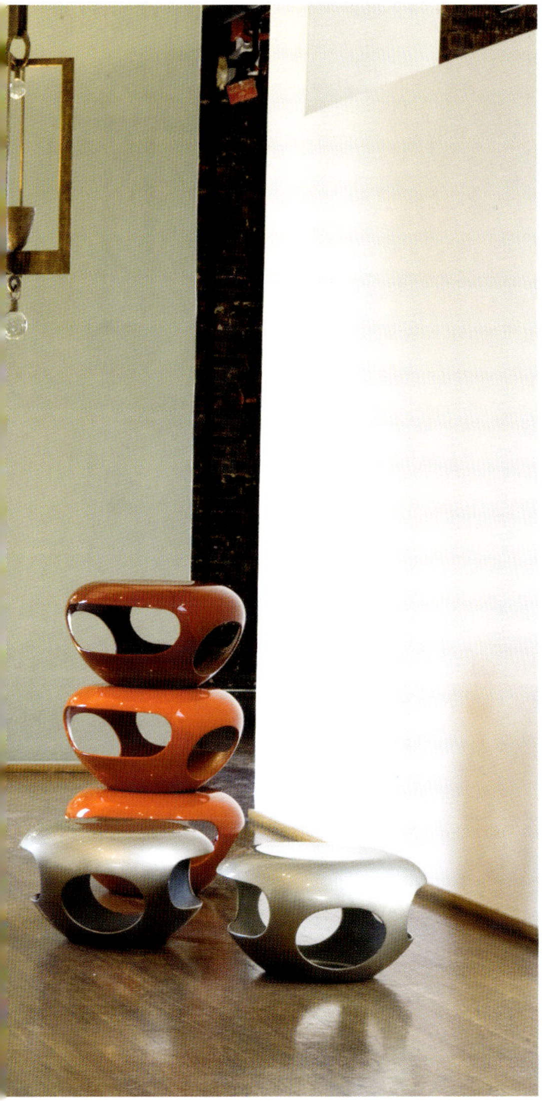

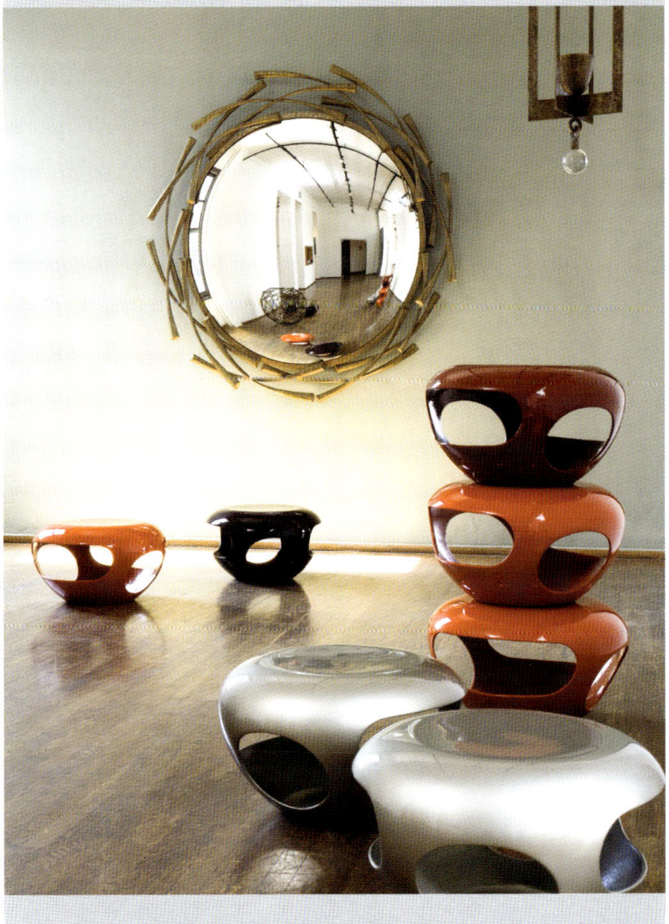

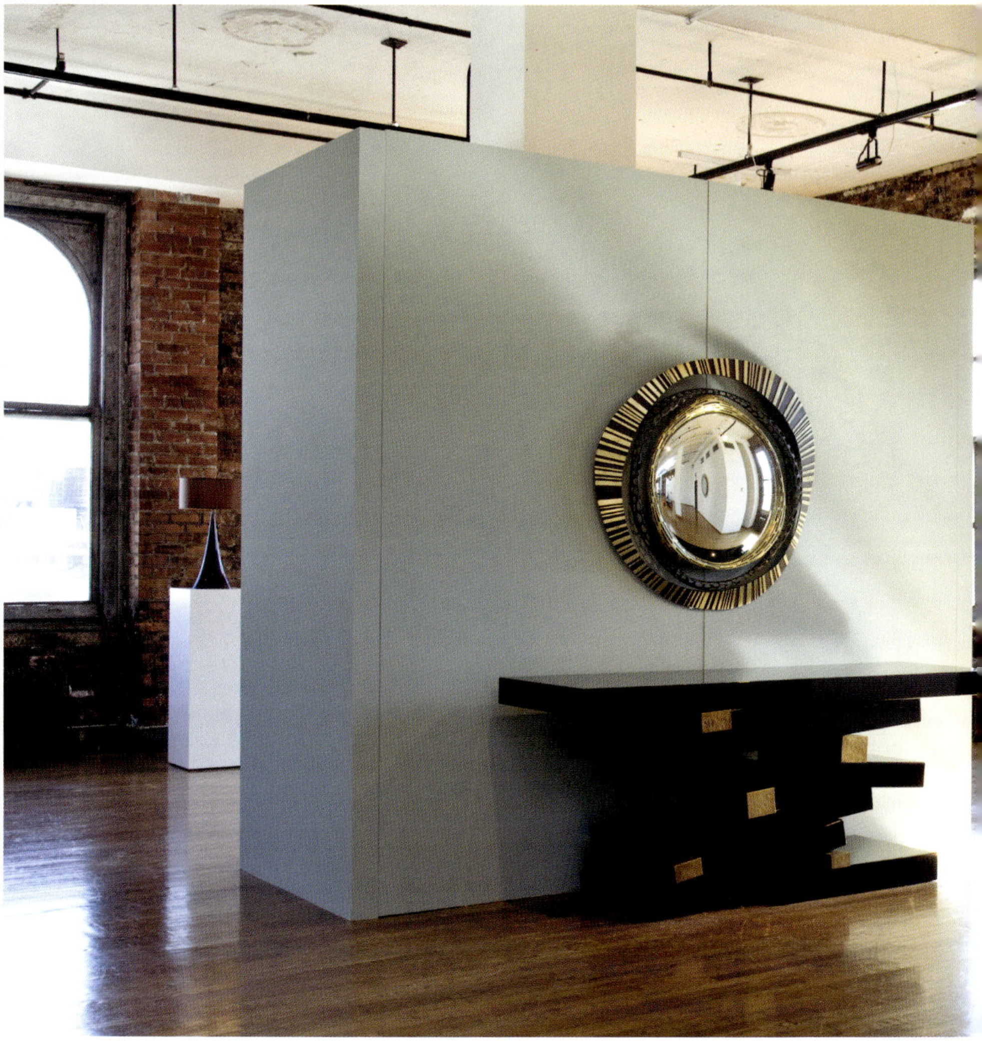

"Turbulence," 2007

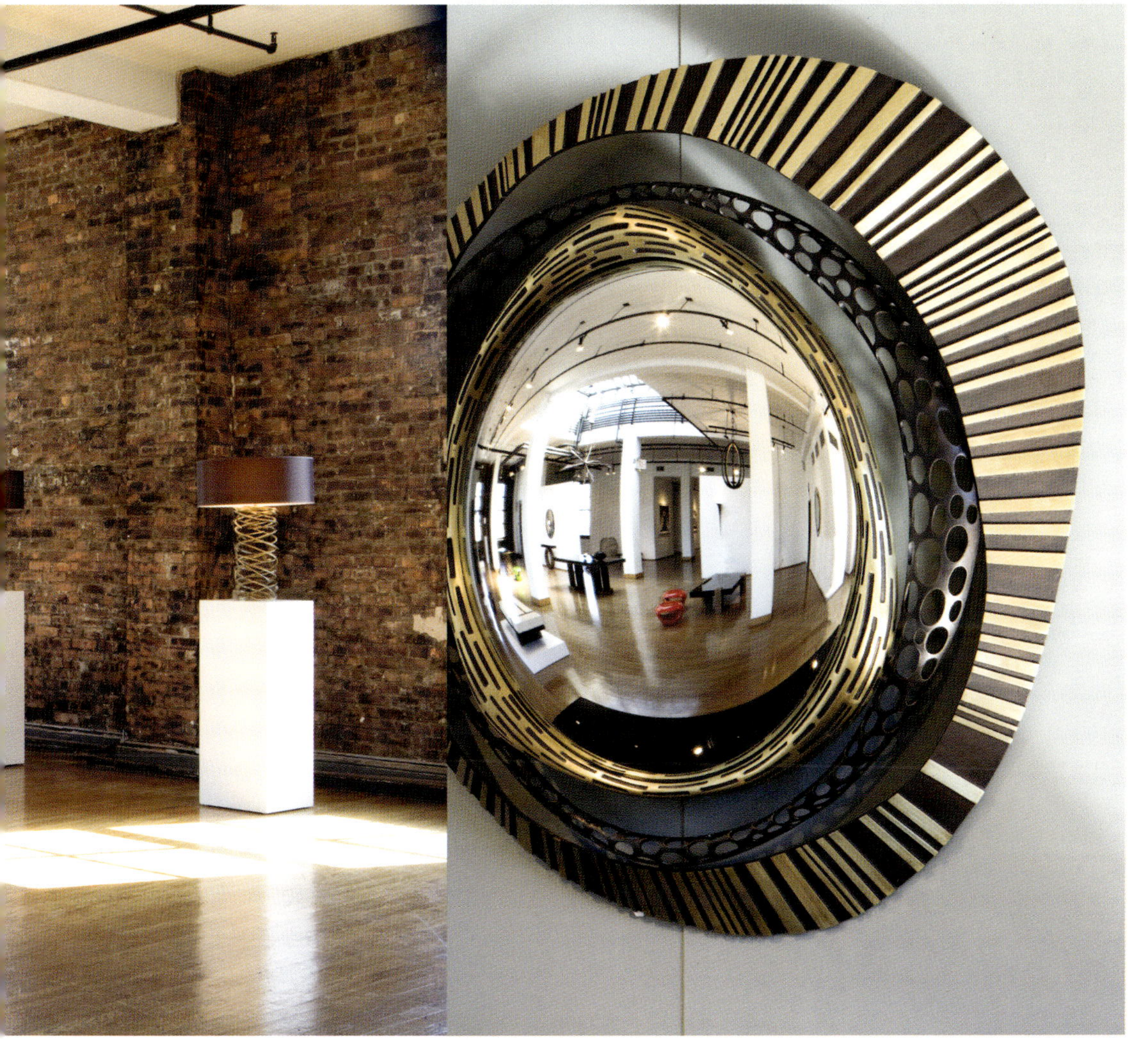

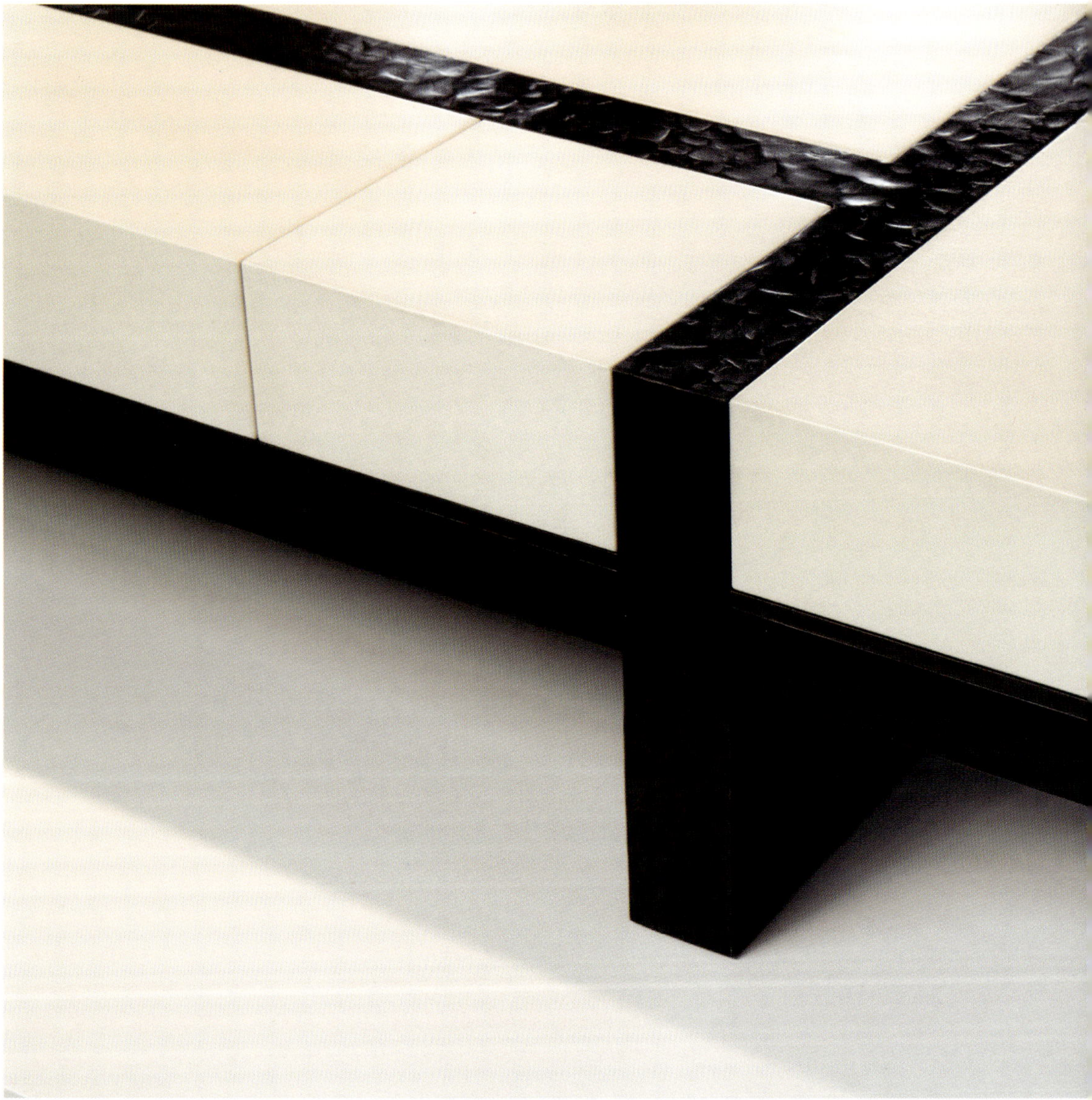

"Turbulence," 2007

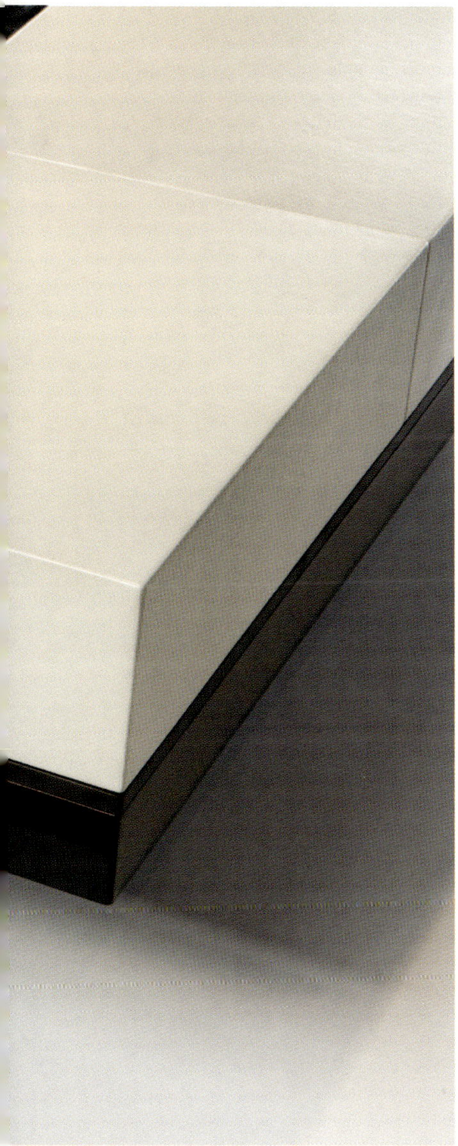

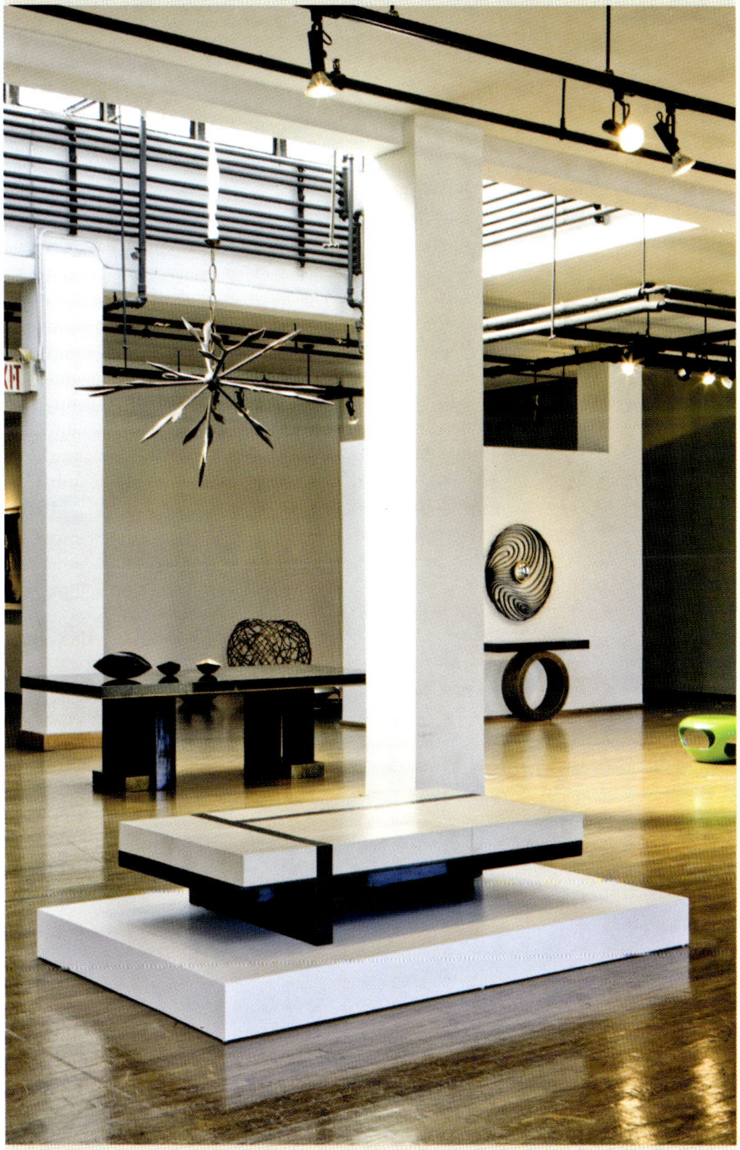

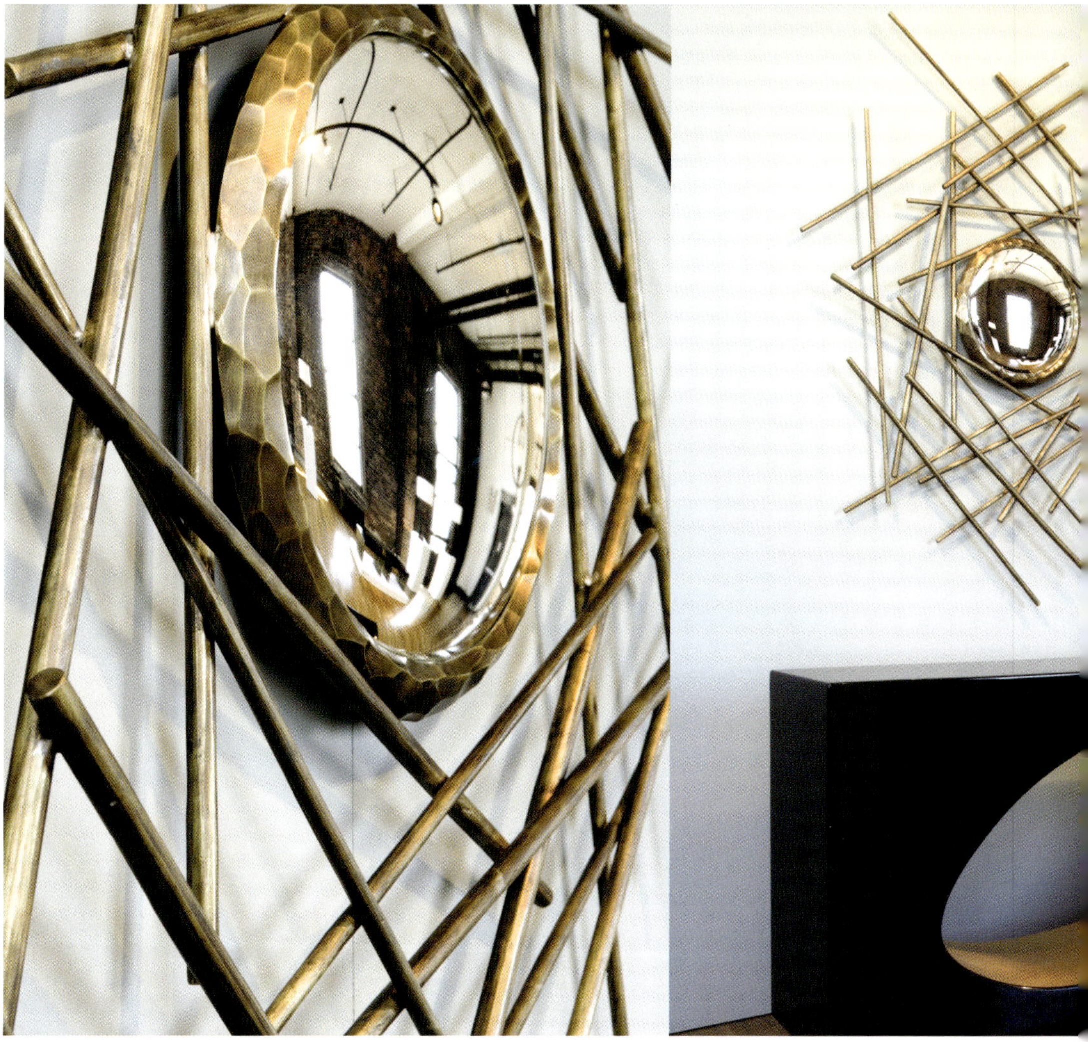

"Turbulence," 2007

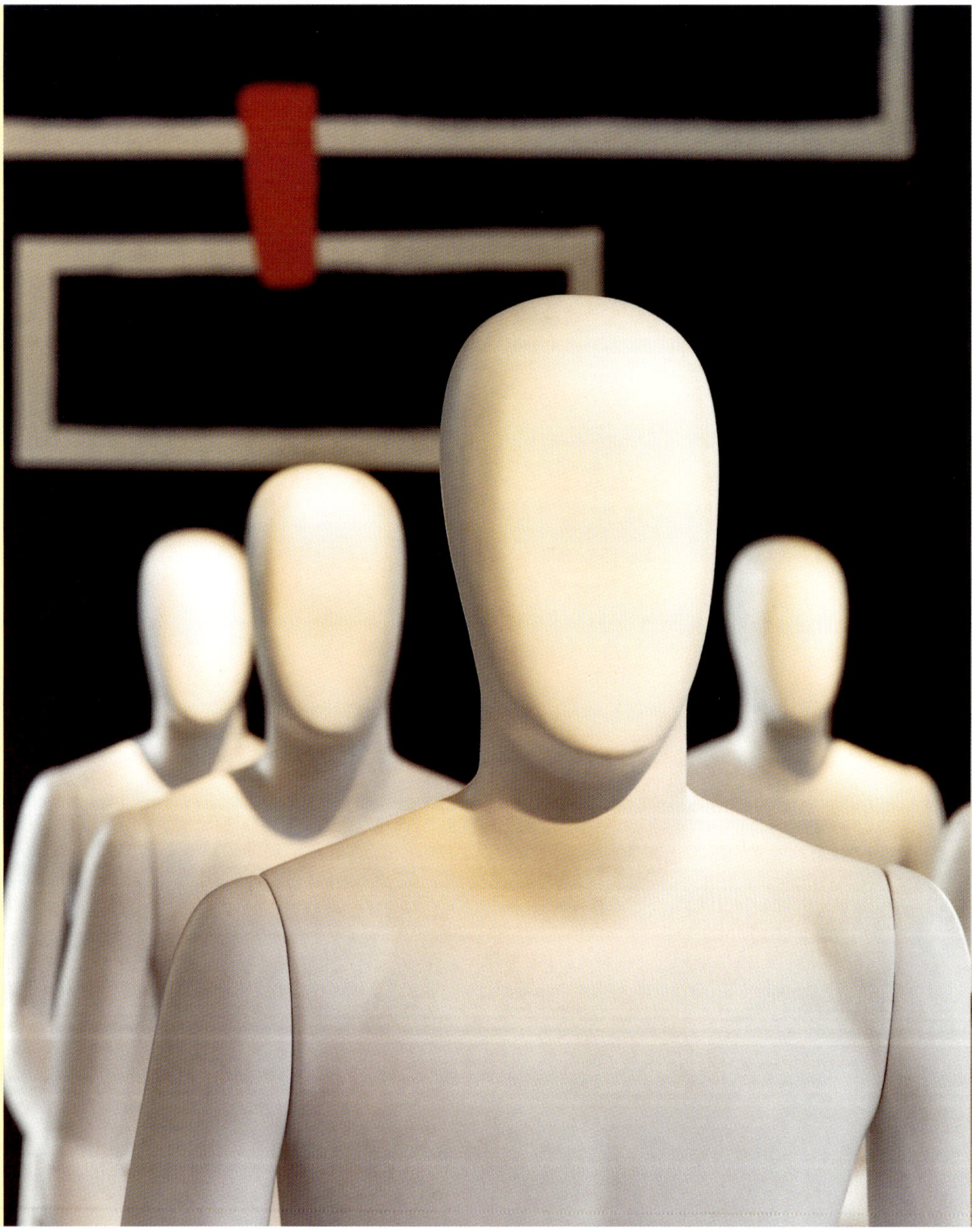
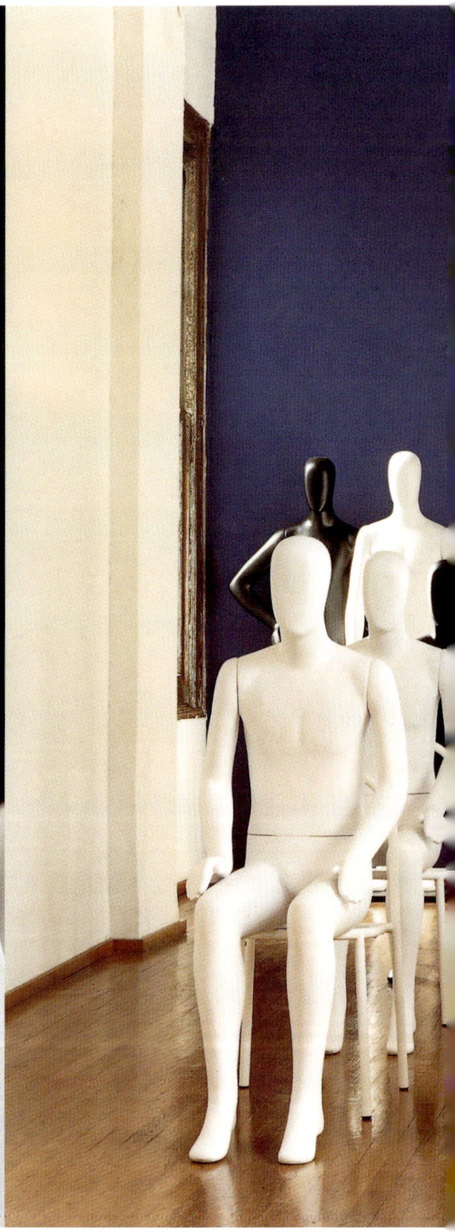

ralph pucci *BLANK* male mannequins, 2001, mural by Nicholas Howey

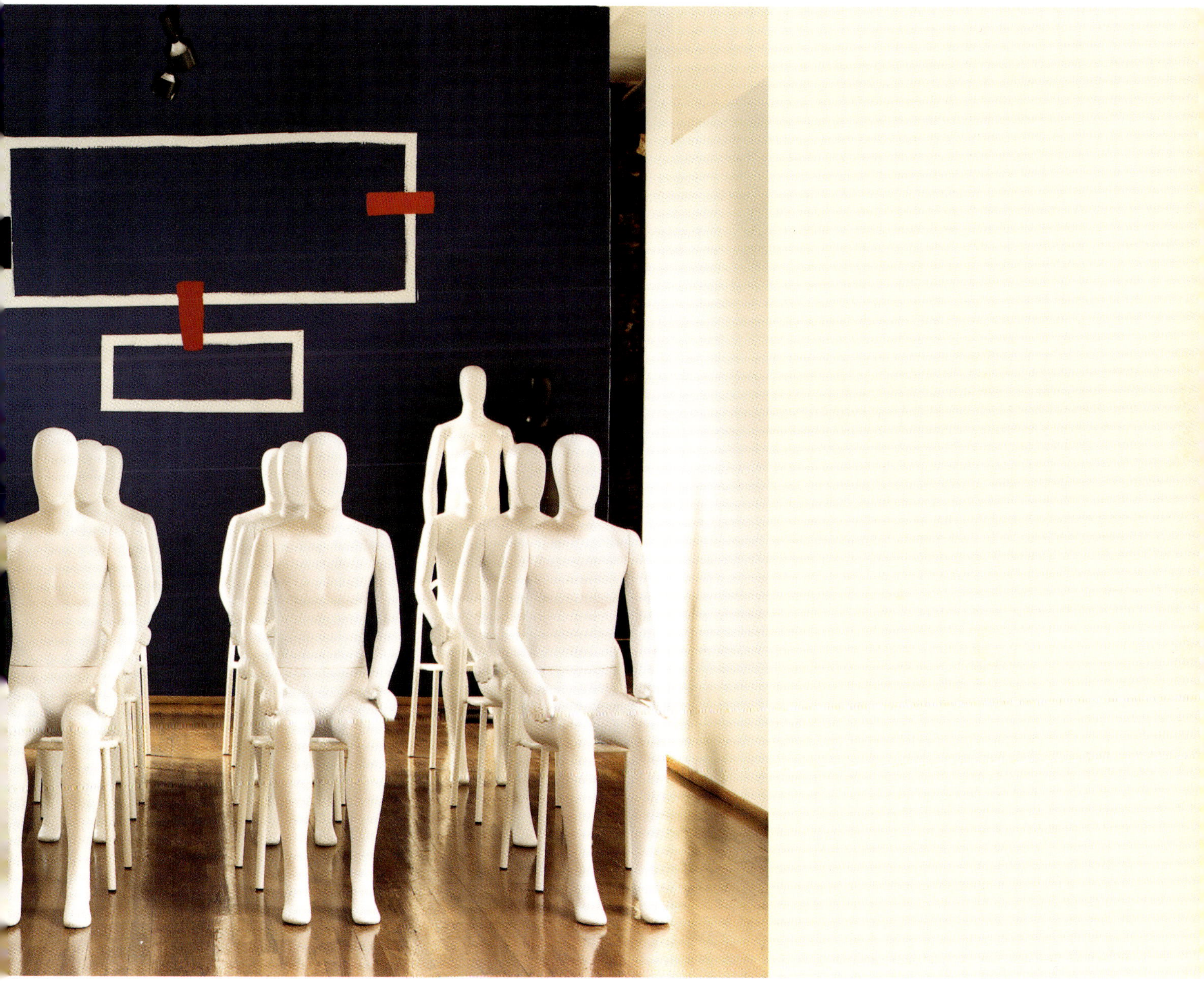

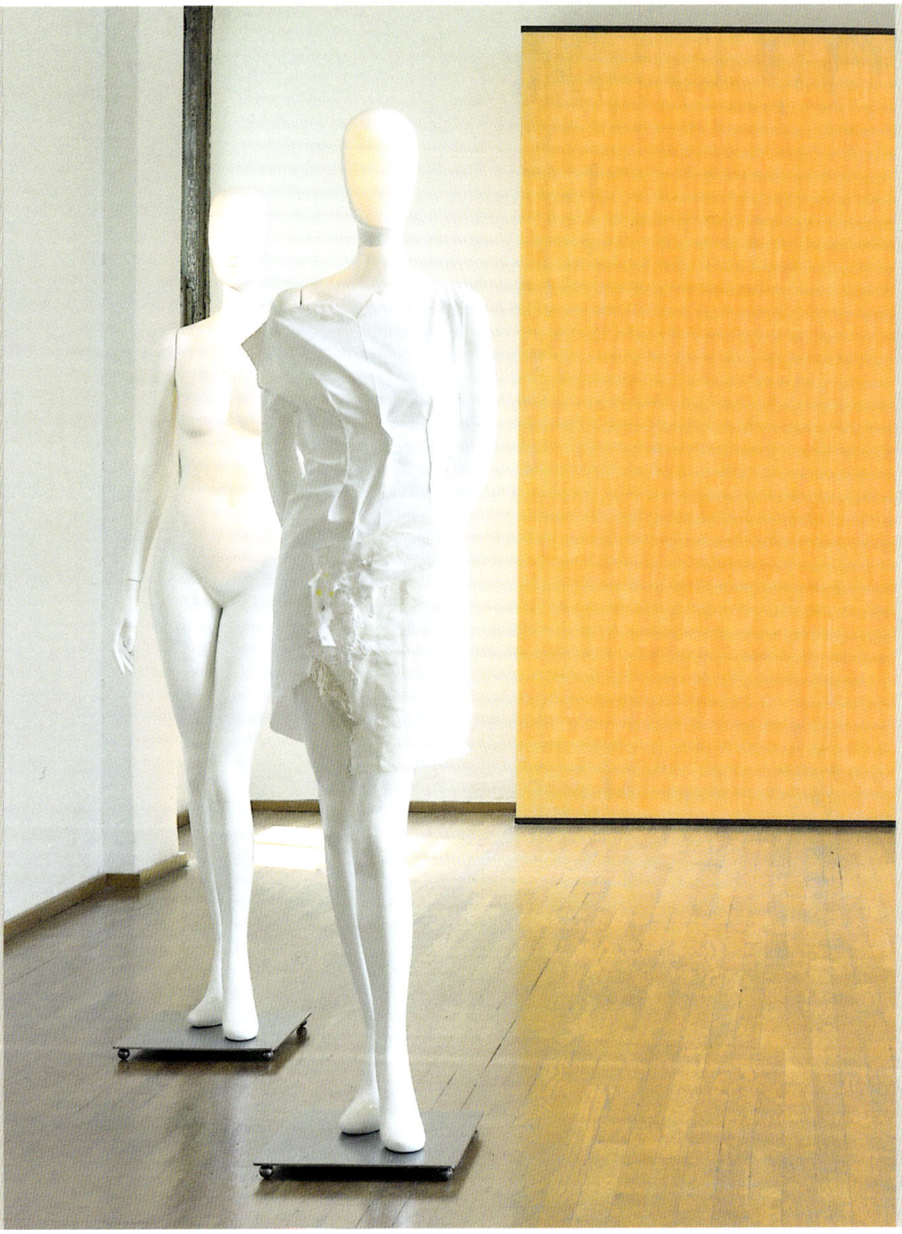

BLANK female mannequins, 2001

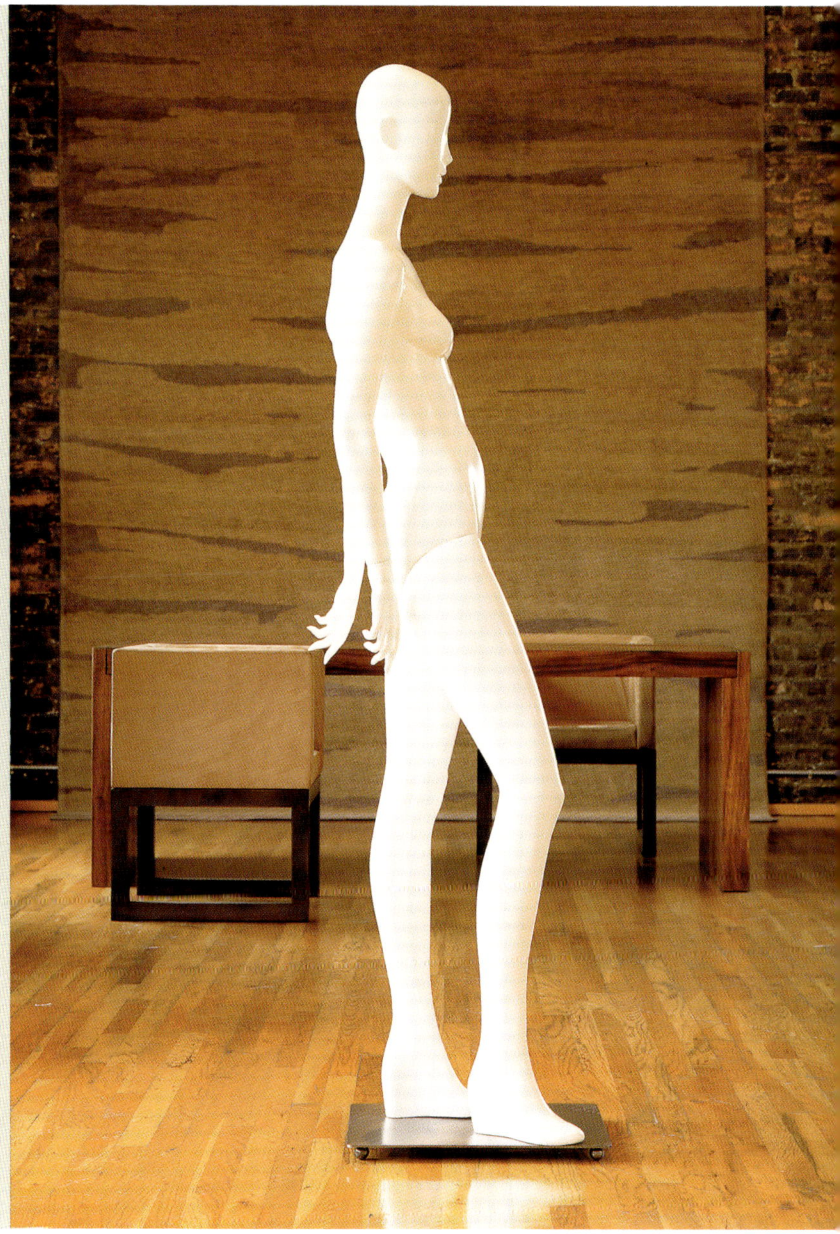

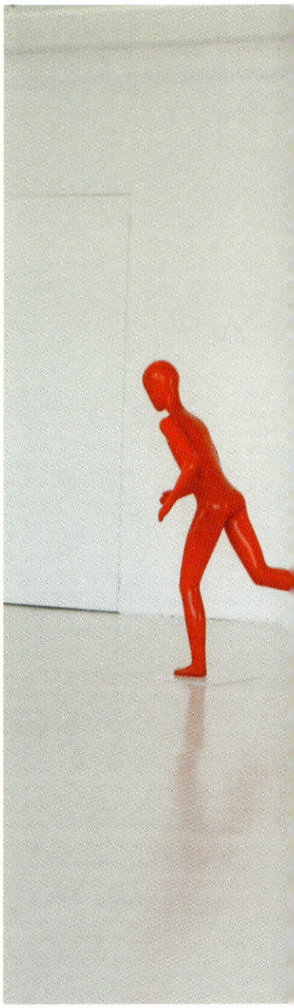

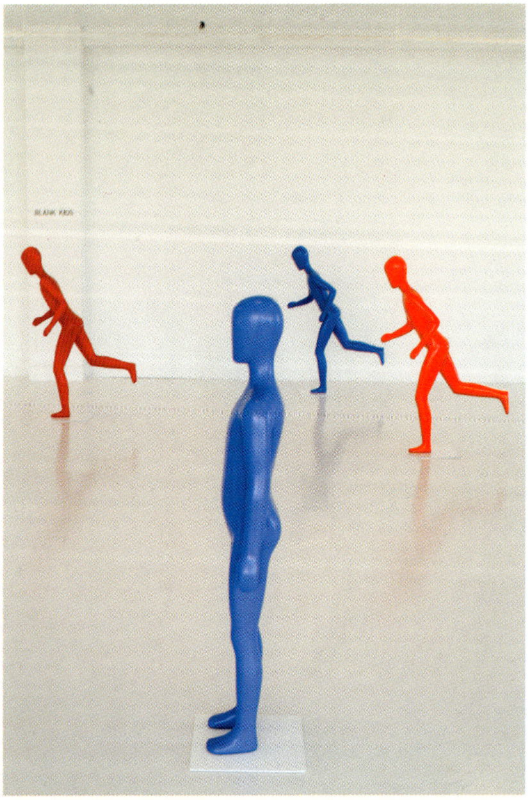

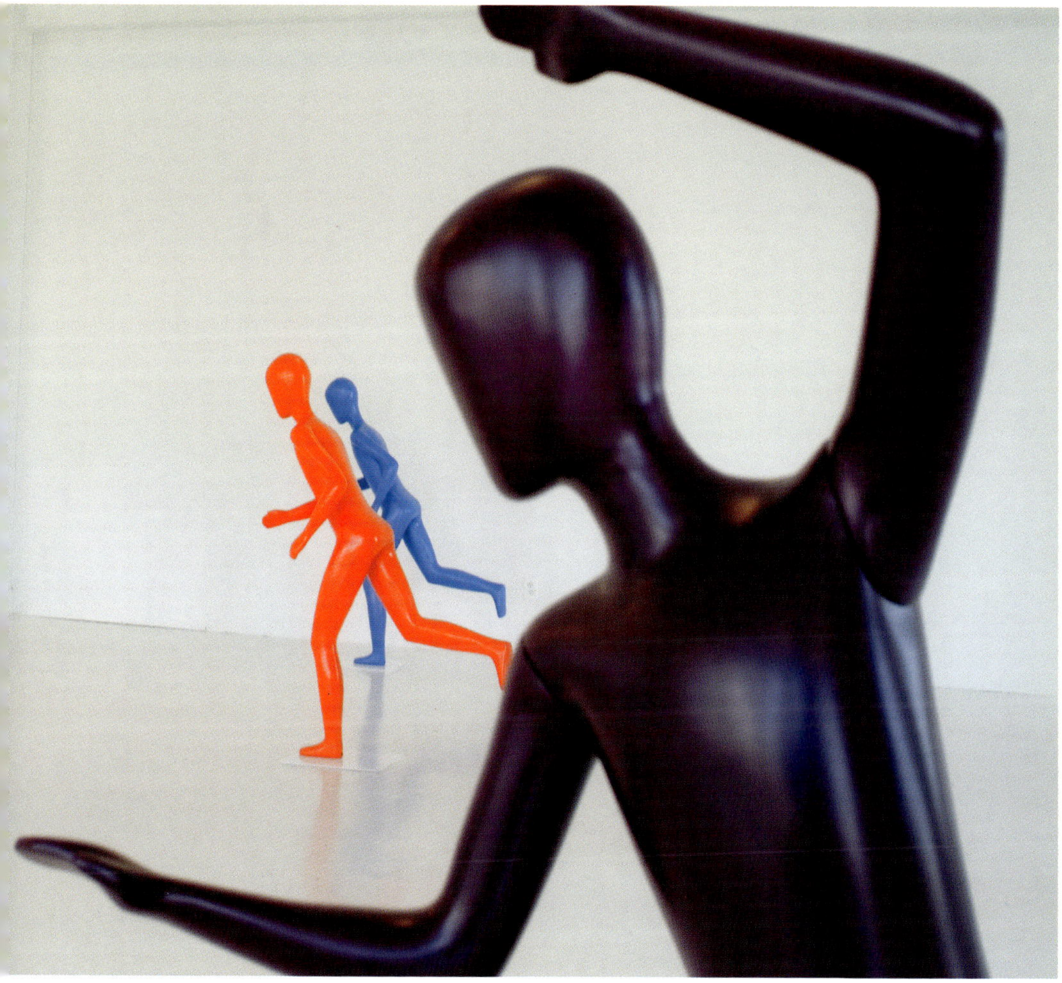

BLANK kids mannequins, 2003

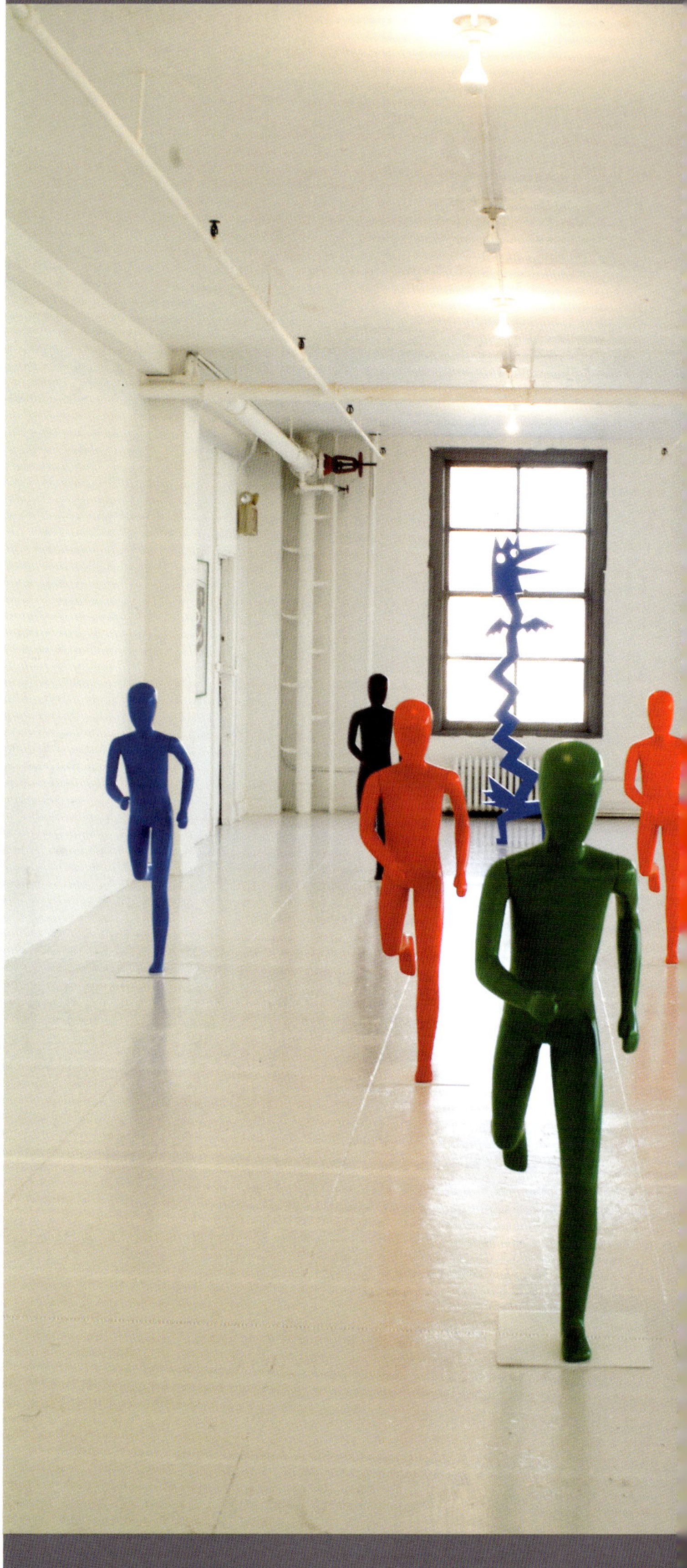

BLANK kids mannequins, 2003

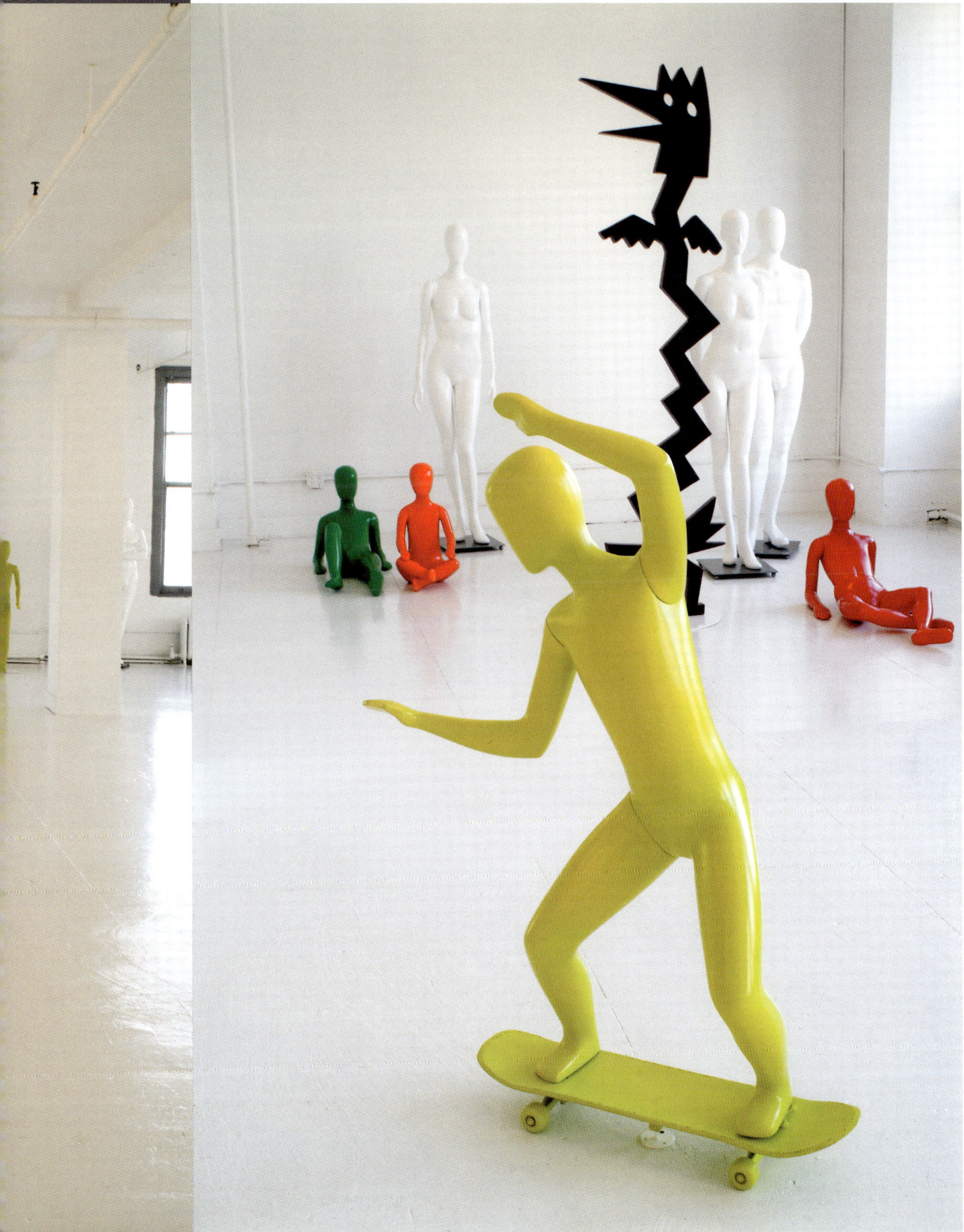

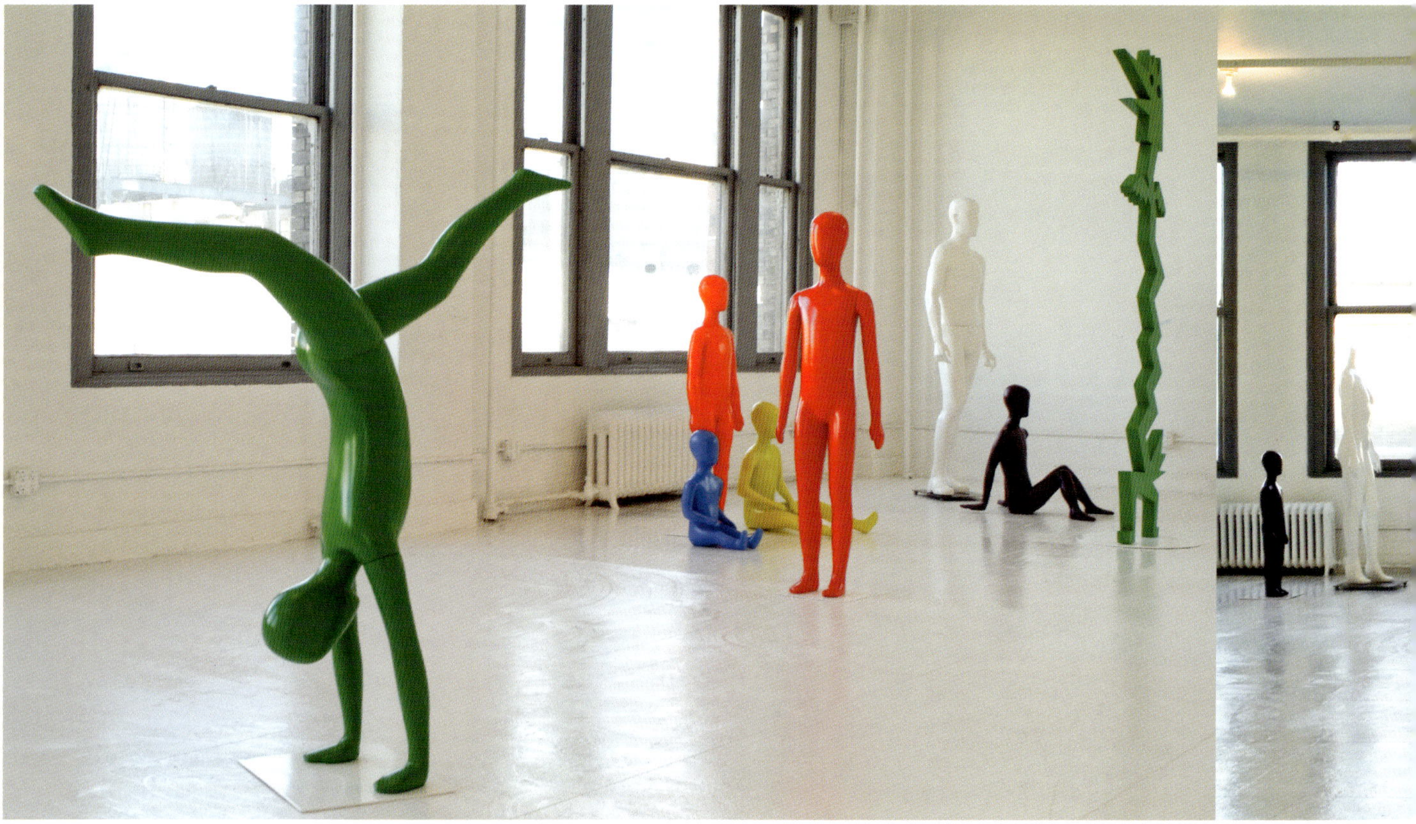

BLANK kids mannequins, 2003

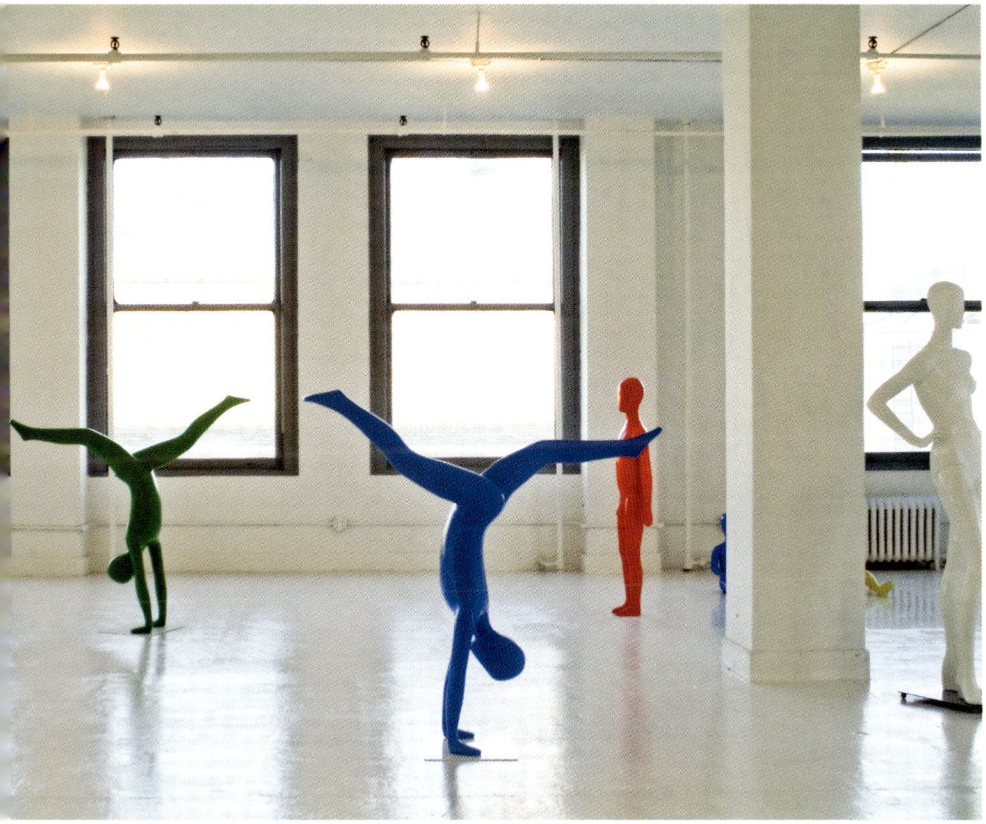

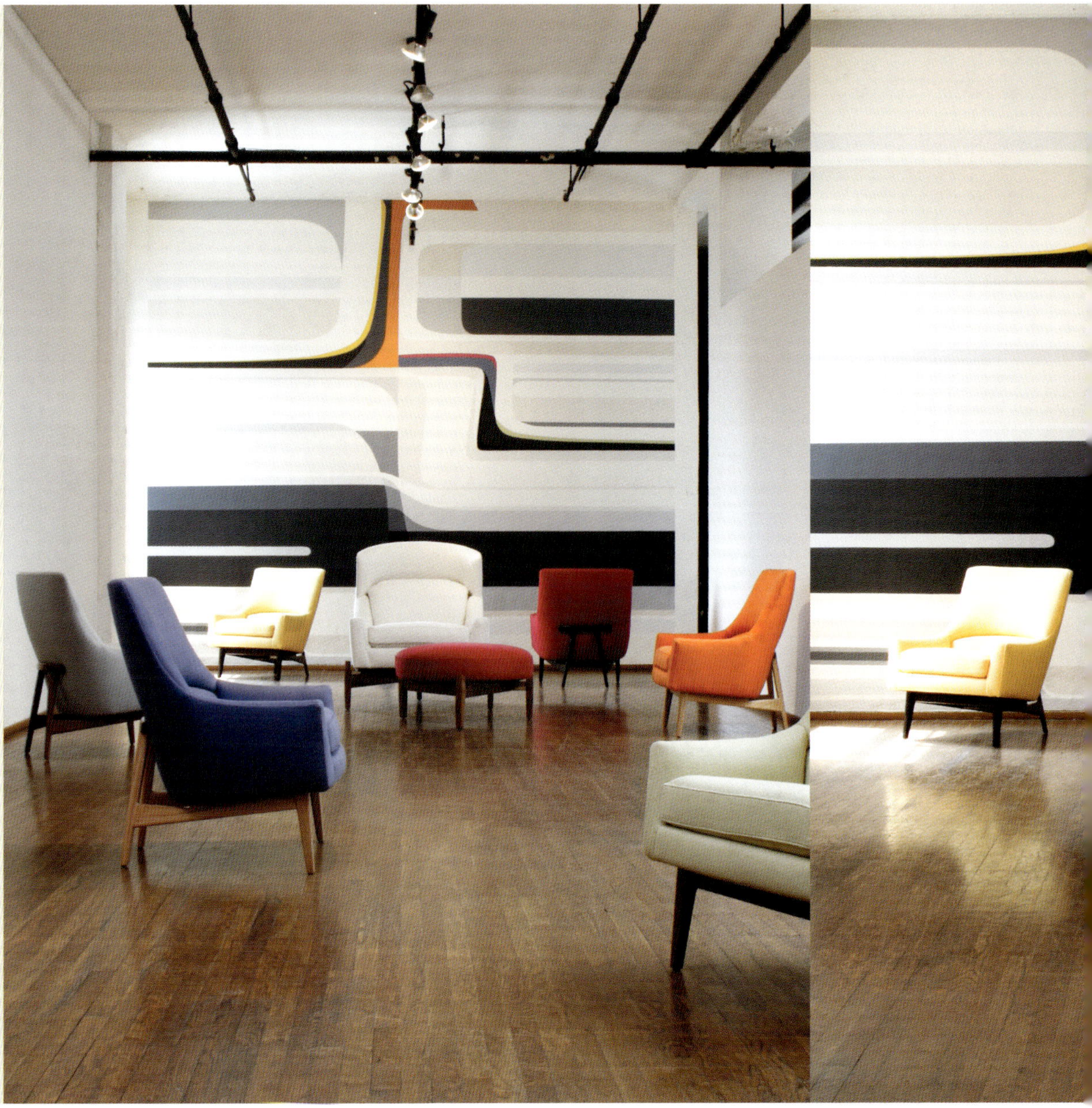

jens risom *A Chair*, 2007 (left and center), *Easy Armless Chair*, 2005 (right).
Murals by Malcolm Hill.

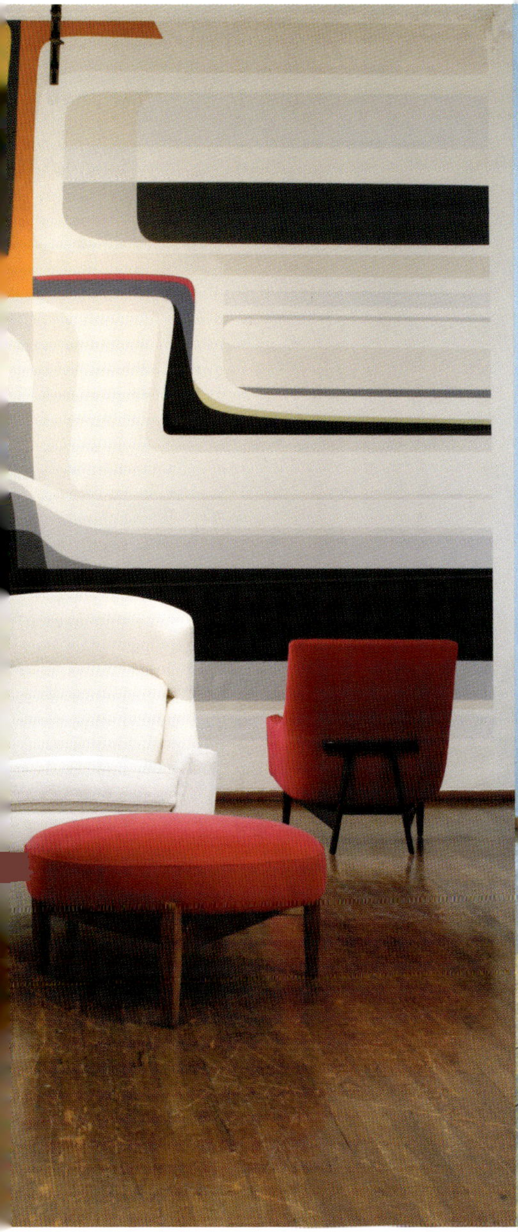
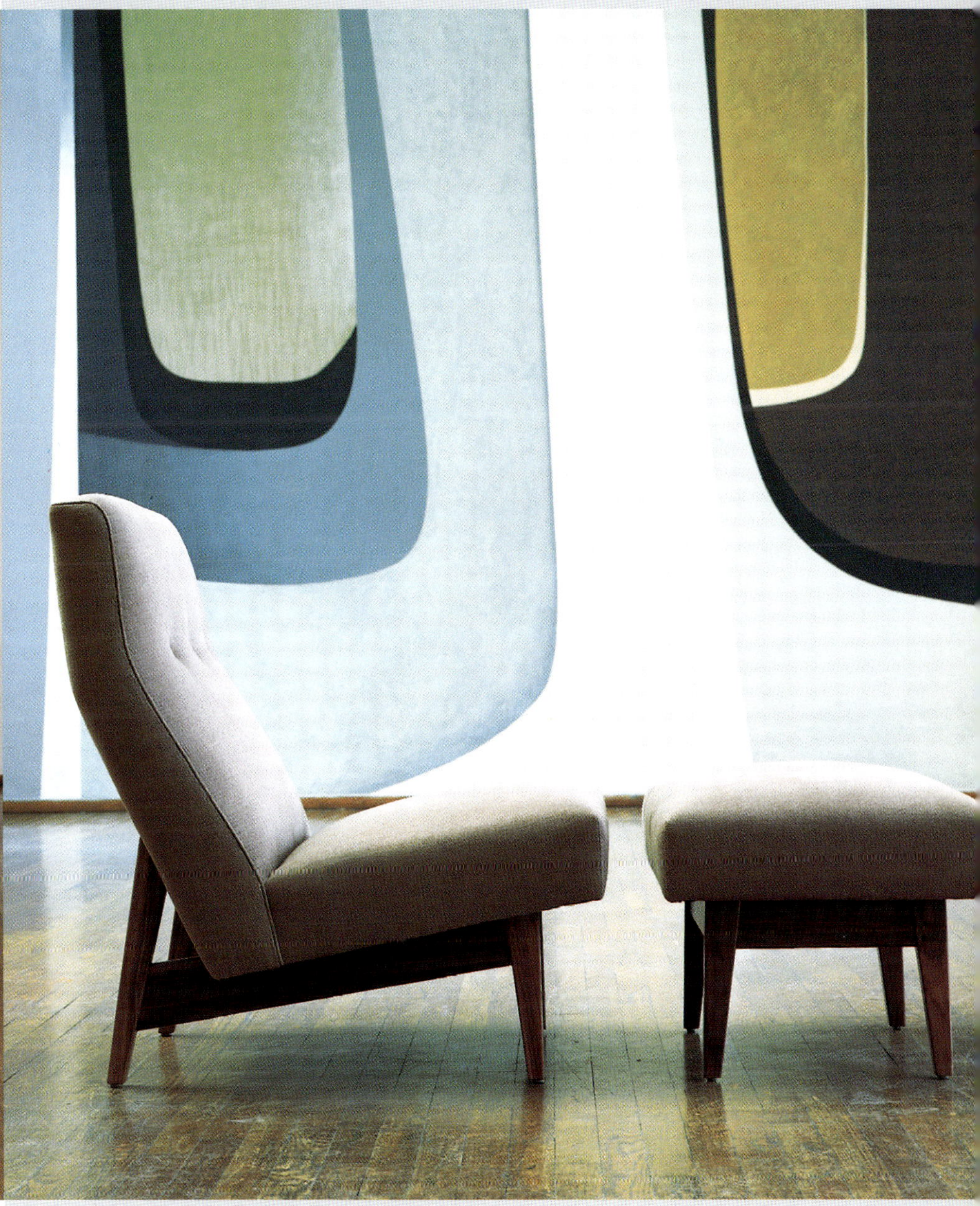

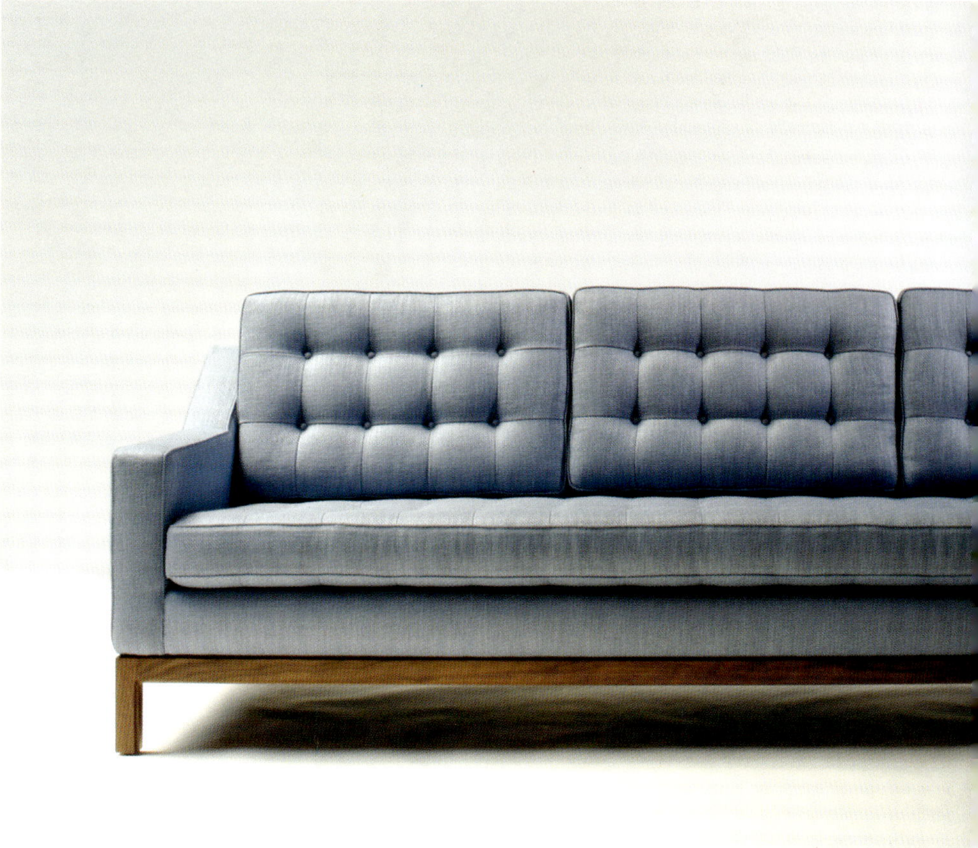

"Jens Risom²," *Structure* sofa and *Structure* chair, 2007

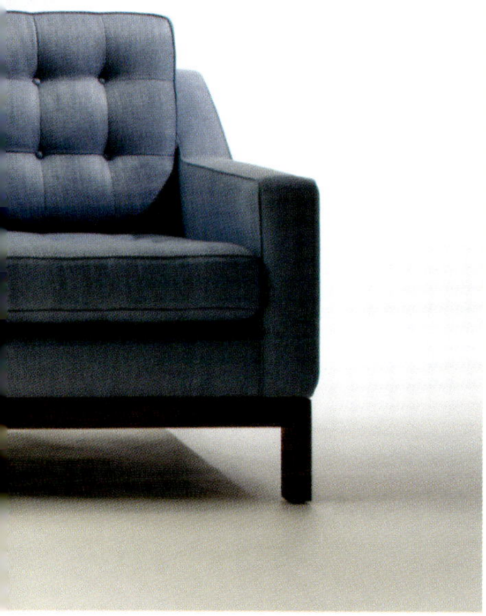

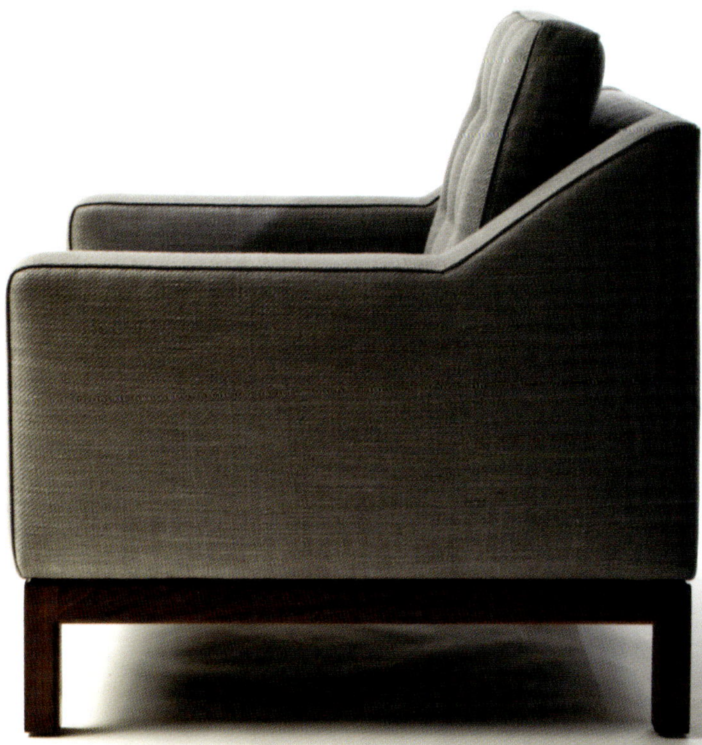

Easy Sofa and *Chair*, 2005

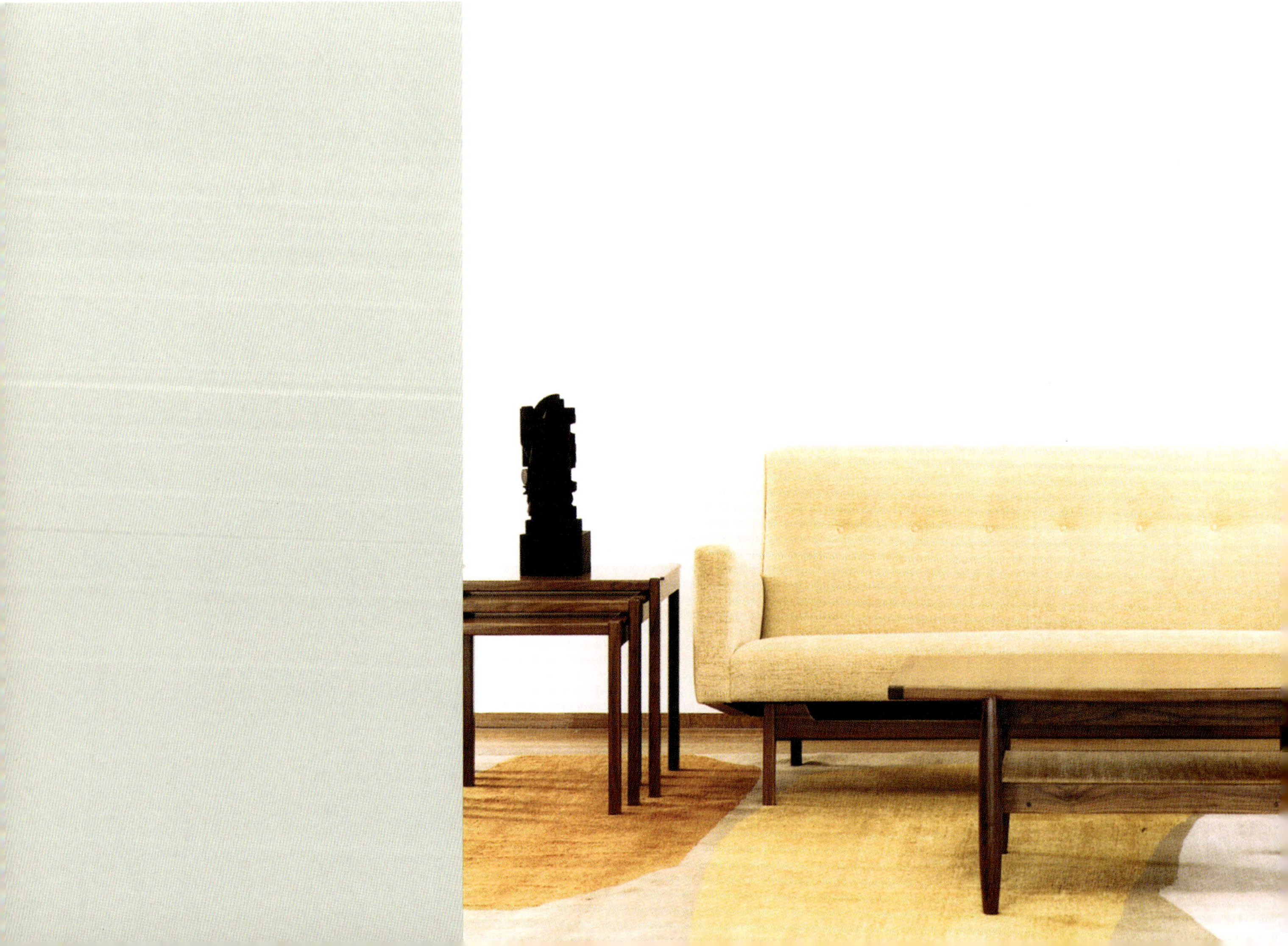

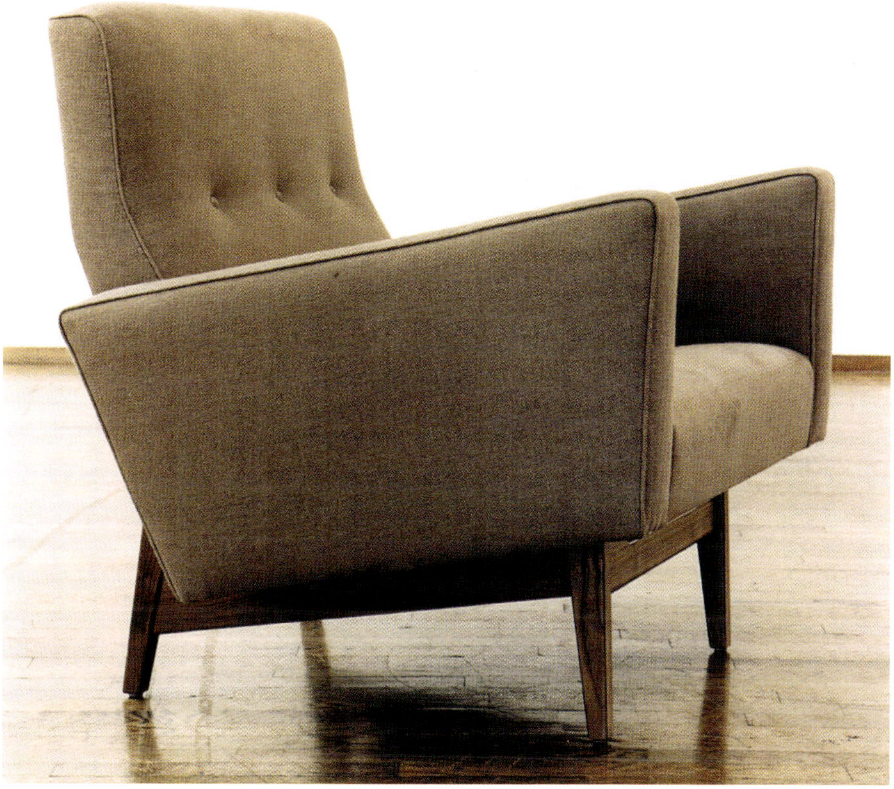

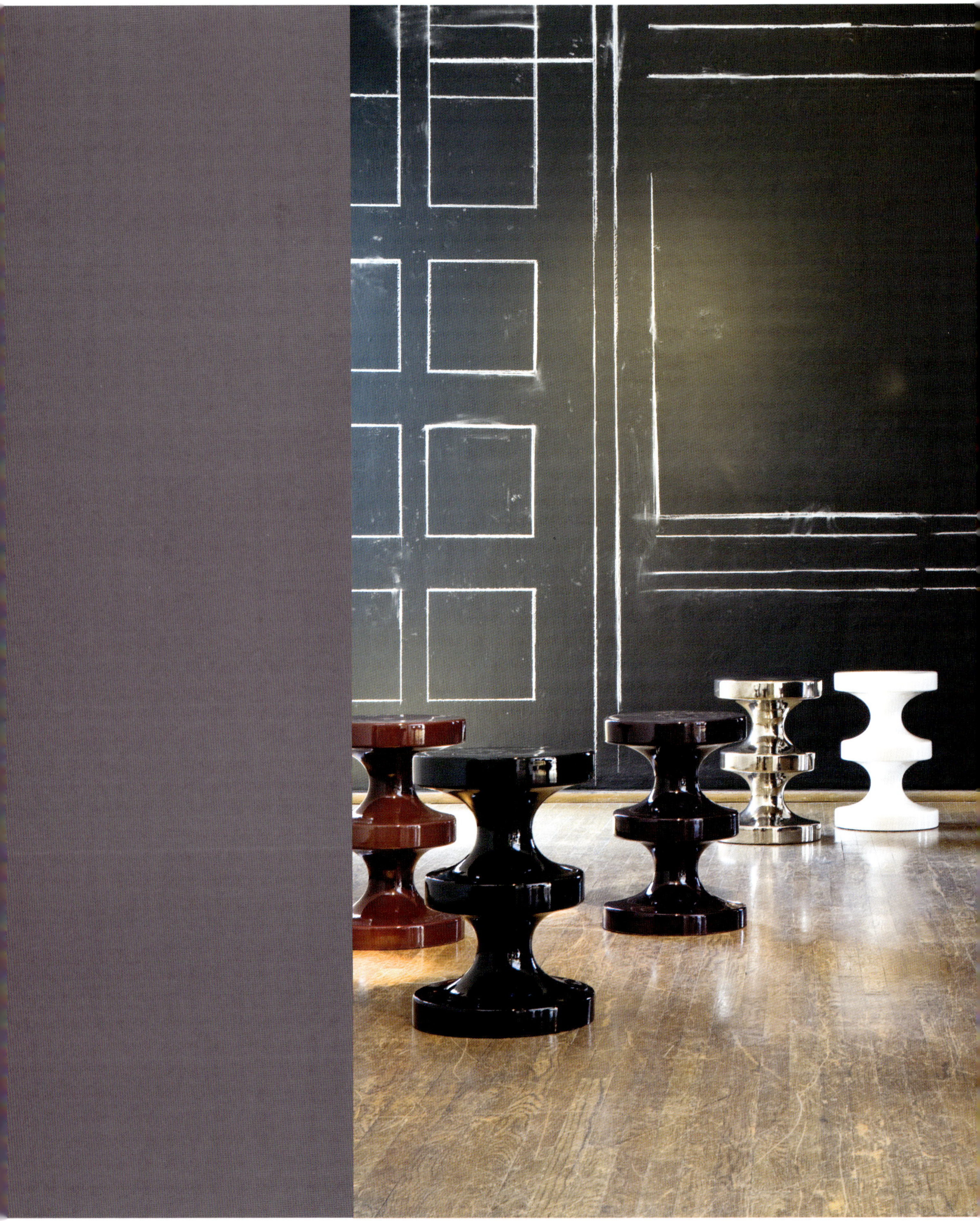

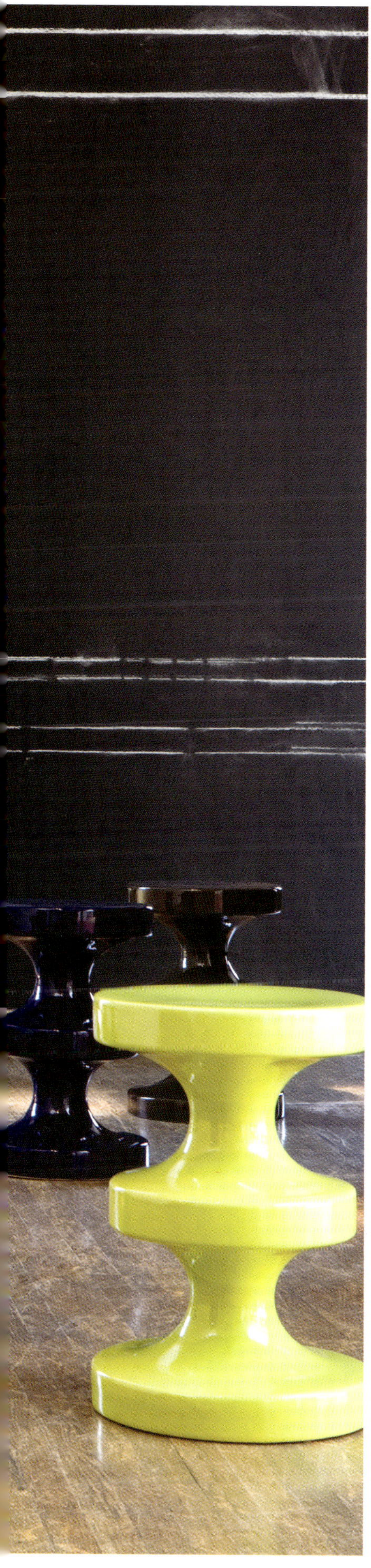

india mahdavi furniture collection, 2008, mural conceived by India Mahdavi

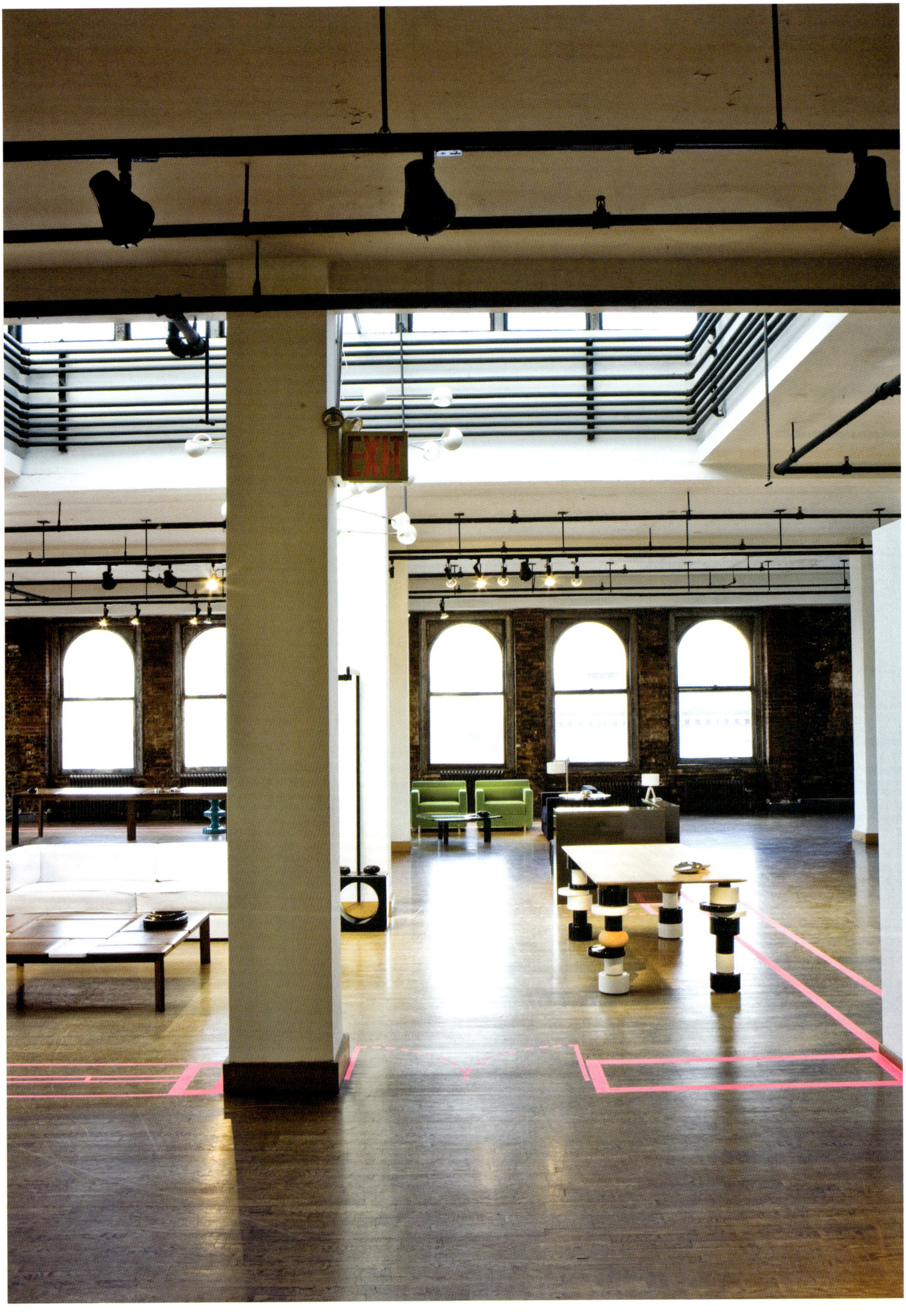
EXIT

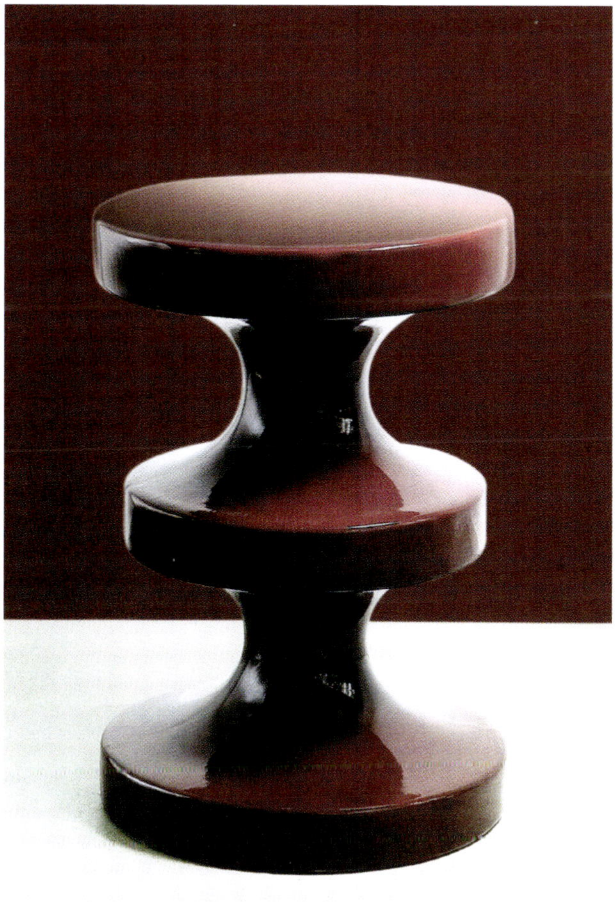

Furniture collection, 2008 (left); *Bishop*, 2008 (above)

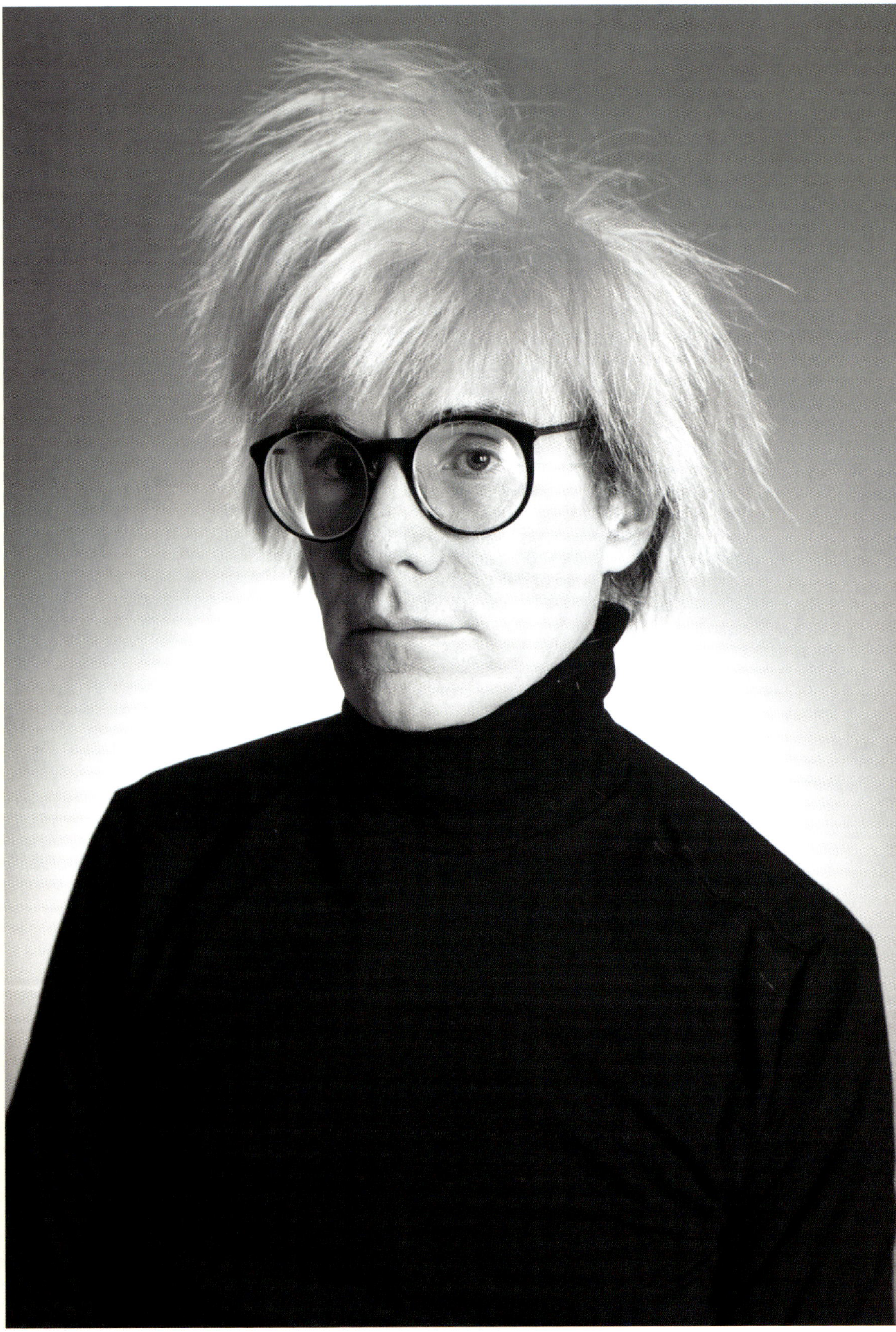

christopher makos *Andy Warhol* photographs, 2007

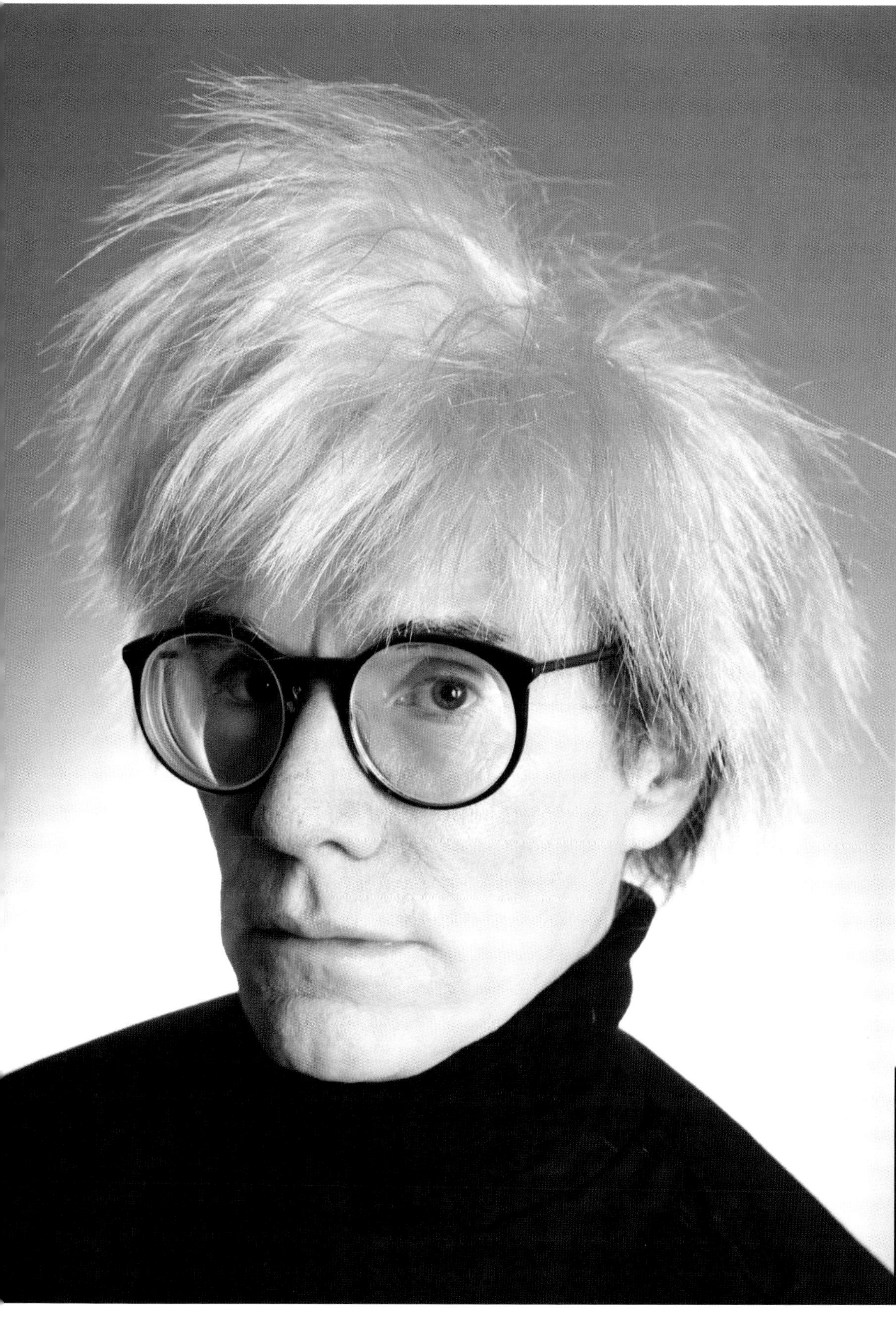
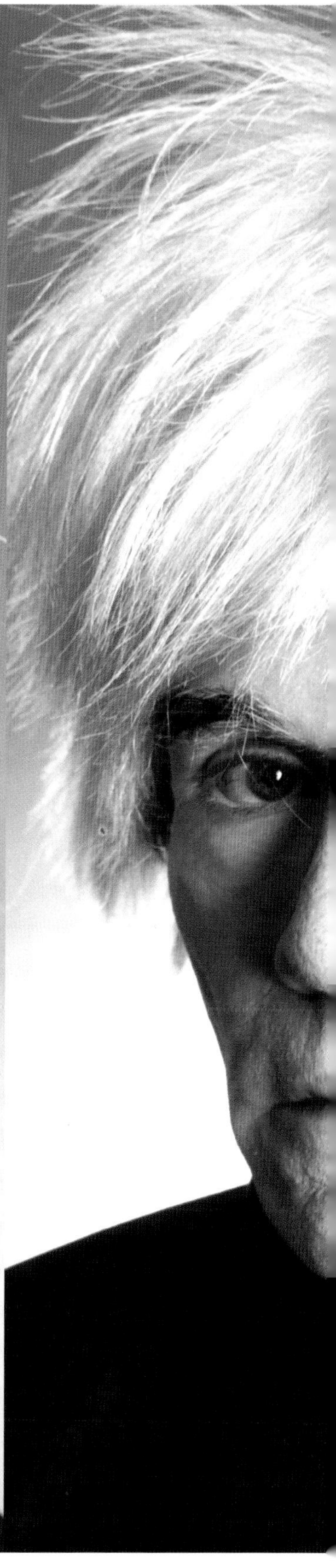

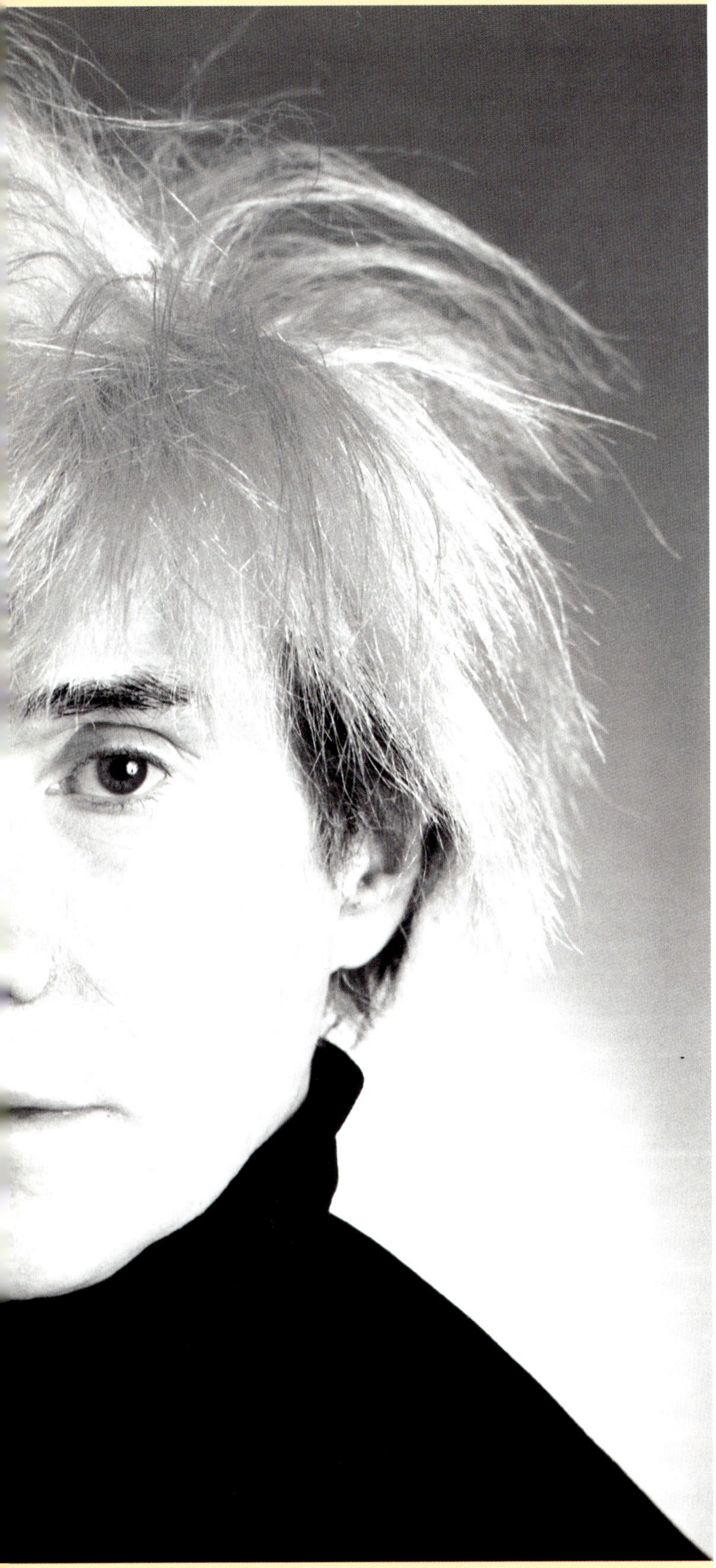

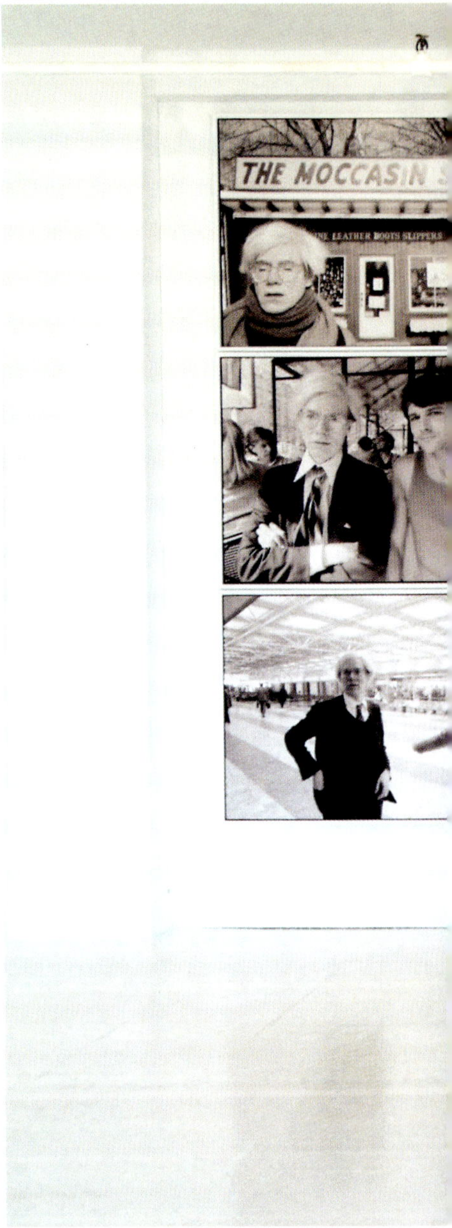

"Forever Andy" photographs, 2004,
chair and ottoman by Trace Simple,
end tables by Robert Bristow

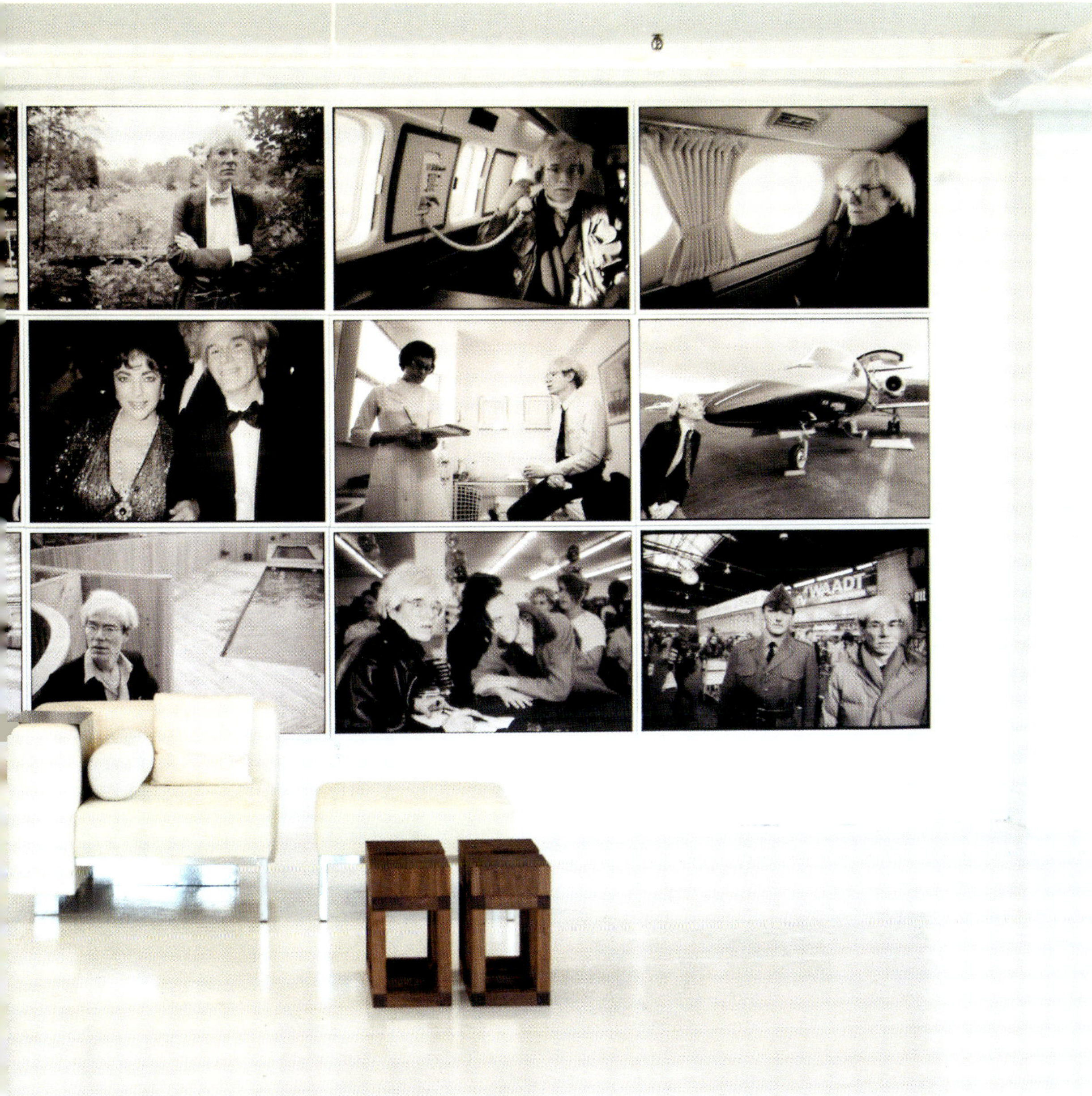

"Great inspiration always is 'the meeting' of abstract thoughts at the moment when they collide with concrete matter."

—Christopher Makos

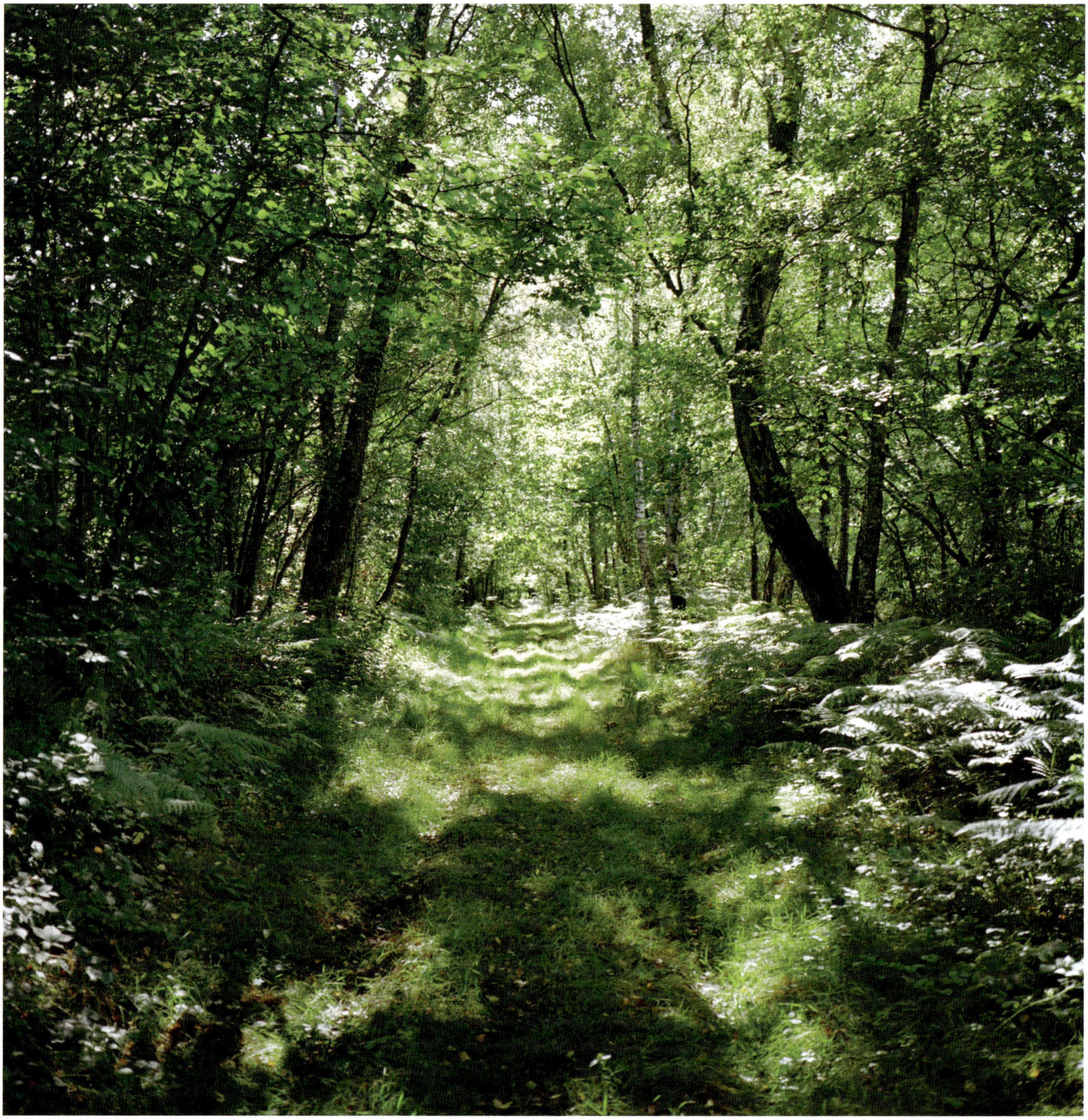

antoine bootz *Path* photographs, 1999

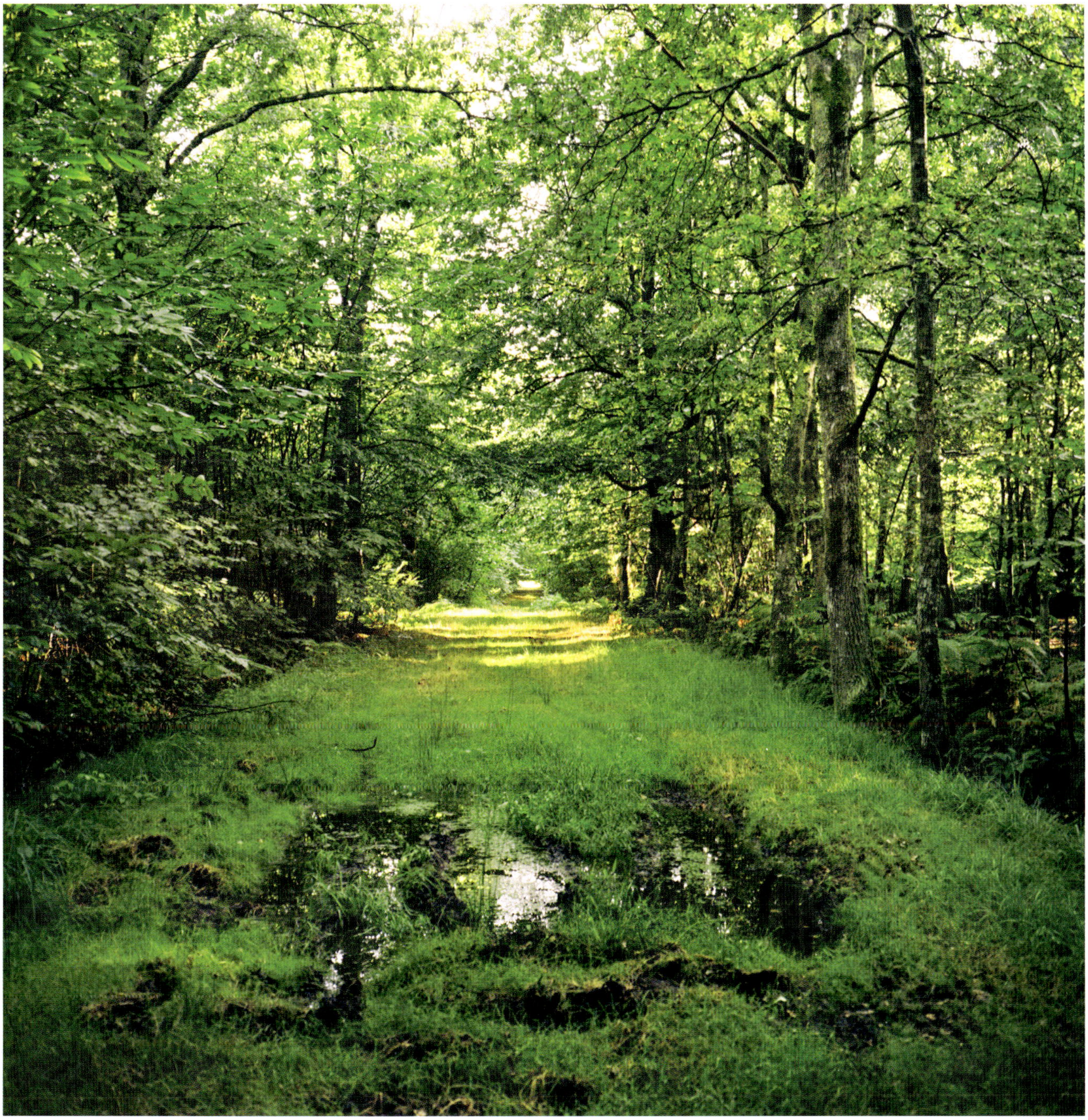

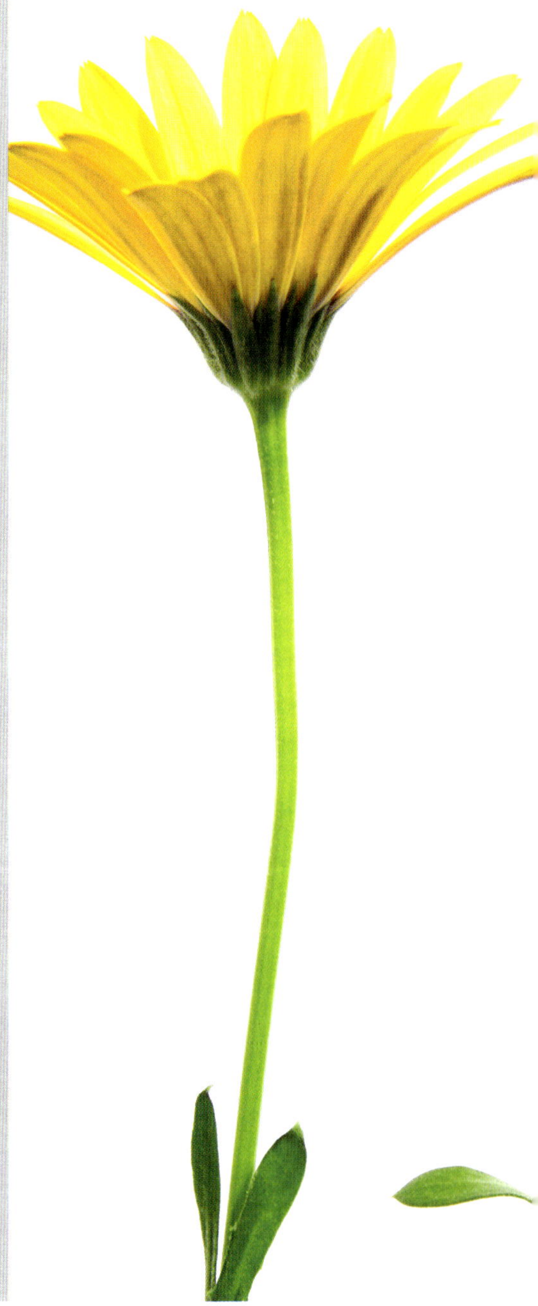

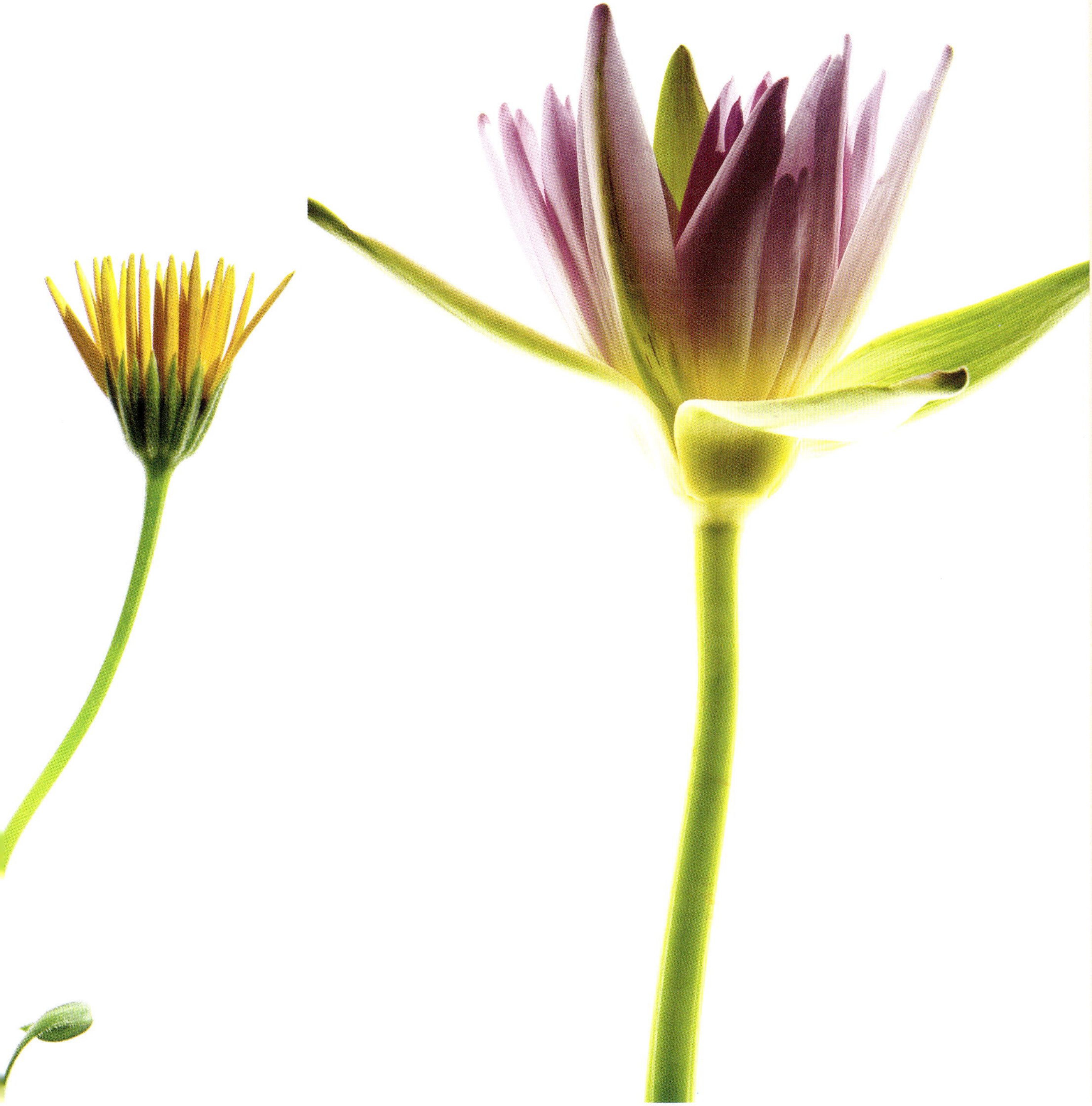

paul solberg *Bloom* photographs, 2005

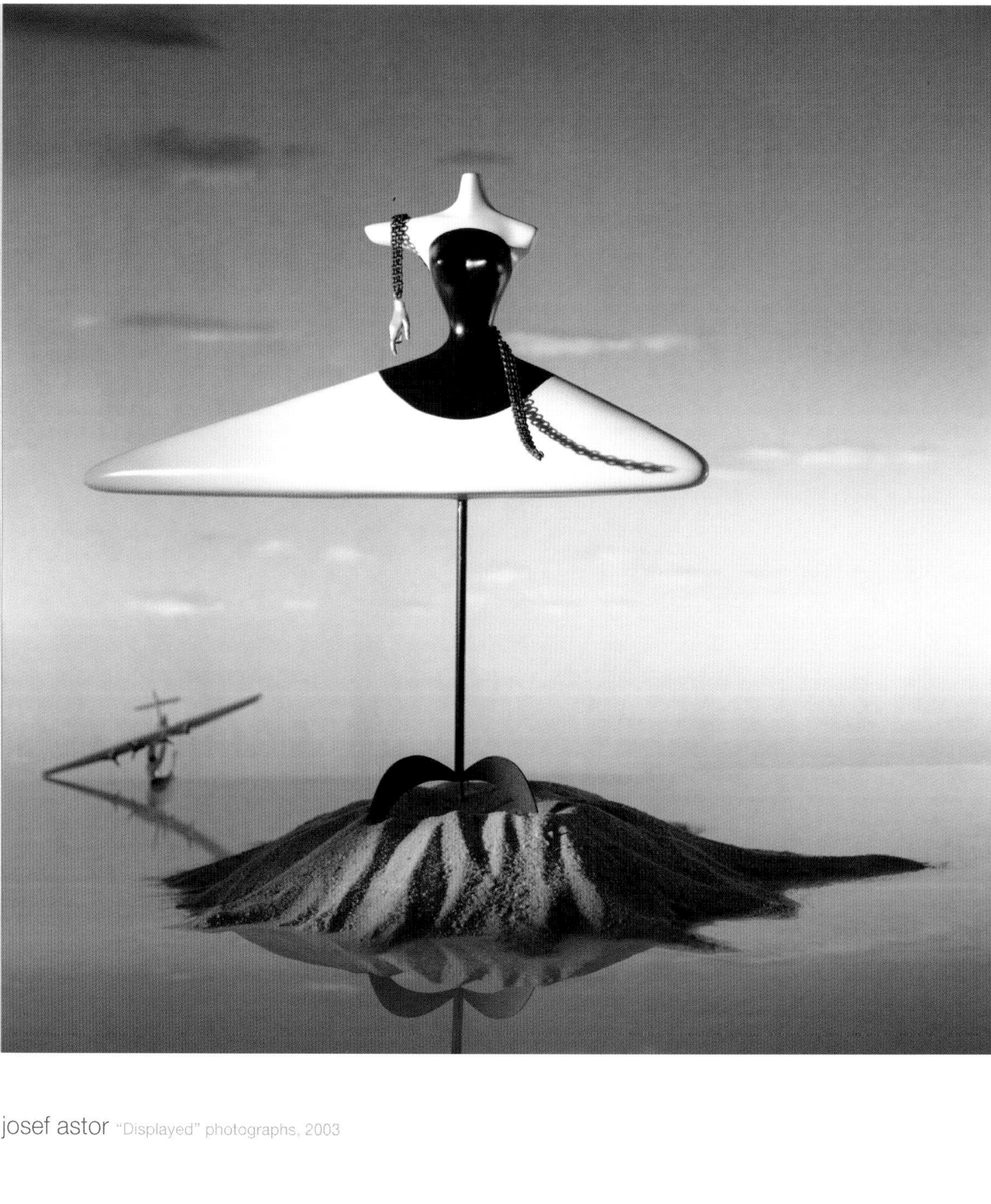

josef astor "Displayed" photographs, 2003

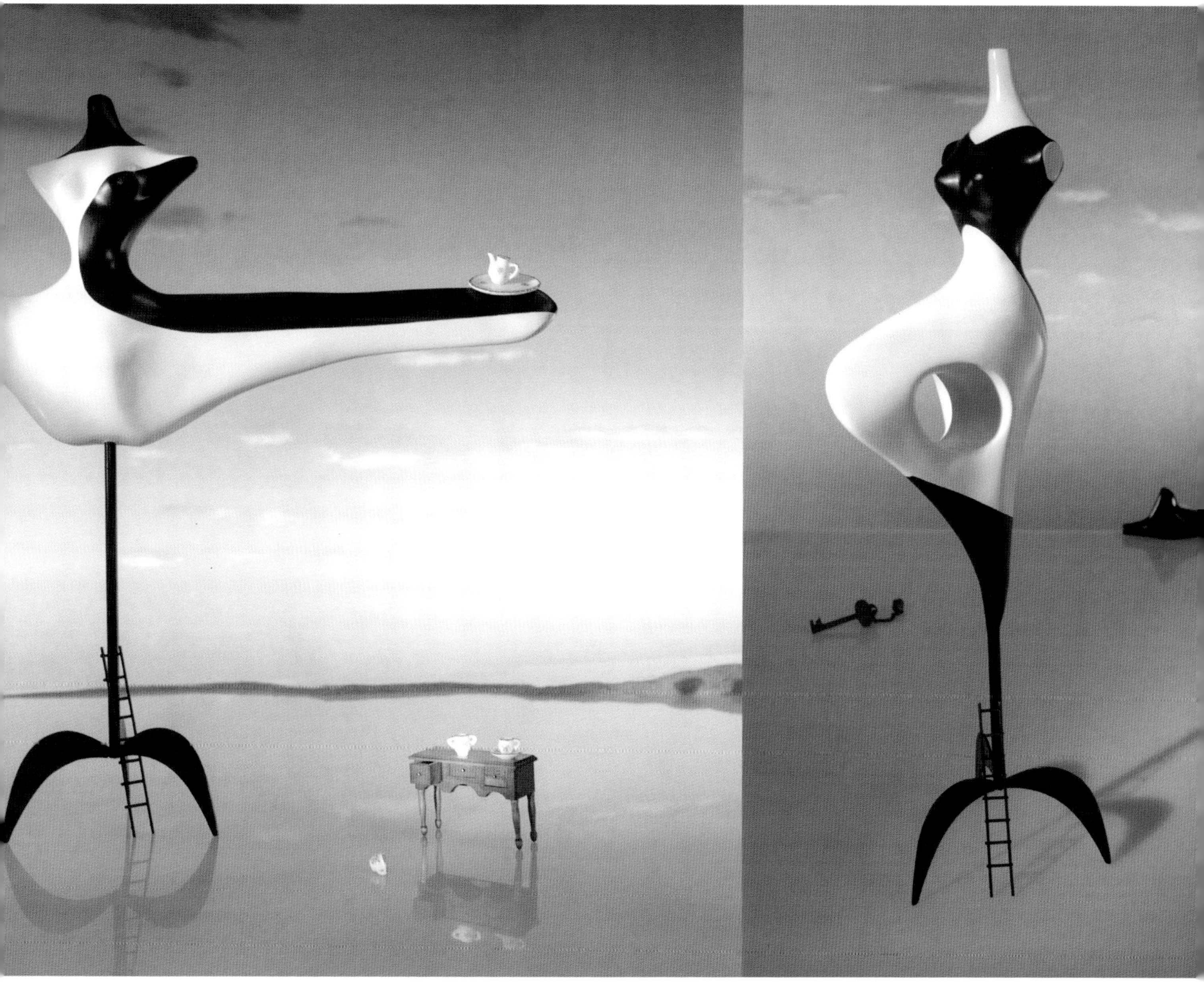

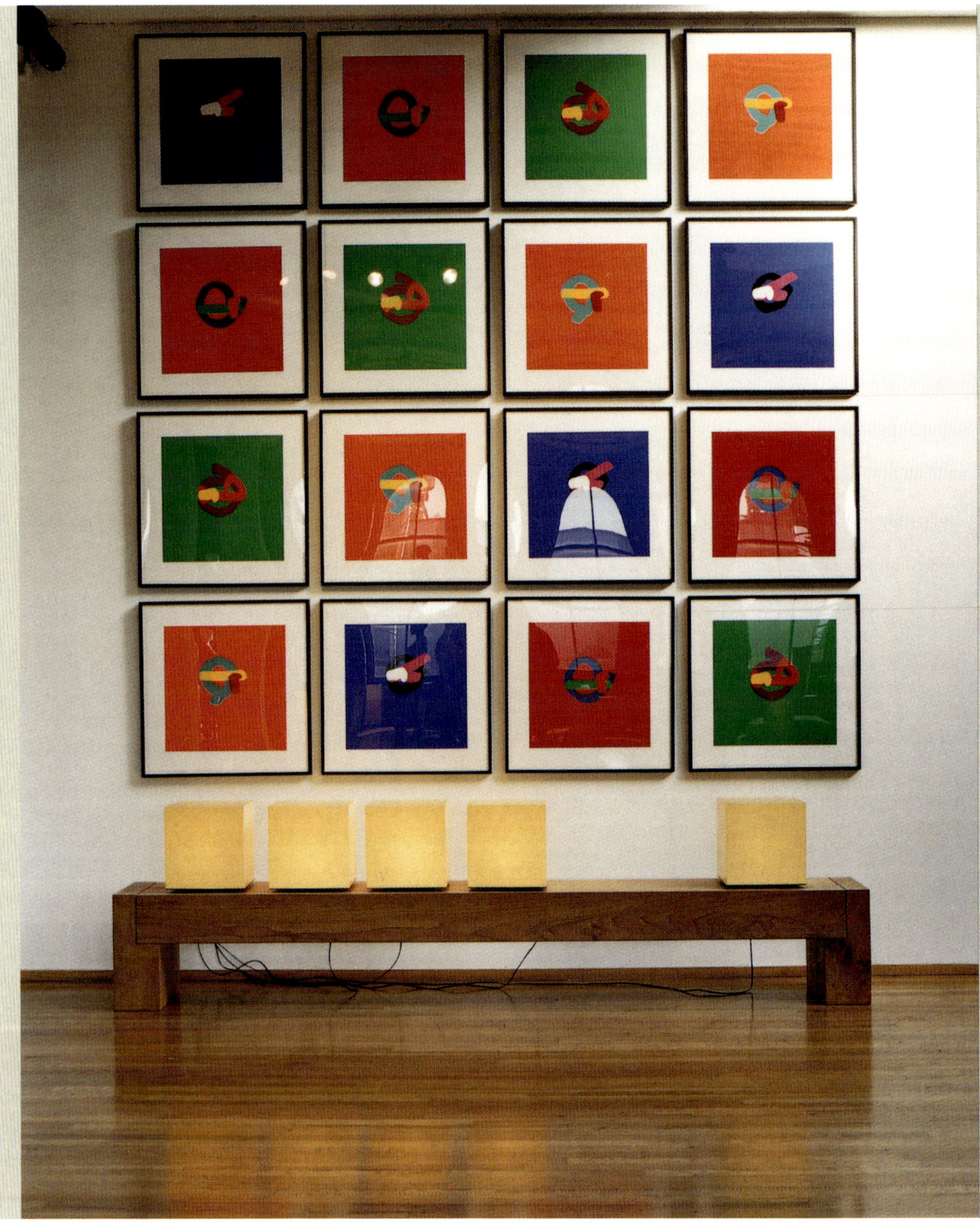

nicholas howey paintings, 2001

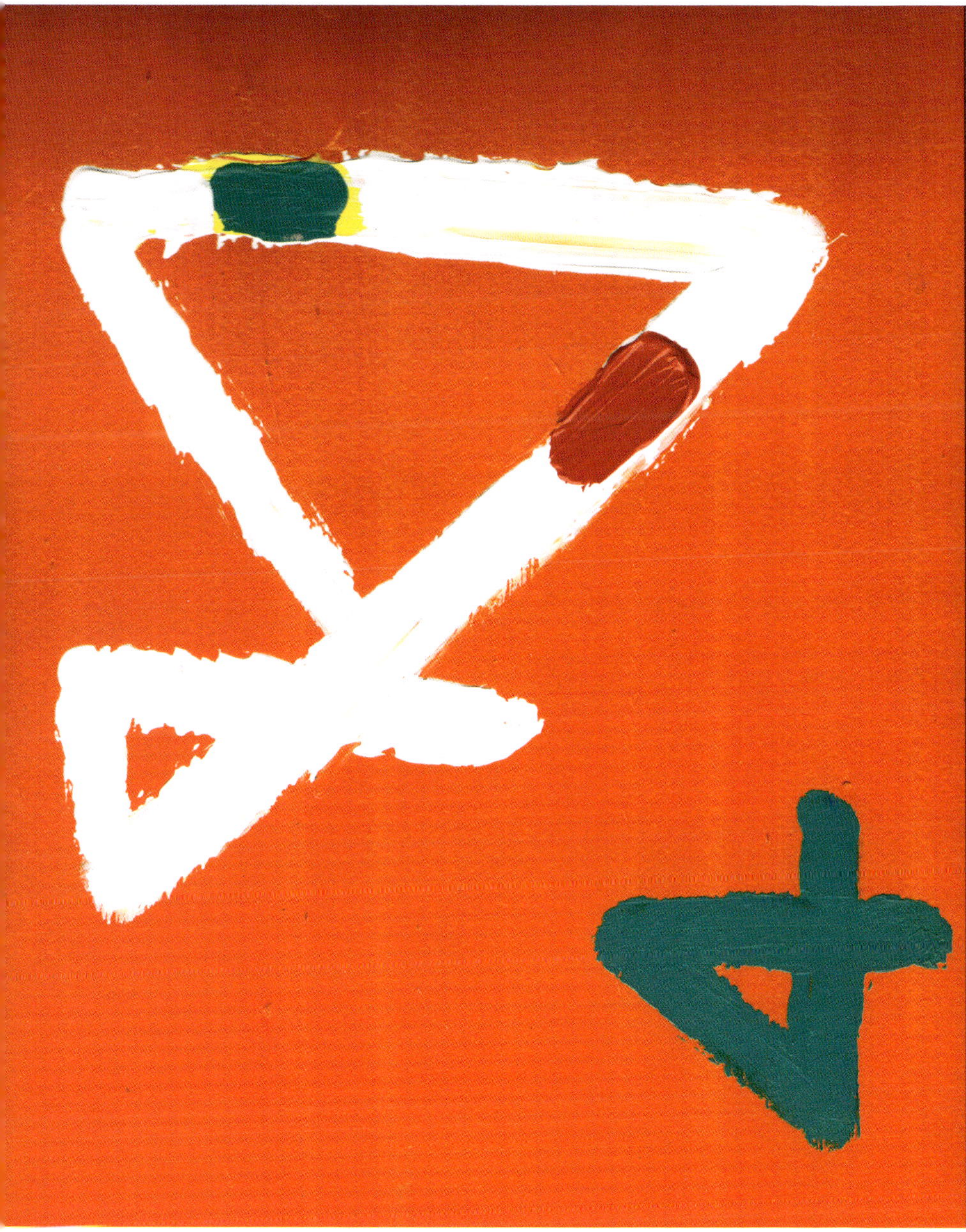

"My work is about
pure
emotion,
saturated color, special relationships, and human instinct. It's a language that melts its own history through creating an economic and very personal alphabet."

—Nicholas Howey

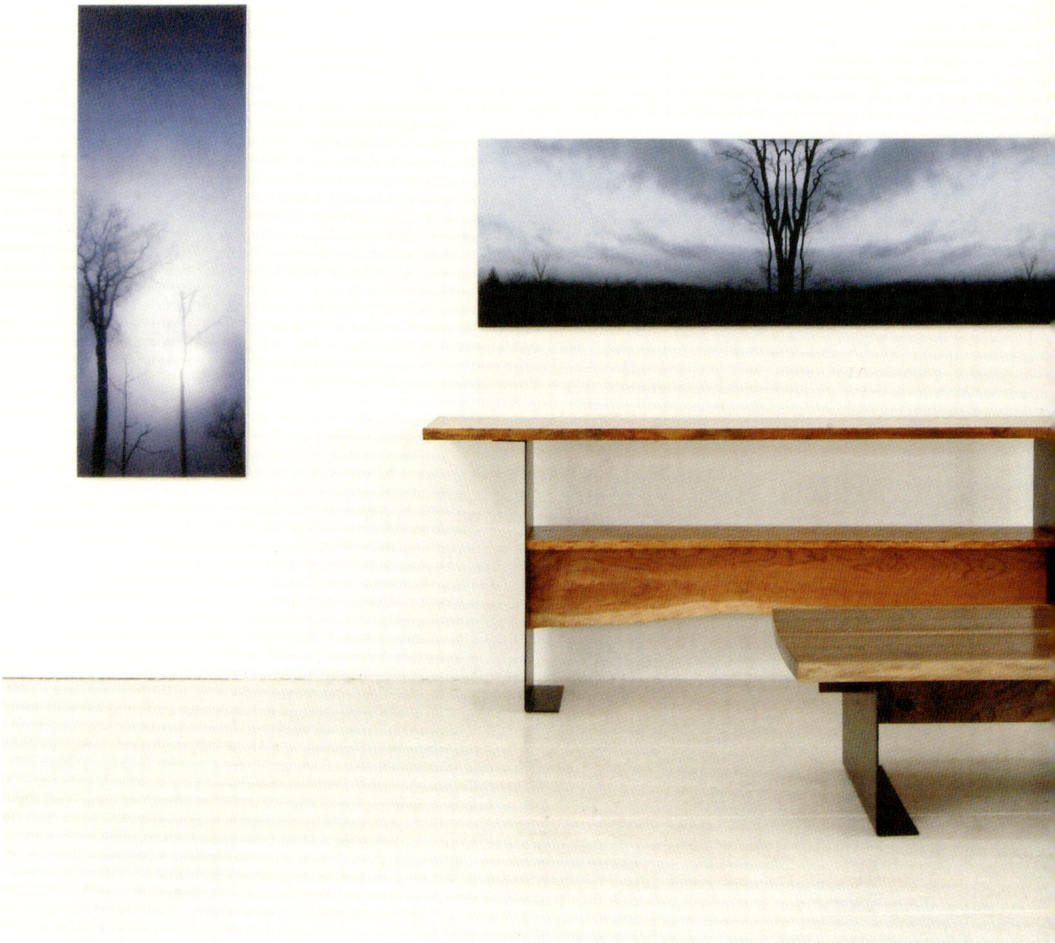

gail leboff "Atmosphere," photographs, 2005, tables by Chris Lehrecke

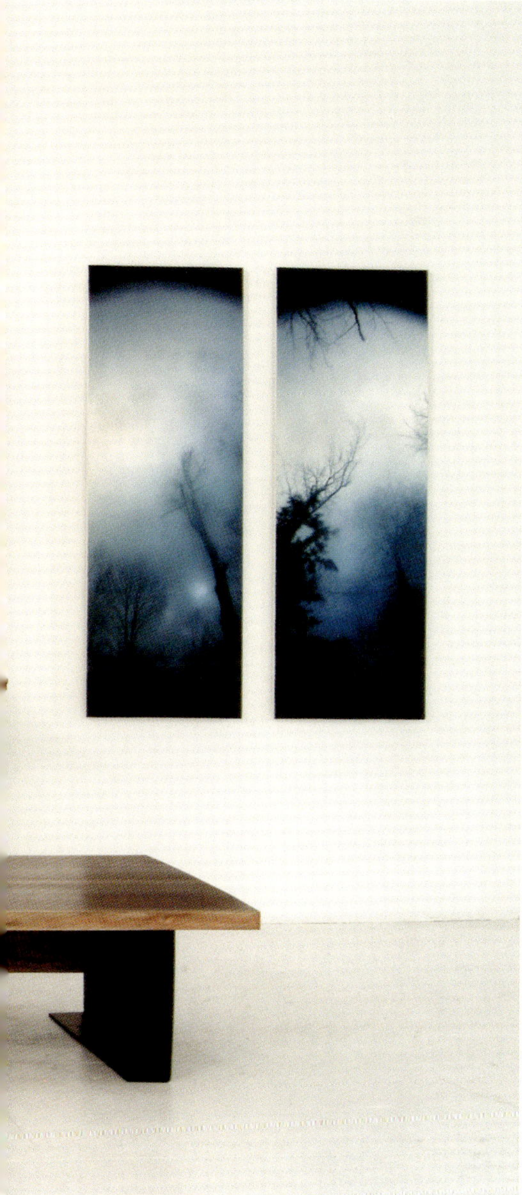

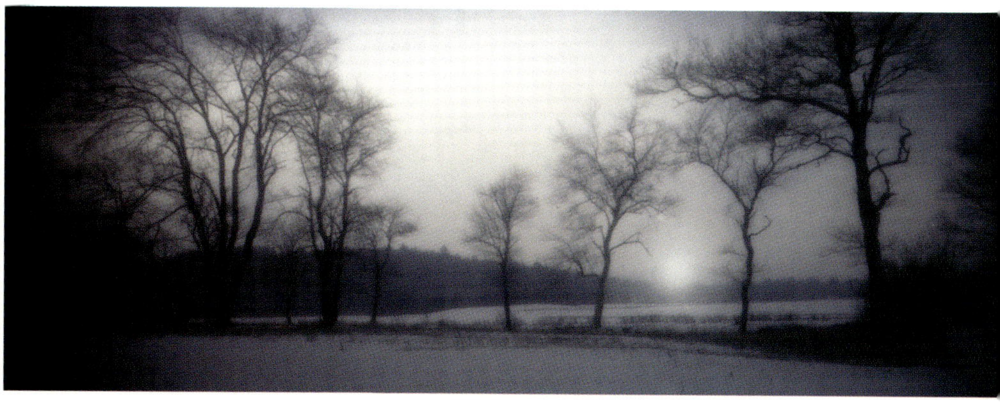

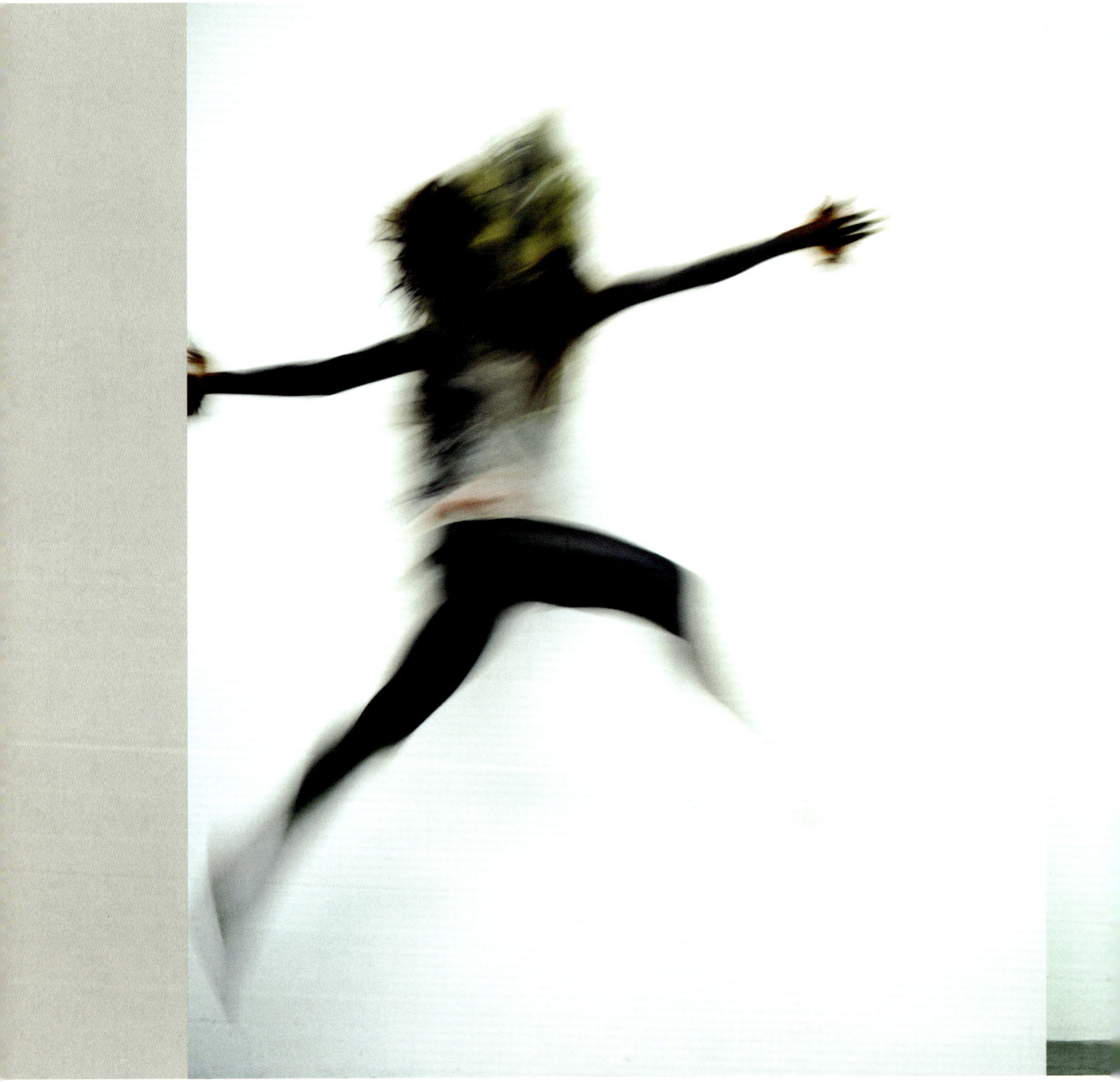

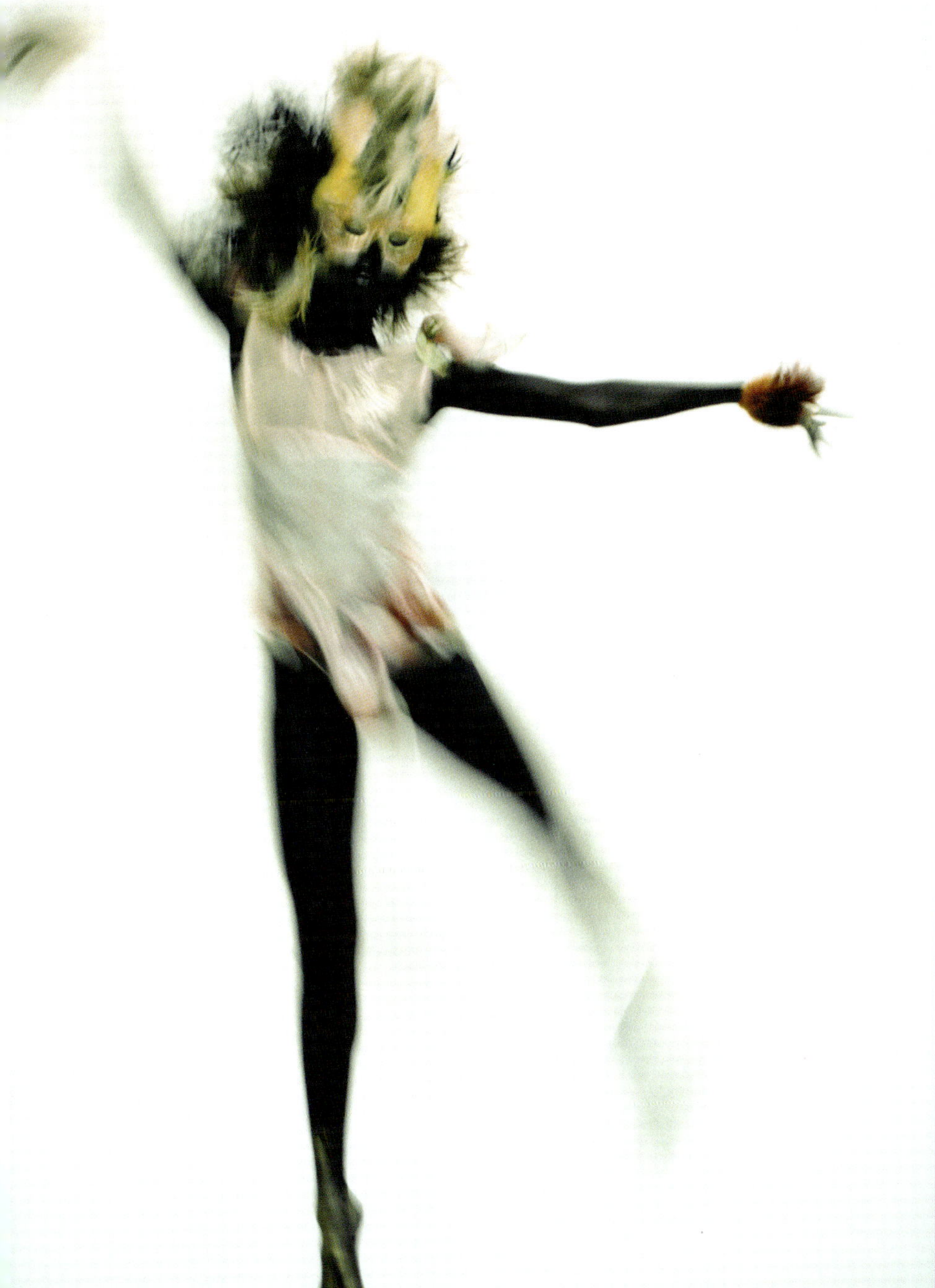

"When we passed through 'art to design' and back again through 'design to art,' we often think of Ralph Pucci and his thoughtful magic that provokes these unexpected encounters."

—James Brown

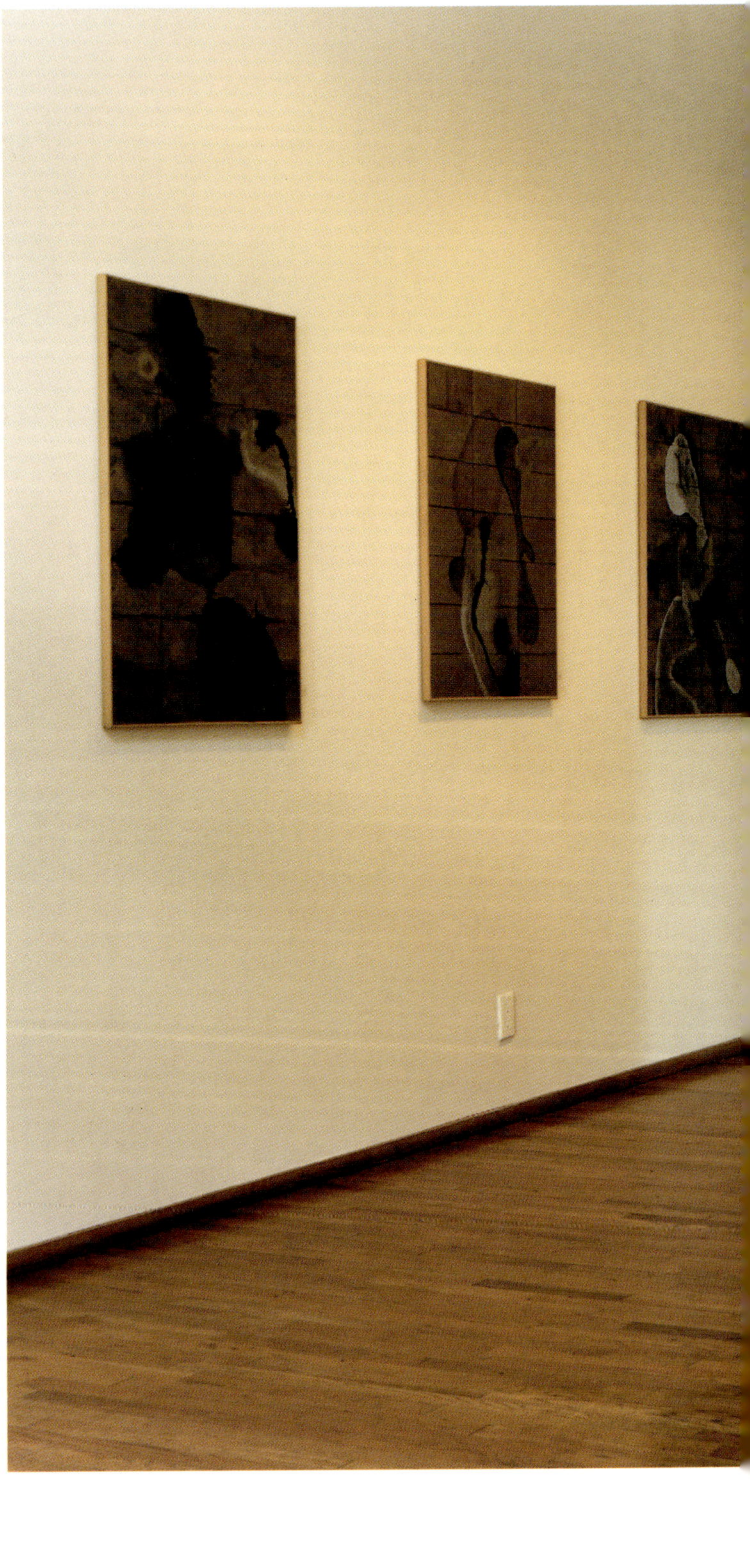

james brown paintings and sculpture, 2001

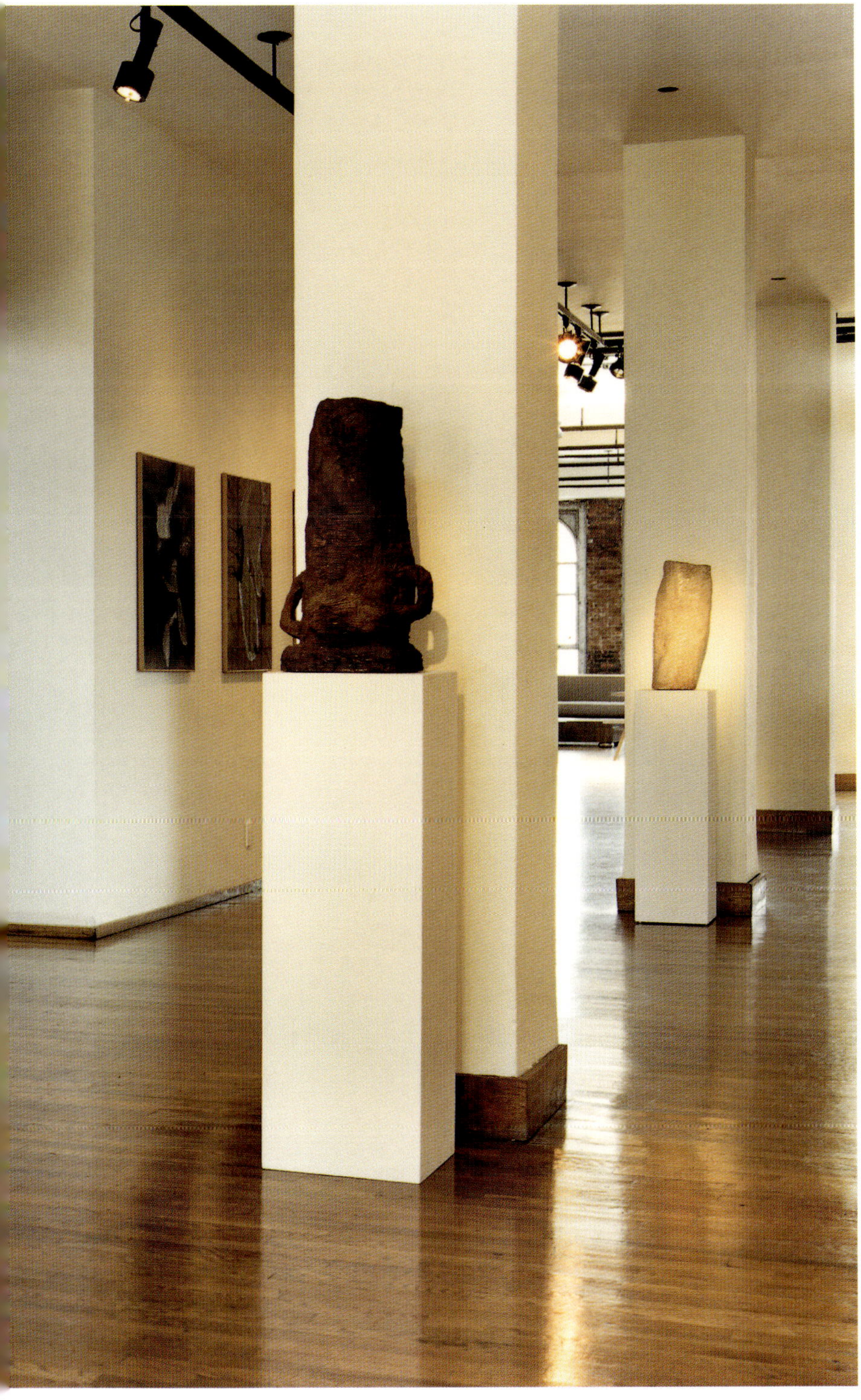

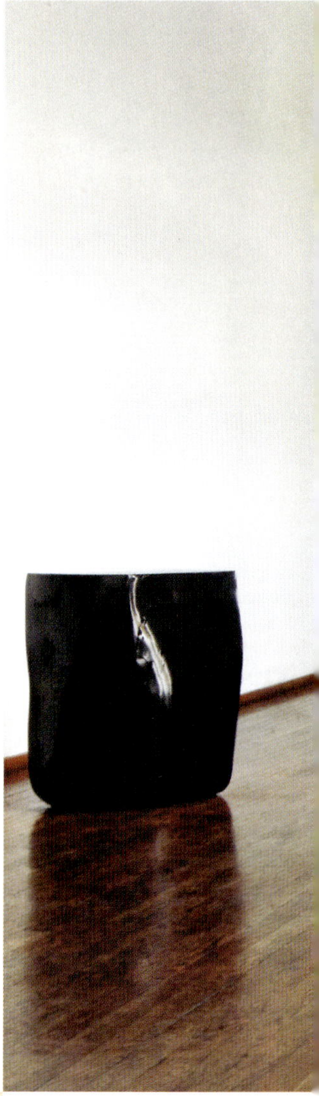

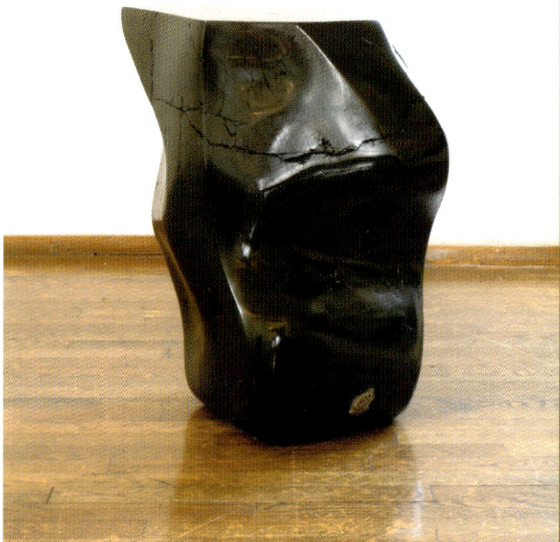

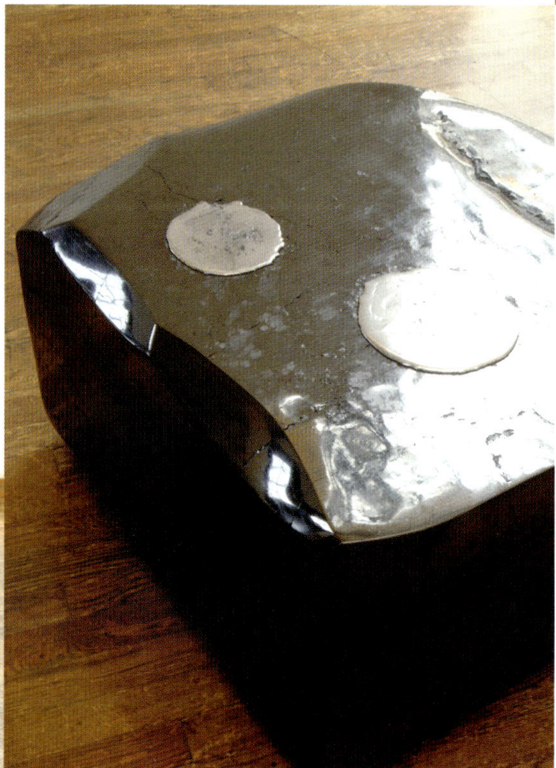

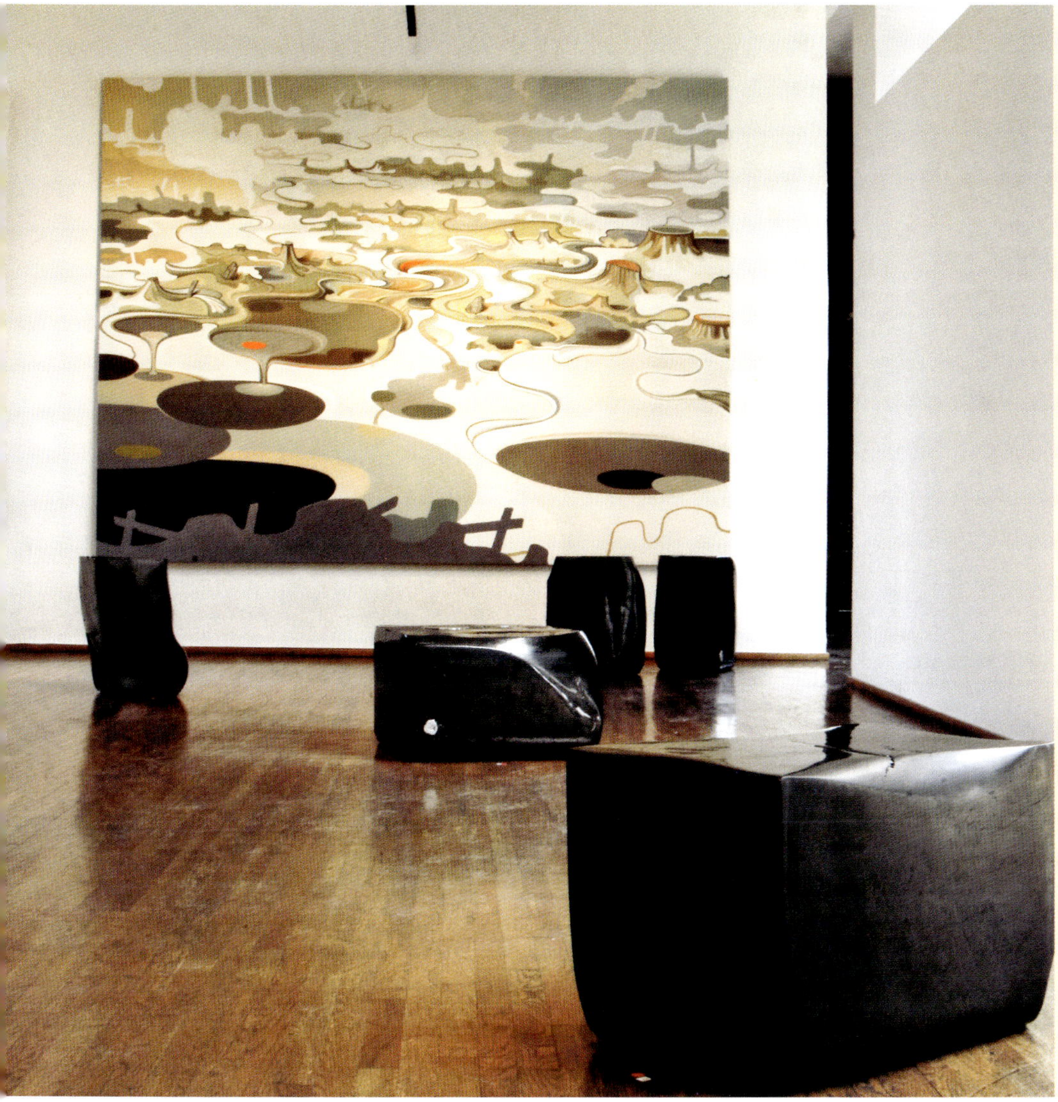

jim zivic "Coal," 2005, painting by Jeff Quinn

"tribute to noguchi" 2006: John Tanji Koga, stone sculpture; Franco Salmoiraghi, photographs; Jeff Roth, wooden surfboards; Randall Shiroma, stone and terraza; Lonny Tomono, wood

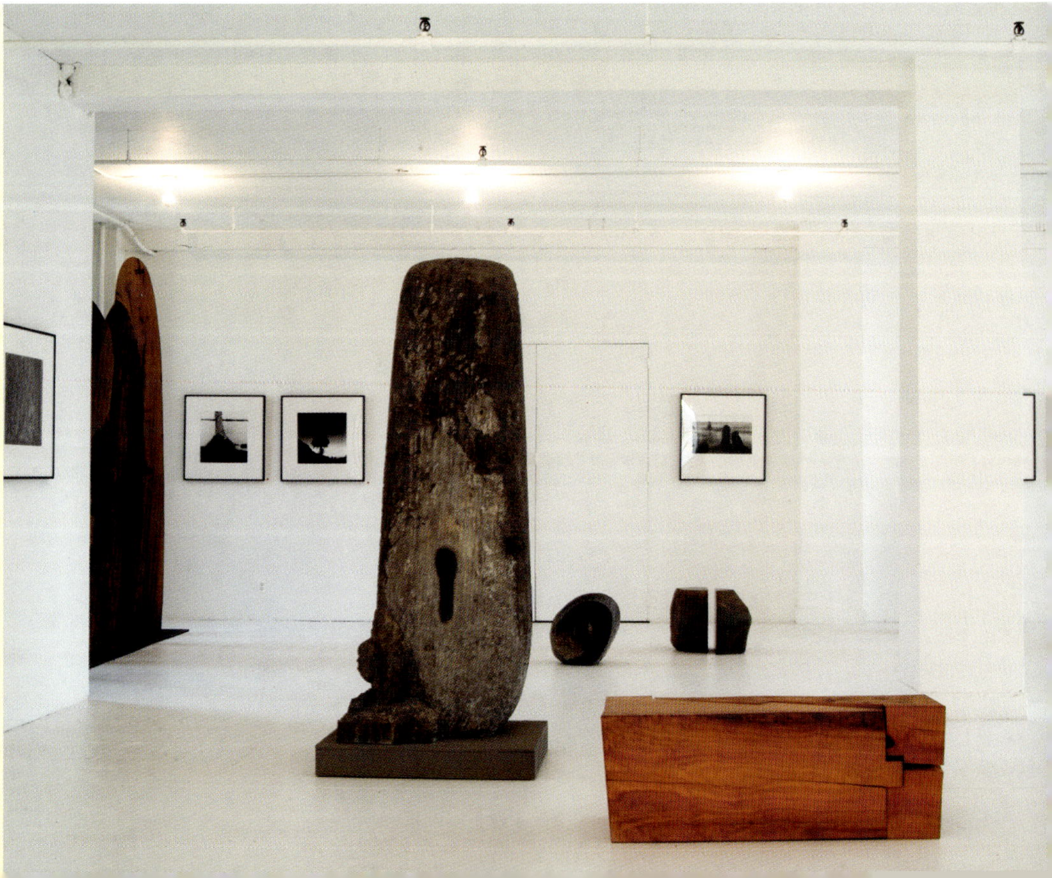

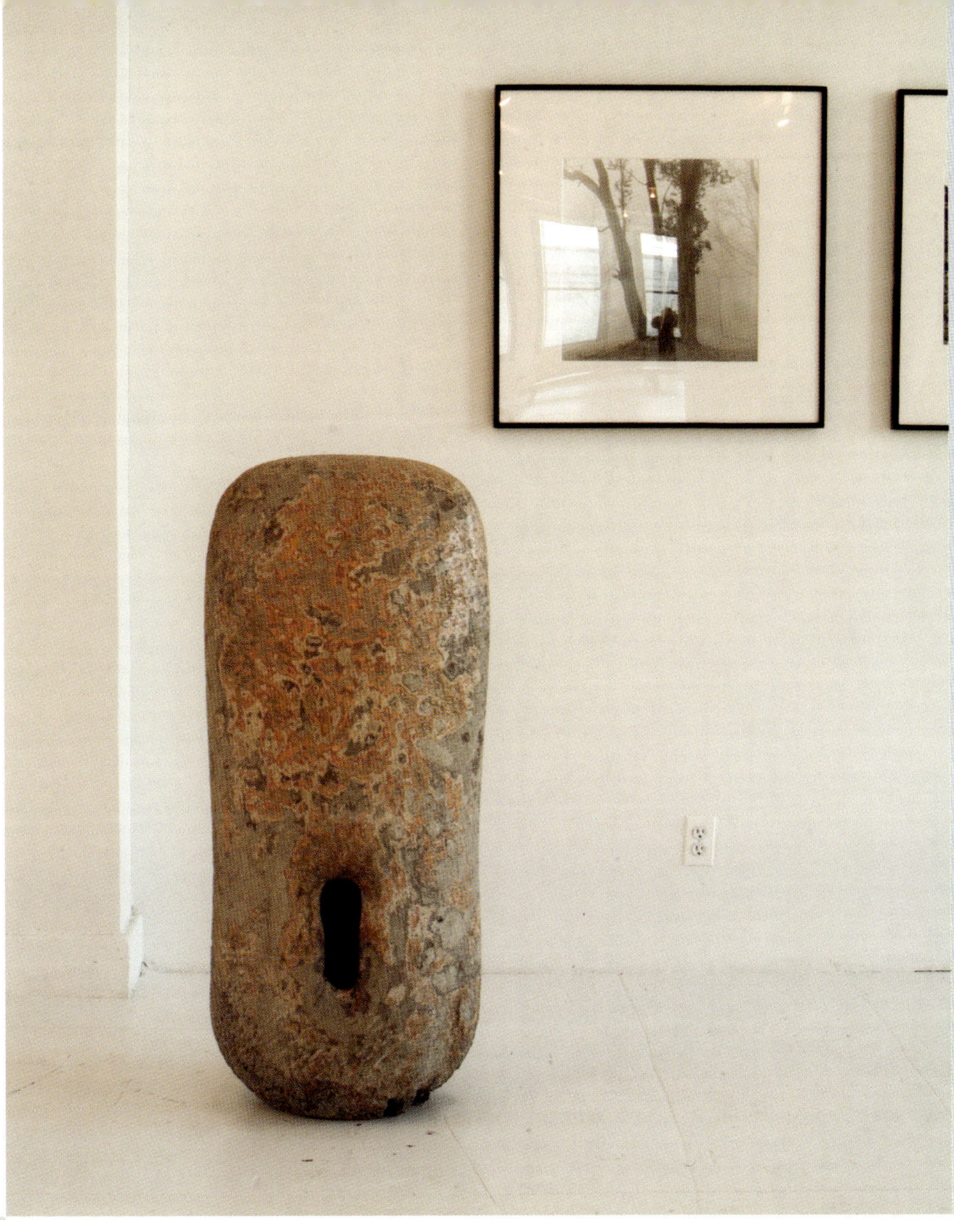

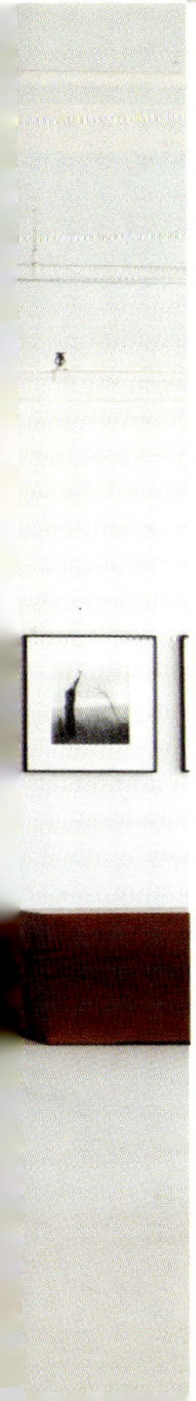

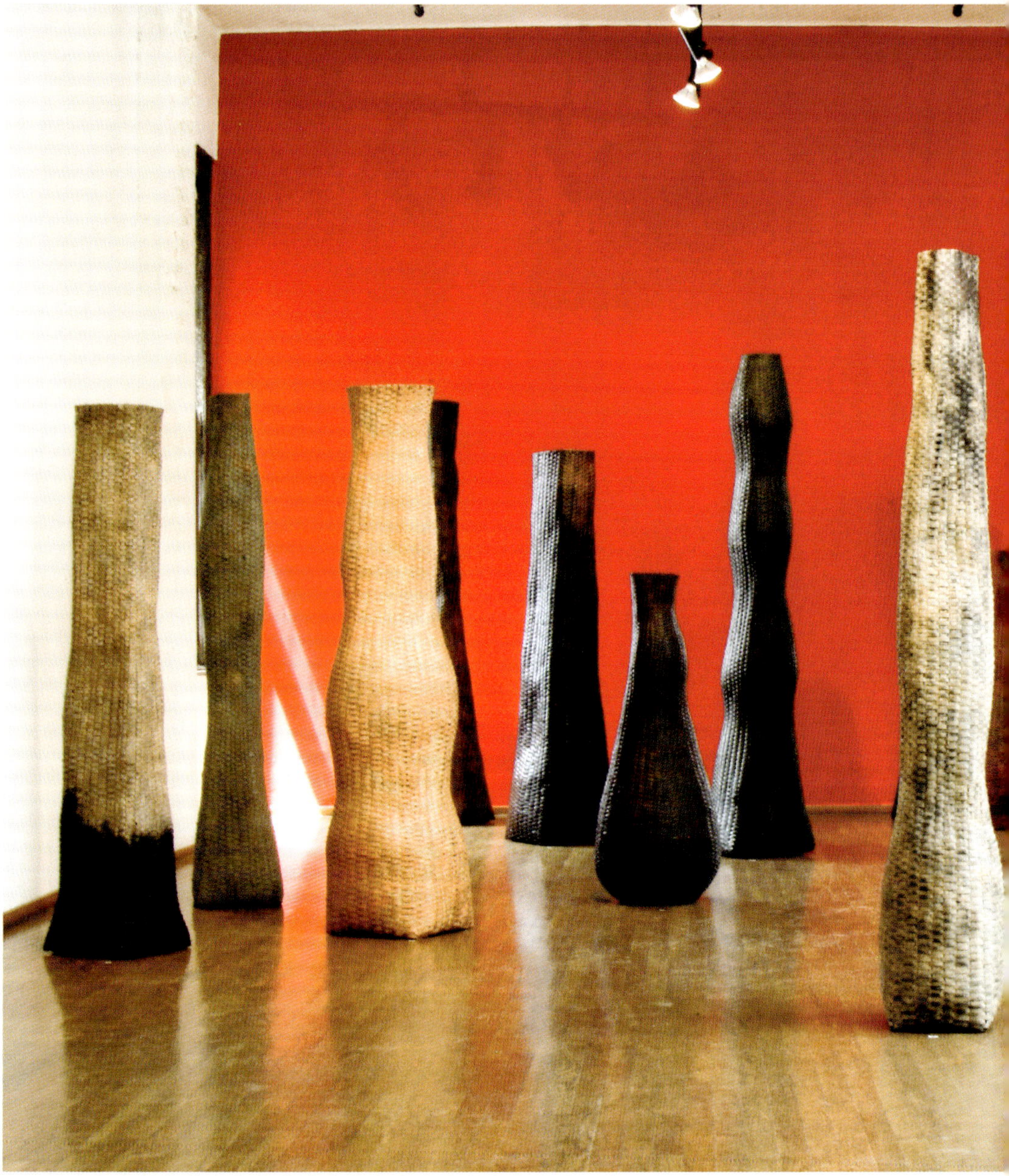

jonathan kline "Woven Vessels," 2005

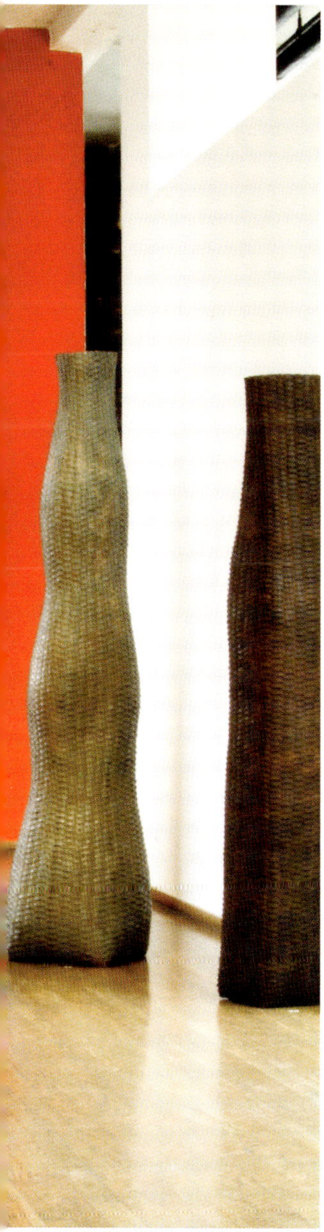

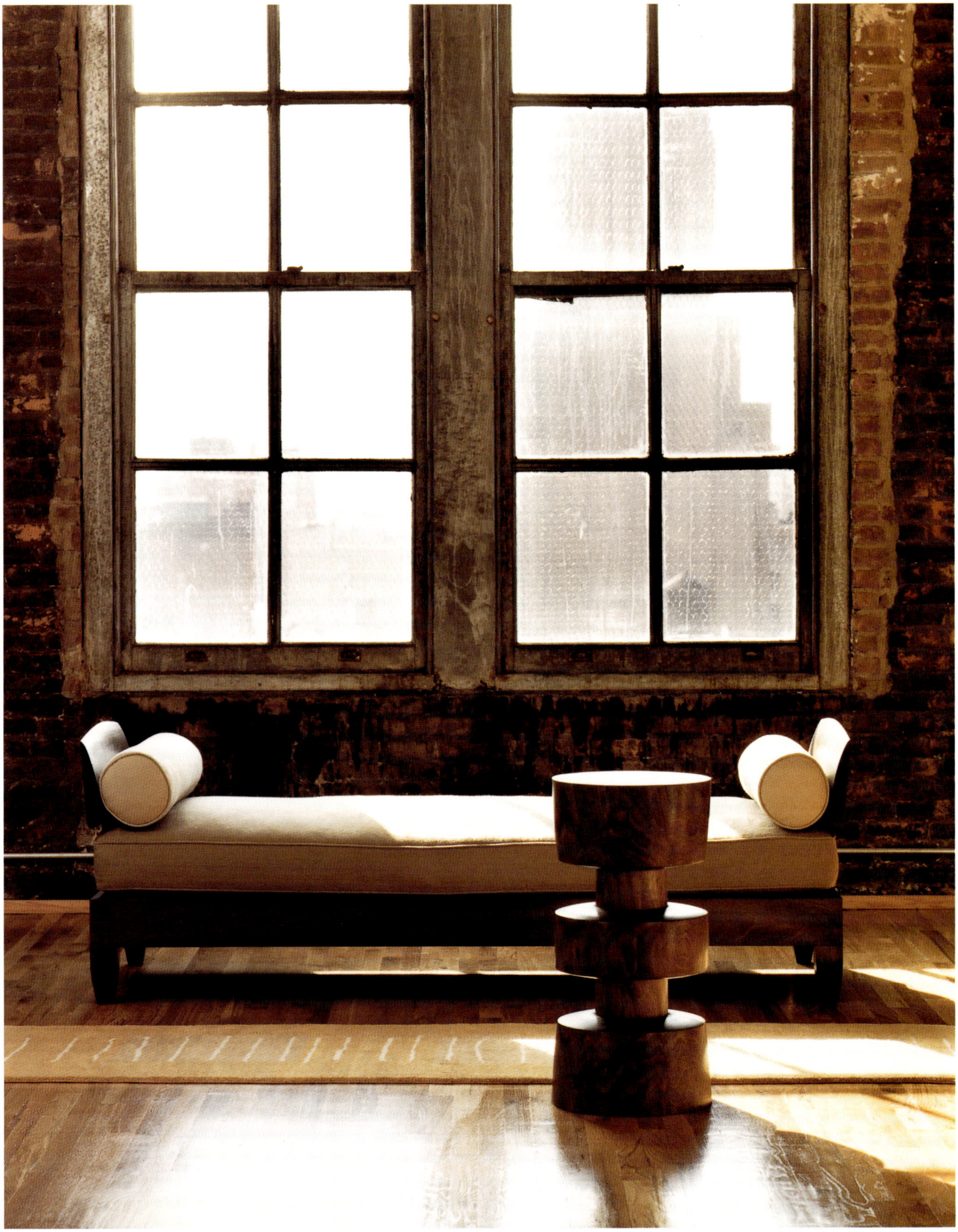

chris lehrecke daybed and pedestal, 1997; "Chinese," 2003 (right)

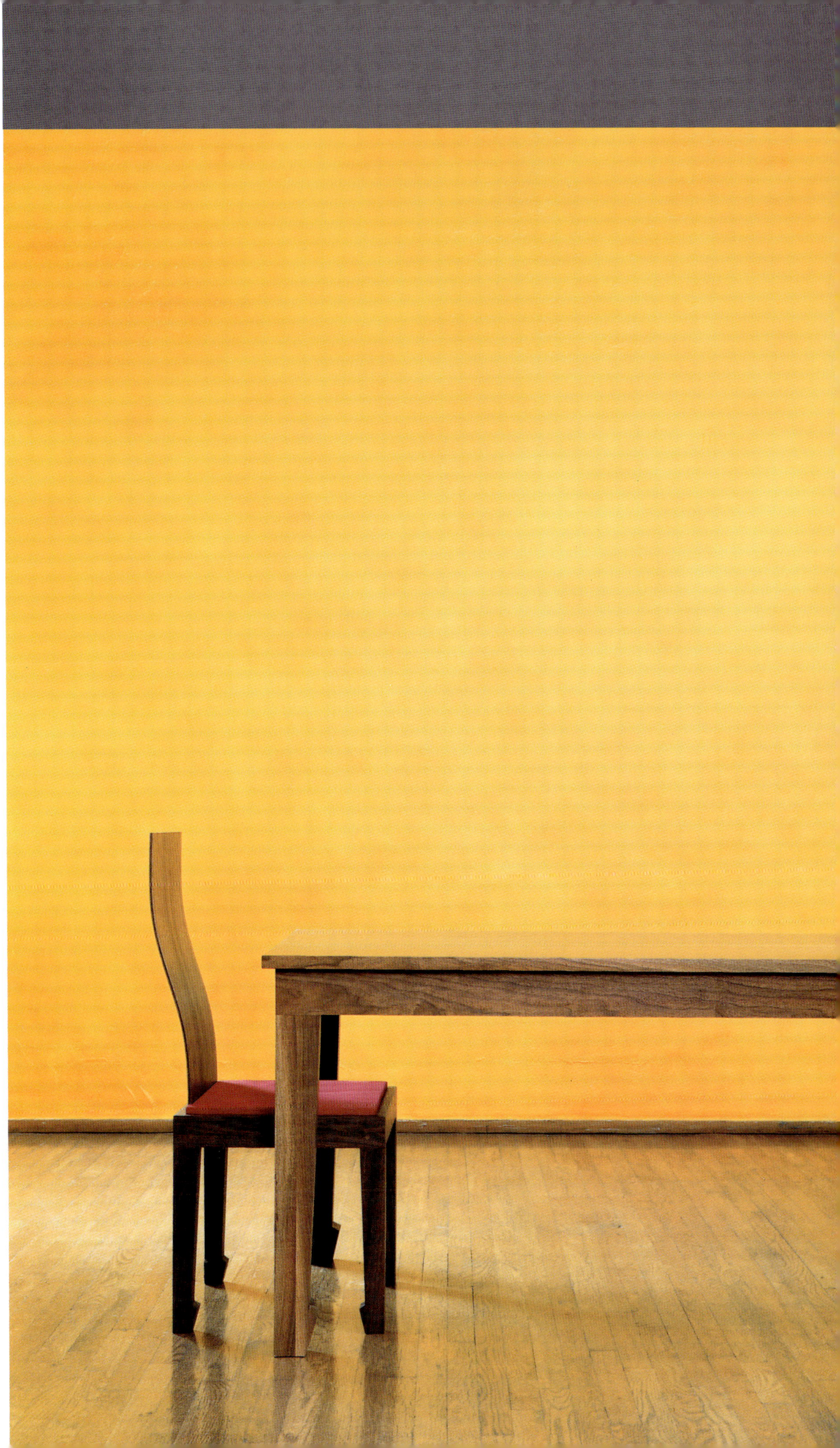

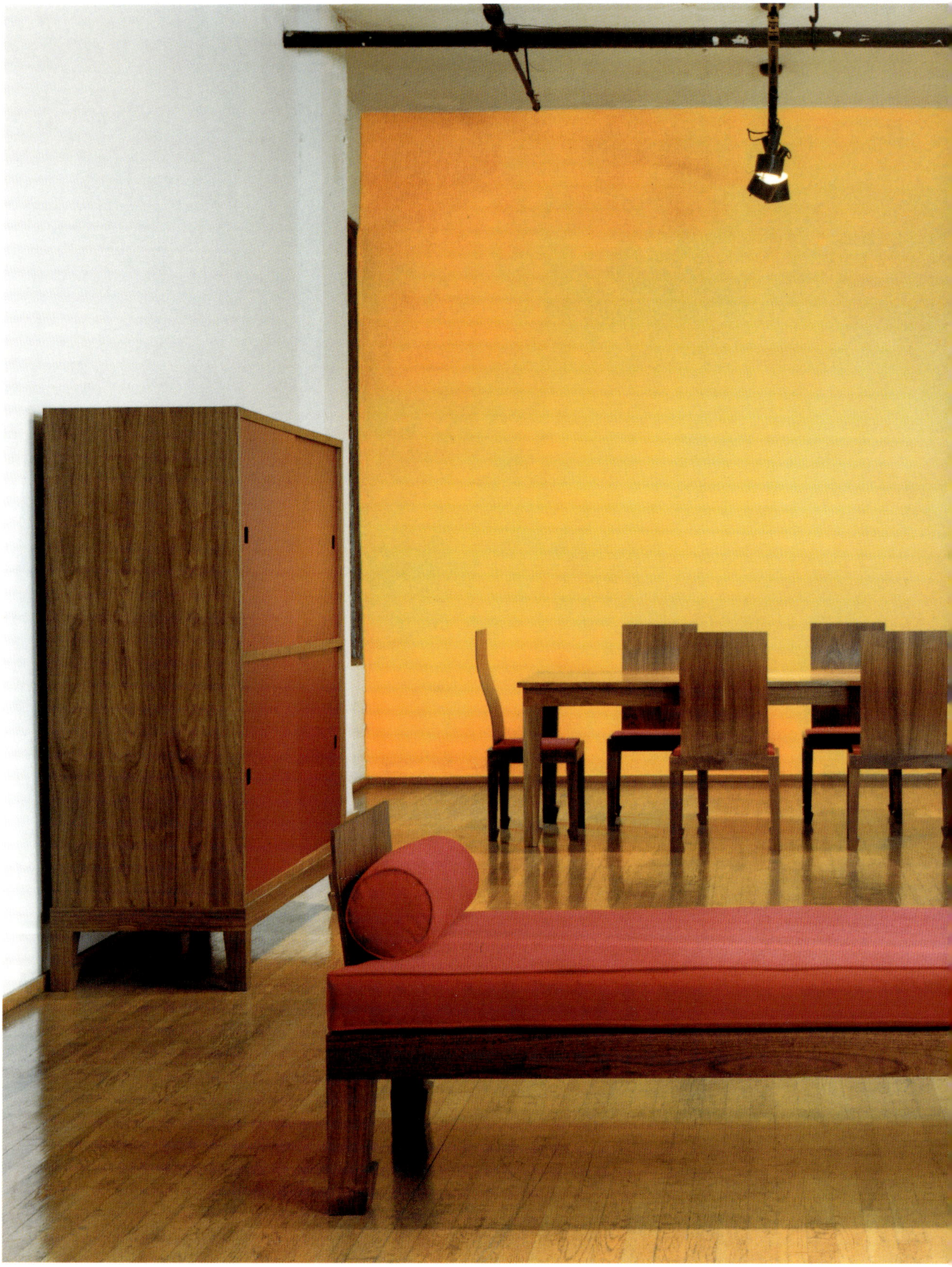

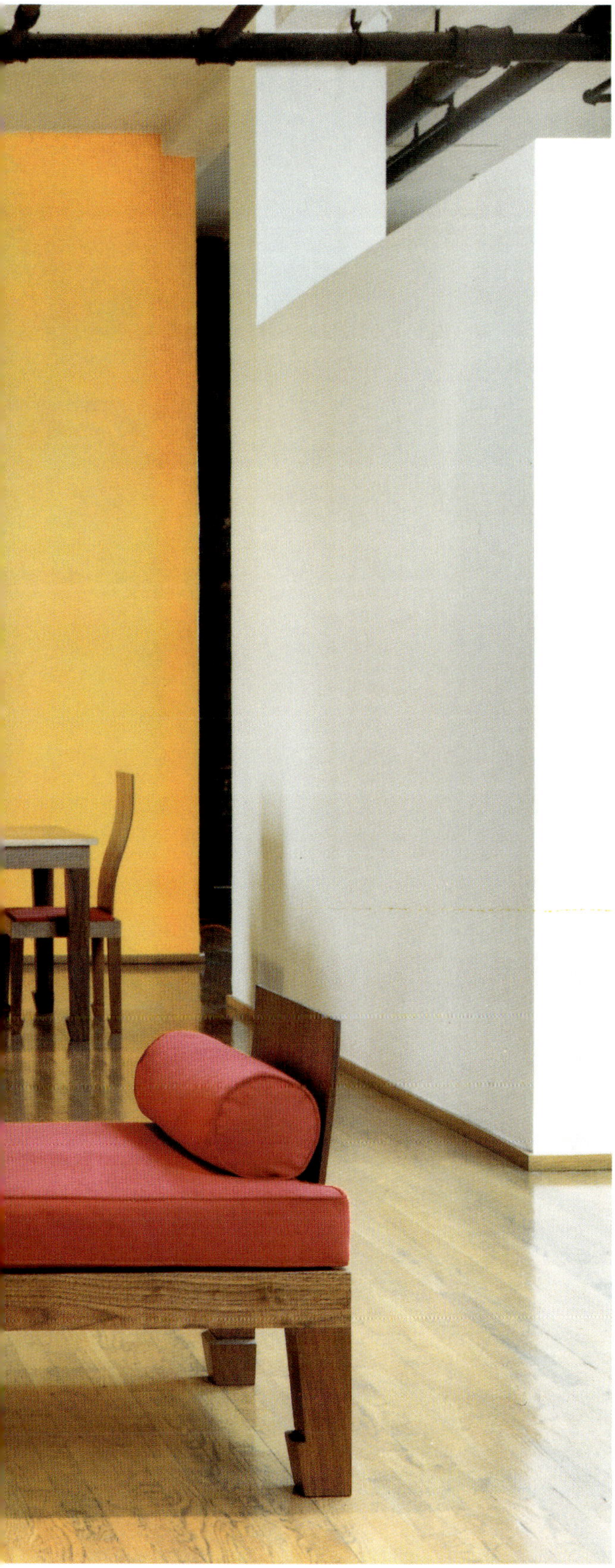

"My work during this period has had many different influences and inspirations. In addition, I have been inspired increasingly by materials and nature."

—Chris Lehrecke

"Chinese," 2003

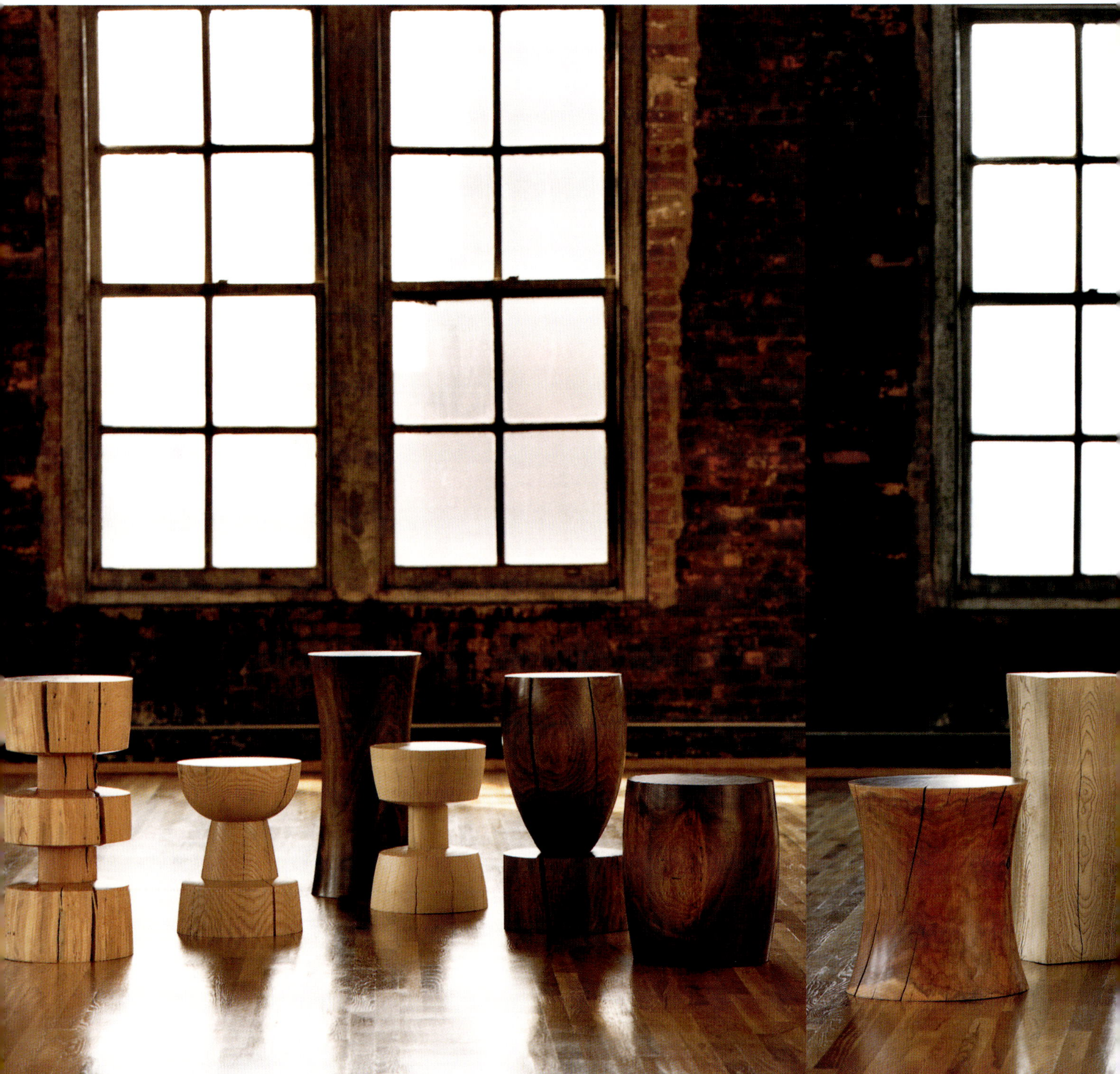

 Wooden pedestals, 1997

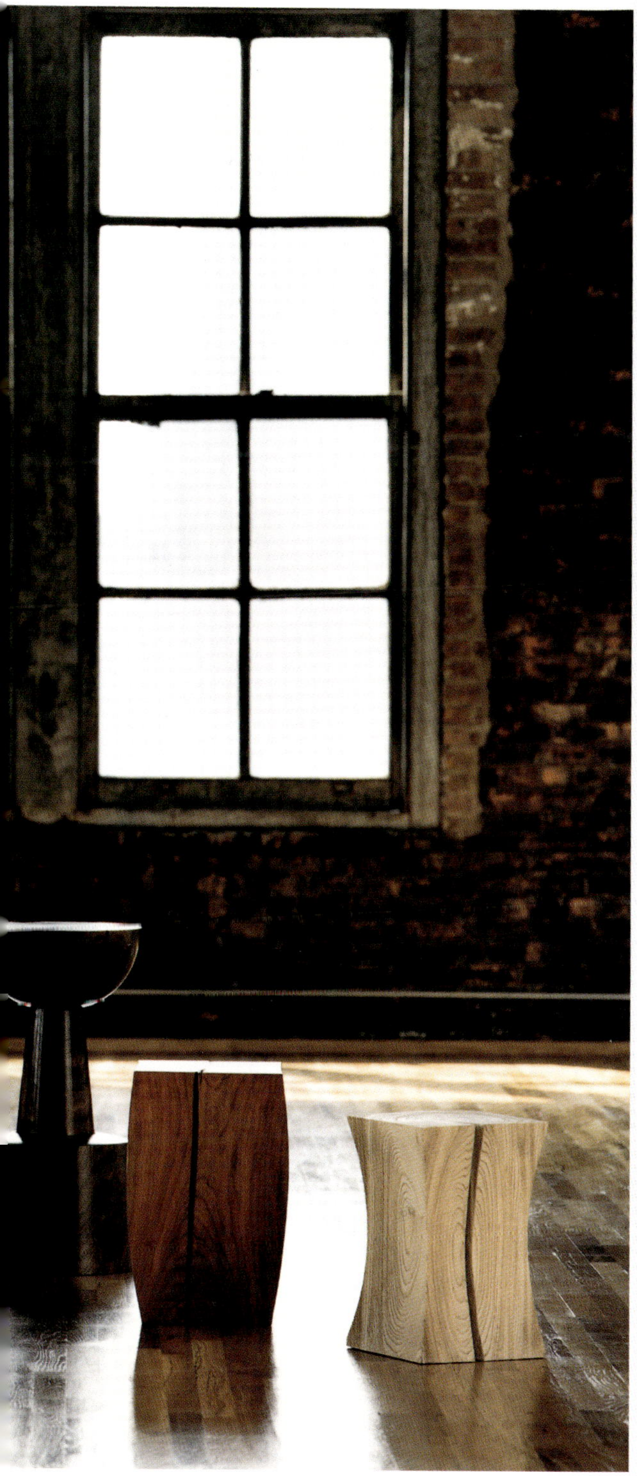

"I envisioned that my mission as a furniture designer was to interpret my Century, not simply to emulate the past."

—Vladimir Kagan

vladimir kagan "A Lifetime of Avant Garde Design," 2004

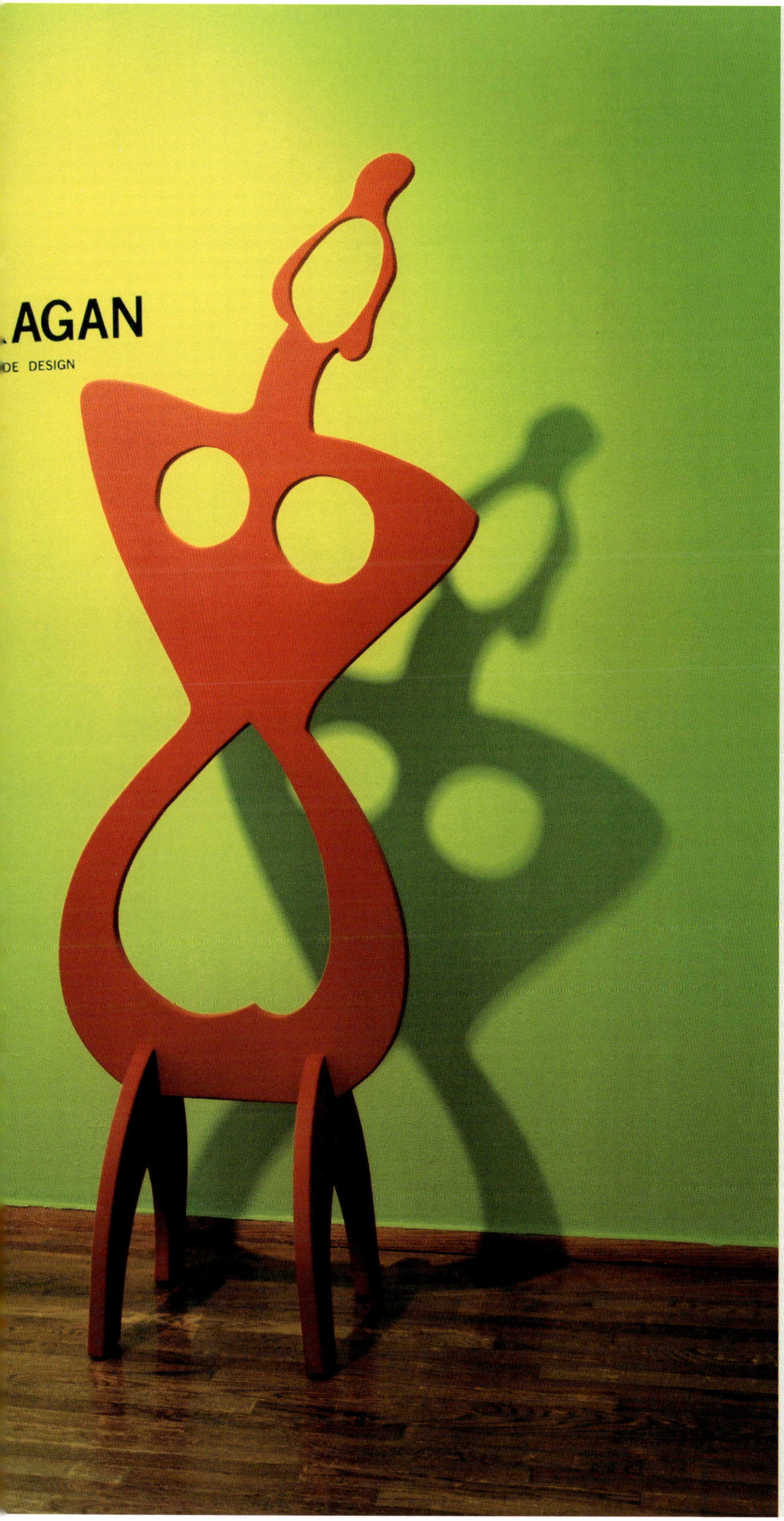
AGAN
DE DESIGN

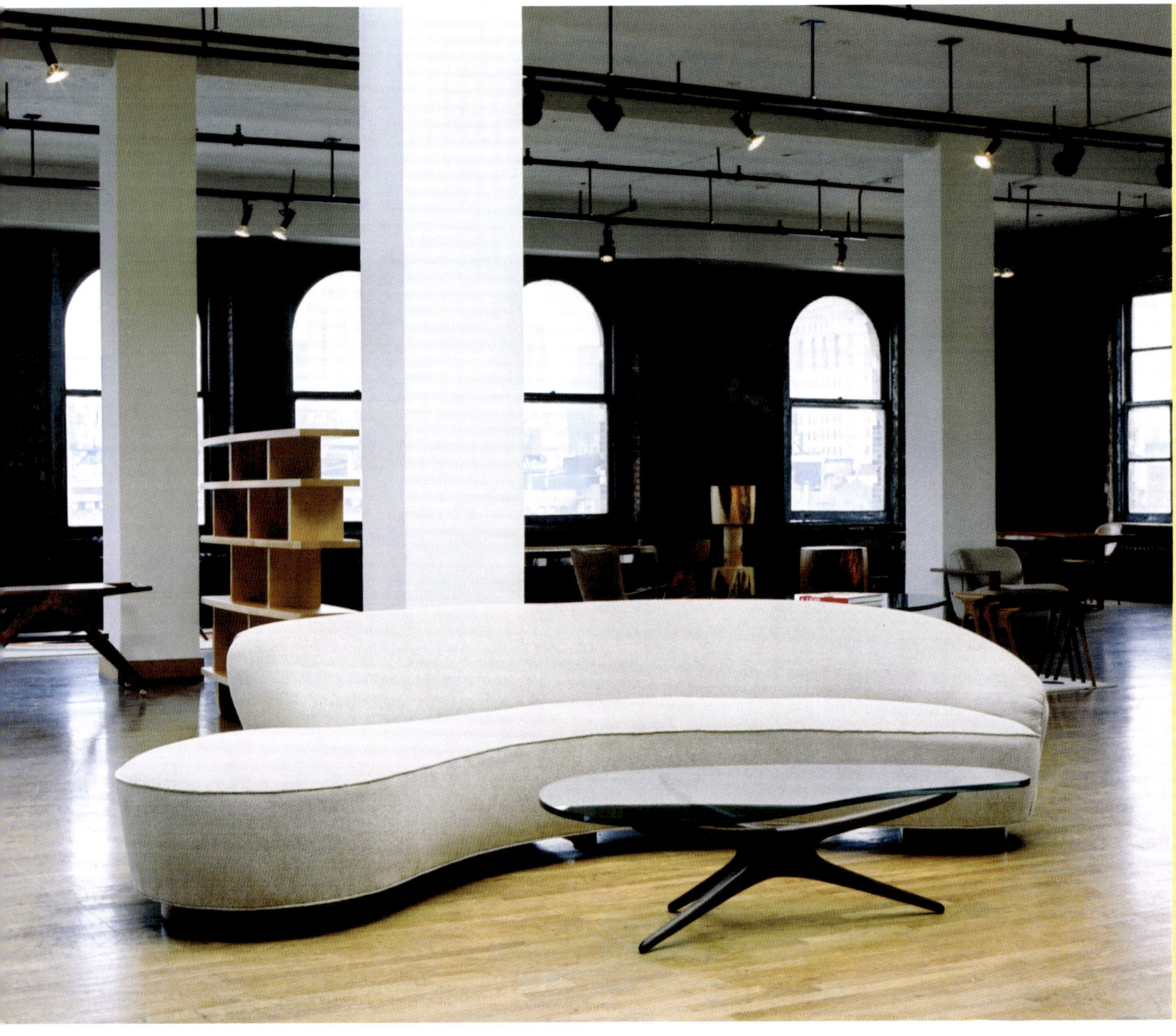

"Kagan Collection #1," 2002

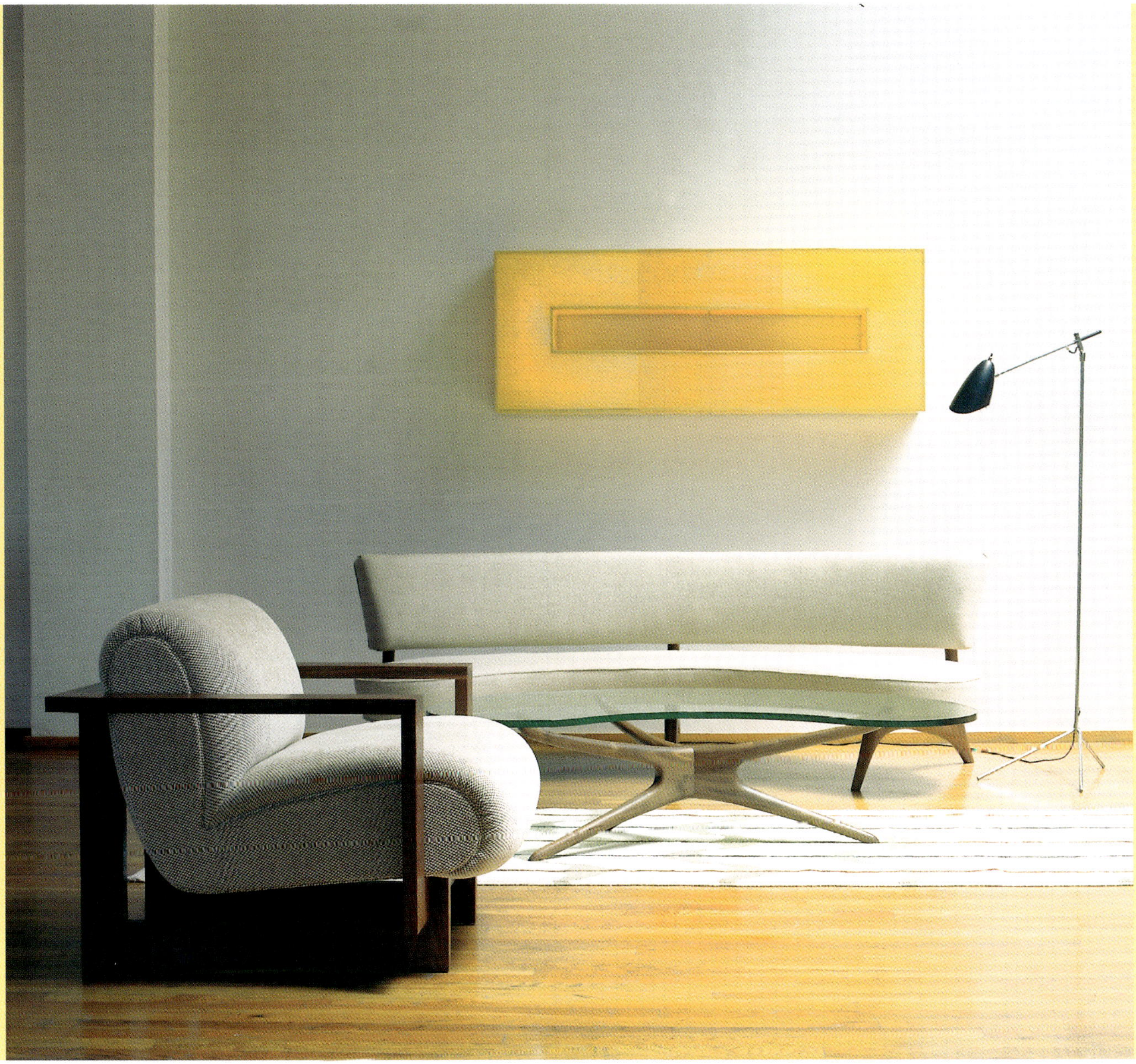

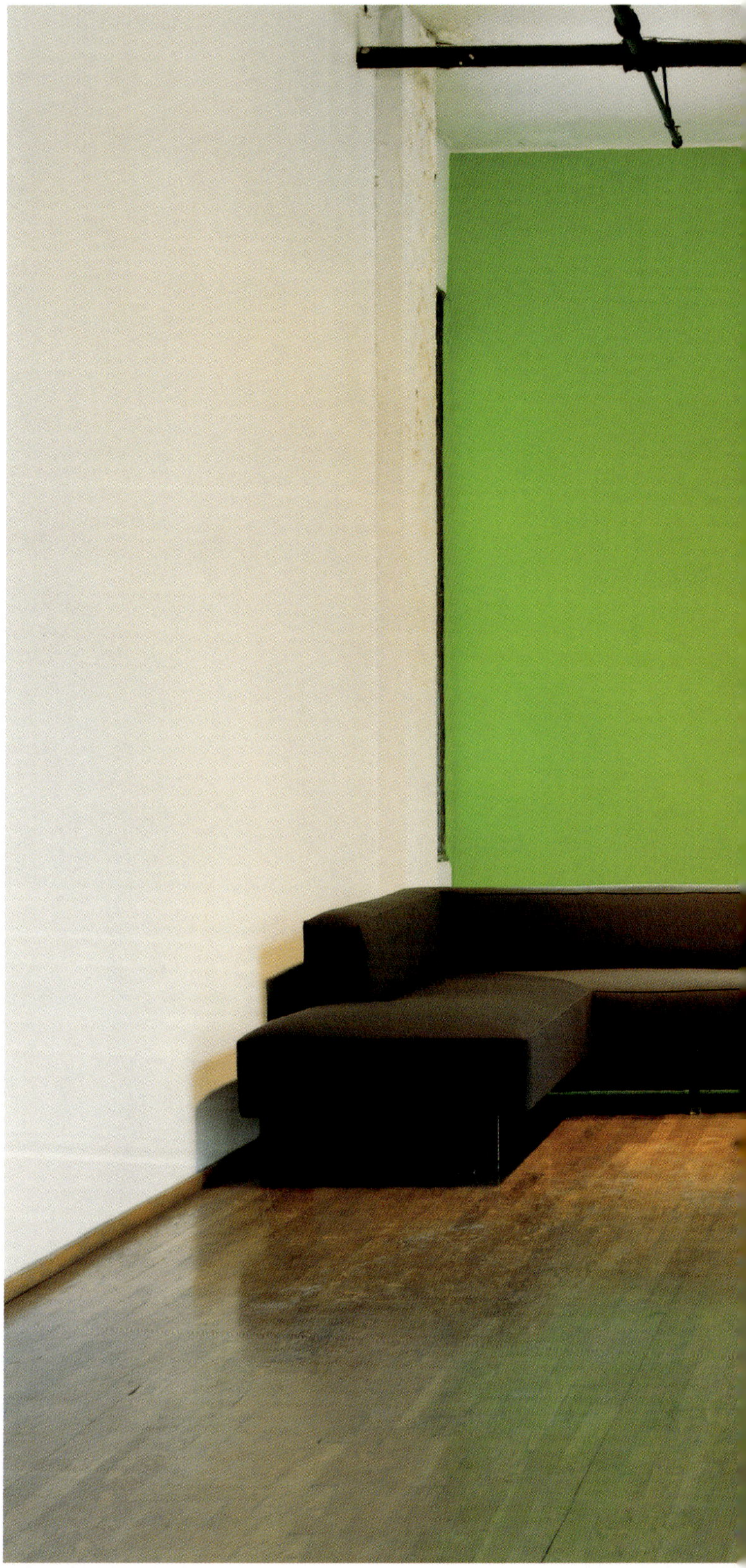

"A Lifetime of Avant Garde Design," 2004

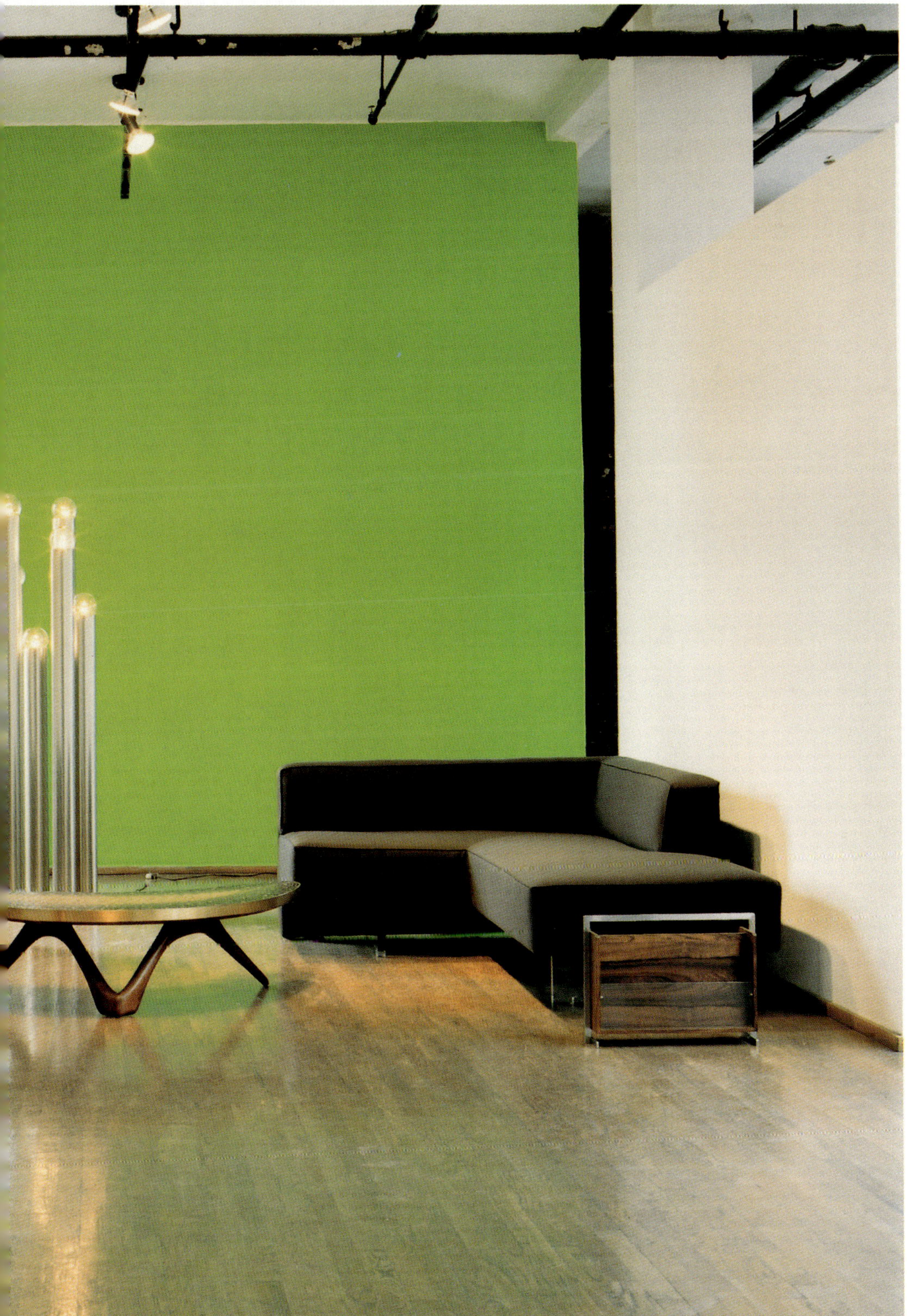

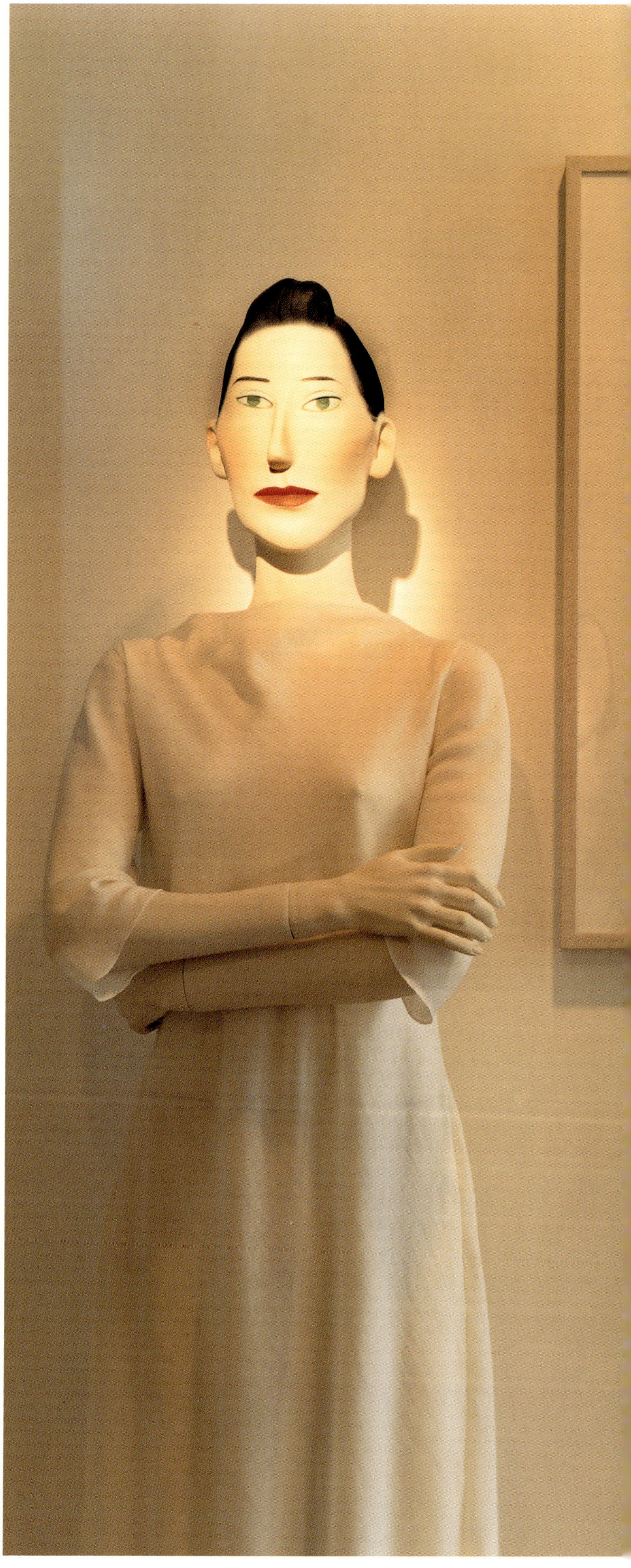

maira kalman *Tango* mannequin collection and drawing, 1994, fashions by Adeline Andrée

Itchy Club mannequin collection, 1996 (right)

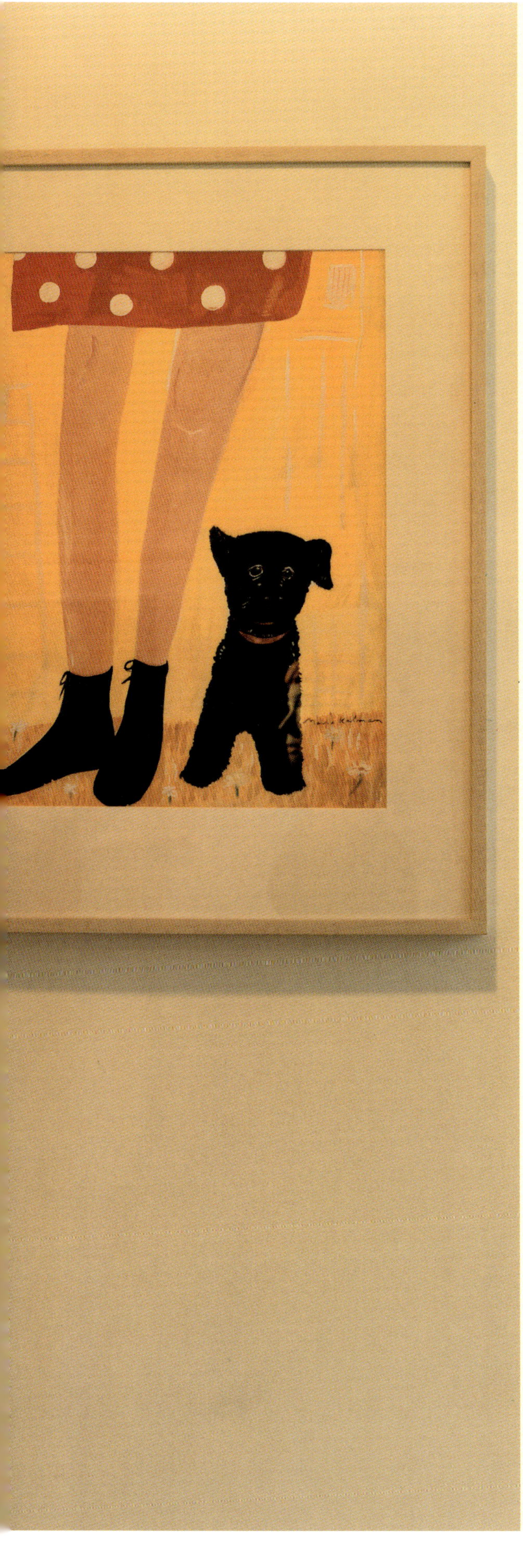

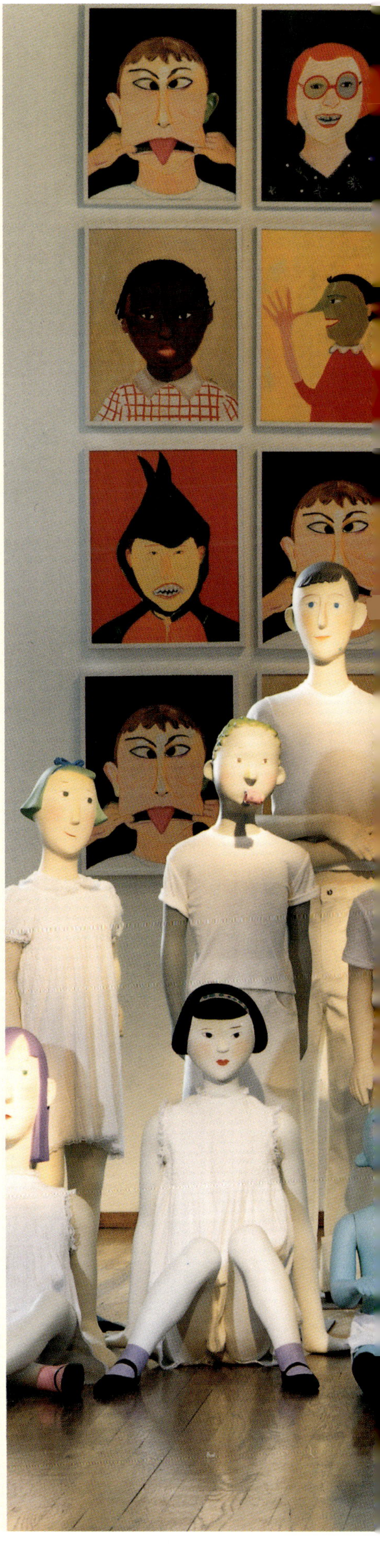

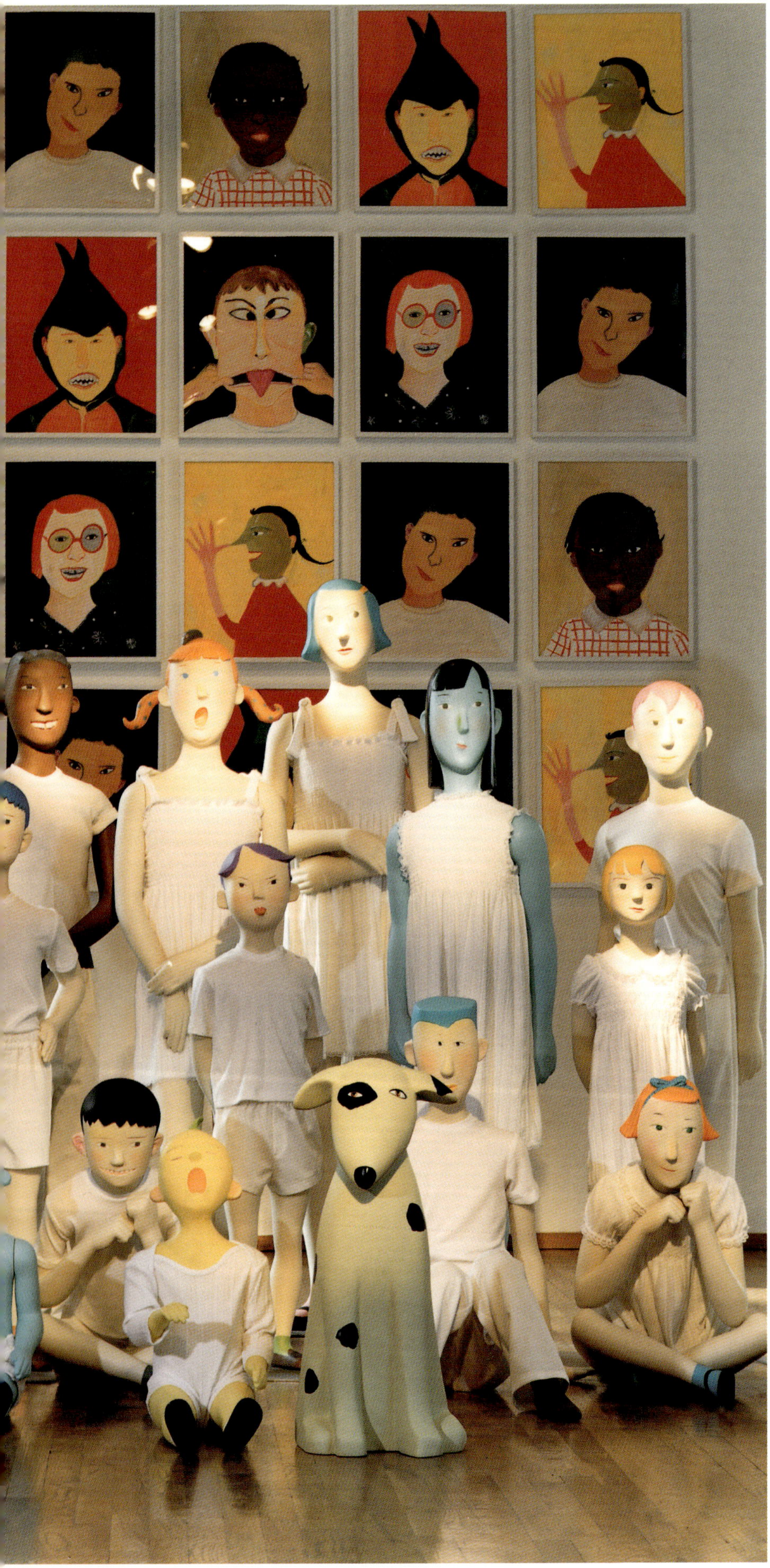

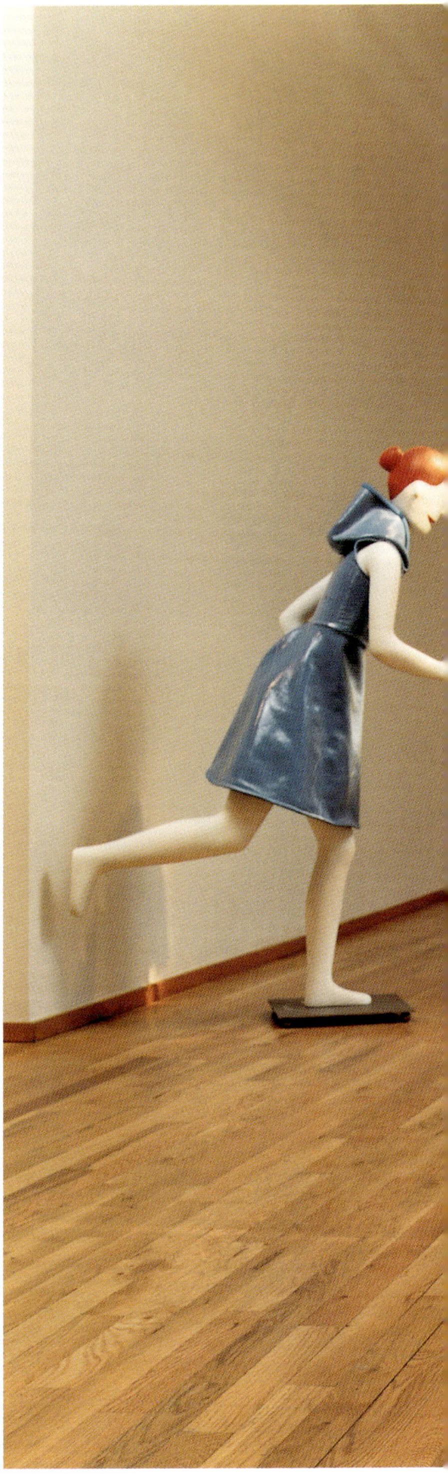

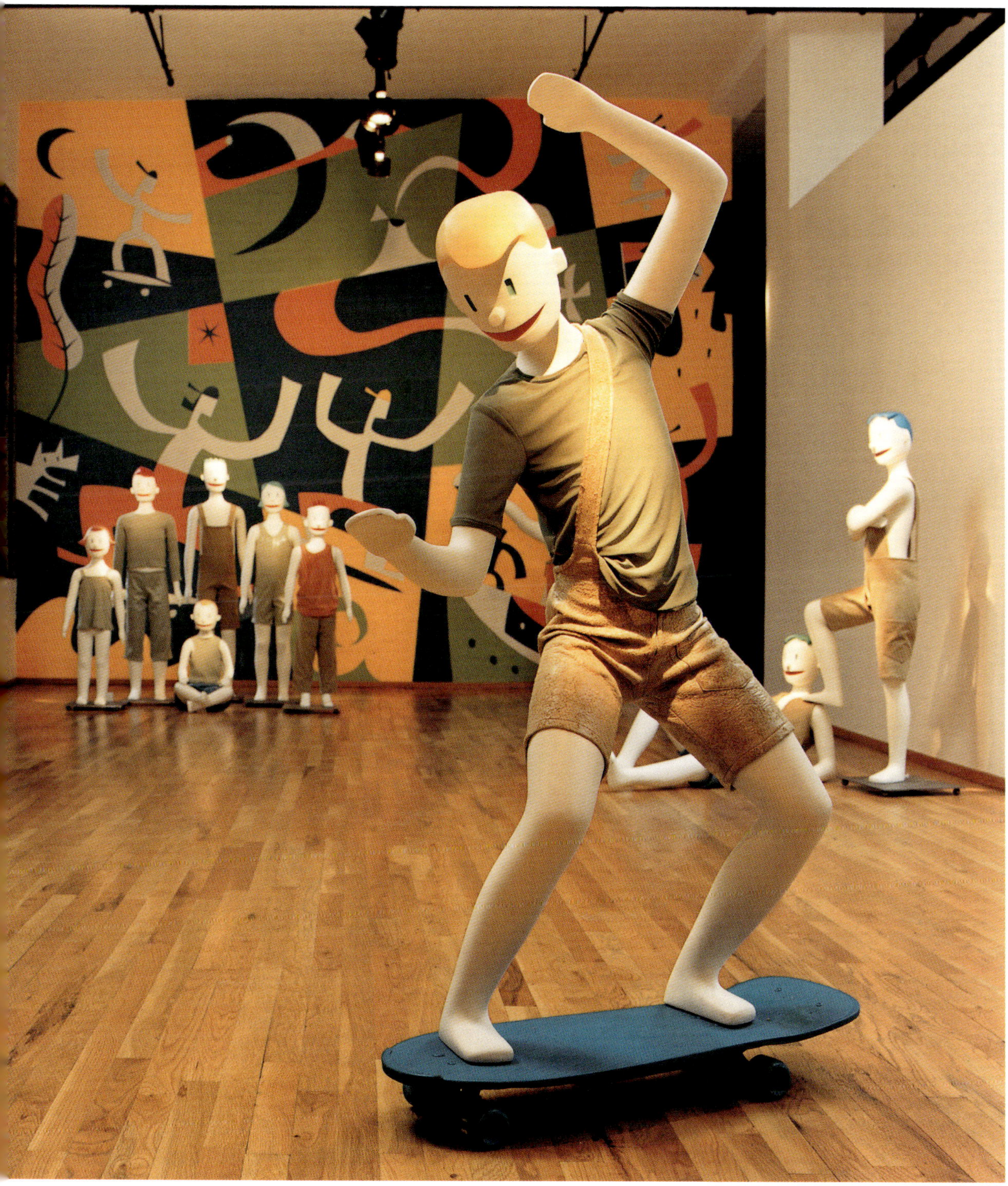

michael bartalos *Whiz Kids* and mural, 1993, fashions by Manolo

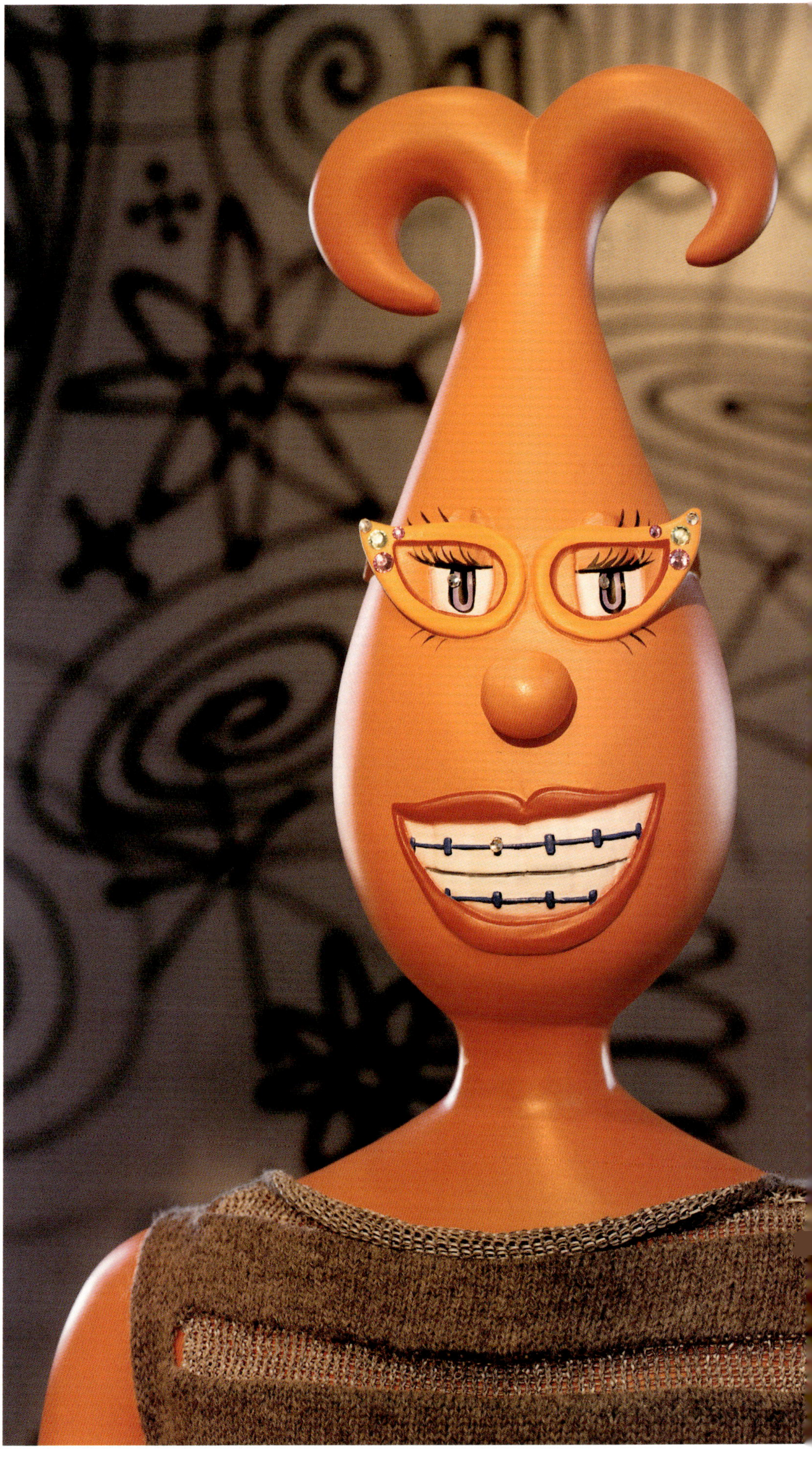

kenny scharf *Universal Offspring* collection, 1998, fashions by Liz Collins

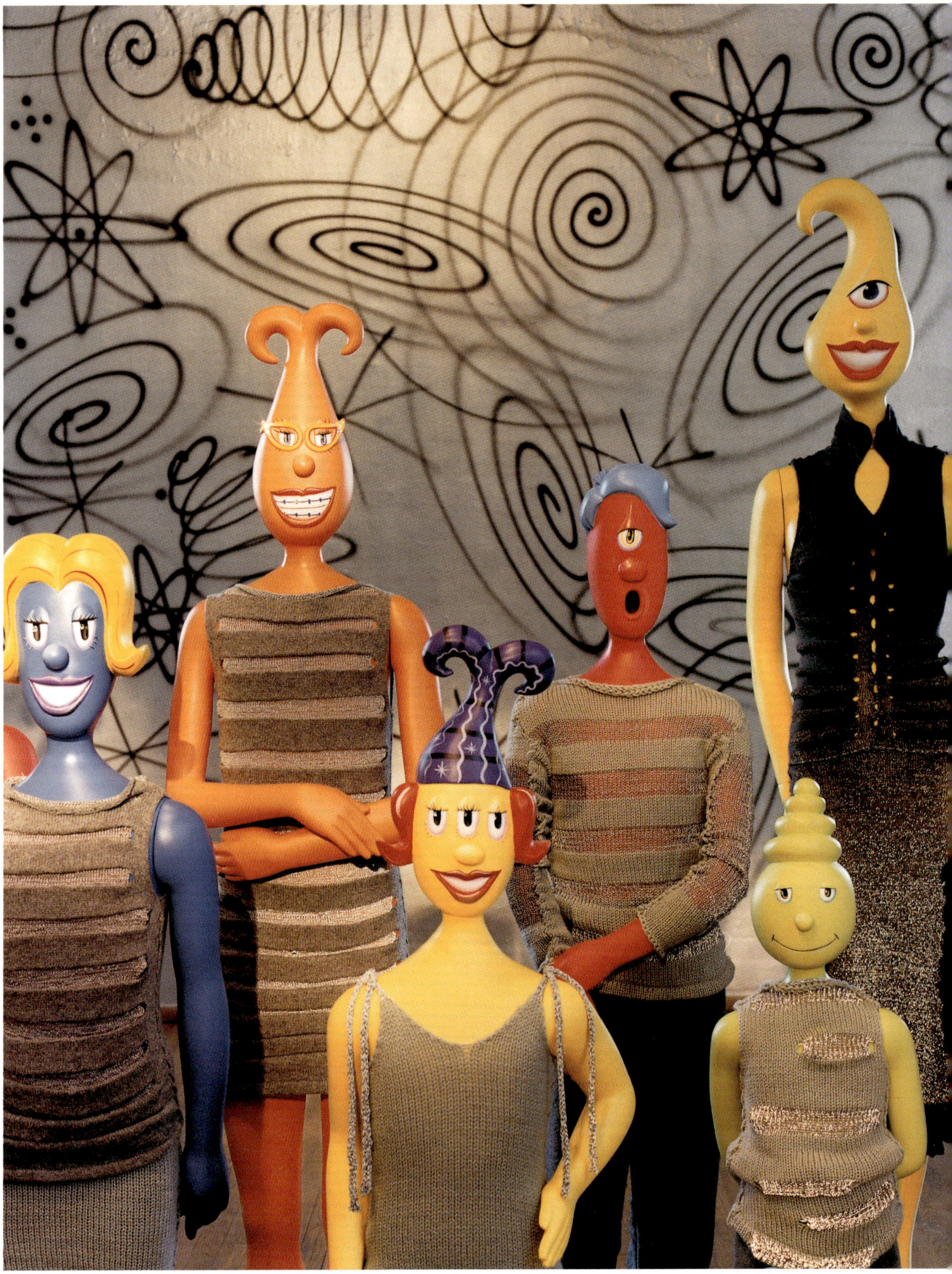

Universal Offspring, 2000, mural by Kenny Scharf

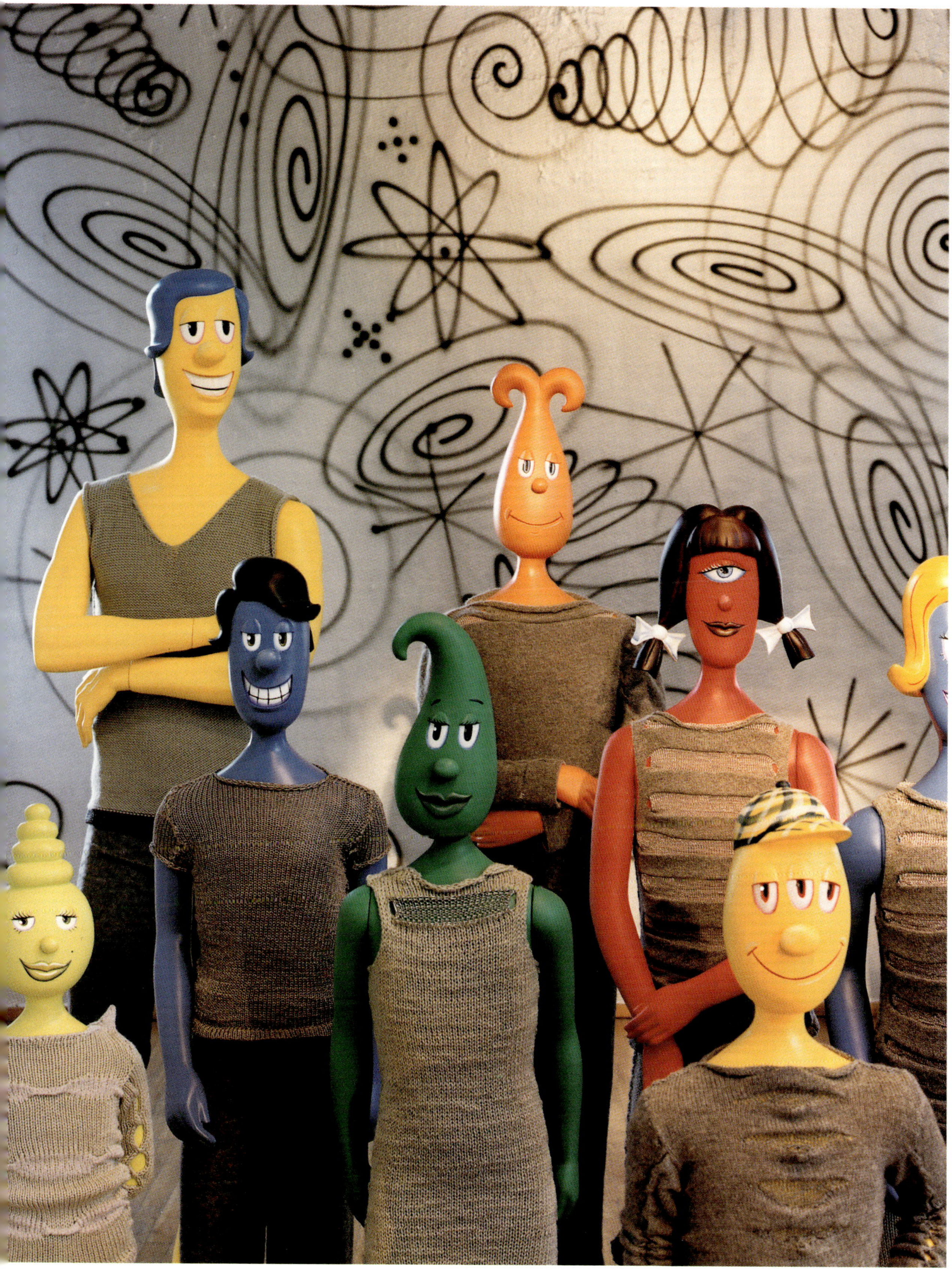

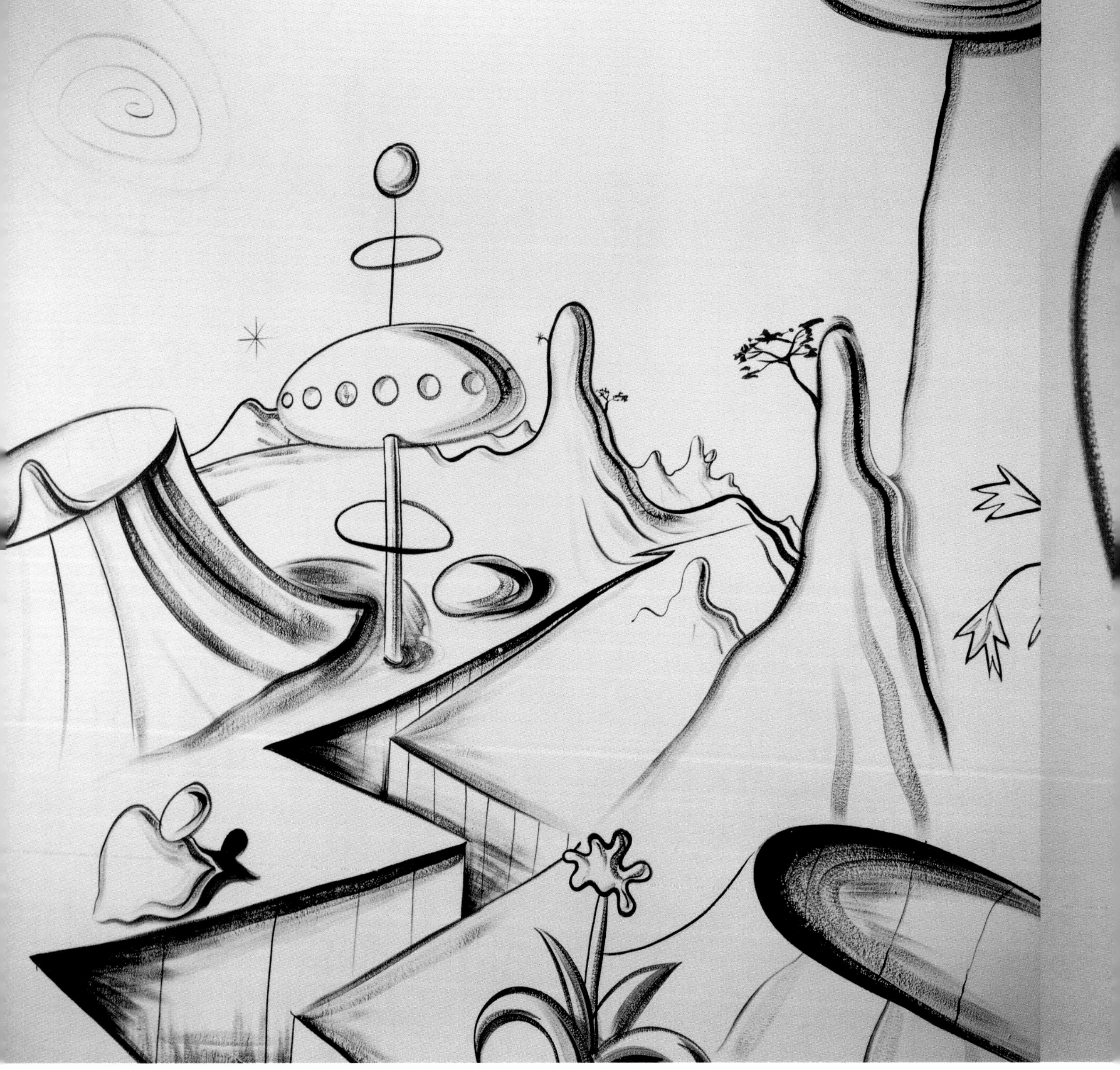

 Kenny Scharf with wall mural, 1998

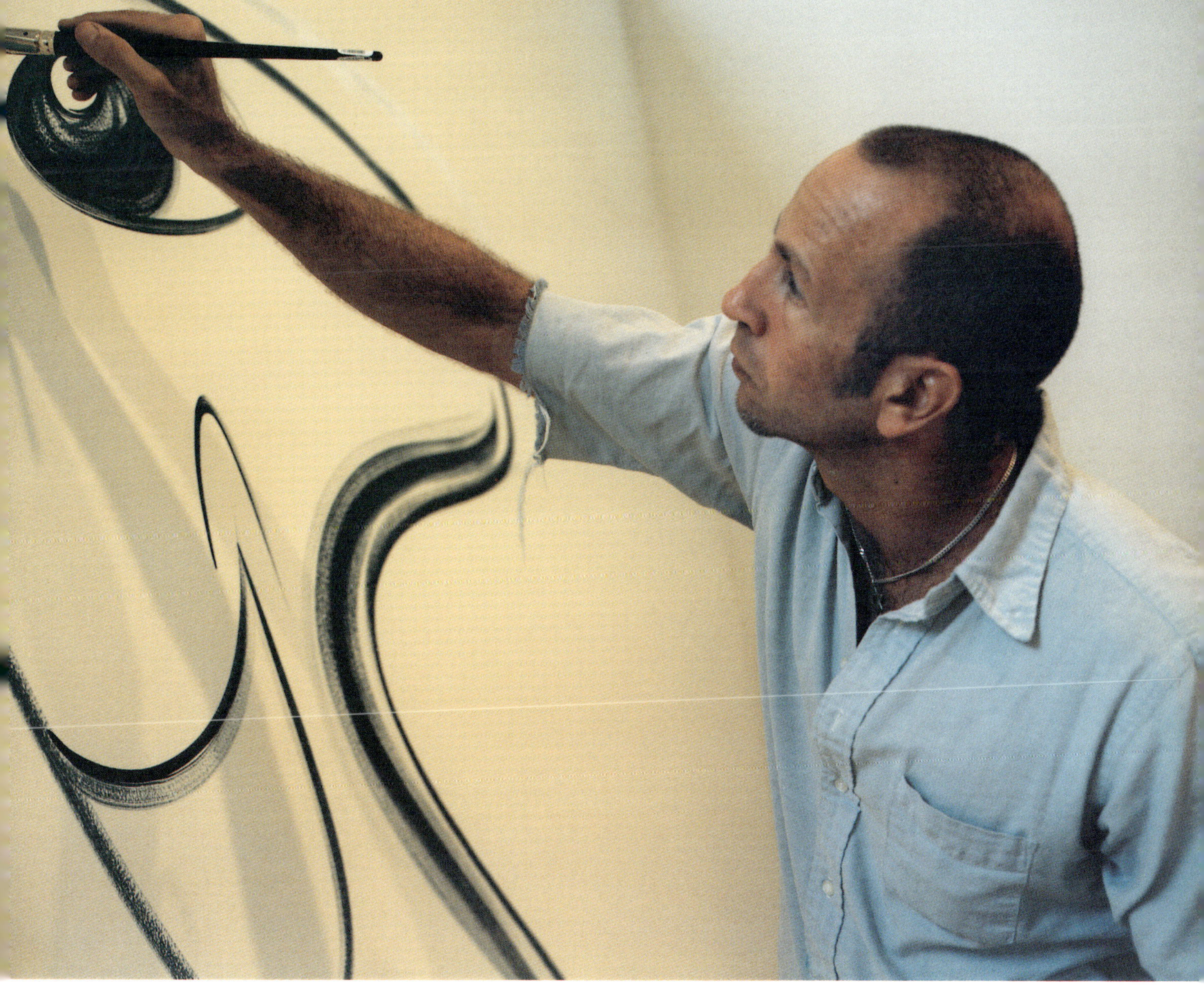

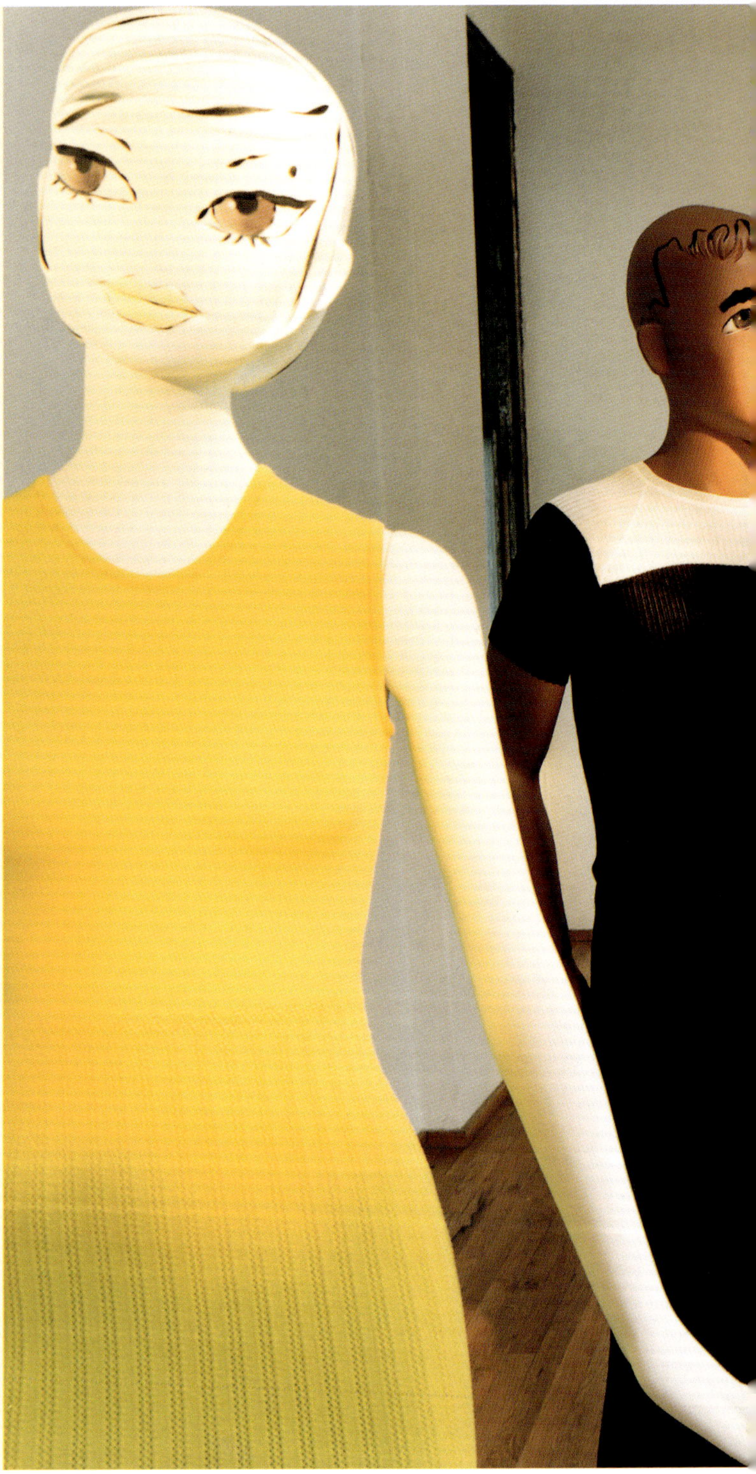

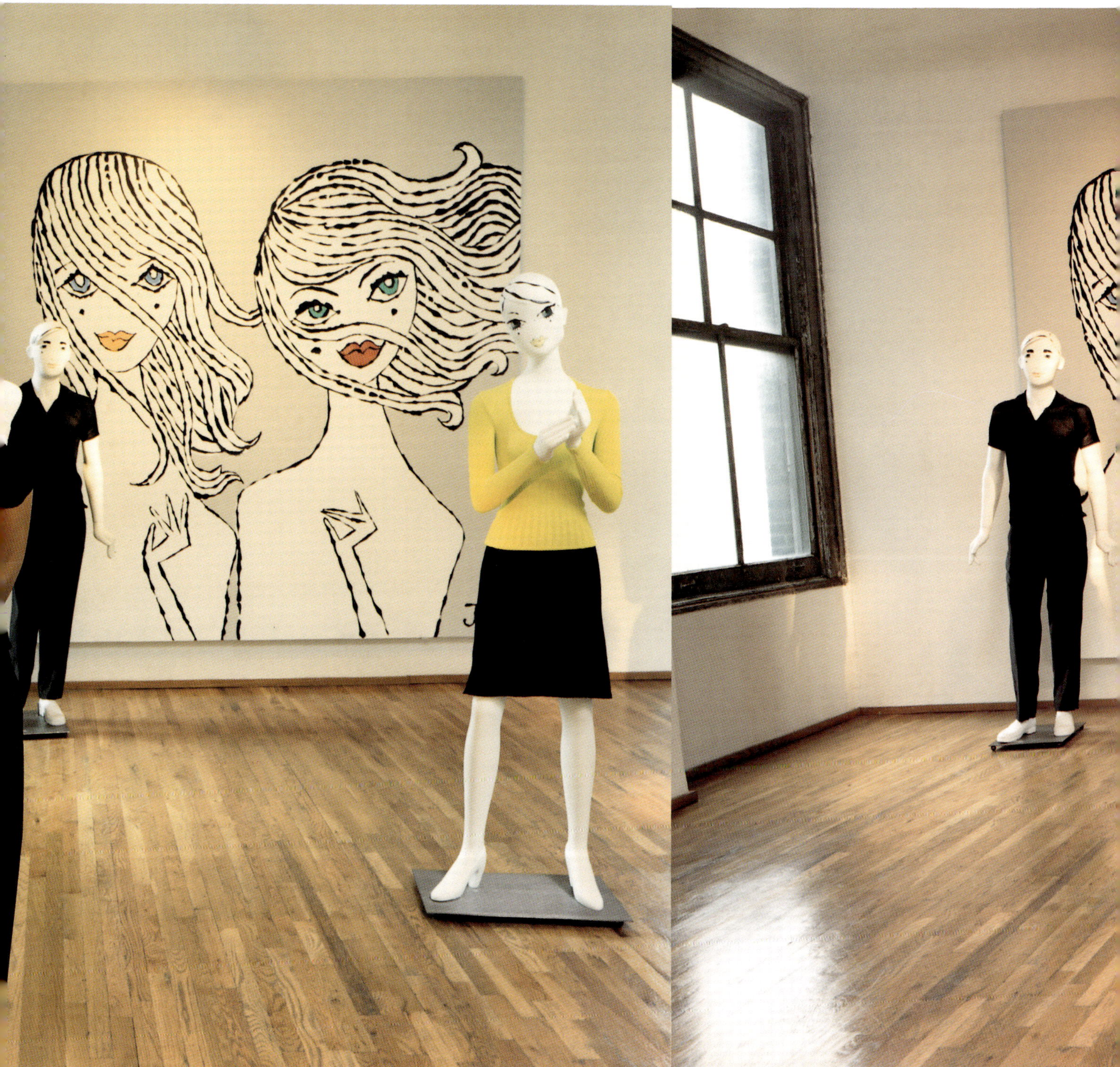

jeffrey fulvimari mannequins, painting, 1996, fashions by Catherine Malandrino

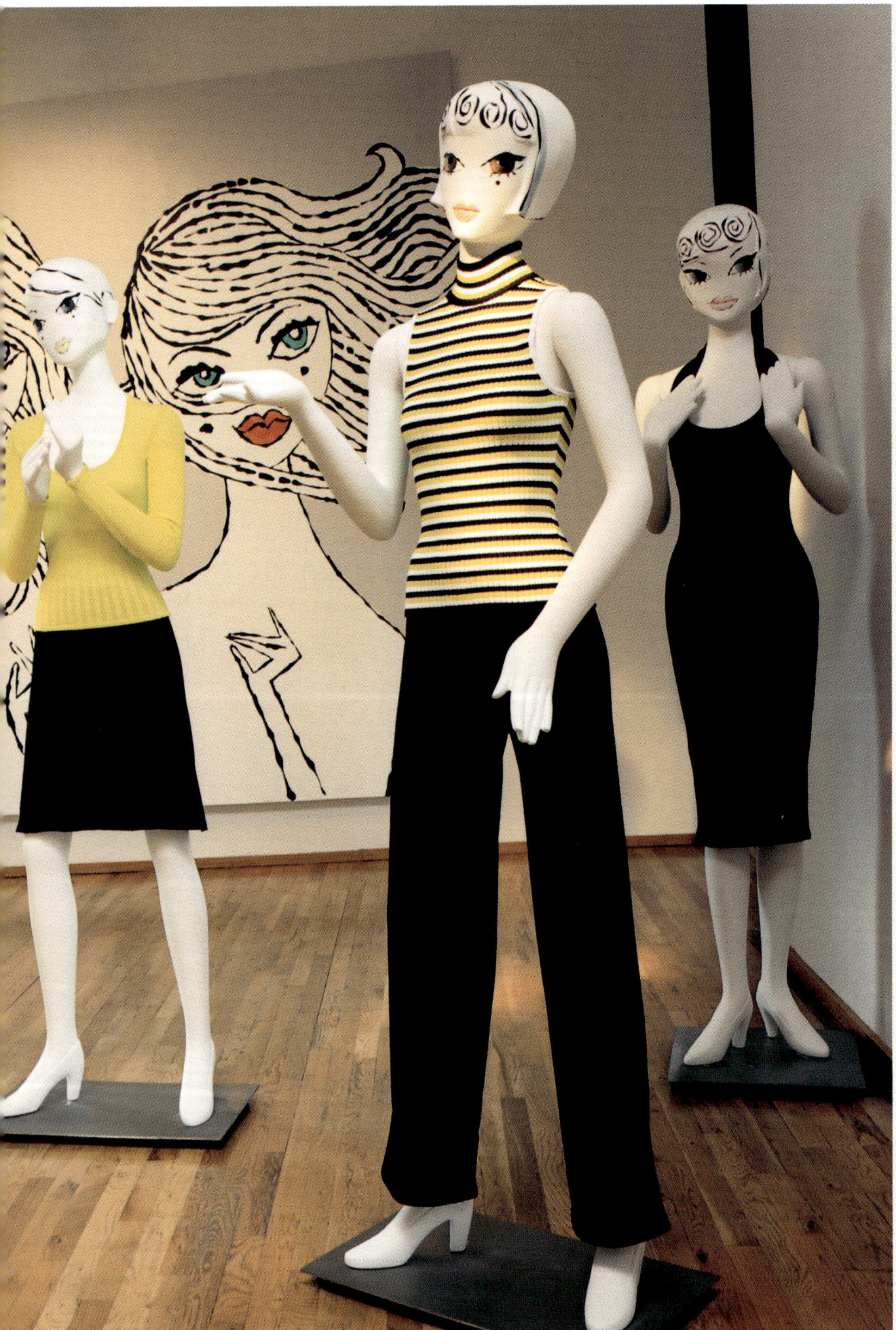

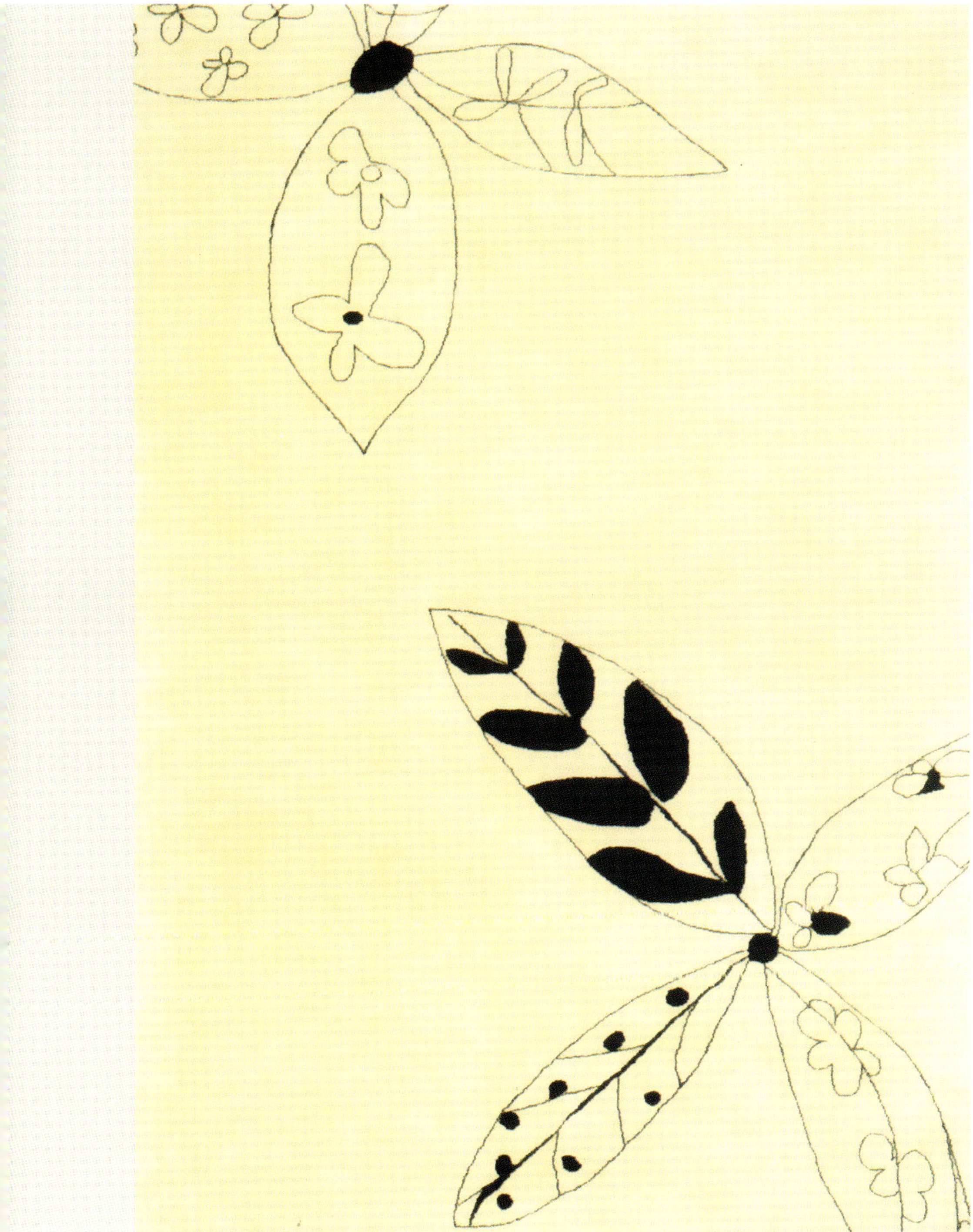

madeline weinrib *Moor* area rug, 2006

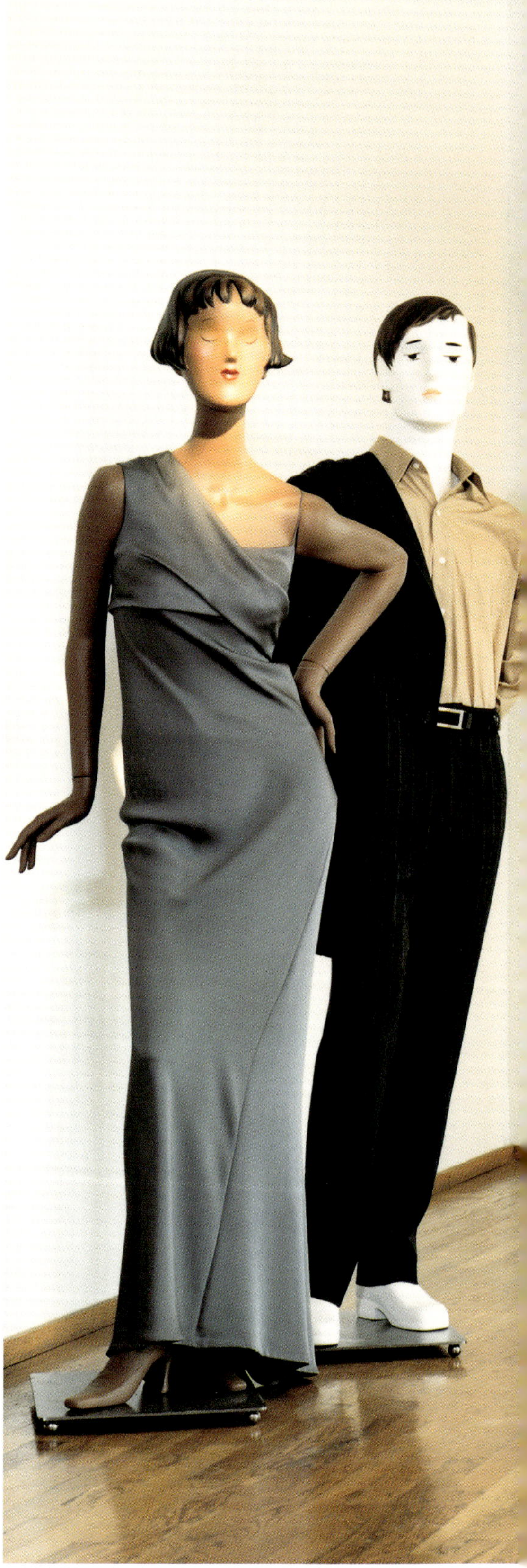

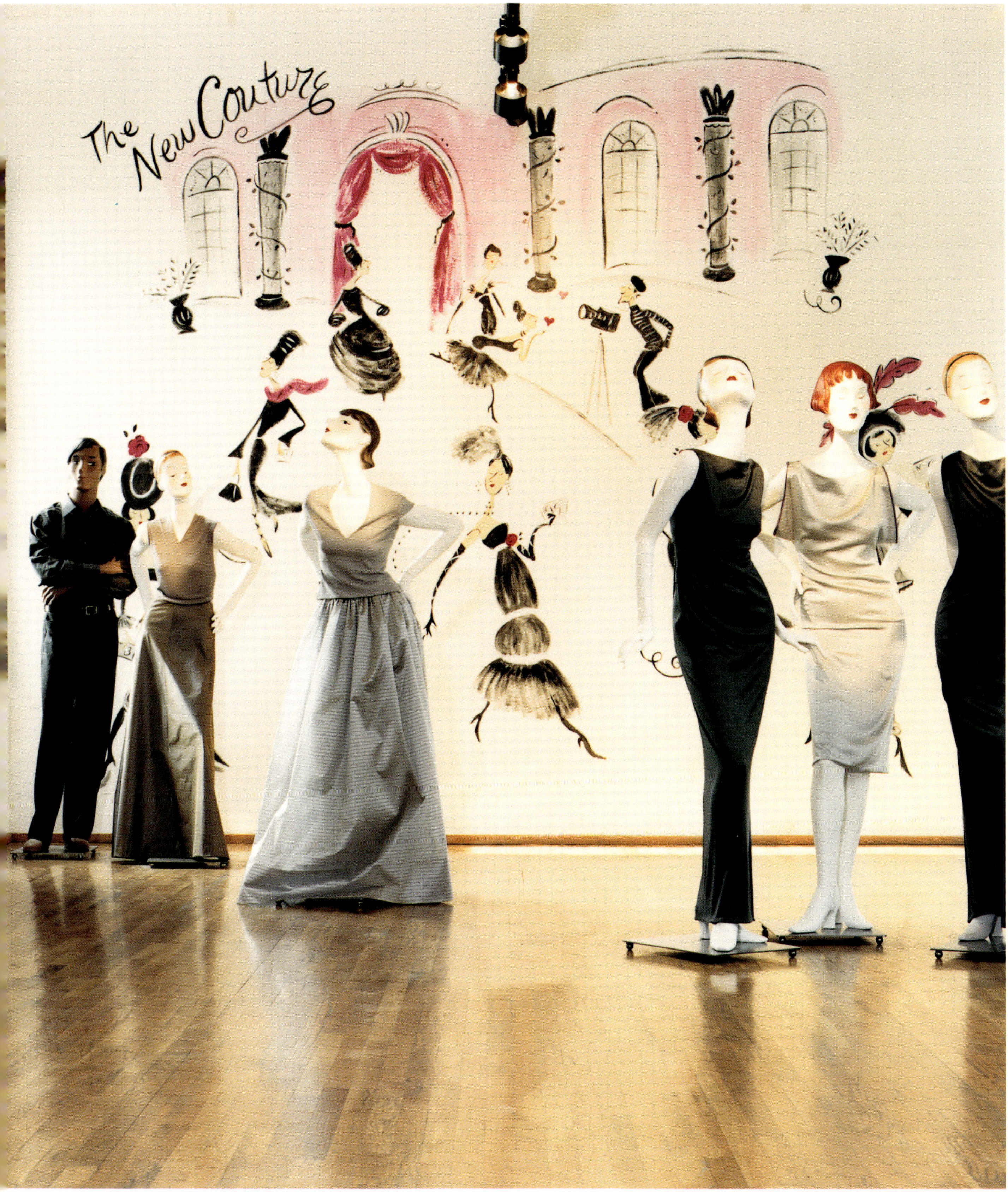

chesley mclaren "The New Couture" mannequin and mural, 1998, fashions by William Calvert

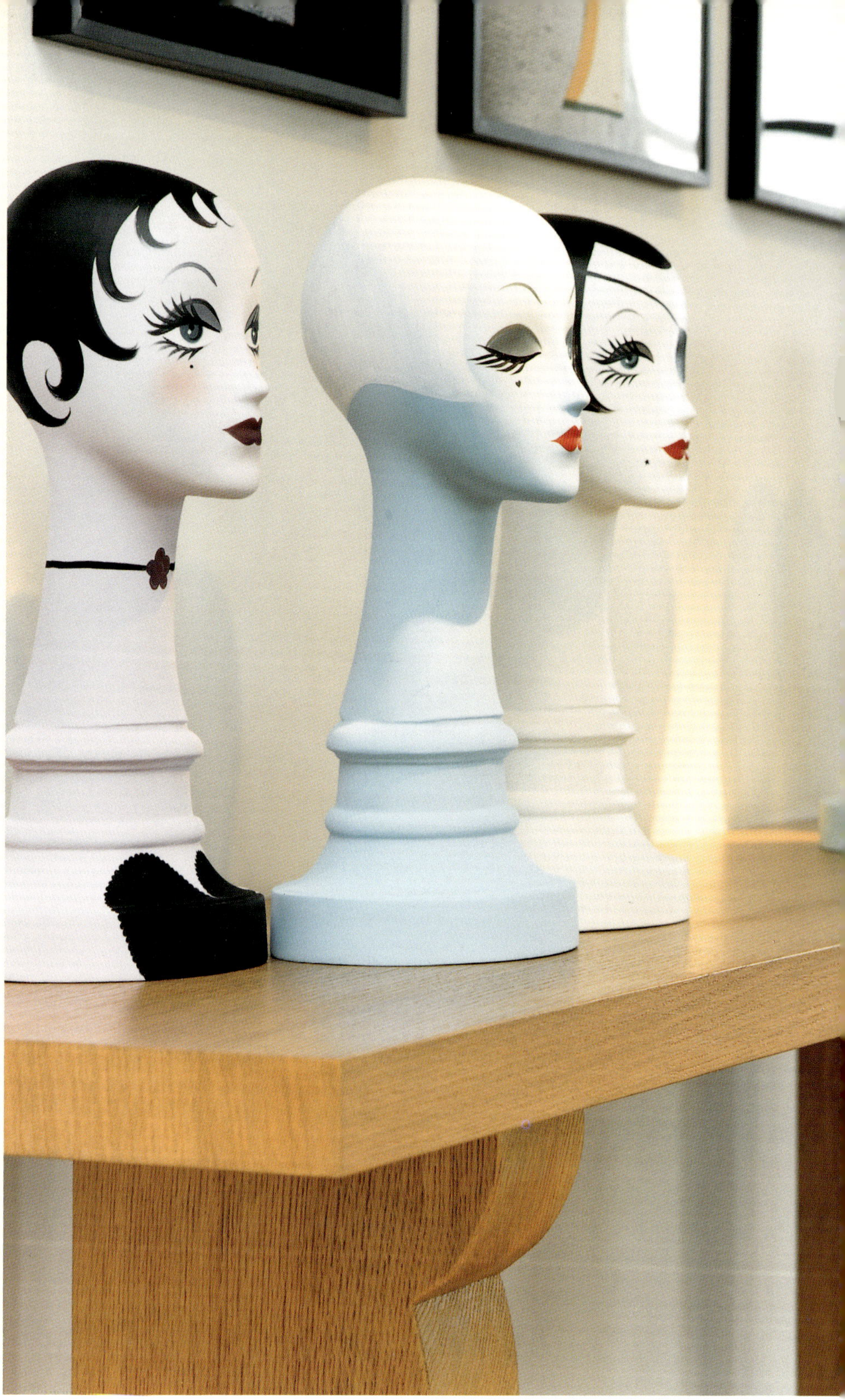

anna sui *Dolly* mannequin, 1997

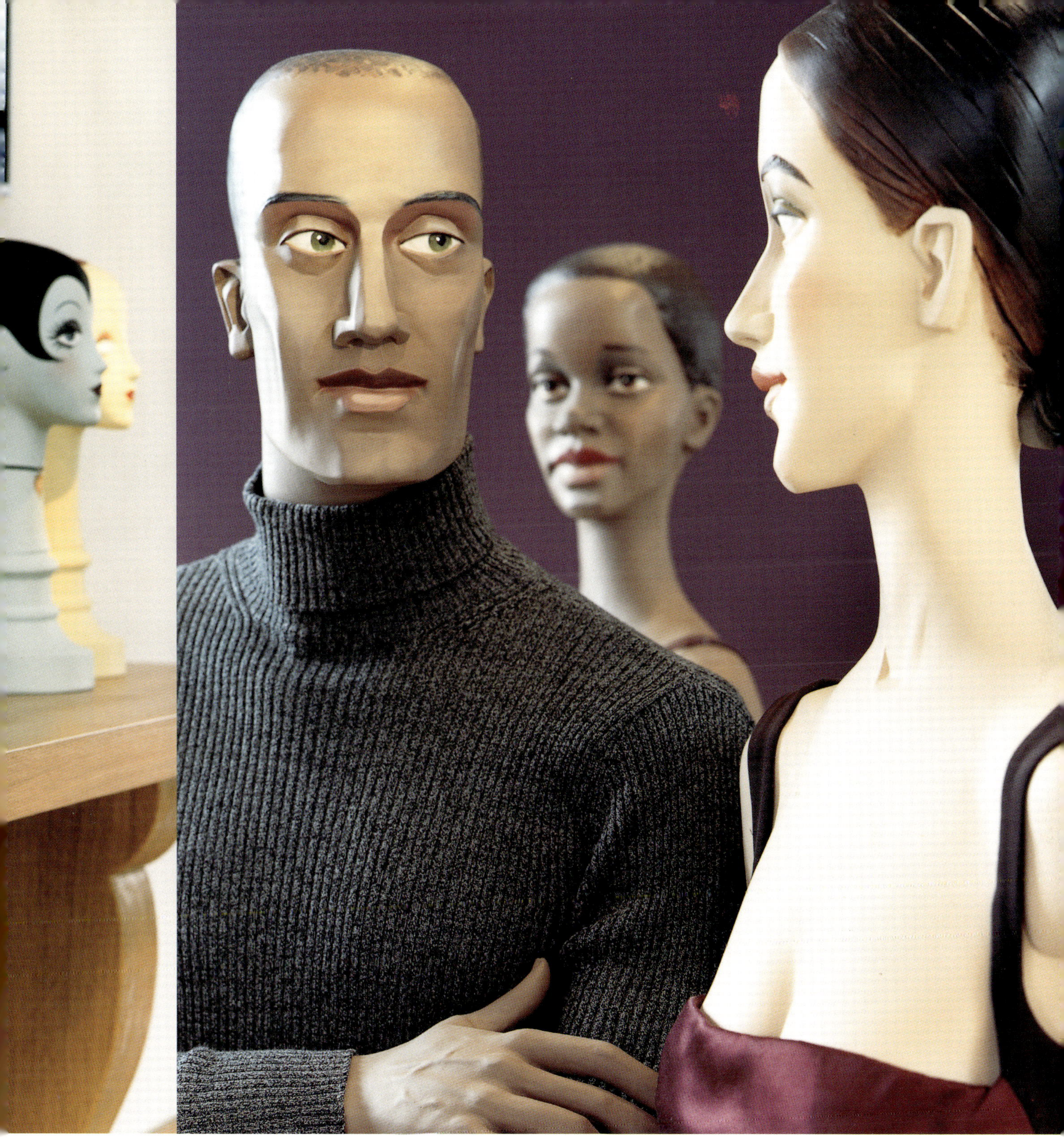

robert clyde anderson *Brownstone* mannequin, 2000

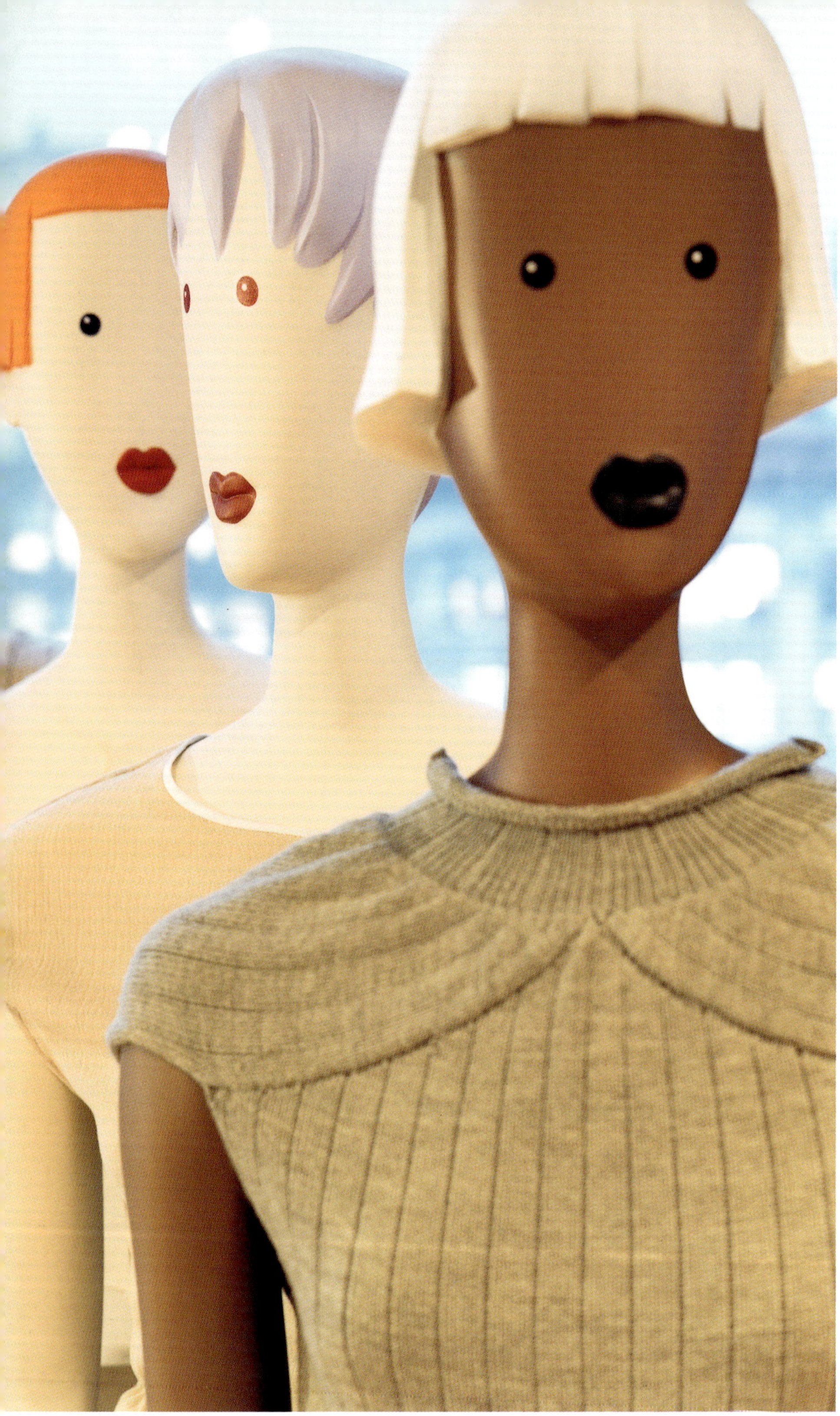

stephen campbell *Nouvelle Vague* mannequins, 2000, fashions by Ruben Chapelle anja kroencke *Goddess* mannequins, mural, 2005, fashions by Jeffery Chow

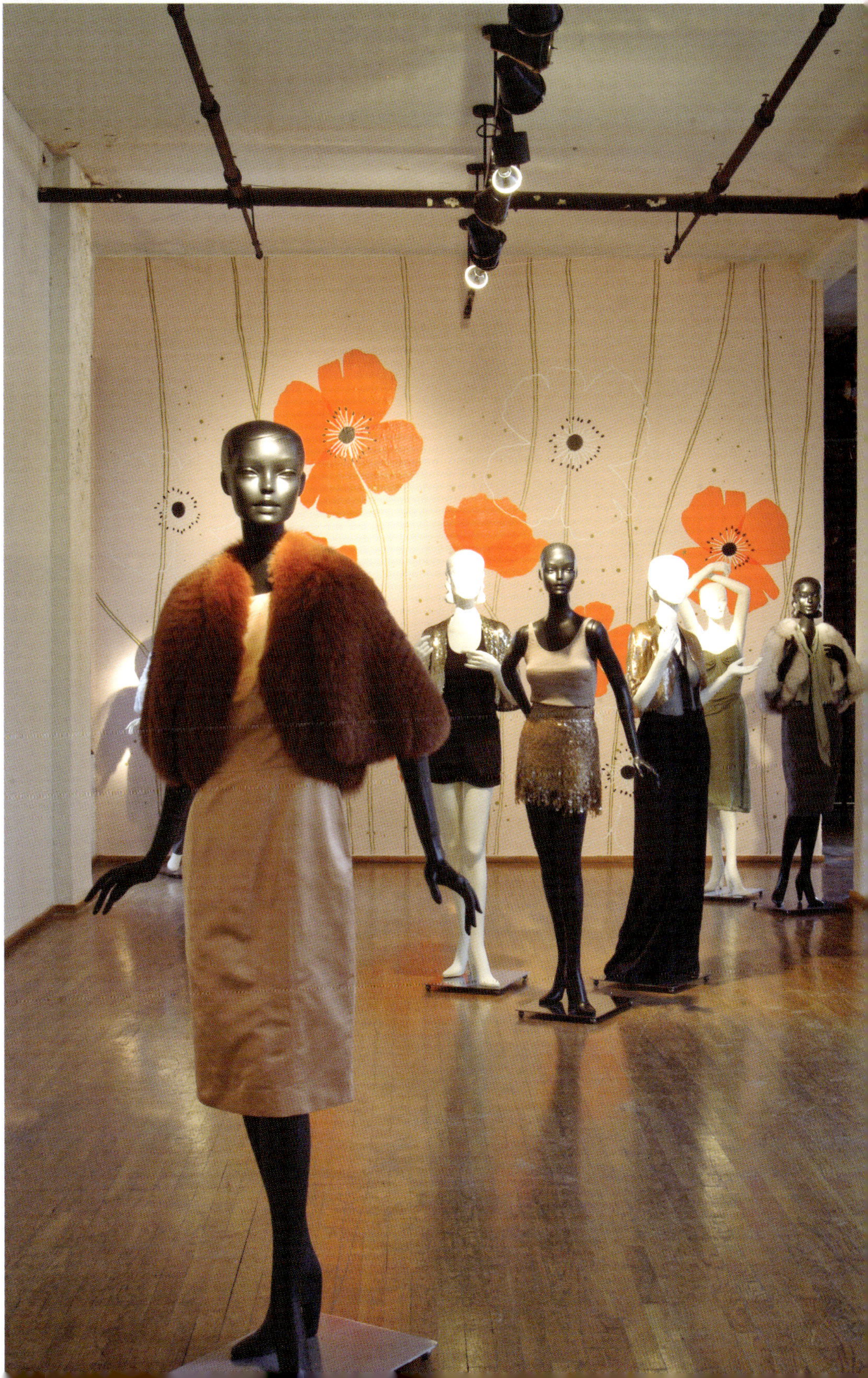

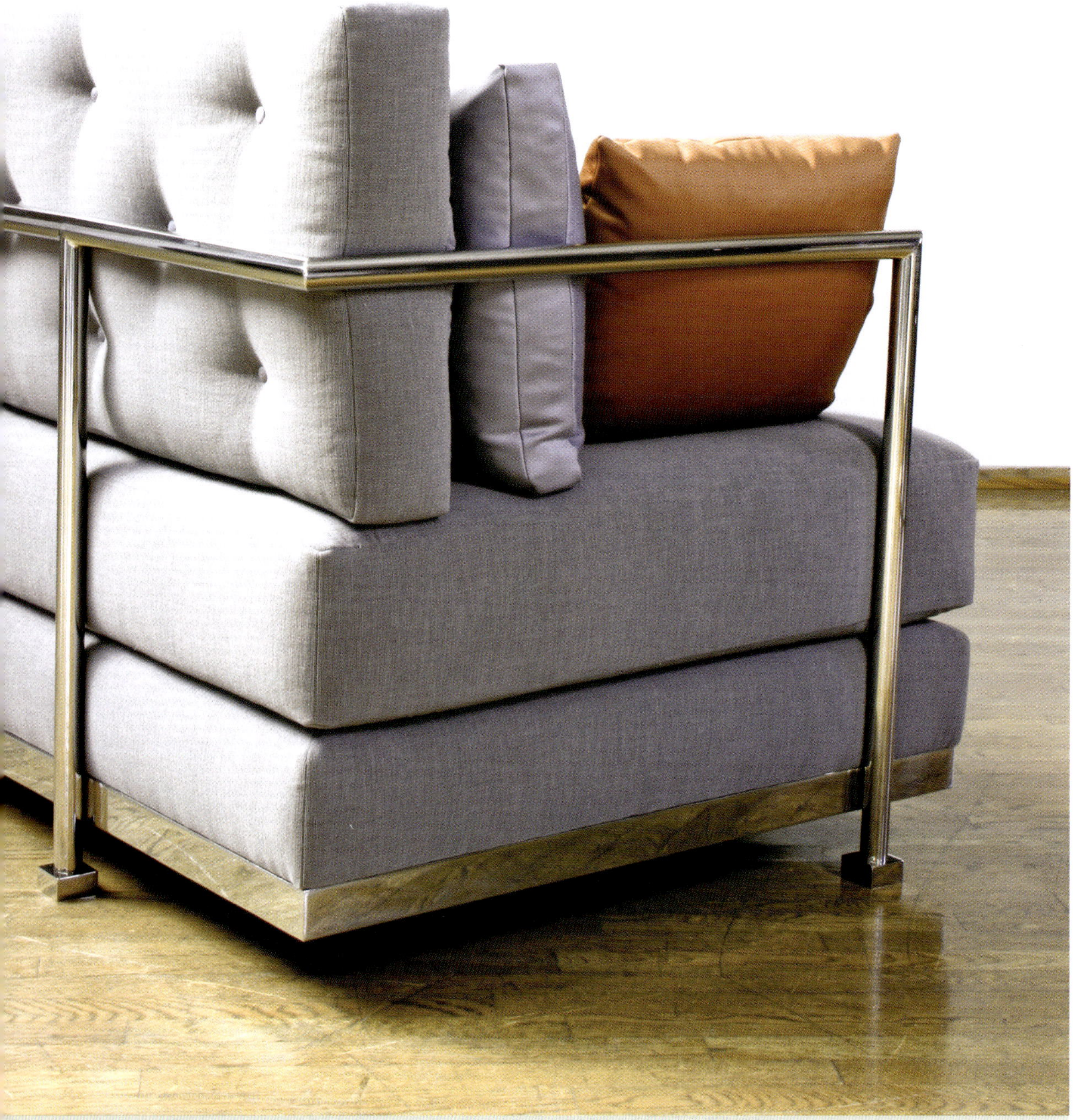

"Good design knows
no boundaries."
—Vincente Wolf

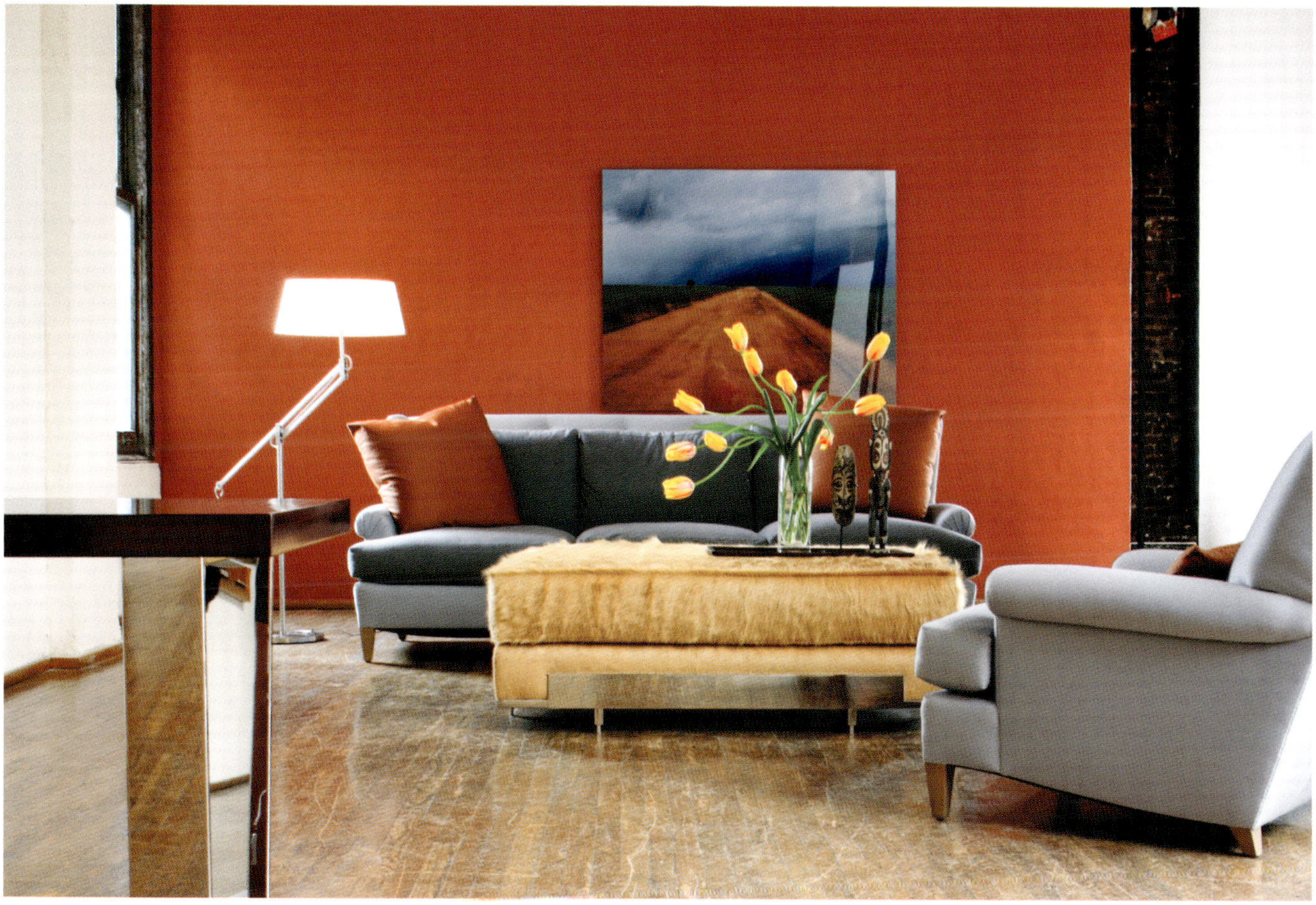

vincente wolf furniture collection and photograph, 2007

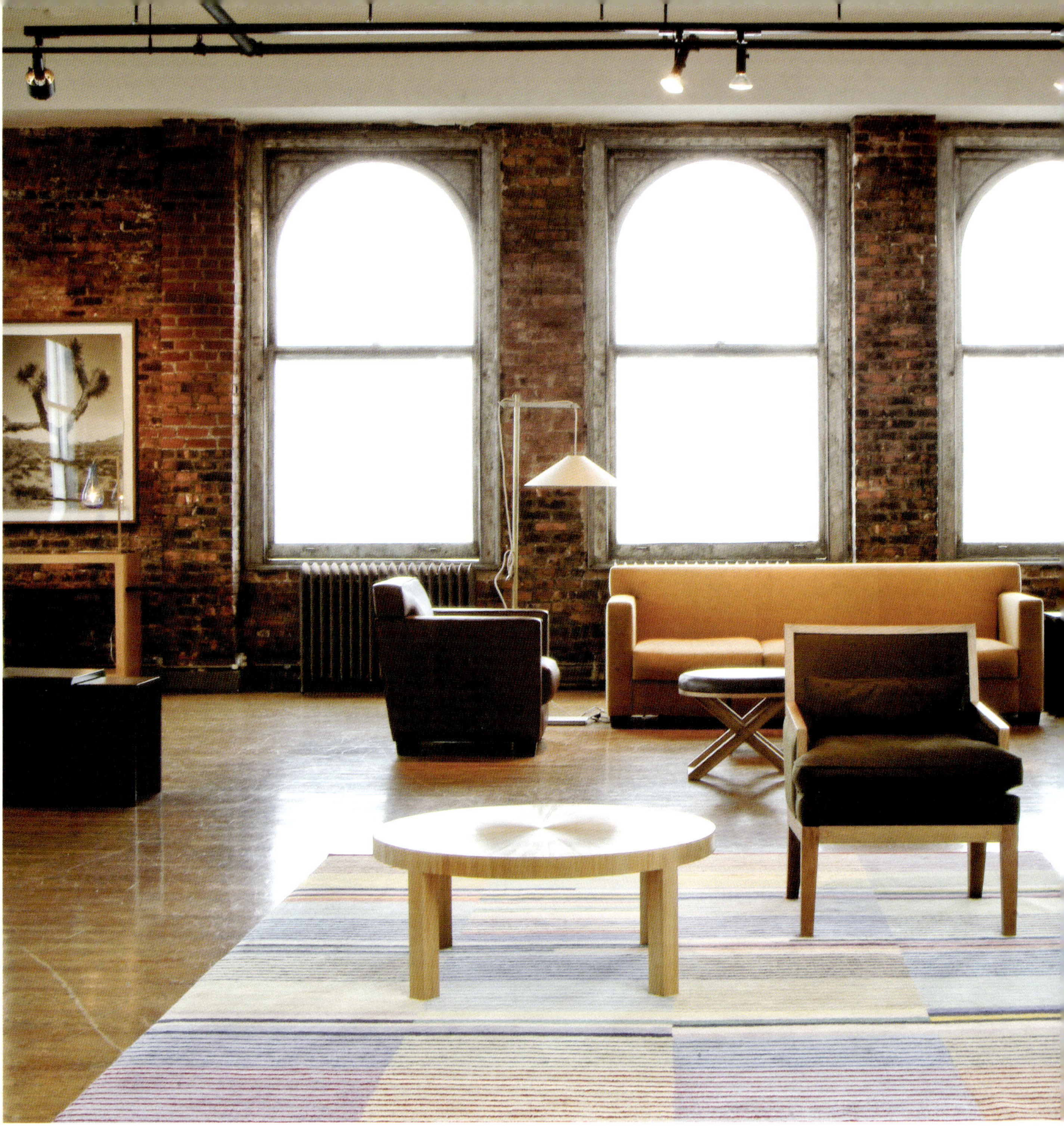

ecart international furniture collection, rug by Gunta Stötzl, 2001

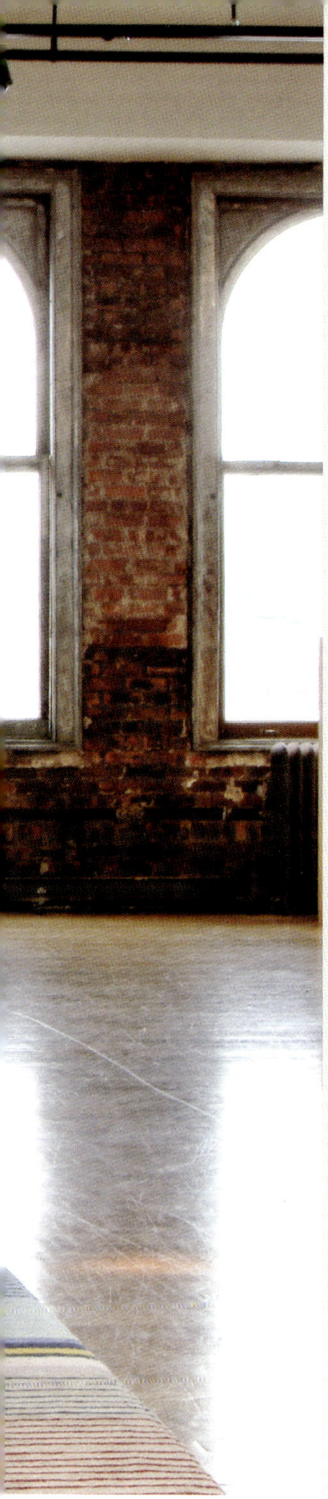

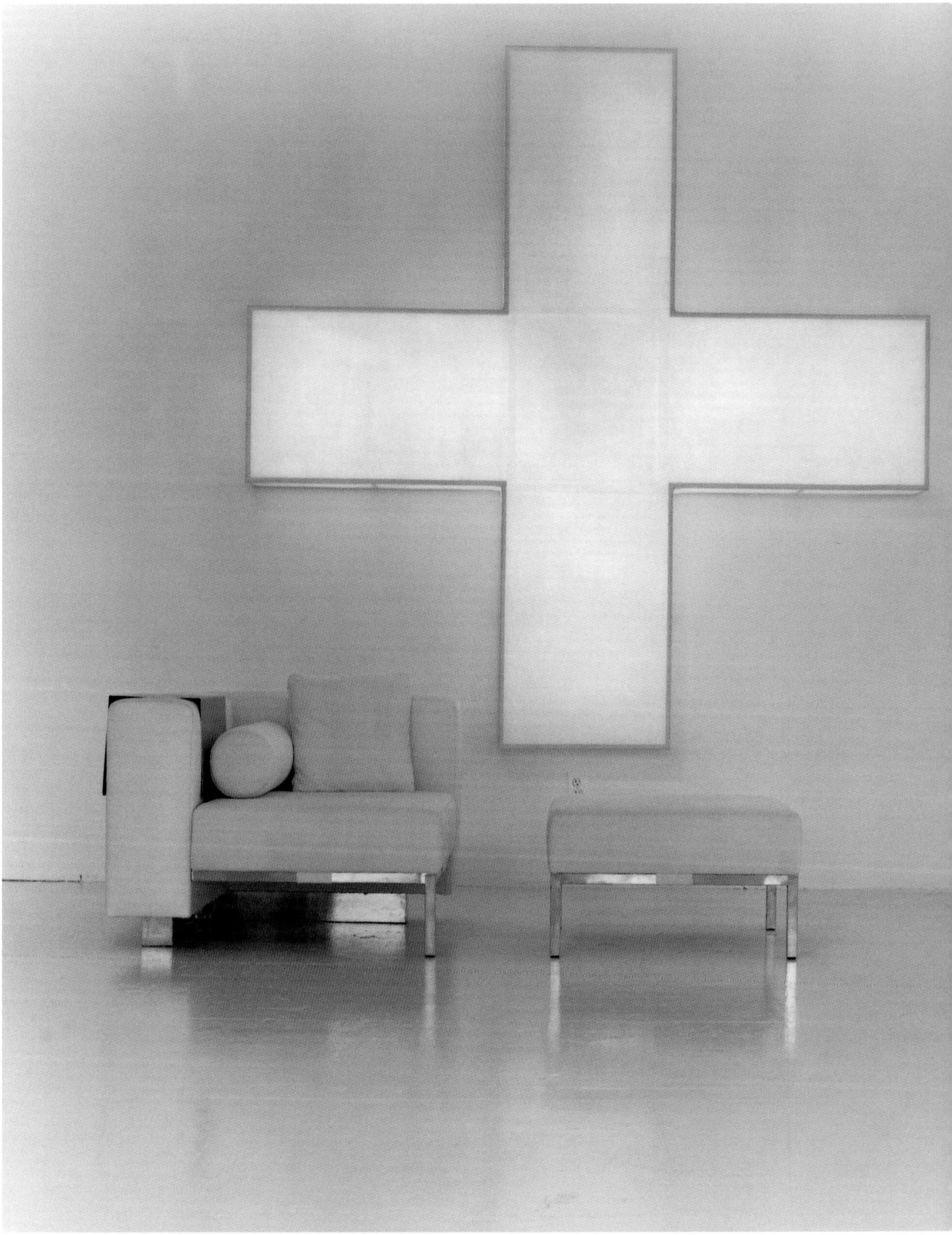

trace simple *St. Germain* club chair and ottoman, 2002

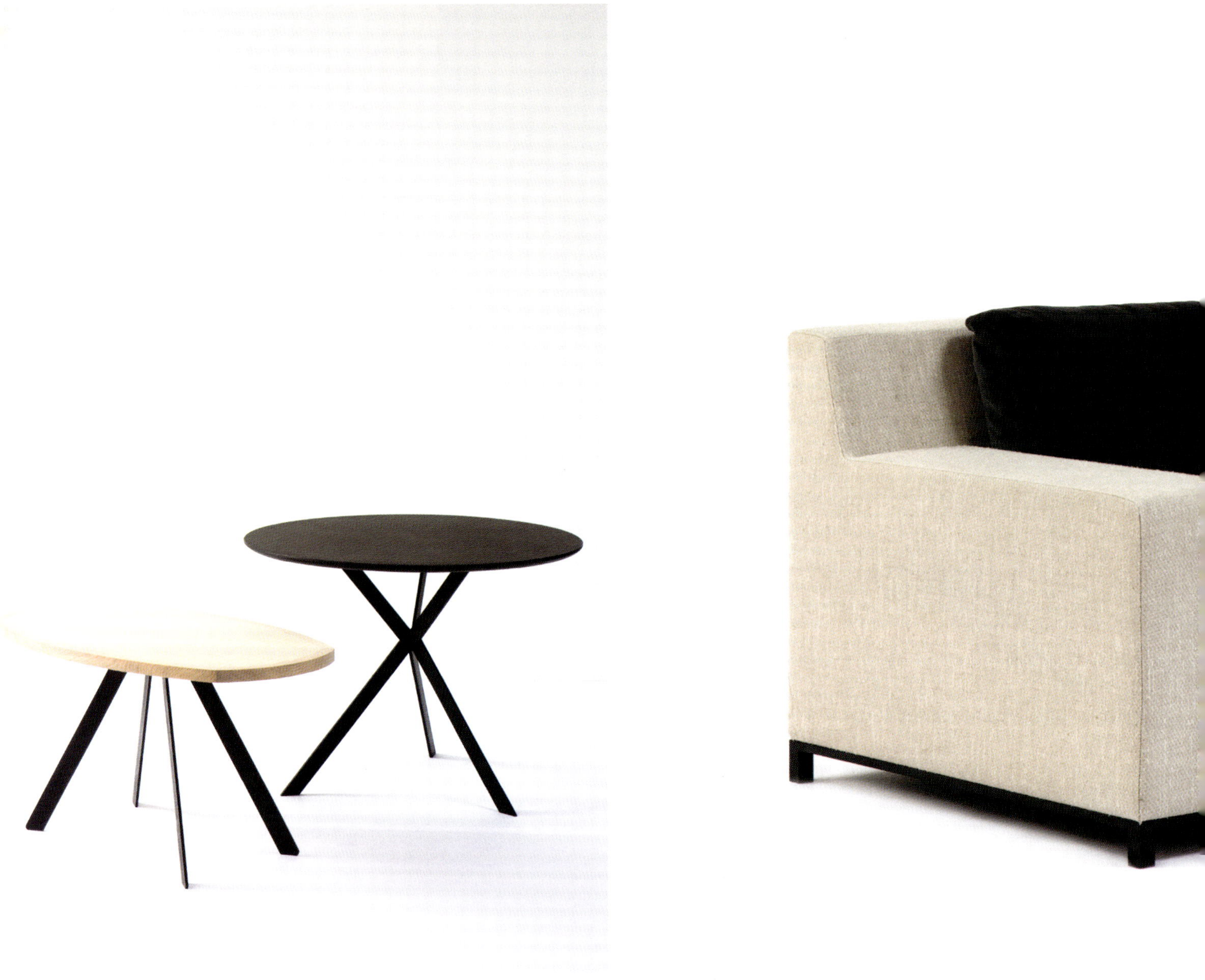

christophe delcourt *OVO* side table and *ANN* chair, 2007

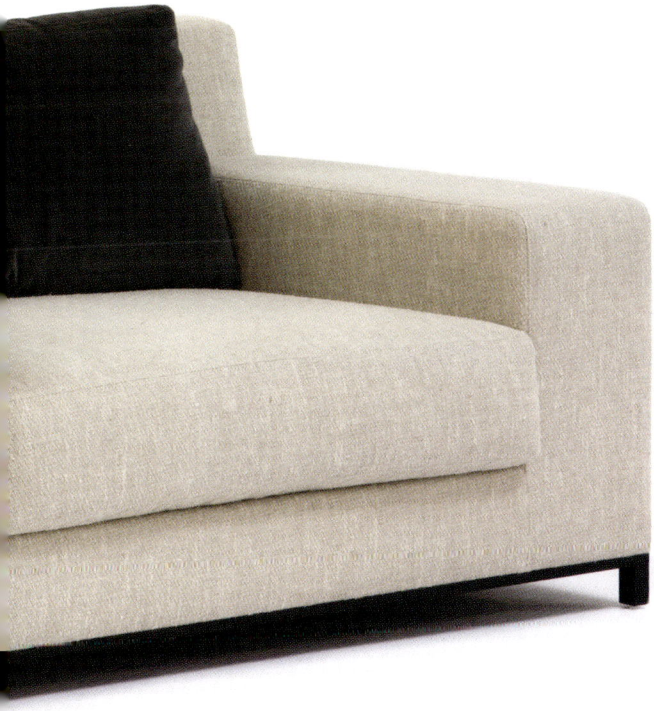

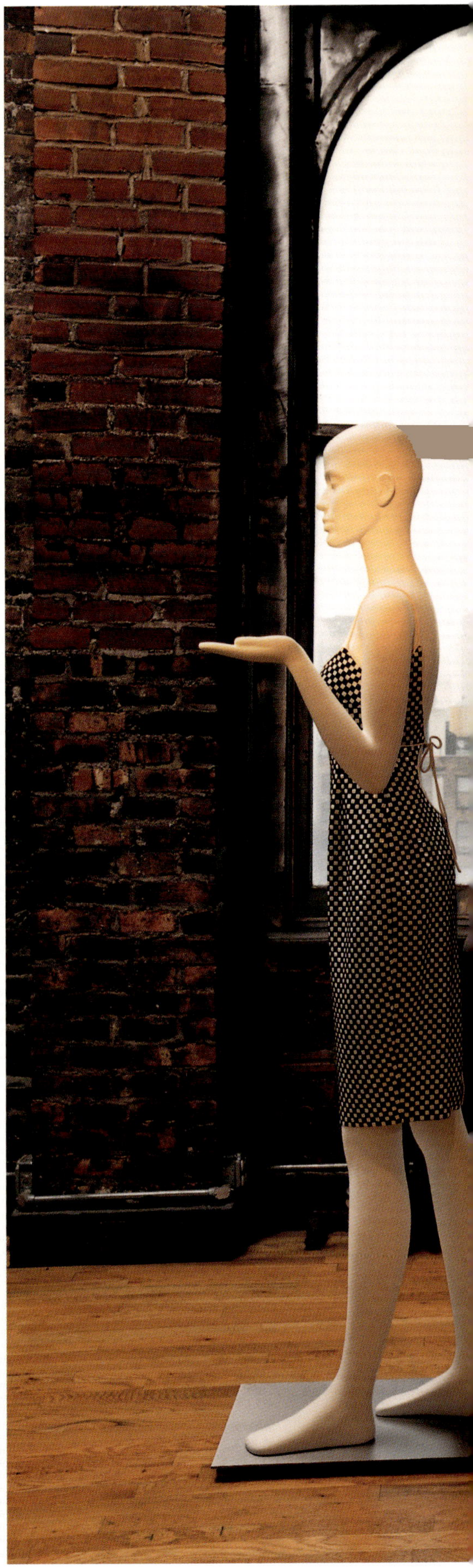

veruschka mannequin, 1996, fashions by Catherine Malandrino

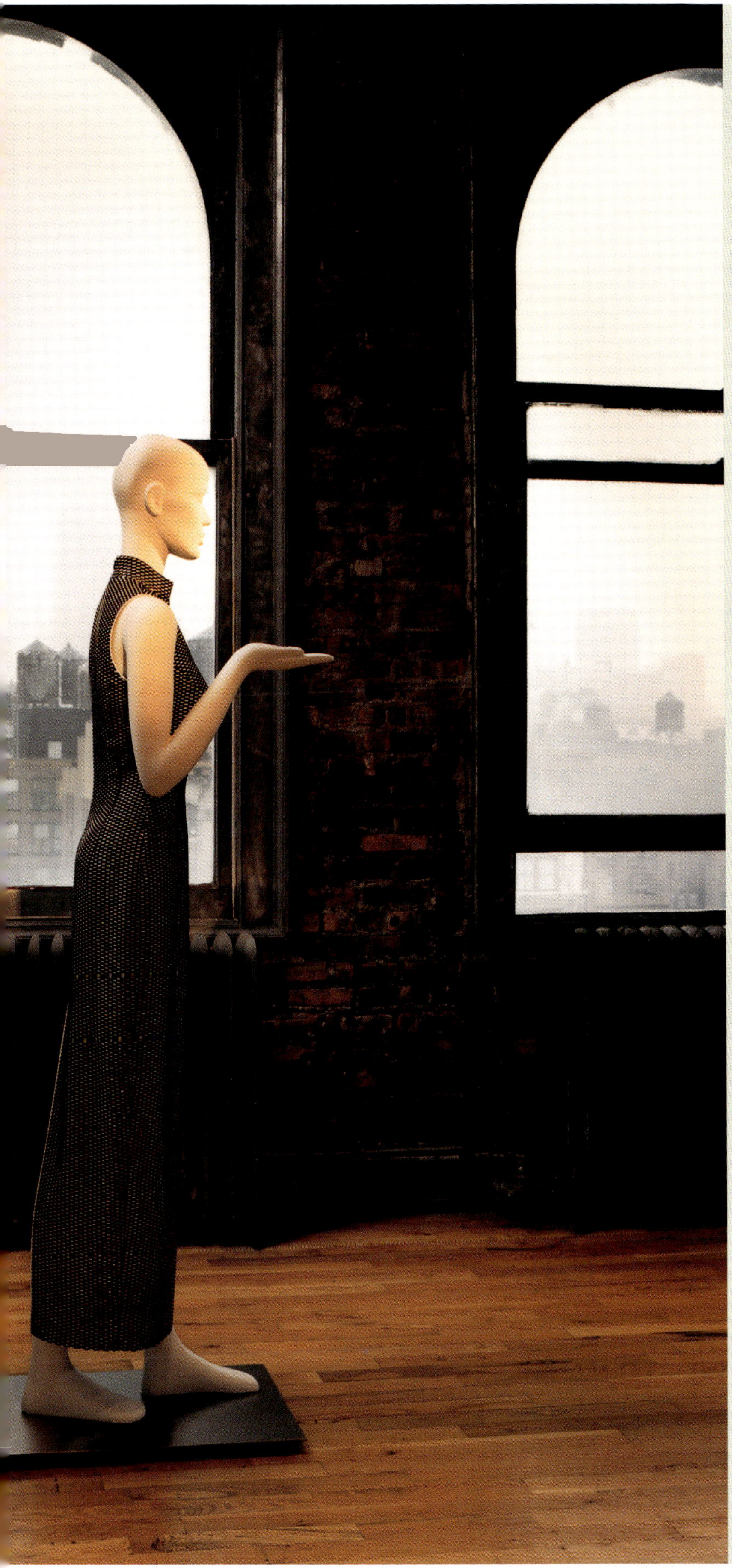

"I insist on the hand of the craftsman to be a visible ingredient. My forms are not tricky, they speak to you slowly, revealing themselves over time."

—Kevin Walz

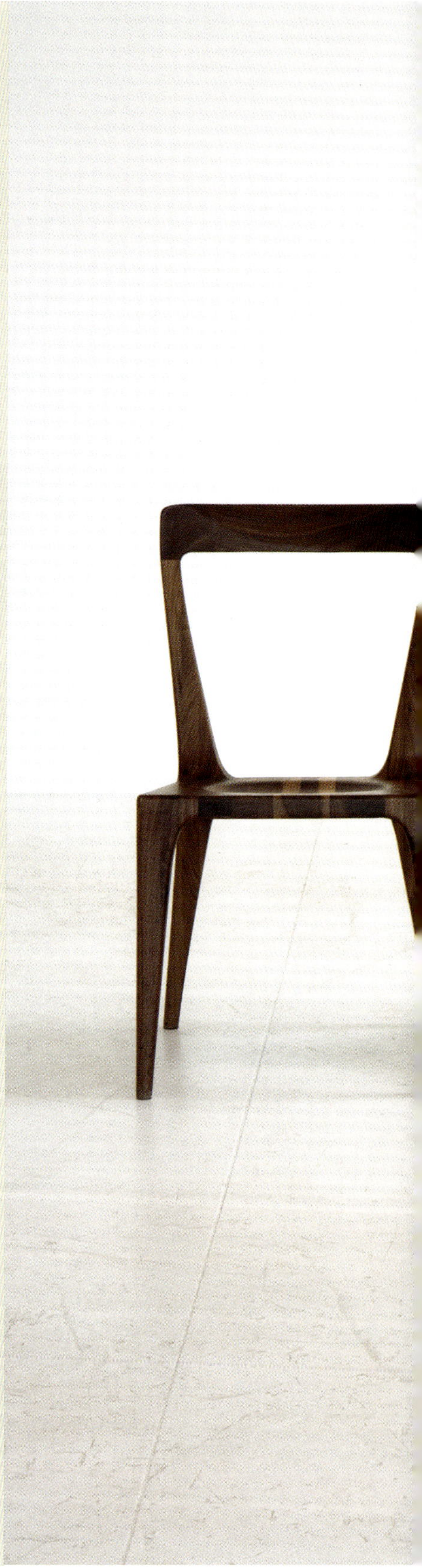

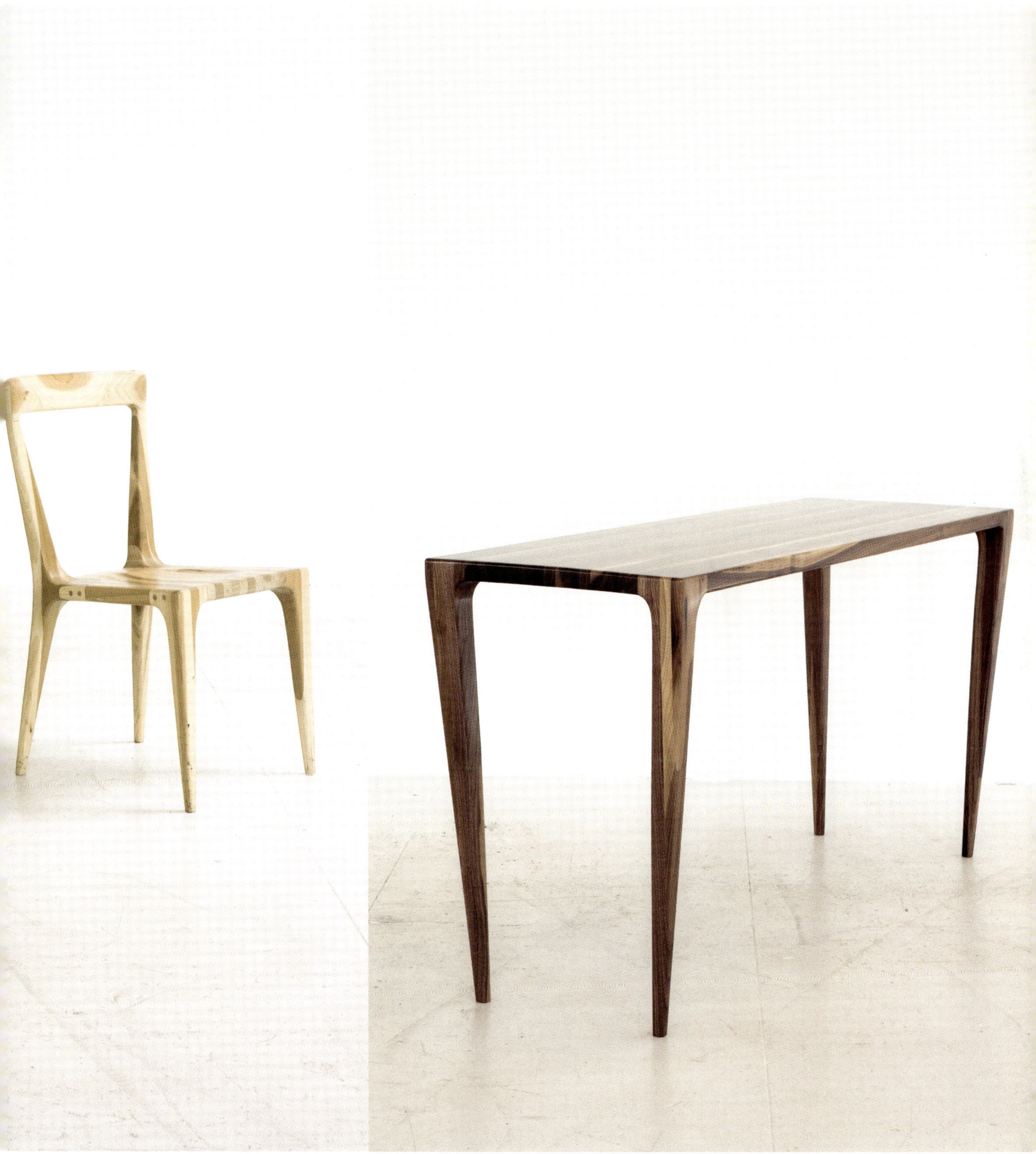

kevin walz "Collection #2," 2008

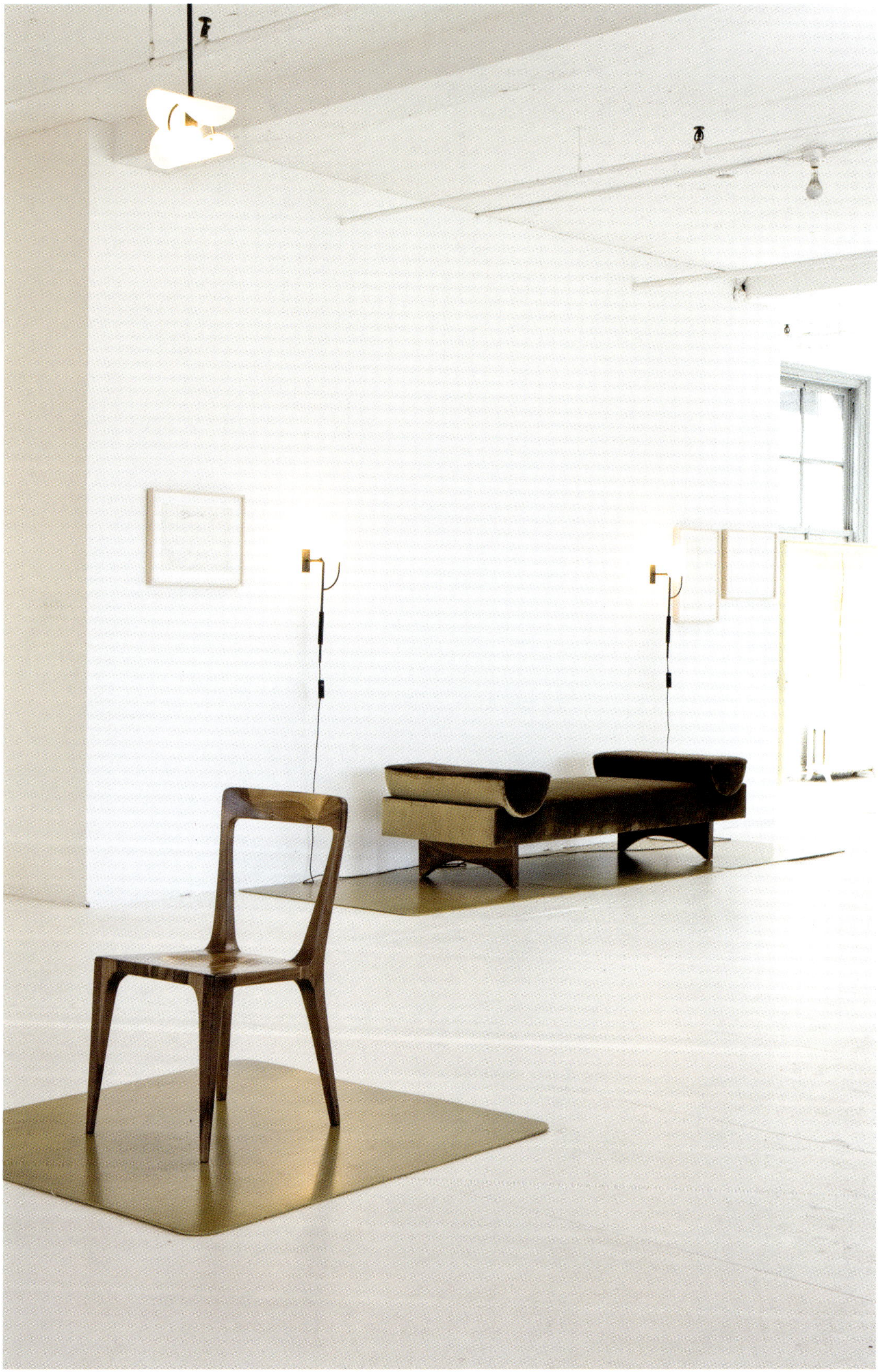

 "Collection #2," 2008

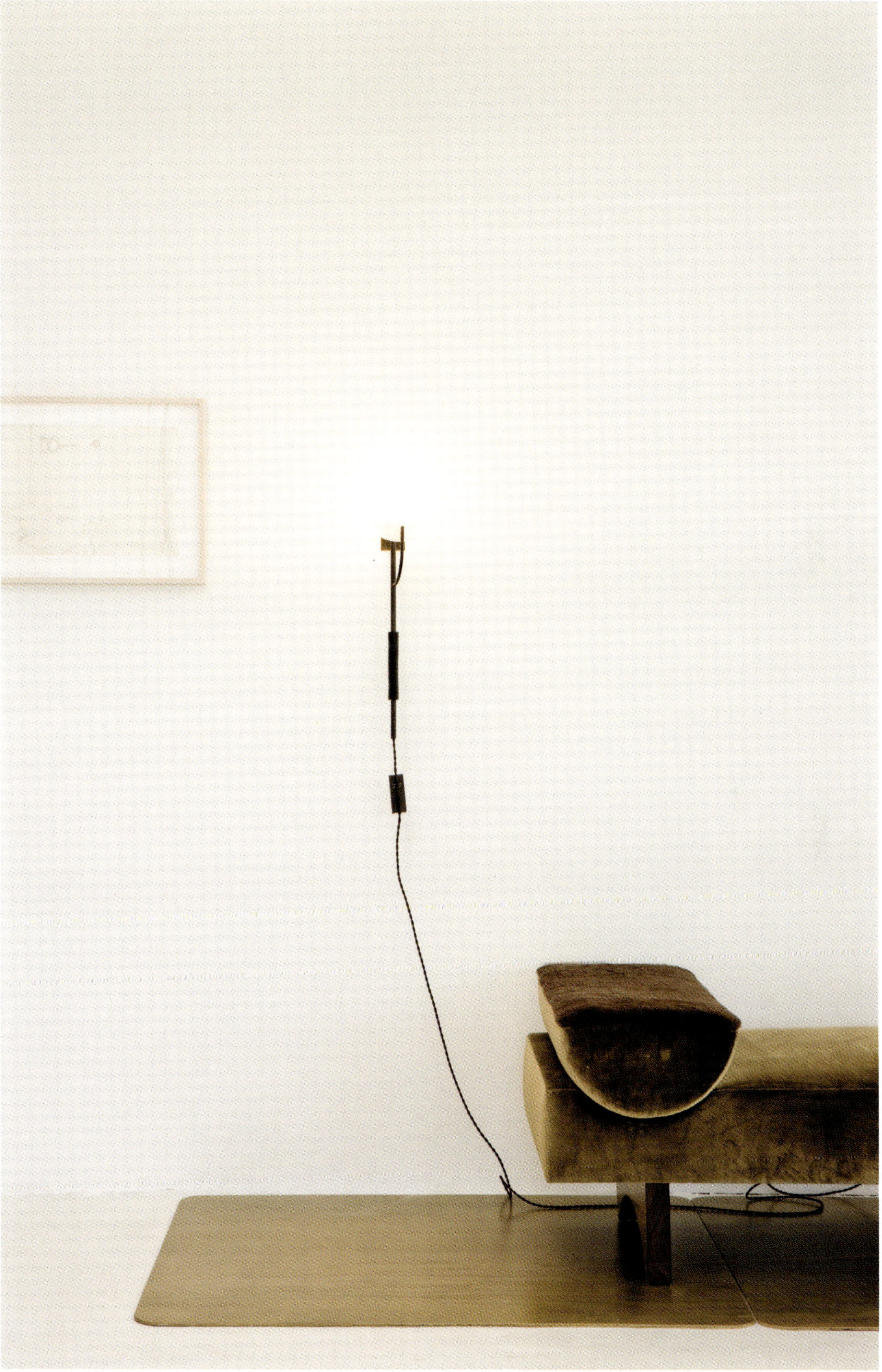

"We want to offer simplicity, strength and clarity. We don't want our furniture to scream for attention: we want it to 'be,' not 'say.'"

—Robert Bristow

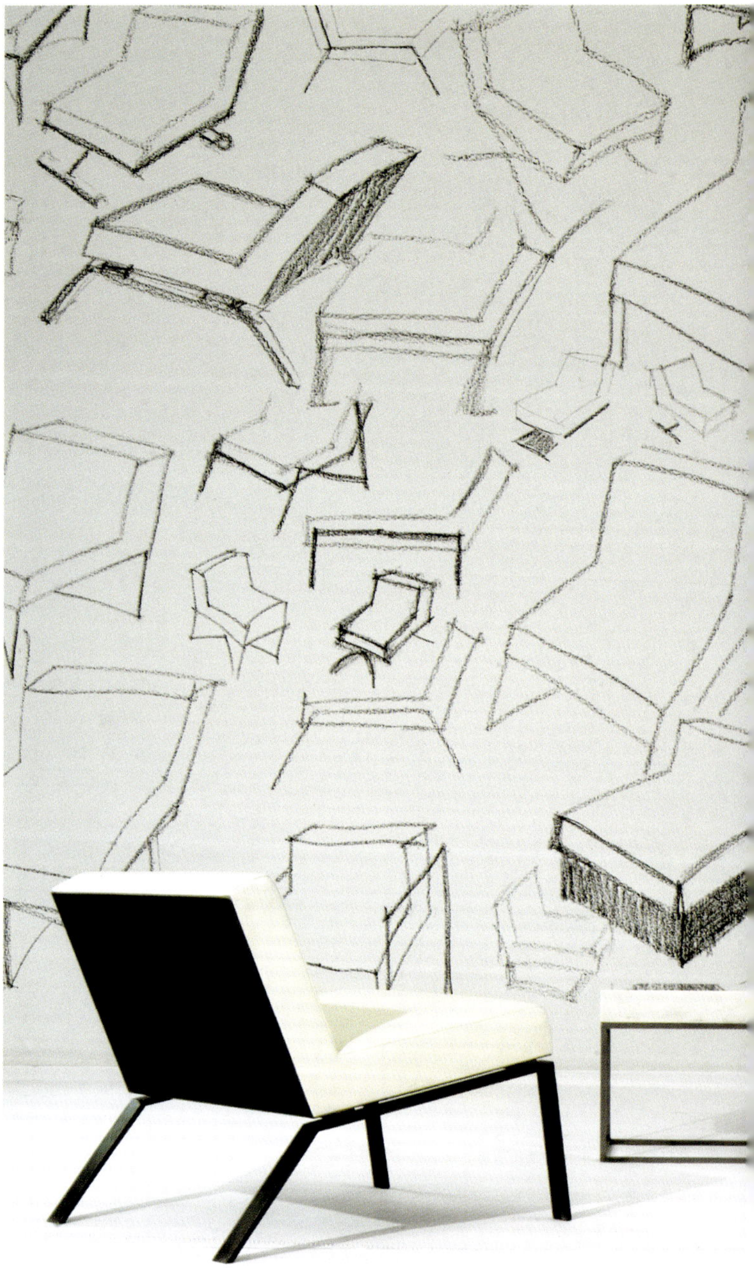

robert bristow *Chair #1, Daybed #1* and mural, 2006

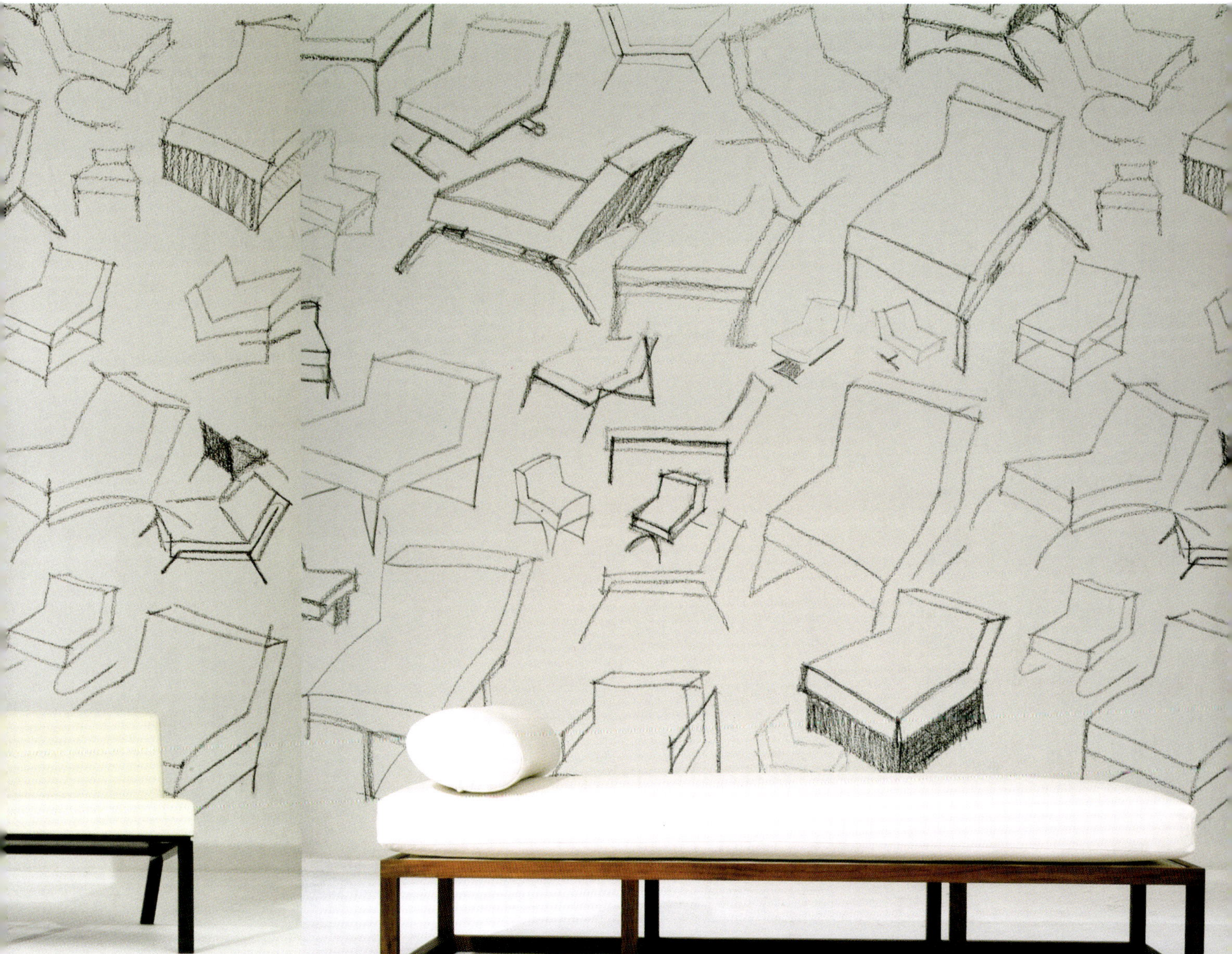

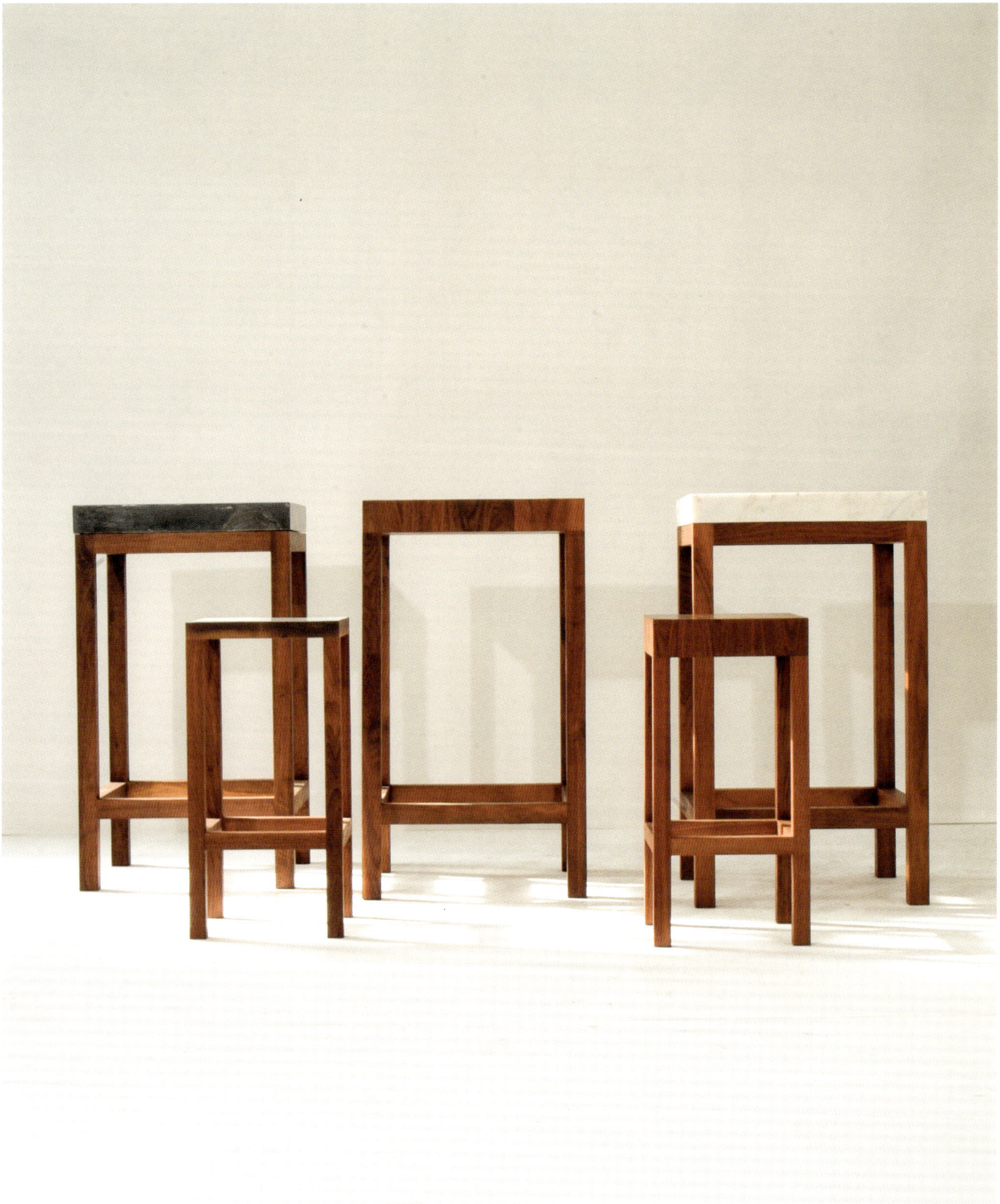

Bar tables and stools, 2004

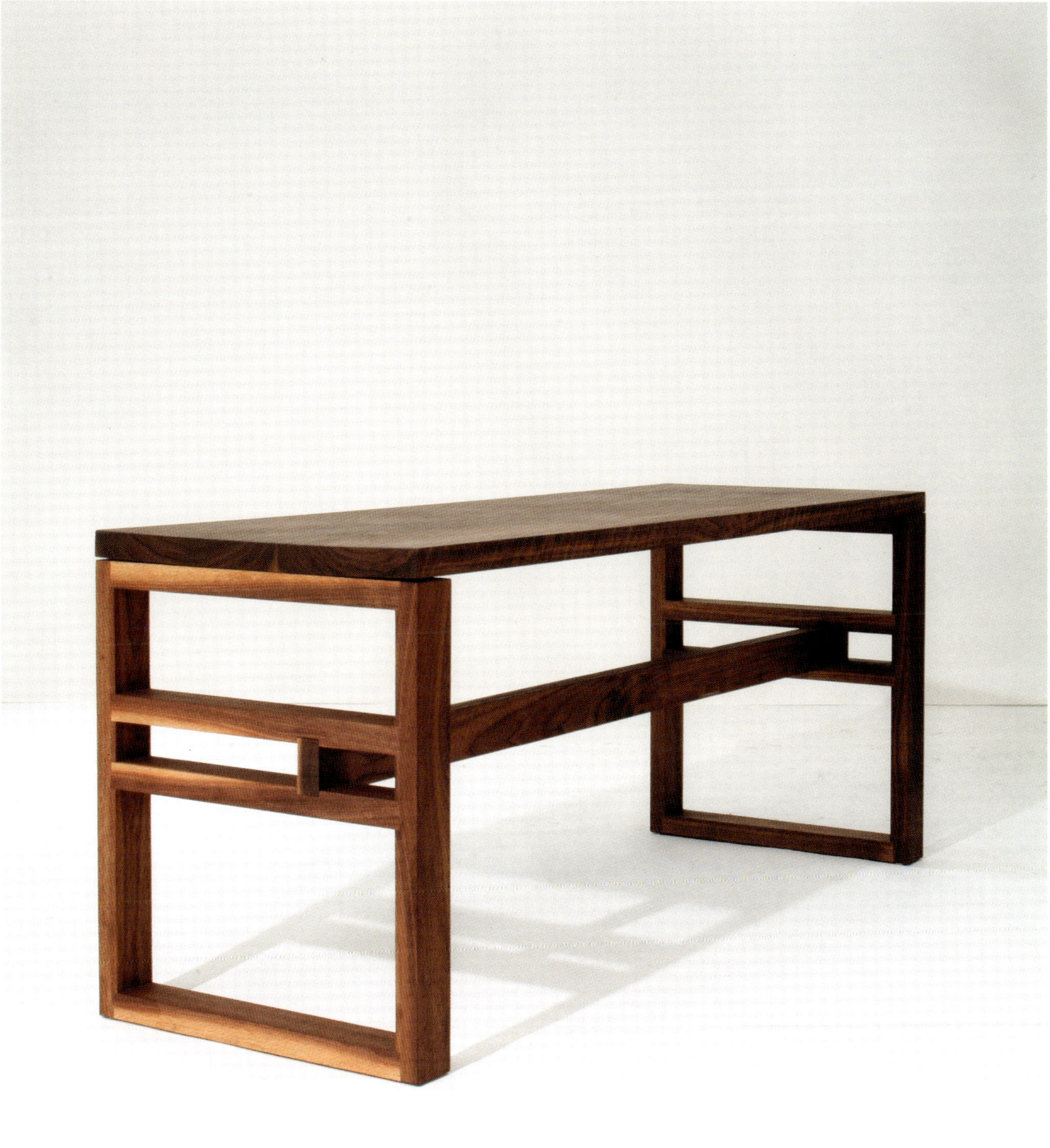

Frame desk, 2004

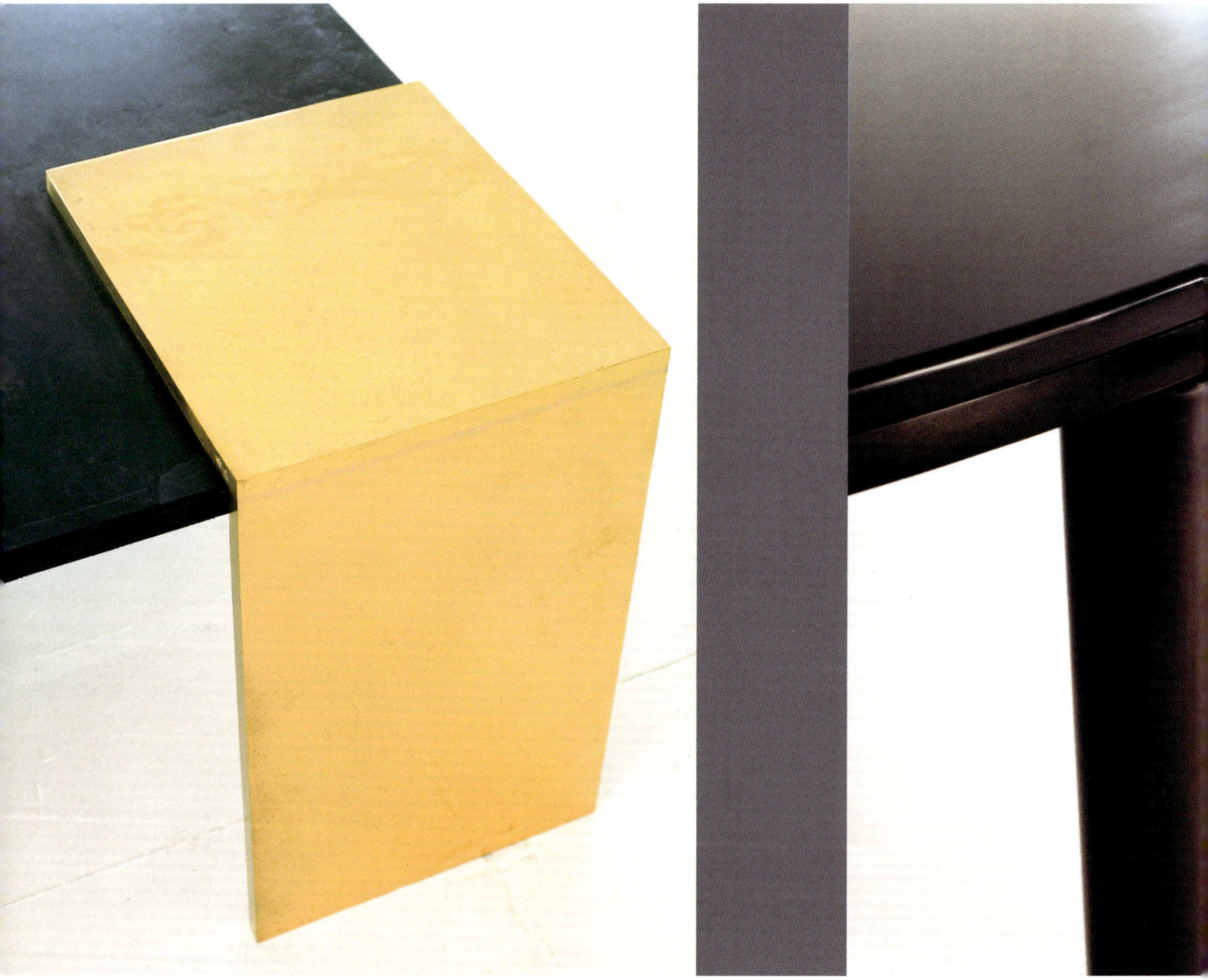

eric schmitt *Bronze*, 2006

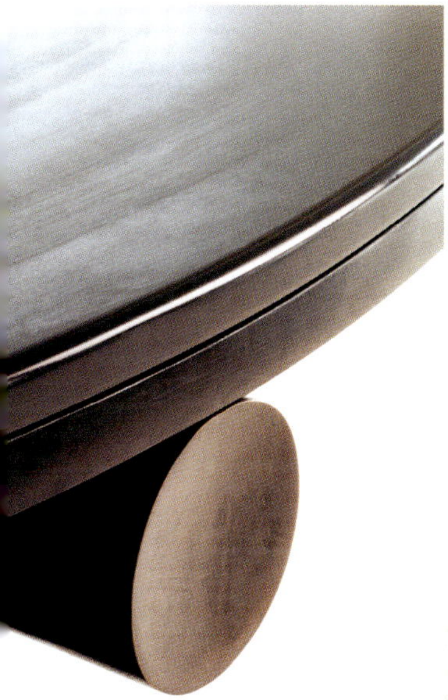

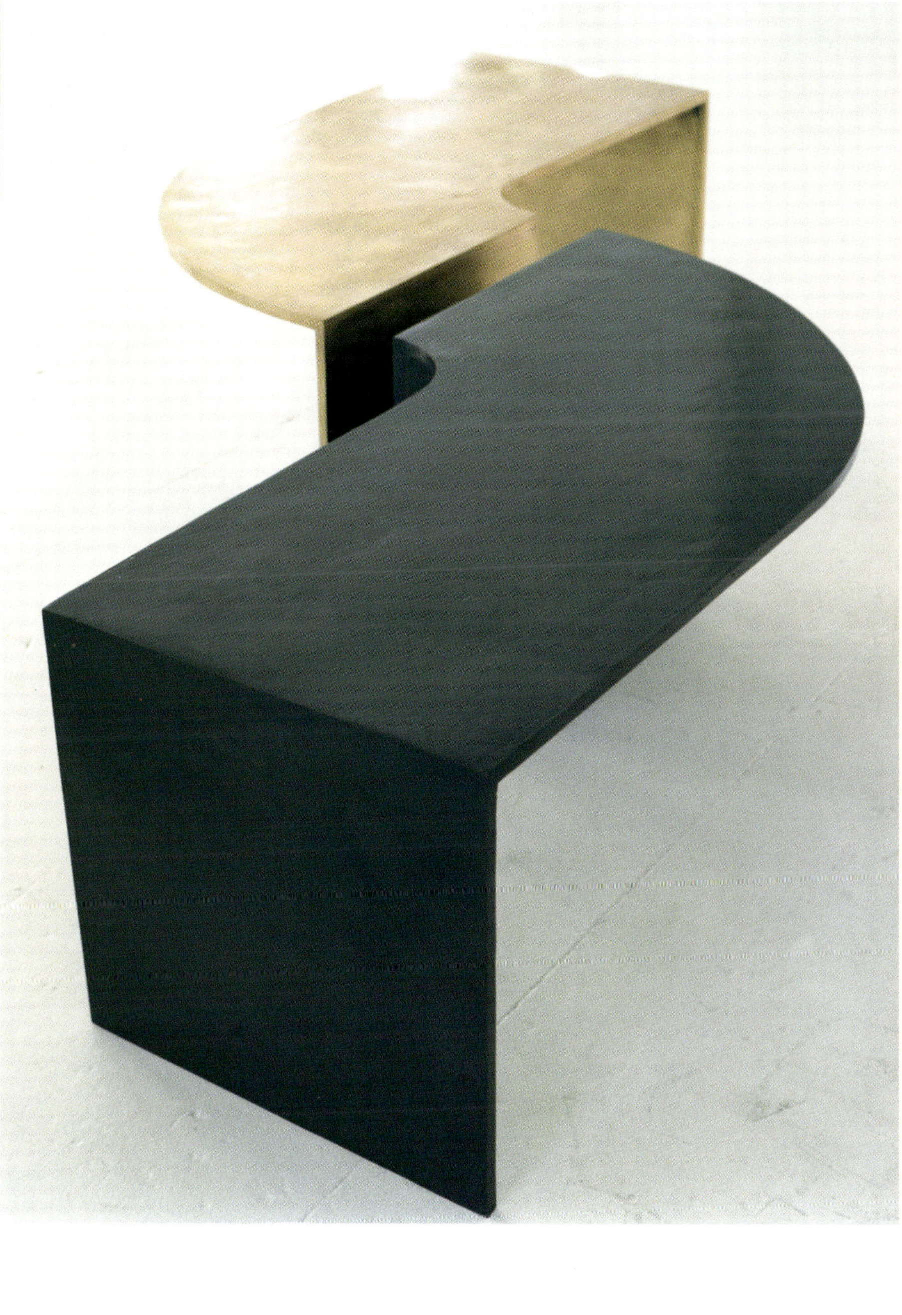

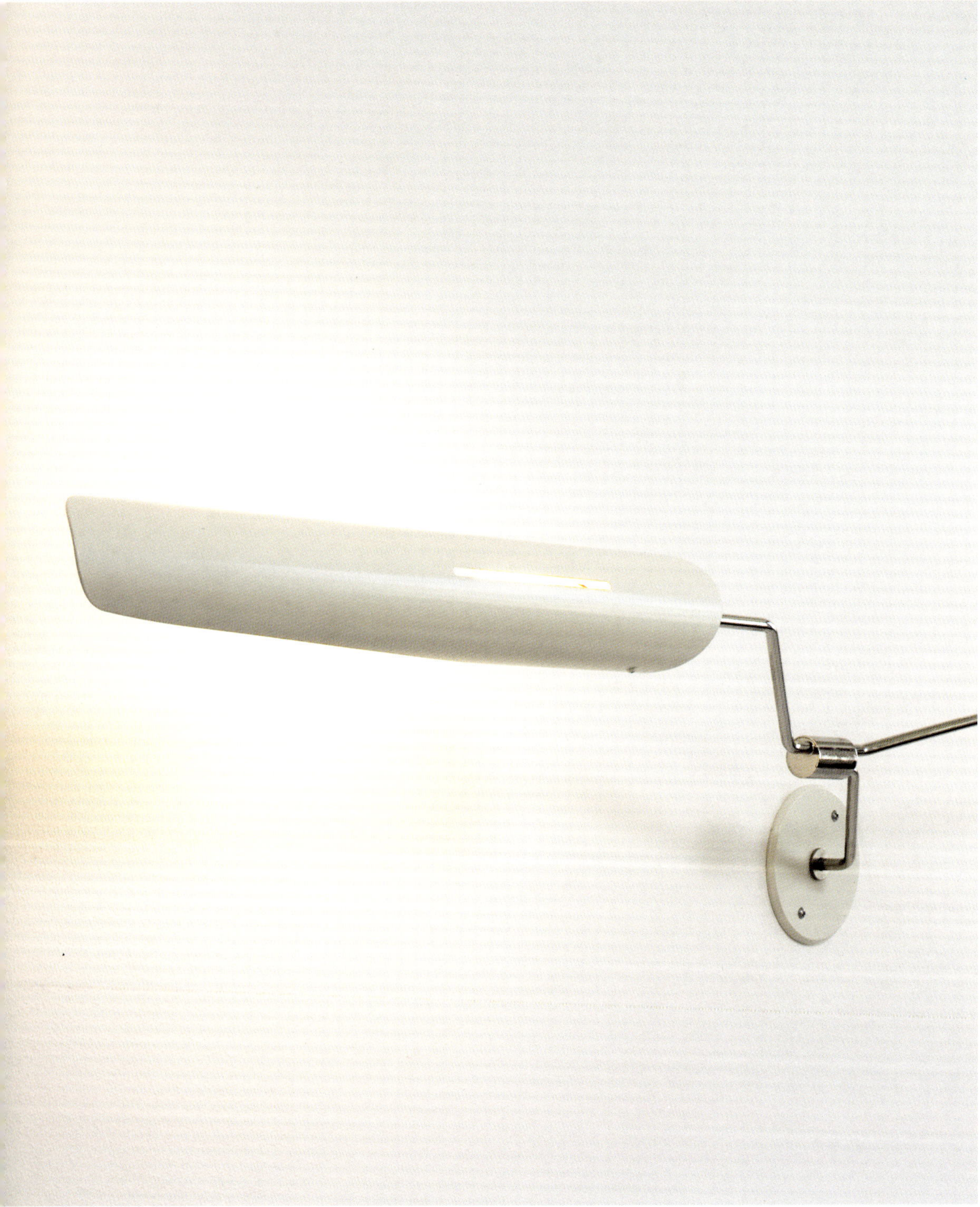

 david weeks *Sarus sconce no. 213, Sculpt sofa*, 2008

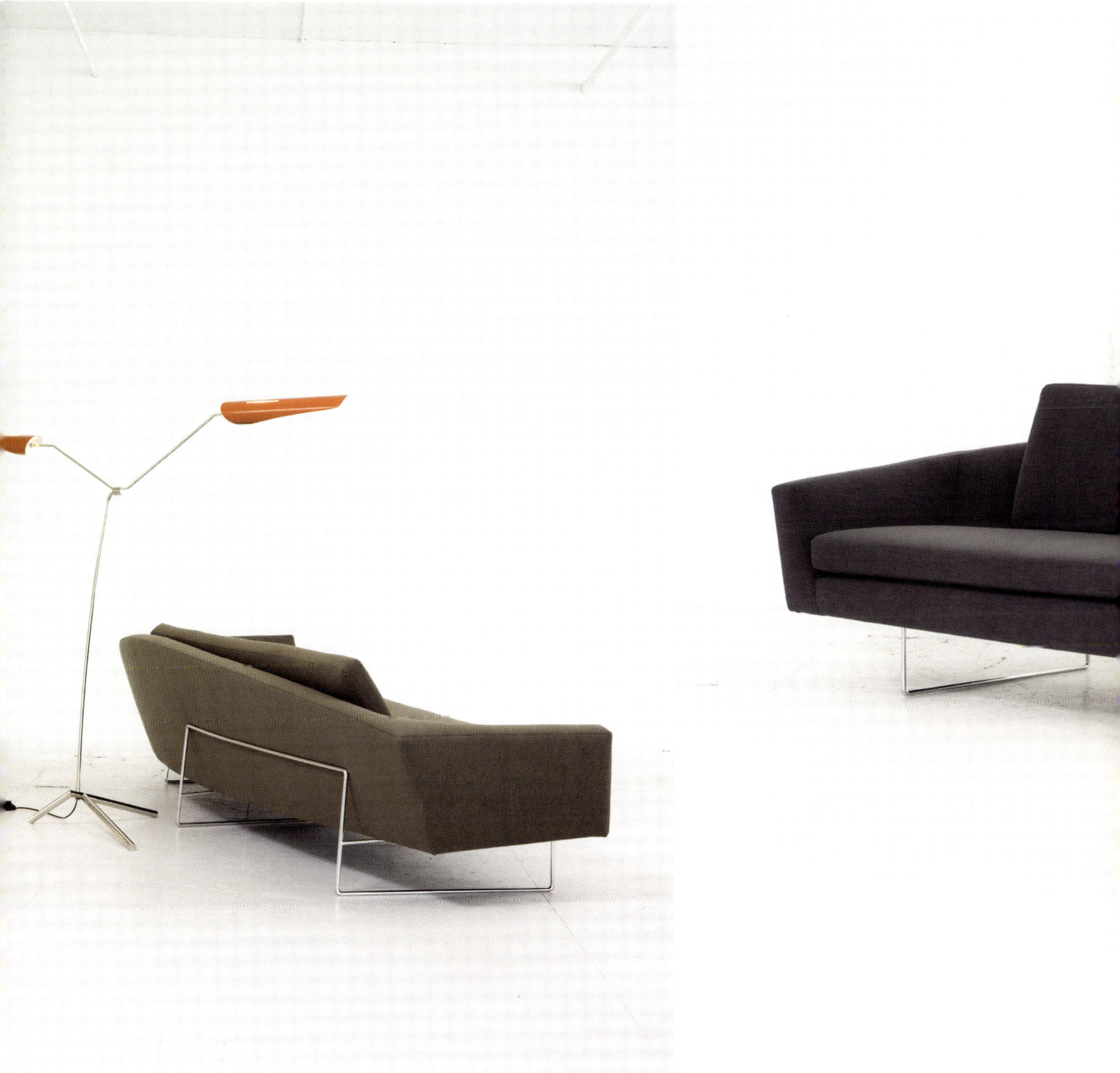

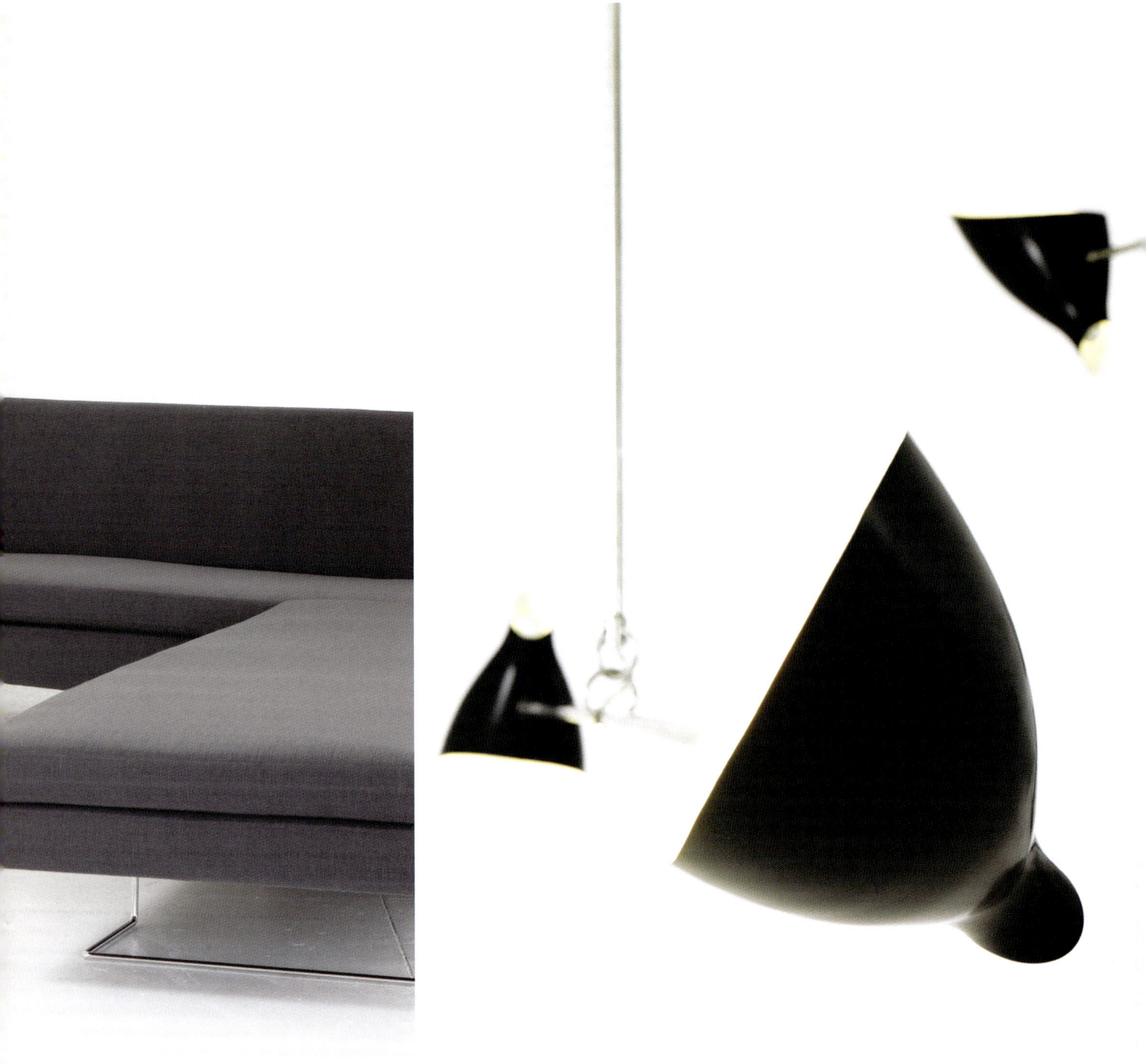

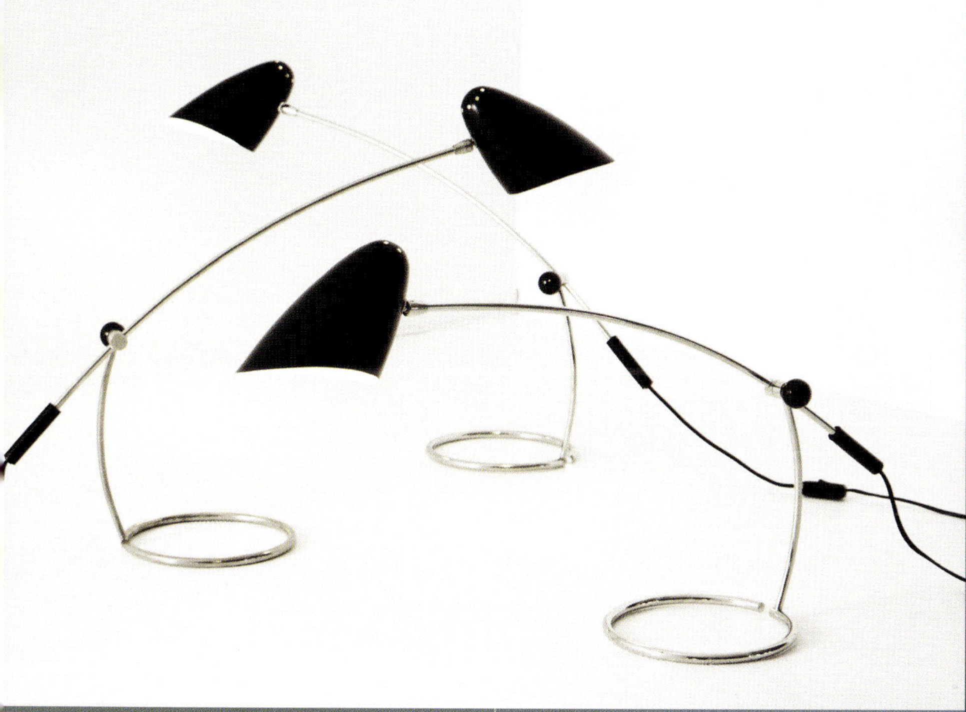

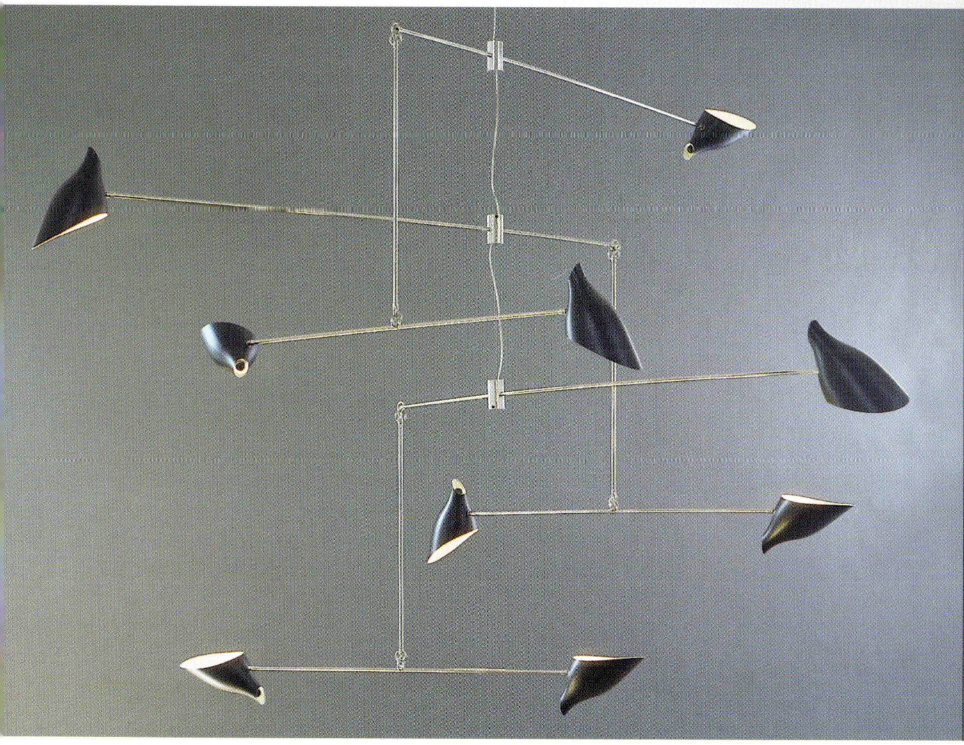

"I am as much a **sculptor** as I am a designer. In the work I've done for Pucci, I have attempted to push the envelope of "product" design; creating large scale fixtures with **details of a jeweler.**"

—David Weeks

Hanging Mobile, and *Adjustable Arc No. 109*, 2003

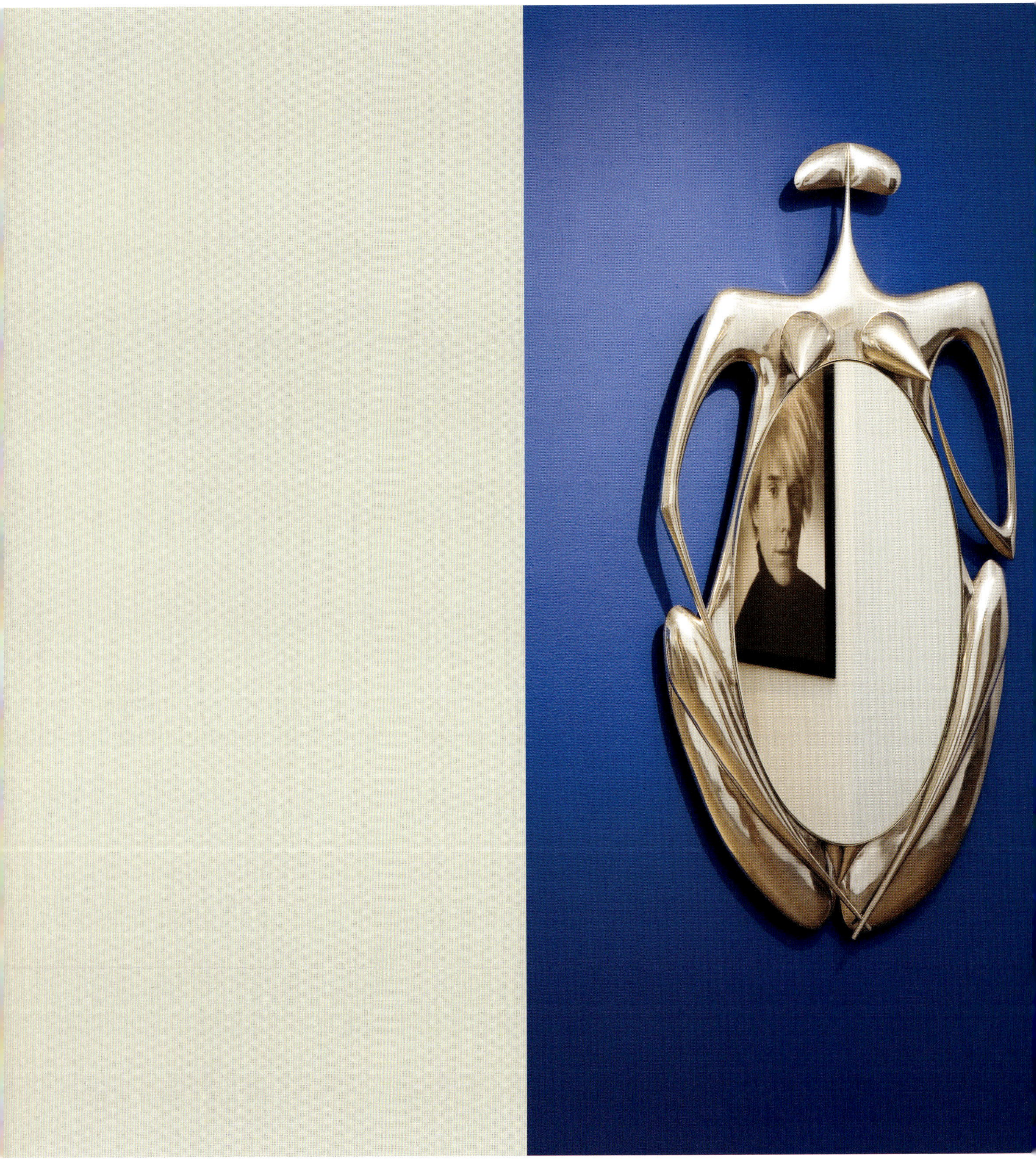

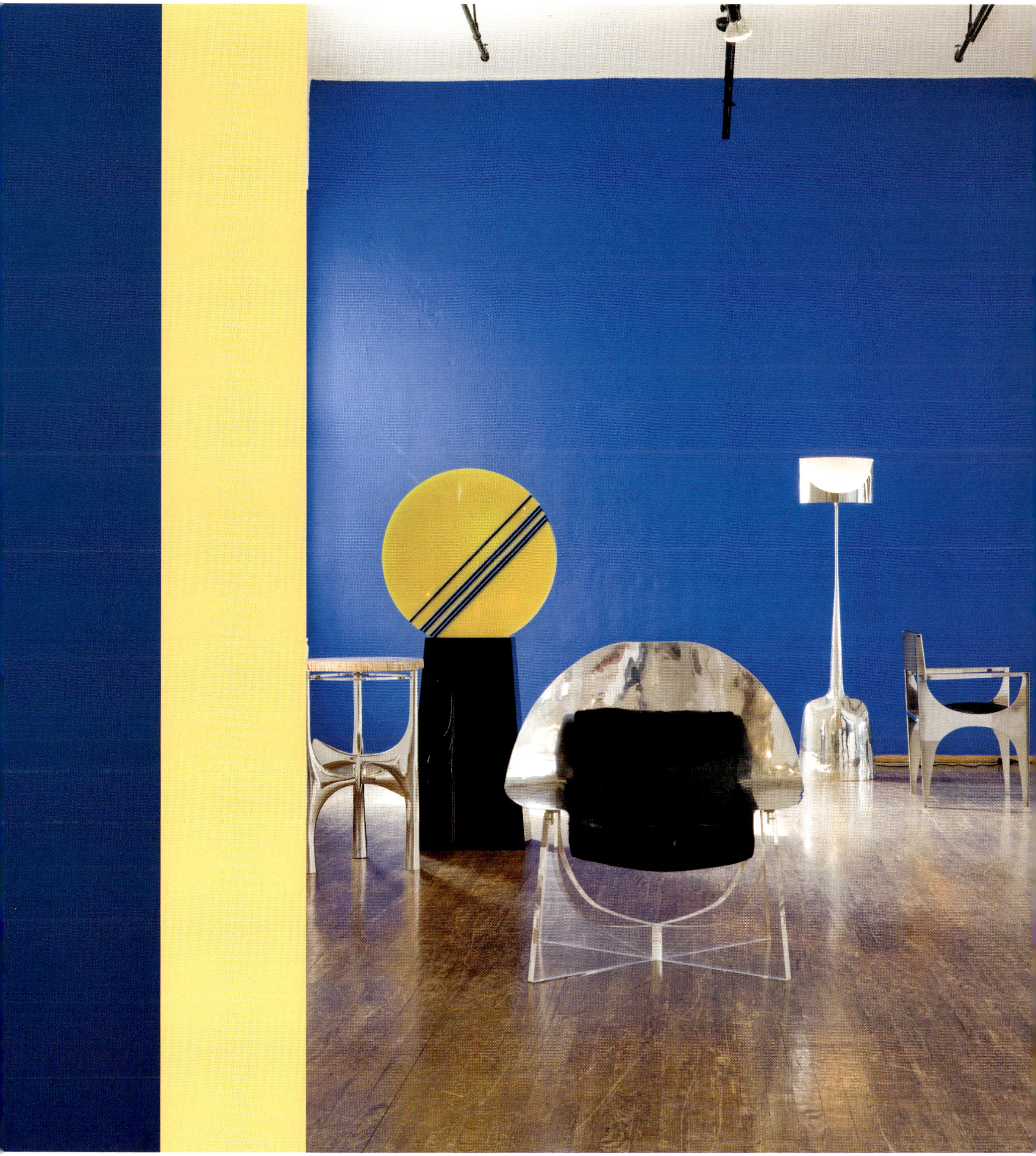

philippe hiquily aluminum collection, 2008, sculpture by Jean-Claude Farhi

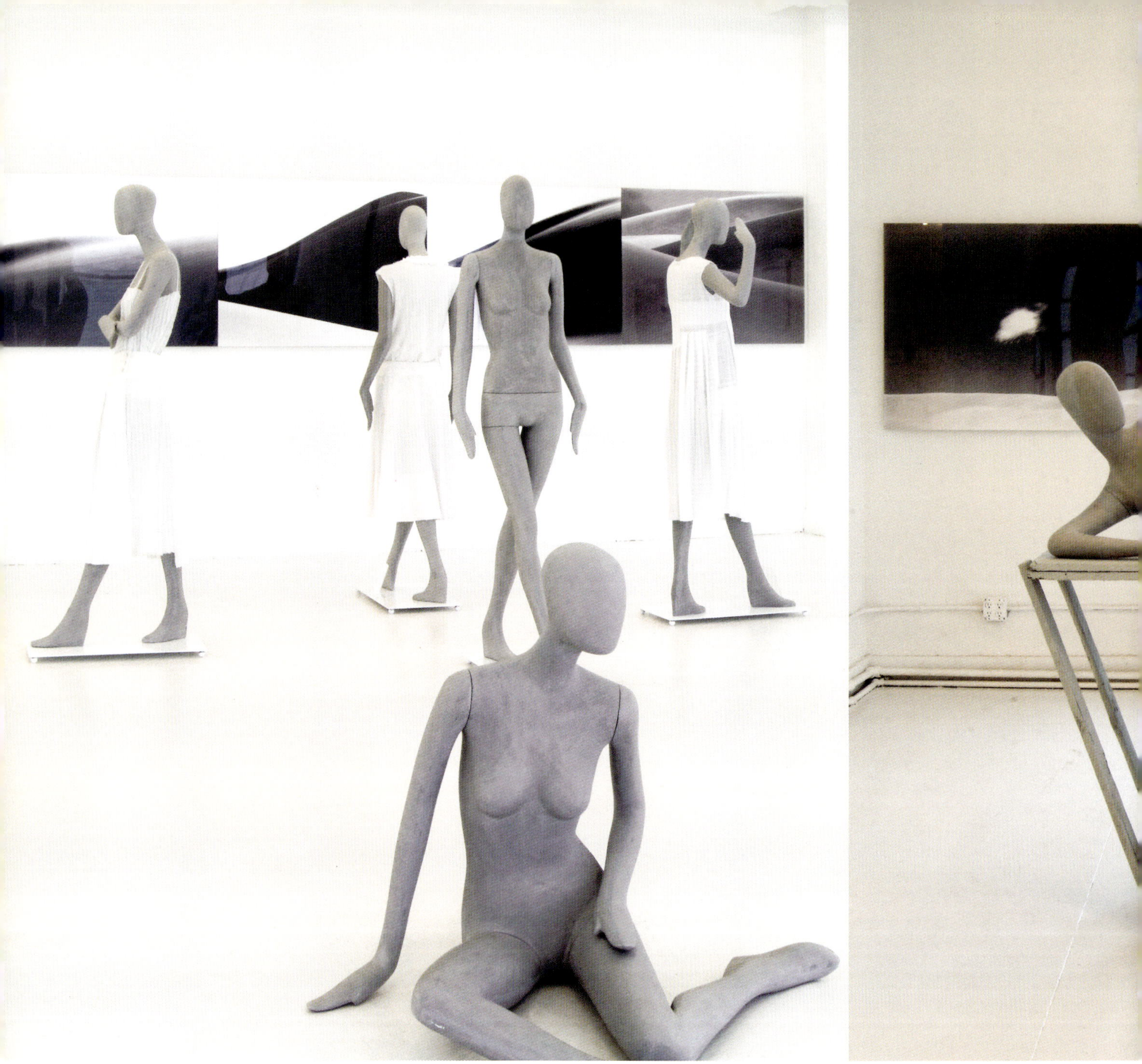

ralph pucci *MANIKIN* mannequins, 2004, fashions by Tess Giberson

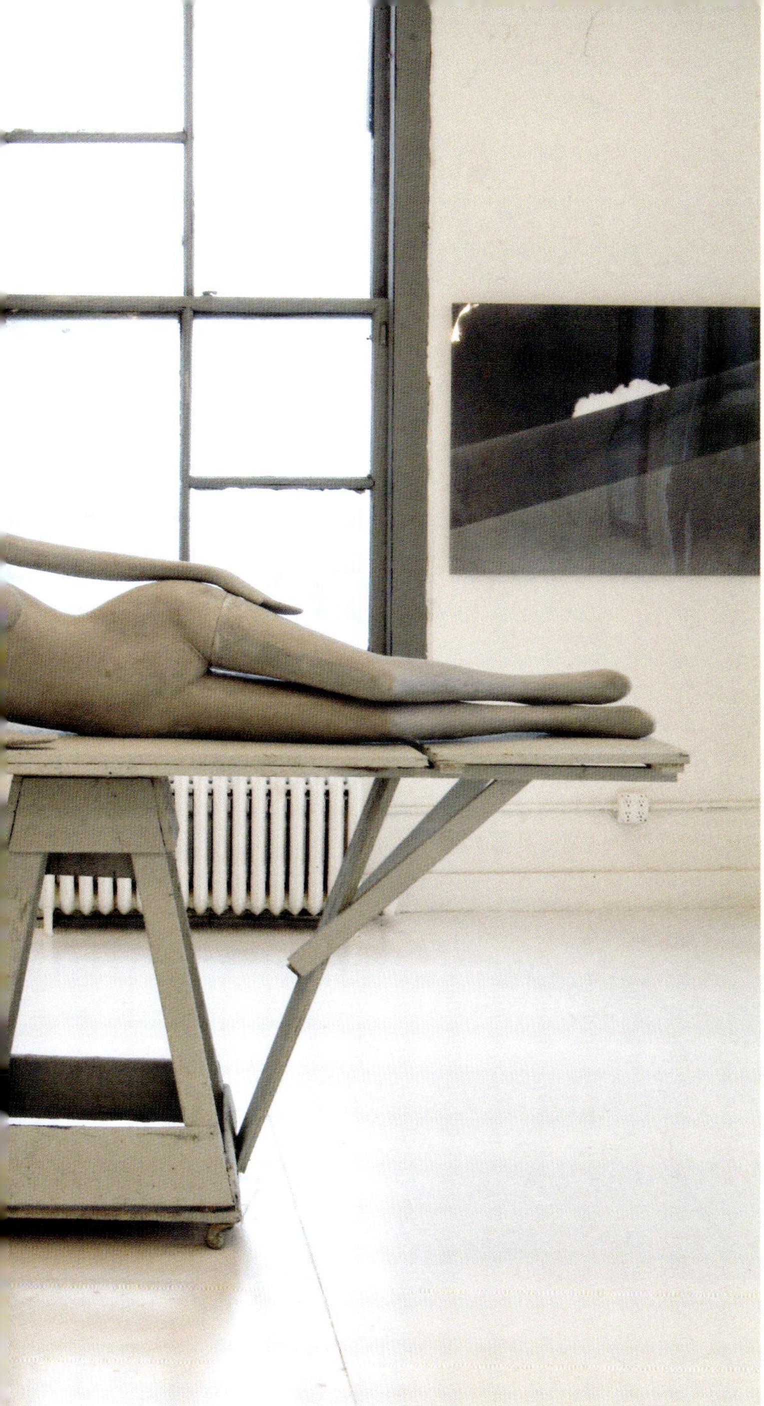

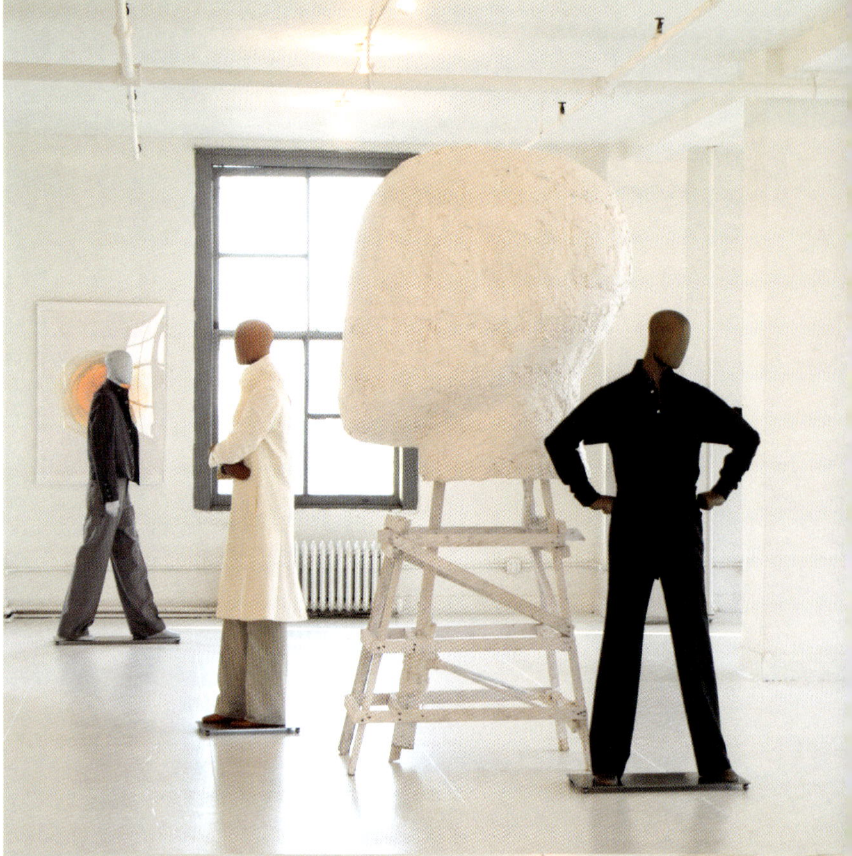

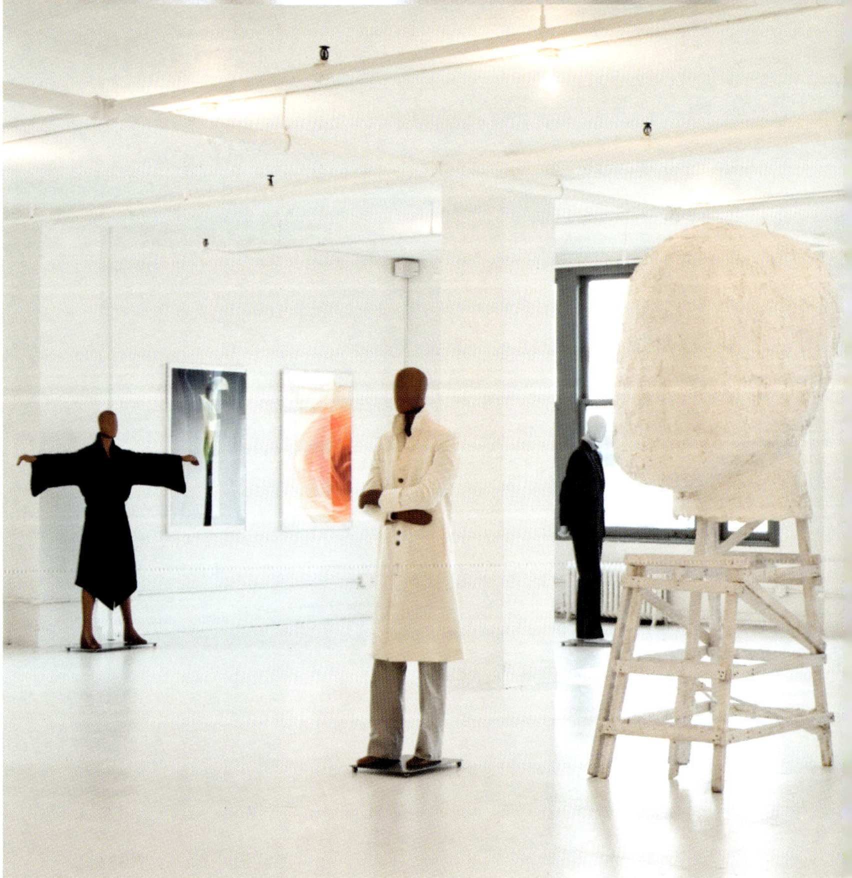

MALE collection, 2005, fashions by Tomer (left, top and bottom). *MALE* collection, 2005, fashions by Tomer, mural by Nicholas Howey (right)

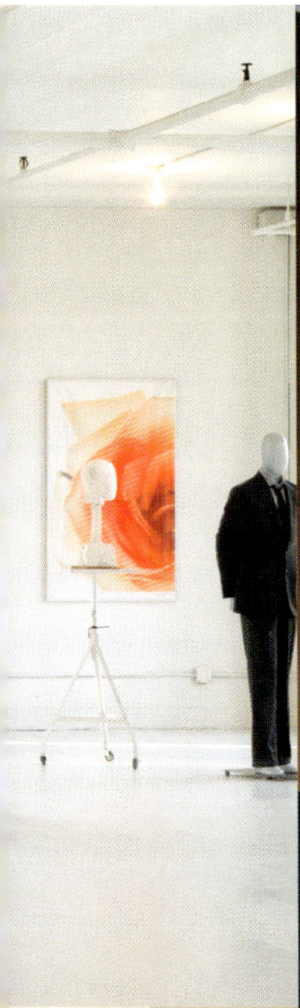

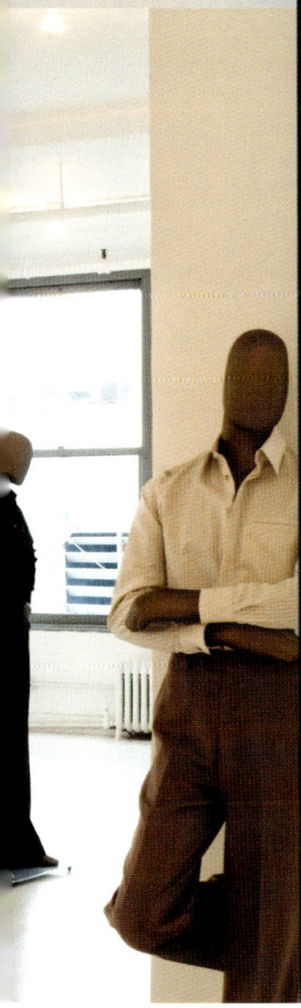

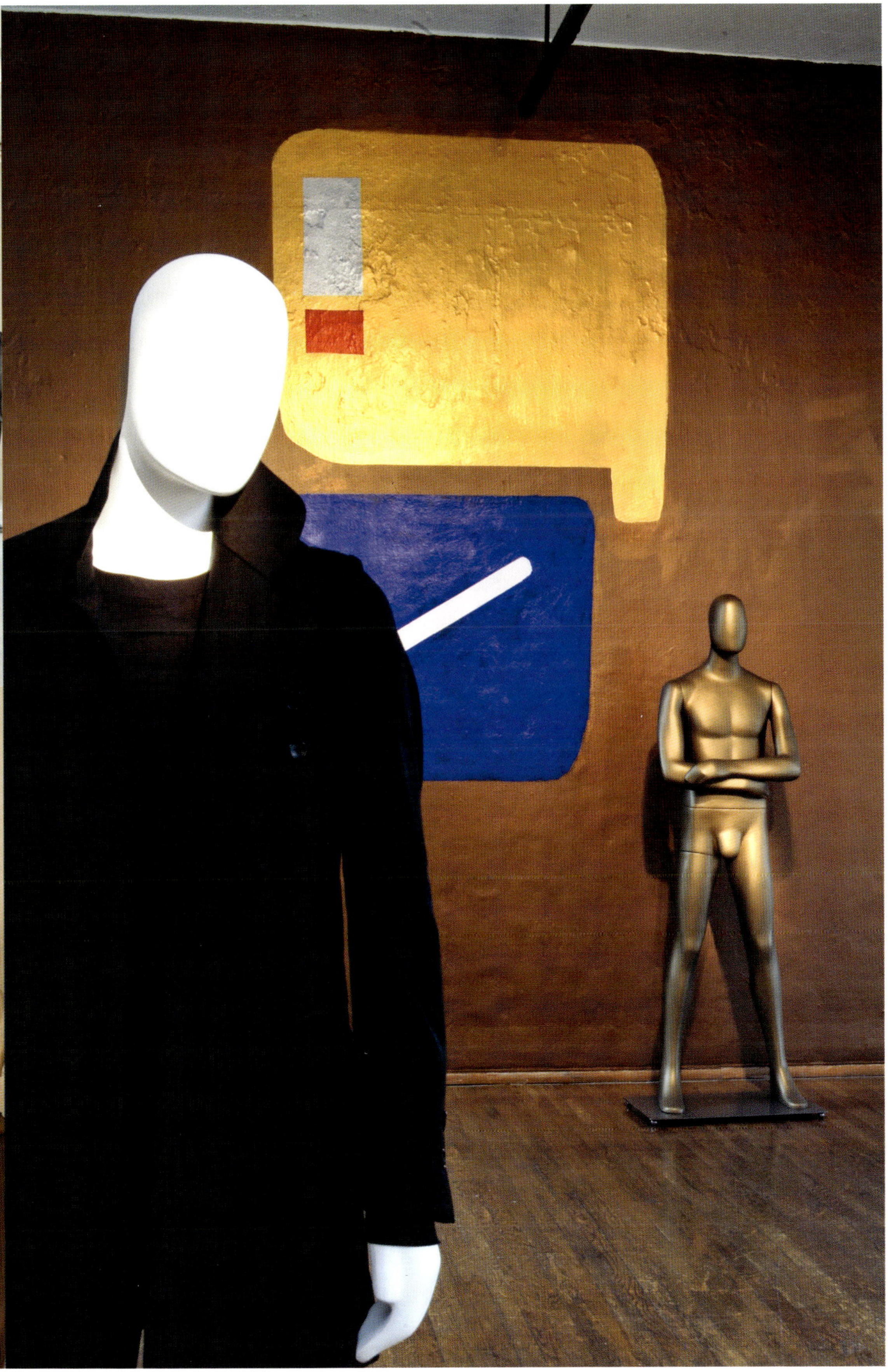

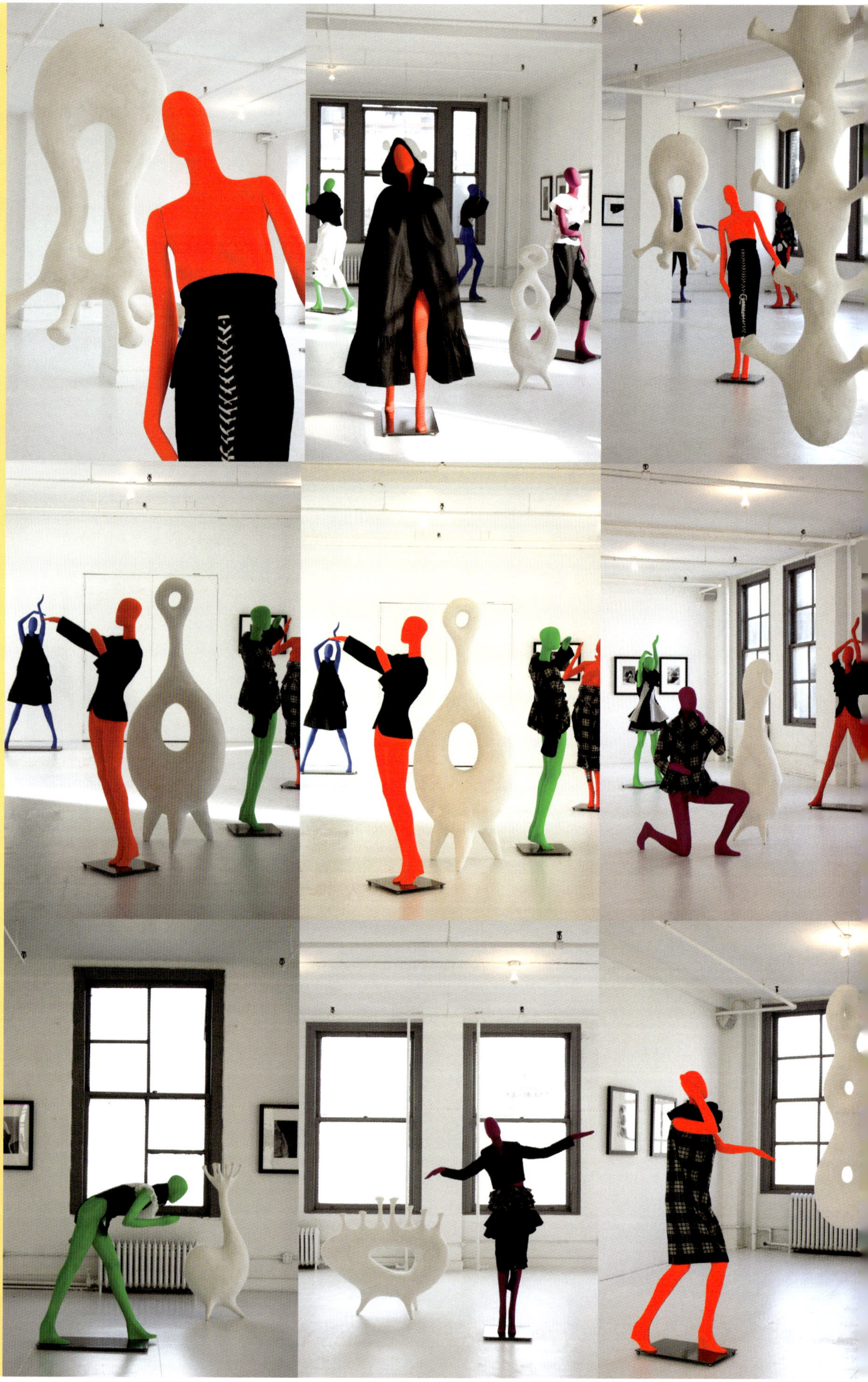

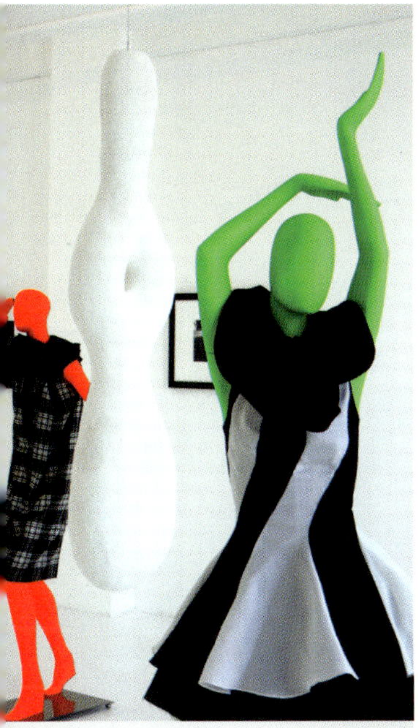

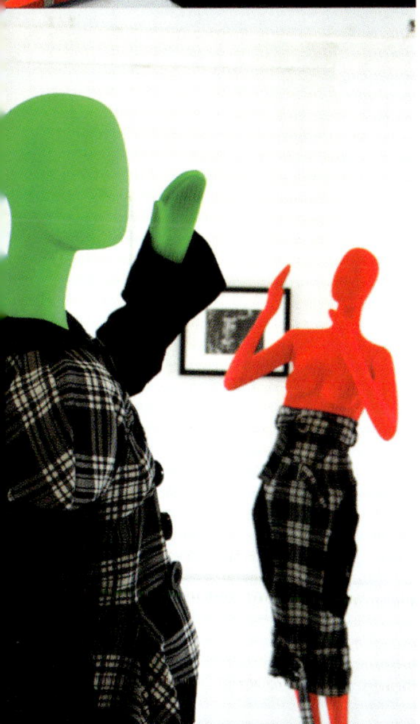

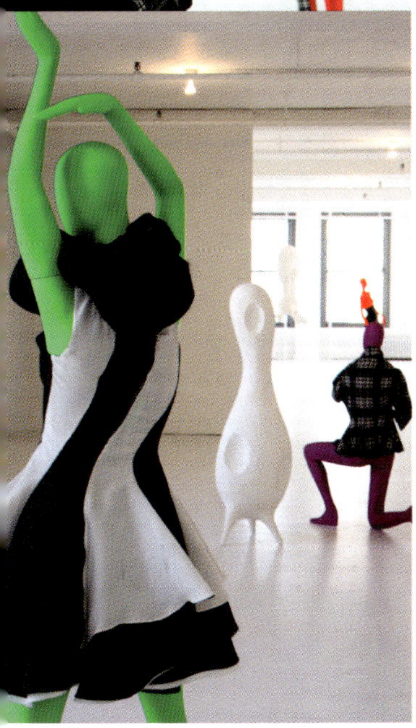

MOTION mannequins, 2006, fashions by Frank Tropiano

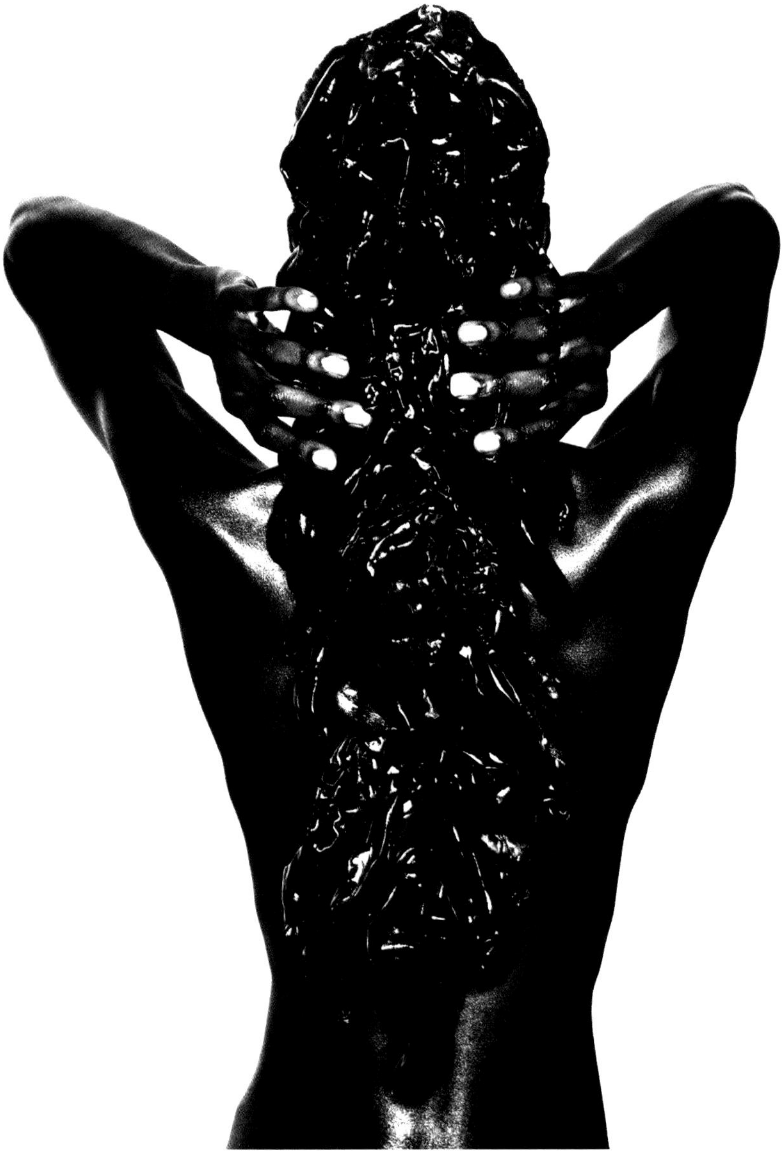

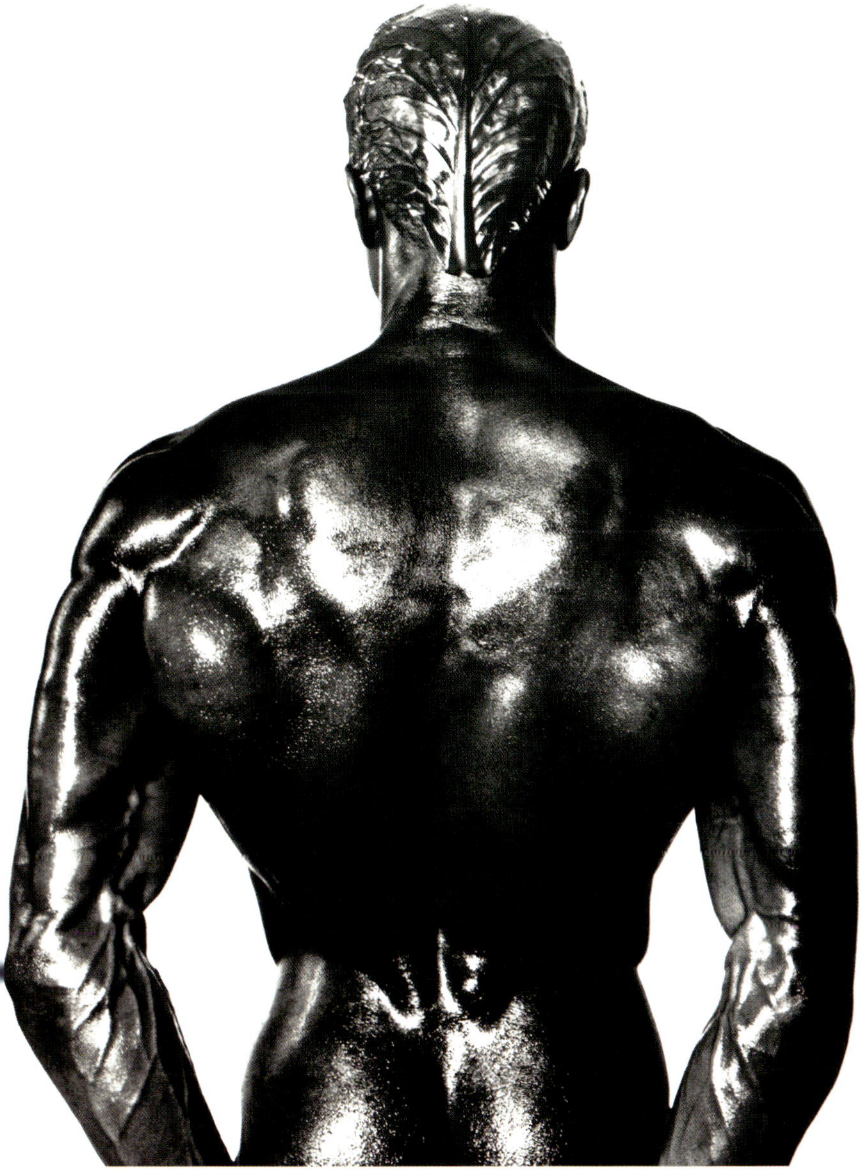

laurent elie badessi photographs, 2007

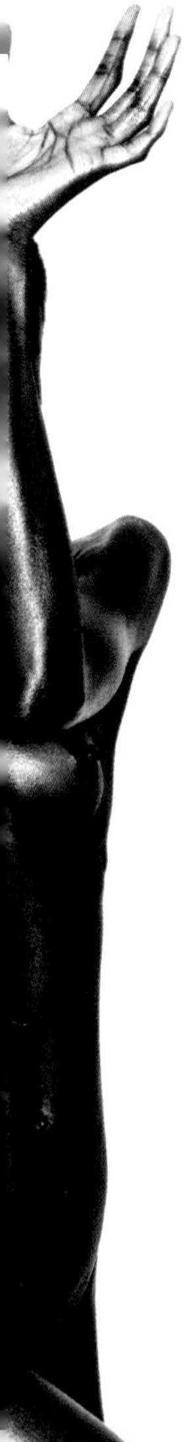

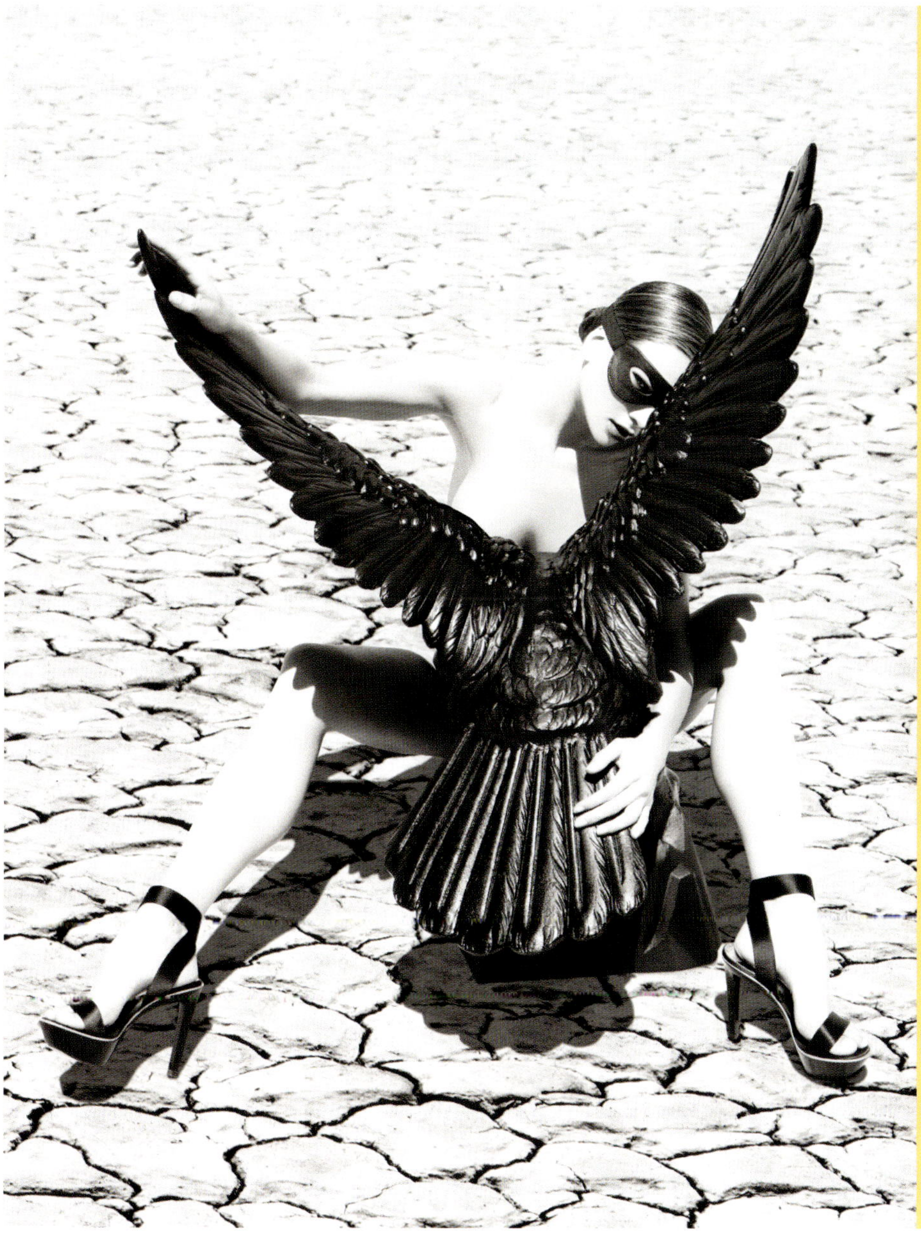

Photograph, 2007

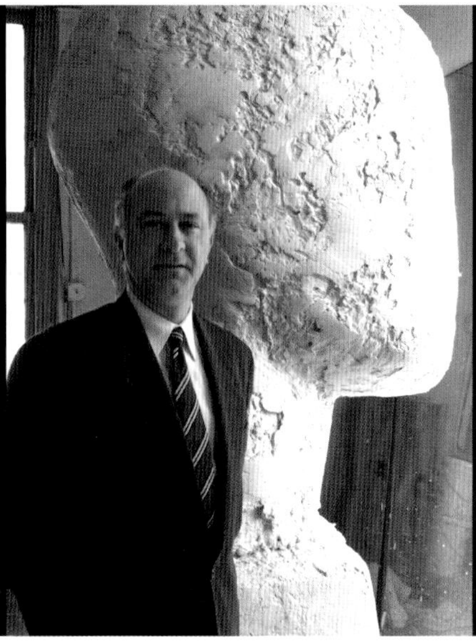

ABOUT THE AUTHOR Ralph Pucci

Ralph Pucci is the major force behind Ralph Pucci International, an innovator in the mannequin industry. He is president of the mannequin company founded by his parents in the 1950s. Operating in a spacious loft, on several floors on West 18th Street, mannequins and furniture are designed, manufactured and unveiled yearly.

His vision for the future of mannequins began when he created the action mannequins, breaking away from the old rigid forms. His new vision continued with a collaboration with international interior designer, Andrée Putman, producing three collections.

Pucci also reached out to the fashion models, mannequin-izing the likes of Jose Borain, Aly Dunne, Anh Duong and Veruschka, among others. A Christy Turlington mannequin was created for the Metropolitan Museum of Art. The Turlington face and body was later recreated in a series of yoga poses. His collaboration with artists, designers and illustrators led to seven series of mannequins with famed illustrator, Ruben Toledo.

He enlisted the talents of many top fashion designers to dress the mannequins, among them, Isabel Toledo, Todd Oldham, Susan Cianciolo, Daryl K, Catherine Malandrino, Anna Sui, William Calvert, Benjamin Cho, Jeffey Chow, Tomer Gendler, Frank Tell and Alpana Bawa.

Ralph Pucci saw the potential of mannequins, furniture and art. They could easily be integrated and presented in his fabulous loft setting. He gained exclusive rights to the French Ecart International collection in the United States, and added collections of many top designers, as well as up-and-coming, talented designers and artists.

Pucci has shown the art works of Chris Makos, Ruben Toledo, Maira Kalman, Antoine Bootz, Gail LeBoff, Diego Uchitel and James Brown. He introduced the art of Hawaiian artists in a show entitled "Tribute to Noguchi." The aboriginal art of Australian Gija Artists celebrating their Gija culture was introduced by Pucci in the United States.

Pucci created mannequins for the Rock and Roll Hall of Fame with Stephen Sprouse, and with Ruben Toledo created the first VH1 award. Pucci mannequins have been featured in museums and galleries, and Ralph Pucci International has been honored by the *Robb Report* as "the best in furniture and furnishings" and *Wallpaper* selected it as "the best showroom."

Ralph Pucci International has showrooms at the Pacific Design Center in West Hollywood, California and the J. Batchelor DCOTA Design Center in Fort Lauderdale, Florida. Pucci lives with his family in Connecticut.